D1483739

*The publisher and the University of California Press
Foundation gratefully acknowledge the generous support of
the Eric Papenfuse and Catherine Lawrence Endowment
Fund in Film and Media Studies.*

ABC Sports

SPORT IN WORLD HISTORY

Edited by Susan Brownell, Robert Edelman,
Wayne Wilson, and Christopher Young

This University of California Press series explores the story of
modern sport from its recognized beginnings in the nineteenth
century to the current day. The books present to a wide
readership the best new scholarship connecting sport with broad
trends in global history. The series delves into sport's intriguing
relationship with political and social power, while also capturing
the enthusiasm for the subject that makes it so powerful.

ABC Sports

THE RISE AND FALL OF NETWORK SPORTS TELEVISION

Travis Vogan

UNIVERSITY OF CALIFORNIA PRESS

University of California Press, one of the most distinguished university presses in the United States, enriches lives around the world by advancing scholarship in the humanities, social sciences, and natural sciences. Its activities are supported by the UC Press Foundation and by philanthropic contributions from individuals and institutions. For more information, visit www.ucpress.edu.

University of California Press
Oakland, California

Library of Congress Cataloging-in-Publication Data

Names: Vogan, Travis, author.
Title: ABC Sports : the rise and fall of network sports television / Travis Vogan.
Description: Oakland, California : University of California Press, [2018] | Includes bibliographical references and index. |
Identifiers: LCCN 2018017673 (print) | LCCN 2018021121 (ebook) | ISBN 9780520966260 (ebook) | ISBN 9780520292956 (cloth : alk. paper) | ISBN 9780520292963 (pbk. : alk. paper)
Subjects: LCSH: ABC Sports. | Television broadcasting of sports—United States—20th century.
Classification: LCC GV742.3 (ebook) | LCC GV742.3 .V6155 2018 (print) | DDC 070.449796—dc23
LC record available at https://lccn.loc.gov/2018017673

27 26 25 24 23 22 21 20 19 18
10 9 8 7 6 5 4 3 2 1

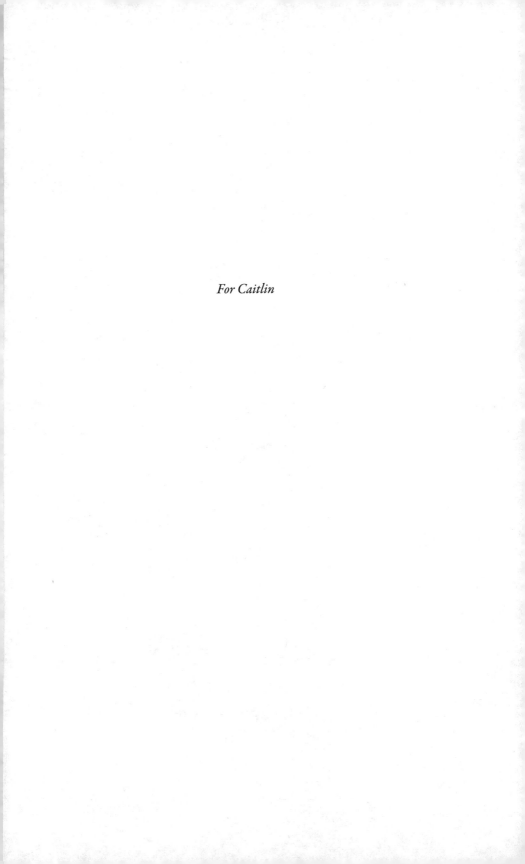

For Caitlin

CONTENTS

ILLUSTRATIONS

ACKNOWLEDGMENTS

It is humbling to reflect on a years-long project—one that winds up as a book that displays only my name on the cover—and realize how many others contributed. Some pitched in directly and with very specific favors and tips; some asked good questions in the midst of chatting about other topics; and some were just encouraging. Despite the size and nature of these contributions, I can say with total confidence that I could not have completed this project entirely on my own. I appreciate the support and promise to pay it forward.

But I do want to single out some folks and organizations that took the time to help out. First of all, I have to give a giant thanks to sports broadcasting legend and model Hawkeye Ken Aagaard for connecting me with some of the sources who helped me piece together this history. The book would not be nearly as good without their memories and voices, and Ken got the ball rolling by vouching for me. Thanks to Jack Gallivan, Roger Goodman, Rick Kaplan, Dennis Lewin, Robert Lipsyte, Williams Liss, John Martin, Geoff Mason, Sean McManus, Al Michaels, the late Don Ohlmeyer, Dorrance Smith, Jim Spence, Steve Solomon, Alex Wallau, Fred Williamson, and Doug Wilson.

I always thought the University of California Press would be an excellent landing spot for this project. I started out working with Mary Francis, who left UCP not long after we began. But Mary left me in the expert hands of Niels Hooper and Bradley Depew, and we were able to press on without missing a beat. I am grateful to Mary, Niels, and Bradley for believing in the project and helping out with it. Thanks also to Jessica Moll, Nicholle Robertson, and Susan Ecklund for the assistance as we moved into production and copyediting. We ultimately decided to include this in the Sport in World History series. I'm glad we did. I particularly appreciated the feedback from series editors Bob, Chris, Susan, and Wayne. Thanks also to Robert Bellamy and Dick Crepeau for their comments, which helped immensely as I was putting the book together, revising, and polishing.

Archivists and librarians are my favorite people in academe. They organize, protect, and make available the raw materials that are eventually mined to create more and different resources (that librarians then organize, protect, and make available, and so on). They often seem to know more about topics than the researchers they aid, and they are mostly content to stay behind the scenes. Almost without fail, the archivists who helped me wound up bringing materials I had not thought to consult or that weren't obviously relevant from the catalogs. No database has the passion these folks possess for their work. Thanks to Columbia University's Rare Book and Manuscript Library, New York University's Special Collections, the New York Public Library, the Chicago Public Library, the Paley Center for Media, University of Southern California's Cinematic Arts Library, the UCLA Library's Special Collections, the LA84 Foundation Sports Library, the University of Illinois Archives, the Wisconsin Historical Society, the University of Buffalo Library's Special Collections, the University of Massachusetts Library's Special Collections, Vanderbilt University's Television News Archive, the Smithsonian Archives of American Art, and the LeRoy Neiman Foundation. I want to give a special shout-out to Tara Zabor and the Neiman Foundation for helping me to secure the rights to use several Neiman images. Finally, and most of all, thanks to the University of Iowa Libraries.

Though I traveled a good bit to write this book, the project started and ended in Iowa City. Fortunately, I'm surrounded by a bunch of benevolent geniuses who tolerate questions about and mentions of all sorts of things— often non sequiturs like "You know, Howard Cosell appeared on an episode of *The Partridge Family*" that make me a slightly less cute version of that kid from *Jerry Maguire*. Thanks to Tom Oates, Rebecca Raw, Brian Ekdale, Melissa Tully, Nick Grossman, Alyssa Prorok, Andy Todd, Erin Syoen, Kajsa Dalrymple, Jeff Kritzman, Dylan McConnell, Becca Neel, Ben Cooper, Dan Berkowitz, Frank Durham, Gigi Durham, Rachel Young, Gabe Bodzin, Andrew Willhoit, Emily Brown, Steve Bloom, Dave Dowling, Deborah Whaley, David Ryfe, Mike Gibisser, Hannah Givler, Steve Warren, Susan Birrell, Ann Haugland, Tim Havens, and Nick Yablon. Thanks also to Becky Kick, Michele Ketchum, Rosemary Zimmerman, Jennifer Cooper, Laura Kastens, Ericka Raber, and Mike Hendrickson for helping me to navigate important details concerning books, funding, and technology. Part of this research was supported by a UI College of Liberal Arts and Sciences Flexible-Load Assignment. I also had research assistance from Mallory Miranda and Eloisa Valenzuela-Mendoza. The UI School of Journalism and Mass Communication generously ponied up the money to pay for my index, which was nice because I have no idea how to put one together.

Beyond Iowa, I benefited from questions and comments at conferences such as those of the Society for Cinema and Media Studies, the North American Society for Sport History, the American Studies Association, the International Communication Association, and the Association for Education in Journalism and Mass Communication. Vicky Johnson, as always, offered brilliant comments as I was conceptualizing, researching, and writing the project. Frank Durham and Danny Nasset gave me feedback on my proposal. Nick Yablon read the entire manuscript and provided some insights that helped me to make improvements before I turned in the final draft. Fragments of the book were piloted in articles published in *American Art* and *Television & New Media*. I am grateful to Marie Ladino, Emily Shapiro, and Diane Negra for guidance that helped get those works into shape and eventually sharpen the book.

Finally, big thanks to my friends and family. You guys are always helping me out with big and small stuff—and most times you don't even know it.

Introduction

ABC SPORTS AND NETWORK SPORTS TELEVISION

IN SEPTEMBER 1994, *Sports Illustrated* published a list of the forty most influential sports figures in the forty years since the magazine's launch. Its top two selections—Muhammad Ali and Michael Jordan—were no great surprise. At the height of their respective careers, Ali and Jordan were arguably the most recognizable people on Earth. *Sports Illustrated*'s third-ranked selection—the American Broadcasting Company's sports television mastermind Roone Arledge—was comparatively obscure. Arledge never fronted for global ad campaigns, had a shoe line, or divided a nation with his politics. But the magazine might have underestimated the influence of this producer and executive. During Arledge's thirty-eight-year stint at the network, ABC built and codified the media infrastructure that made possible global sport celebrities of Ali and Jordan's unprecedented magnitude.

ABC Sports is behind some of network sports television's most significant practices, personalities, and moments. It created the weekend anthology *Wide World of Sports*, transformed professional football into a prime-time spectacle with *Monday Night Football*, and fashioned the Olympics into a mega media event. It helped to turn Ali, the sportscaster Howard Cosell, and the daredevil Evel Knievel into stars and captured now-iconic instances that include Tommie Smith and John Carlos's raised-fist protest at the 1968 Olympics, the terrorist attacks at the 1972 Munich Games, Billie Jean King and Bobby Riggs's 1973 "Battle of the Sexes" tennis match, the US hockey team's 1980 "Miracle on Ice" victory over the Soviet Union, and the 1999 Women's World Cup final. *ABC Sports: The Rise and Fall of Network Sports Television* offers a cultural and institutional history of ABC Sports from its beginnings to its 2006 rebranding as "ESPN on ABC." It uses the division to examine network sports television's development in the United States; the aesthetic, cultural, political, and industrial practices that mark it; and the changes it endured along with the new sports media environment it spawned.

. . .

Sports drove TV's ascendance into a commonplace appliance after World War II. By 1947 the trade publication *Variety* was hailing live sports as the new medium's "greatest contribution."[1] But TV confronted widespread resistance among many in the sports industry who believed it would decimate ticket sales—anxieties radio and print also faced when they emerged. A 1952 report commissioned by the National Collegiate Athletic Association (NCAA) concluded that television had an "adverse effect on college football attendance." That same year, the Radio-Television Manufacturers Association—a group devoted to boosting the medium—trumpeted TV as "a constructive force" that "helps to stimulate new interest" in sports and that "promotes while it entertains."[2]

Despite the NCAA's reluctance, college football was popular enough to endure—and ultimately benefit from—television. But less prominent sports did suffer. Minor-league baseball attendance sunk by 30 percent during the 1950s, and the *New Yorker's* A.J. Liebling blamed TV for eviscerating his beloved boxing: "The clients of the television companies, by putting on a free boxing show almost every night of the week, have knocked out of business the hundreds of small-city and neighborhood boxing clubs where youngsters had a chance to learn their trade and journeymen to mature their skills. . . . Neither advertising agencies nor brewers, least of all the networks, give a hoot if they push the Sweet Science back into a period of genre painting. When it is in a coma they will find some other way to peddle their peanuts."[3]

Beyond television's impact on boxing's viability and quality, Liebling charged that TV broadcasts dulled the rich social experience of attending matches in crowded, smoky clubs. "Television gives you so plausible an adumbration of a fight, for nothing," he wrote, "that you feel it would be extravagant to pay your way in. It is like the potato, which is only a succedaneum for something decent to eat but which, once introduced to Ireland, proved so cheap that the peasants gave up their grain-and-meat diet in favor of it."[4] TV, as Liebling saw it, sapped live boxing's humanity. Regardless, television established itself as the United States' dominant mass medium by the end of the 1950s. Accordingly, it became a permanent fixture in sports and a necessary ingredient in sports organizations' financial health.

The youngest of the United States' three major networks, ABC ranked a distant last among them in the 1950s. It used sports to build a distinct image and attract a steady audience. The network initially contracted its sports programming to Edgar Scherick's Sports Programs Inc. The subcontractor then hired Arledge—who had never before worked in sports—to produce ABC's autumn 1960 slate of college football broadcasts. The rookie producer made up for his greenness with ambition and confidence. He audaciously proclaimed that ABC would revolutionize the staid representational method guiding sports TV. It would "take viewers to the game" and provide what the network eventually branded as an "up close and personal" view of events and participants through innovations that borrowed from documentary, journalism, and even drama. As Arledge decreed, "We are going to add show business to sports!"[5]

Arledge aspired to capture the vitality Liebling accused the medium of depleting. ABC Sports broadcasts privileged building stories over displaying events and assumed viewers might watch the tales it packaged no matter their interest in sports. It humanized competitions by presenting them through familiar narratives (rivalries, records about to be broken, battles against the elements) and by making their participants relatable. These often-simplistic tropes—such as the pregame profile of an athlete desperately yearning to bounce back after an injury—quickly became clichés. As such, they are easy to discount as commercialized pandering. But they function through engaging the cultural codes that make TV so important. "In order for television to achieve its work," writes media scholar Herman Gray, "it has to draw upon and operate on the basis of a kind of generalized societal common sense about the terms of the society and people's location in it."[6] This common sense, of course, reflects existing power relations. Like all mass media, then, television has tremendous potential to reinforce and reshape culture. Arguably the medium's most visible, durable, and valuable genre, sports TV is a key voice in the culture industries. It flexes this clout as much through the resonant stories it tells—and the ways of looking at the world they create—as through the events and people it exhibits.

ABC Sports expanded sports television's previously narrow aesthetic scope into the realm of cinematic storytelling. It also looked beyond the genre's traditionally rose-tinted promotional ethos to report on the sometimes-divisive social issues—many of which its sponsors and clients would have preferred that it overlook—informing and surrounding the competitions it covered, such as the Cold War tensions that marked international events and the discrimination faced by female and nonwhite athletes. These controversies made compelling narratives that lent ABC's coverage drama and newsworthiness. ABC Sports, in fact, boldly denied broadcast partners influence over its content or personnel—a unique policy at the time that gave the network greater creative and editorial leeway than its more docile competitors. Apart from sporadic commentaries by on-air columnists like Cosell, ABC Sports remained neutral on the more prickly issues it reported. It both allowed Ali to express his dissident point of view on *Wide World of Sports* and made space for Ronald Reagan to recite jingoistic platitudes during its 1984 Summer Olympics coverage. But ABC Sports provided a forum that raised important questions about sport's sociopolitical contours while demonstrating the crucial role media play in showcasing, fortifying, and questioning them.

Network television was particularly potent when ABC Sports emerged and thrived. Between the 1960s and 1980s, ABC Sports' regular Saturday afternoon programming—from football to bowling—drew total audience numbers that rival those for the most popular programs in the fragmented, digitized, and multiplatform media environment that has replaced the network era. Not coincidentally, many of the twentieth century's marquee sporting moments appeared via ABC airwaves and gained their status through the expansive visibility and distinctive shape ABC Sports gave them. Besides reflecting Arledge's creative approach, these representations and the cultural work they performed grew out of ABC's efforts to create a brand, compete for market share, and promote content—industrial priorities that extend beyond the network's involvement in sports. Both ABC Sports' history and the larger story of network sports television emerge from these intersecting aesthetic, cultural, and economic concerns.

Media studies scholarship has painstakingly detailed television's profound cultural power and the historical, political, industrial, institutional, and technological contexts that inform it. However, and surprisingly, this robust body of work pays only scant attention to sports television, one of the medium's most popular genres. Sports television is—unfortunately and short-sightedly—an intellectually suspicious section of a medium that is already traditionally dismissed as a "bad object" of scholarly inquiry.[7] Despite its evidently questionable cultural status, sports television informed and, in some cases directly shaped, television programs and practices that have attracted substantial scholarly treatment—scrutiny that can be enriched by the lessons sports TV teaches. Similarly, scholarship on sport culture and history typically gives television only superficial consideration despite its crucial role in showcasing and shaping sport. When this work does comment on TV, it tends only to offer textual analyses of productions and largely ignores the industrial, institutional, and technological circumstances that make possible those ideologically loaded productions. These traditional approaches to studying television and sports, in short, miss a lot. But they can accomplish a lot when brought together. This book uses ABC Sports to demonstrate sport's vital role in shaping what television does, and television's crucial part in impacting what sport does. It unites these intertwined but rarely conjoined areas of study and demonstrates the fruits their articulation can yield—benefits that span far beyond this study's scope.

This project offers a mostly chronological account of ABC Sports through a vast collection of archival sources, programming and marketing materials, popular and trade press commentary, and interviews with those who worked at and with the organization. It begins by examining the economic, industrial, and institutional circumstances that prompted ABC to invest heavily in sports during the late 1950s and charge Arledge with overseeing this programming. Chapter 2 turns to *Wide World of Sports*, ABC Sports' signature show and the primary testing ground for its creative approach. The Saturday afternoon anthology possessed a meager budget that permitted it to secure rights to televise only the most marginal sports. Ski jumping and demolition derbies, for instance, were commonplace during its early years. The Cold War provided a way to dramatize many of *Wide World*'s prerecorded and otherwise unpopular events. The program established its popularity and culled much-needed acclaim through carrying a series of track meets between the United States and the Soviet Union that at once emphasized sports television's capacity to cultivate international harmony and advertised ABC Sports as innovative and edifying.

Chapter 3 discusses how ABC adapted *Wide World* to cover the Olympics. *Wide World* offered year-round promotion for the athletes who would eventually compete in the Olympics, while the high-profile quadrennial event built interest in *Wide World*'s weekly installments. *Wide World* introduced two of its biggest stars—Ali and Cosell—between ABC's first Olympics in 1964 and 1968, when it began to cover the event consistently and bill itself as "the Network of the Olympics." The duo's many appearances capitalized on Ali's polarizing views and Cosell's similarly divisive defense of the boxer. A key thread in ABC's coverage of the 1968 Summer Olympics in Mexico City concerned whether the United States' African American athletes—many of whom were inspired by the outspokenness Ali exhibited on *Wide World*— would use the Games to protest the racism they faced in the country they represented. Tommie Smith and John Carlos's infamous demonstration composed ABC's biggest story of the event, much of which aired during prime time. *Wide World*'s creative approach, programming practices, and stars fueled ABC's investment in and identification with the Olympics.

Emboldened by the success its 1968 Olympics coverage enjoyed in prime time, ABC teamed with the National Football League to launch *Monday Night Football* in 1970. *Monday Night* extended Arledge's lavish aesthetic to fashion a spectacle that would attract a broader audience than typical weekend telecasts. It particularly set its sights on women—a necessary audience for any successful prime-time show. While *Monday Night* grew out of ABC's Mexico City broadcasts, it avoided discussing racial tensions that might splinter the consistent prime-time viewership it sought. ABC used *Monday Night*'s popularity to create successful TV events that utilized the programing flows it forged and reproduced its pasteurized racial politics, such as the 1971 made-for-TV movie *Brian's Song* and, more significantly, the 1977 miniseries *Roots*. Chapter 4 contextualizes *Monday Night*'s development and explains how it informed the depiction of race on network TV events beyond sports broadcasts.

ABC's coverage of the 1972 Munich Olympics amplified its reputation as the Network of the Olympics and took advantage of the consistent space *Monday Night* forged for sports in prime time. But Munich was overshadowed by the Palestinian terrorist group Black September taking as hostage and eventually killing eleven members of Israel's Olympic team. ABC Sports' marathon coverage of the incident became the department's most celebrated achievement to date. This success eventually convinced ABC to entrust Arledge with its languishing news division in 1977, which he revamped by modifying the recipe he developed at ABC Sports. Chapter 5 uses Munich to explore how ABC Sports composed a template through which the network reinvented ABC News, and network sports TV more broadly.

ABC Sports capitalized on the notoriety it achieved during the 1970s by licensing an eclectic collection of items and producing nonsports programming. Along these lines, the subsidiary demonstrated that it did not need preexisting events to create popular sports television by developing made-for-TV specials, including Billie Jean King and Bobby Riggs's Battle of the Sexes, Evel Knievel's bone-shattering stunts, and *The Superstars*, which featured athletes competing in sports outside their areas of expertise. Though commercially successful, these programs were widely belittled as "TrashSports" that degraded the respectability ABC Sports had steadily built. Amid ABC Sports' investment in TrashSports, the division became embroiled in a scandal surrounding the 1977 US Boxing Championships, in which elements of the competition were fabricated to ensure its value as a TV spectacle. Chapter 6 examines how ABC's brand extensions and involvement in TrashSports took its sports programming to lengths that no longer necessitated preexisting events and uses the controversial Boxing Championships to investigate the limits to which ABC could manufacture engaging sporting content.

Cable outlets emerged in the mid-1970s and used the practices ABC Sports had established to gain a toehold in the new industry. To mitigate the effects of this competition, ABC acquired majority ownership of ESPN, the first all-sports cable channel and the biggest threat to its market share. But traditionally reliable ABC Sports programs like *Wide World* and *Monday Night* sank in popularity as the sports TV market expanded. Adding to these changes—and reflecting the upsurge of corporate consolidation that marked the 1980s—Capital Cities Communications acquired ABC in 1985 and implemented a swell of budgetary, procedural, and personnel changes that saw ABC Sports give up both Arledge and the Olympics. Chapter 7 considers how these shifts altered ABC Sports' previously secure place within the reconstituted American Broadcasting Company, sports TV, and popular culture while contextualizing the broader industrial transformation they foretold.

As ABC Sports' metamorphosis continued, ESPN established itself as TV's most lucrative cable outlet and one of the most recognizable brands in media—sports or otherwise. ESPN's rising value prompted the Walt Disney Company to purchase Capital Cities in 1996. Immediately after the acquisition, Disney began to position ESPN as the company's featured sports TV brand while it adjusted to the Web-driven and convergent sports media ecosystem that was replacing the network era ABC Sports represented. These changes culminated in 2006 when Disney moved *Monday Night* to ESPN and rebranded all ABC Sports programming as "ESPN on ABC." The book concludes by tracing Disney's reinvention of ABC Sports in the image of ESPN and probing the network division's scattered remnants in postnetwork media culture.

In telling ABC Sports' cultural and institutional history, this project touches on several topics that have inspired their own books, documentaries, and even big-budget feature films like *Ali* (2001), *Munich* (2005), and *Battle of the Sexes* (2017). It sheds new light on these familiar subjects by reading them through the lens of ABC and sports television. Likewise, it offers a more nuanced treatment of ABC Sports figures and programs that have received individualized treatment—Roone Arledge, Howard Cosell, *Monday Night Football*, and so on—by piecing together the broader cultural contexts out of which they emerged and avoiding the nostalgia, selective memory, and cronyism that marks the memoirs and popular histories that compose most of the literature on these topics. Moreover, it demonstrates sports television's intimate relationship to and influence on other TV genres and the broader industry—connections scholarship on sports media has been slow to identify. This book, then, explains how ABC Sports grew out of and reshaped the diverse circumstances surrounding it and suggests historical approaches to understanding such media institutions should tend carefully to these intersecting contexts and how they change over time.

· · ·

"One of the happiest relationships in American society is that between sports and the media," wrote James Michener in 1976. "This interface is delightfully symbiotic, since each helped the other survive."[8] Today, this remains truer than ever. However, sport and media's relationship has become more complex in the internet-driven media landscape that has replaced the network era ABC Sports dominated. Live sports broadcasts maintain special status as appointment viewing in an industry increasingly organized around on-demand content. But alternatives have emerged that allow consumers to skirt traditional distribution channels and enable content providers to serve as their own media producers. The economics and cultural meanings of sports television have changed apace.

Tracing sports TV's emergence, properties, and transformation, then, demands careful scrutiny of the diverse elements that constitute it. The history of ABC Sports helps to do this work. Network sports television is a shared site of cultural production that informed which types of people receive popular media attention, propelled the Super Bowl into a veritable national holiday, and cemented the Olympics' status as a global festival on which entire nations pin their geopolitical identities and aspirations. ABC Sports was the key institutional force in establishing sports TV's conventions, visibility, and power. The storied network sports division tells a larger story about sport, media, and culture from the 1950s into the present.

ONE

The "Almost Broadcasting Company" and the Birth of ABC Sports

Sports programming put ABC on the television map.

BERT SUGAR, journalist and historian[1]

ACCORDING TO BROADCAST HISTORIAN WILLIAM BODDY, "The American television industry underwent its deepest and most lasting changes in the middle years of the 1950s."[2] Of the three major networks that survived the decade, ABC—the youngest of the bunch—endured the most drastic shifts. It nearly folded, was sold to United Paramount Theaters, and was forced to develop inventive strategies to counteract its comparative feebleness. Sports became one of its chief survival techniques. The network's annual commitment to sporting content increased 600 percent over the 1950s and culminated with its March 1961 creation of ABC Sports—the first network sports division.[3] ABC Sports gave the traditionally unpopular network an identity and became the laboratory at which Roone Arledge developed his foundational aesthetic.

HARD ROCK

ABC was born the bastard child of the Radio Corporation of America's (RCA) National Broadcasting Company. The "Second Depression" of 1937—a recession within the Great Depression that deflated what few strides the economy had made since the 1929 stock market crash—compelled the US government to intensify its scrutiny of the large trusts and monopolies blamed for the financial crisis. The film and radio industries composed high-profile targets that signaled no entity would evade inspection. The Federal Communications Commission (FCC) specifically began to investigate chain broadcasting—the practice of programming multiple radio stations to air the same content simultaneously. Its 1941 *Report on Chain*

Broadcasting ruled that no single organization could broadcast on more than one network.

Two years later, the FCC deemed RCA's ownership of both the NBC Red Network and the NBC Blue Network anticompetitive and forced it to sell one of the properties. Unsurprisingly, RCA owner David Sarnoff opted to unload the less popular Blue Network, which focused on public affairs programming and was limited to low-power stations in small markets. Sarnoff found an eventual buyer in Edward J. Noble, the Life Savers Corporation owner and entrepreneur who thought a radio network might compose a promotionally rich complement to his many other ventures. Noble procured NBC Blue in October 1943 for $8 million, the highest price paid for a broadcasting entity to that date. The network, which came along with 168 affiliates and 715 employees, went by "Blue" until Noble purchased and adopted the name American Broadcasting Company in June 1945. Despite the title change, ABC retained Blue's comparative unpopularity and was distinguished only by its lower ratings, less prominent advertisers, and fewer affiliates. The network, wrote *Forbes*, "scraped along on the crumbs that fell from the table at which the big two were feasting."[4] As a result, ABC was known throughout the industry as the "Almost Broadcasting Company" and was constrained to engage in activities its competitors considered déclassé. "To get a modicum of income and to show a modest profit," explained eventual ABC president Oliver "Ollie" Treyz, "ABC took a relaxed view of standards established by NBC and CBS. We took spots for deodorants and laxatives, which the other guys wouldn't take."[5] As part of the struggling network's efforts to subsist, ABC followed CBS's, NBC's, and the short-lived broadcasting upstart DuMont's entrances into the new medium of television.

As with RCA, the FCC found Paramount Pictures Inc.—which comprised a movie studio and theater chain—to be restricting trade. The 1948 *United States v. Paramount Pictures Inc.* ruling, colloquially known as the Divorcement Decree, forced Paramount to separate its studio and theater arms into separate entities, Paramount Pictures Corporation and United Paramount Theaters (UPT), so it could not simply fill its theaters with the movies it produced and ignore competitors' products. Media historian Douglas Gomery calls the ruling "one of [the twentieth] century's more bitter and drawn-out antitrust battles," which permanently altered Hollywood's distribution and exhibition practices.[6] Beyond extricating itself from Paramount Pictures, United Paramount Theaters had to reduce its theater chain from 1,395 to 650 within five years. The windfall it received from selling those theaters poised the company to collect new assets. UPT president Leonard H. Goldenson, who joined Paramount as a lawyer in 1933 and took over after the divorcement, figured television would be a sensible place to invest the proceeds given the medium's similarities to, shared audience with, and ability to promote film.

But much to Goldenson's chagrin, it was impossible for prospective broadcasters to secure station licenses at the time. The FCC's Sixth Report and Order initiated a station freeze the same year as the Divorcement Decree. Originally slated for six months, the freeze extended more than three years—from September 30, 1948, until April 14, 1952. Aside from blocking potential station owners like UPT, the freeze solidified industrial hierarchies. The less popular ABC and DuMont networks continued to lose money during this period while CBS and NBC maintained their long-standing supremacy. "Given the station allocation plan contained within the FCC's Sixth Report and Order," explains broadcast historian Stewart Lewis Long, "most observers felt it was only a matter of time before either ABC or DuMont, or both networks, would go out of business."[7] Goldenson sought television stations, not necessarily ABC. But the only way he could acquire stations at this time was by purchasing an entity that already owned them. Though "only a skeleton of a network," ABC had five stations—the maximum the FCC permitted at the time—in five of the United States' top six markets.[8]

Noble—a notorious cheapskate who reportedly gave employees Life Savers candies as Christmas bonuses—demanded $25 million for ABC, far more than the losing venture's projected value.[9] He bargained with UPT by averring that CBS president William S. Paley expressed an interest in his struggling company. Though Goldenson reasonably argued that such a deal would never gain FCC approval, necessary for any acquisition involving the sale of licensed stations, the UPT president finally budged in 1951. "I knew it was too much," Goldenson shrugged years later, "but I was also pretty sure there wouldn't be another television network coming on the market anytime soon." In February 1953, after a protracted hearing that included thirteen hundred pages of documents and five hundred exhibits, the FCC approved UPT's acquisition. Goldenson initially retained ABC president Robert E. Kintner (whom he replaced with Treyz in 1956), and Noble chaired the network's board of directors. The FCC ratified the merger in part because it determined that ABC otherwise could not realistically vie for market share without some help: "ABC has been unable to compete effectively with NBC and CBS, principally because it lacks the financial resources, the working capital, and the diversity of revenue-producing activities of the other network of companies with which they are associated." Upon the acquisition, UPT infused ABC with $30 million it could use to secure new programming and upgrade its comparatively shabby facilities.[10]

ABC's good fortune accelerated DuMont's demise. The UPT-ABC merger "in effect sacrificed the DuMont Network in order that ABC might survive and prosper to offset the obvious dominance which NBC and CBS had gained during the 'freeze' years." "The minute the FCC approved the merger our fate was sealed," lamented DuMont president Theodore Bergman.[11] DuMont ceased broadcasting in 1955. ABC seized on this new void to turn its first profits. Though DuMont was even less prominent than ABC, sports programming composed one of its few strengths. DuMont's presentation of the 1951 National Football League championship, for instance, was the earliest live national TV broadcast of professional football. DuMont also aired non-live weekend anthology programs, the outdoor show *Fishing and Hunting Club* (1949–50), and the first prime-time pro football broadcasts, which anticipated, respectively, ABC's *Wide World of Sports*, *American Sportsman*, and *Monday Night Football*.

Despite UPT's infusion of capital and DuMont's folding, ABC remained television's least distinguished network. It held stations in New York, Chicago, Los Angeles, Detroit, and San Francisco but otherwise had just fourteen primary affiliates. NBC, by contrast, had sixty-three and CBS possessed thirty. ABC's affiliates were also often on less powerful UHF stations. While CBS and NBC offered a nearly continuous stream of programming, ABC did not schedule more than two hours of content before 7:00 p.m. until 1956, and it would typically go dark after 10:30. "It was widely believed that ABC could never offer one of the top ten shows," wrote trade journalist Martin Mayer, "simply because it couldn't get on enough stations at enough good time periods." As Goldenson sighed, "We had no hit shows, no stars, and nothing in prospect but struggle." Because of its limited reach and subpar content, ABC gave discounts to those precious few sponsors it secured. Advertisers treated the network as a supplementary service that would reach additional consumers at bargain-basement rates rather than an entity that warranted consistent investment.[12] ABC was consequently dubbed "Hard Rock," in contrast to CBS's "Black Rock" and NBC's "30 Rock." As CBS's nickname came from its jet-black headquarters and NBC's moniker referenced its address at 30 Rockefeller Plaza, ABC was defined by its comparative misfortune.

Most of the sports ABC carried nationally during its early years were schlocky and low-budget events like wrestling and roller derby. In 1948, a group of midwestern ABC affiliates joined to showcase the NFL's Chicago Bears and Chicago Cardinals games—broadcasts that originated from ABC's Chicago-owned station, WBKB. This package caught the attention of Edgar Scherick, a wheeling and dealing Harvard-educated time buyer for the Dancer-Fitzgerald-Sample advertising agency. Scherick noticed that the ABC affiliates covered almost exactly the distribution region of Falstaff Beer, a St. Louis–based client whose account he managed. He arranged for Falstaff to purchase half the spots on these regional broadcasts for the discounted price of $2,000 per game—an acquisition he later proclaimed "the greatest media buy in the history of television" because of its ability to capture so inexpensively and effectively the client's target market.[13]

Based on his success with the NFL broadcasts, Scherick persuaded Falstaff to sponsor a national Major League Baseball package starting in 1953. ABC struck a deal with the Chicago White Sox, Cleveland Indians, and Philadelphia Athletics to broadcast seventeen Saturday afternoon matches in the program titled *Game of the Week*. The following year it expanded to thirty weeks and added the Brooklyn Dodgers, New York Giants, and Philadelphia Phillies.[14] Because of the MLB's blackout rules, the games would appear only in markets without a major-league franchise. Faced with these constraints, *Game of the Week* ensured it would attract a sizable audience by hiring former MLB pitcher Jay Hanna "Dizzy" Dean as its featured announcer. Already a radio star, Dean affected a homespun persona that drew viewers regardless of the featured teams and kept them tuned in no matter the score. Despite the Falstaff-sponsored packages' success on ABC, Scherick moved both to CBS. "They just didn't have the good station hookups in enough cities," he bluntly explained of ABC.[15] The network's inexpensive ad rates, Scherick indicated, did not compensate for its paltry distributional range.

ABC built on this slowly growing identification with sports by securing contracts to air boxing and, more prominently, NCAA football in 1954. Its contract with the NCAA—whose TV rights stood and remain among the most coveted in sports—included twelve contests (along with a Thanksgiving Day game) and would be carried on 150 stations. On top of the football games, the agreement included twenty-six weeks of assorted winter and spring events. ABC made this deal in part by promising the NCAA that its broadcasts would place "emphasis on promoting collegiate football and the college way of life," an effort waged in part to offset negative publicity college sports had incurred after several recent scandals. *Variety* identified ABC's sporting efforts—and the NCAA contract in particular—as a mechanism through which the network might reasonably taper the gap separating it from its competitors.[16] Regardless of the NCAA deal's prestige, ABC was unable to sell sufficient sponsorships. It mistakenly banked that General Motors, the primary sponsor of NBC's NCAA telecasts, would continue advertising on ABC once it got college football. When General Motors declined—perhaps wary of ABC's comparative status—the junior network was forced to lower its rates and wound up losing $1.8 million. It dropped the winter and spring programming that accompanied the football games for fear of losing even more.[17] ABC's brief and unsuccessful efforts to establish a niche in sports programming only solidified its Hard Rock status.

THE WOOLWORTH NETWORK

To help ABC form an identity in network television, Treyz commissioned preeminent Columbia University sociologist Paul Lazarsfeld to conduct a study on the habits of TV viewers. The findings were simple but telling: network television's oligopolistic structure gave ABC space to invest in areas the other two networks were ignoring. Despite broadcast media's pretensions to cut across and unite disparate demographics, ABC developed a philosophy that a network cannot be "all things to all people." It counterprogrammed to attract viewers CBS and NBC underserved or altogether overlooked. "Whatever the audience is not watching at any given time makes for new possibilities," Goldenson explained. "We are not trying to take audiences from CBS and NBC. . . . We are trying to carve our own network character, to create new audiences."[18]

ABC found that programming at CBS and NBC was built primarily around stars from the radio tradition, and, as such, appealed mostly to older audiences. "Lazarsfeld recommended we go after the young audiences," Goldenson recalled. "We should build programs around casts of young, virile people . . . and create programs with stories that younger people would identify with."[19] They found that older audiences were more set in their viewing and purchasing routines and, as a result, were less likely to start watching new networks or sample new goods that might be advertised. "We're after a specific audience," Goldenson concluded. "The young housewife—one cut above the teenager—with two to four kids, who has to buy the clothing, the food, the soaps, the home remedies." Although younger audiences did not have older viewers' purchasing power, Lazarsfeld found that they spent more on average and buy more of the small-ticket products that so heavily populate mass-market advertising.[20] ABC formalized this process by branding itself as "the Network of the Young." "Practically all of the programs developed and/ or acquired by ABC between 1954 and 1956 were geared toward young families," explained media researcher turned executive Fred Silverman, who broke into the industry after writing a master's thesis on ABC's programming strategies. ABC immediately reduced material that did not coalesce with the image it was forging, such as news and public affairs.

Regardless of these shifts, ABC routinely lost its most successful programs. Goldenson opined that sponsors "brought us only their poor programming. They took their best ones to the other networks and when a good one developed at ABC they took that one away." This is precisely what happened with *Game of the Week*. Scherick debuted it on ABC and moved it to CBS after it became a hit with the potential to attract a larger audience than ABC could deliver. The migration of programs, Treyz explained, prevented ABC's lineup from demonstrating "any central network thinking, philosophy or point of view."[21]

ABC prioritized fostering viewing patterns that would stabilize its nascent identity over providing quality content. "First we build a habit factor," Goldenson said, "get them used to watching us, then we can do something about upgrading the programming. We're not interested in the critics." To be sure, critics already had little positive to report about ABC. "The real strength and vitality of television," Goldenson continued, "is in your regular week-in and week-out programs, the strength of motion pictures was always the habit of going to motion pictures on a regular basis, and that habit was, in part, taken away from motion pictures by television."[22] Goldenson thought TV could similarly become a "habit medium" around which consumers organize their everyday routines. ABC wound up teaming with Hollywood studios to nurture these behaviors.

ABC first joined the Walt Disney Company—an organization that possessed a vast archive of content perfect for young audiences. Disney was seeking revenue to help fund its Disneyland theme park, a dream Walt Disney had been pursuing for years. Most investors, however, considered the venture too risky. Disney identified television as a potential partner after producing two successful Christmas specials: *One Hour in Wonderland* (1950) for NBC and *The Walt Disney Christmas Show* (1951) for CBS. It approached all three networks about building a sustained partnership, but only ABC expressed interest. At the time, the network's live clearance rate was only 34 percent. Its consequent amenability to non-live content made Disney's filmed programming a good fit. This material would also be a boon for UPT, since it would advertise a studio whose productions were routinely exhibited in the company's theaters.

Disneyland debuted October 27, 1954. The weekly program showcased classic Disney cartoons and original pieces organized around the theme park's fanciful worlds (Adventureland, Fantasyland, Frontierland, and Tomorrowland). The agreement between ABC and Disney initially called for twenty programs, for which ABC paid $ 50,000 each. The contract also had ABC invest $500,000 in Disney's amusement park, which gave it 35 percent ownership and all profits from Disneyland's concession sales for ten years while helping its partner guarantee the additional loans it needed to complete the project.[23] The deal—which was the biggest programming package in network TV up to that point—gave ABC *Disneyland*'s first refusal rights for seven years.

Fortune celebrated *Disneyland* as "an immediate and smashing success." The show was the network's first top ten hit, which Goldenson called "a turning point in our progress." *Disneyland* attracted nearly half of ABC's advertising sales in 1954 and lured additional sponsors to the programs surrounding it. Just as important, ABC's seven-year contract with Disney ensured that its partner could not simply leave for another network once the show became a sensation.[24]

Goldenson viewed ABC's Disney alliance as a potential source of prestige that would enable the network to benefit from its partner's favorable brand and association with the film industry. Moreover, ABC took advantage of the non-live program's potential to be rerun, scheduled flexibly, and infused with commercial breaks. *Disneyland*'s first year on the air included twenty-five weeks of reruns, twelve weeks of second repeats, and an unprecedented number of commercials. Each of *Disneyland*'s episodes also devoted ten to twenty minutes to promoting Disney's theme park and related products. The following year, ABC and Disney expanded on *Disneyland* with *The Mickey Mouse Club*, a similarly successful afternoon program that the trade magazine *Television* dubbed "TV's most important show" shortly after its debut because it so effectively attracted young viewers.[25]

Allured by ABC and Disney's prosperous deal, MGM and Warner Brothers partnered with the network to create *MGM Parade* and *Warner Brothers Presents*, both of which premiered in 1955 and sold out their advertising spots before even hitting the airwaves. While *MGM Parade* composed a series of short subjects and trailers for MGM's upcoming releases, *Warner Brothers Presents* provided rotating series that adapted the Warner Brothers films *Casablanca* (1942), *Cheyenne* (1947), and *King's Row* (1942). *Cheyenne*, the most popular of the bunch, featured the adventures of gallant frontiersman Cheyenne Bodie and sparked a glut of television westerns like *Maverick* (ABC, 1957–62), *Bonanza* (NBC, 1959–73), and *Rawhide* (CBS, 1959–65). Reflecting *Disneyland*, each *Warner Brothers Presents* episode initially included a six-minute segment called "Behind the Camera" that introduced viewers to the studio's stars and teased the company's upcoming films.

With *Disneyland* airing on Tuesday evenings and *Warner Brothers Presents* on Wednesdays, ABC began to achieve the programming regularity and youthful identity that Goldenson and Treyz sought to cultivate after the merger. The collaborations with high-profile Hollywood studios also set the network apart from CBS and NBC. In 1955, ABC produced only 14 percent of its material, while CBS and NBC manufactured roughly 50 percent of their programs. Despite creating such a small proportion of its programming, ABC's clearance rate increased 24 percent between 1954 and 1955.[26] Taking notice of this success, CBS and NBC began establishing similar Hollywood partnerships. The programming model soon became standard practice across network TV.

Critics, however, expressed befuddlement at ABC's willingness to let content providers so brazenly shop their wares. Goldenson responded to these grievances by appealing to the commercial network's business imperatives. "We're in the Woolworth business," he said, "not in Tiffany's. Last year Tiffany made only $30,000." With a thinly veiled jab at CBS—the so-called Tiffany Network—Goldenson admitted that ABC put profits over prestige. The network's focus on mainstream, promotion-laden entertainments like children's programming and westerns fashioned a brand that—like Woolworth—served the populace rather than lofty cultural goals. "We study public taste hard and carefully," Treyz asserted. "We gear ourselves entirely to what the public wants. And the public wants cowboys. The proof: we're getting the audiences, and we're getting the sponsors. The big two is now the big three."[27]

"A NEW ERA"

ABC built on its Hollywood collaborations by reinvesting in sports. At the time, network sports programming operated out of news departments—a connection that 1950s sports television's stark aesthetics reflected. Tom Moore, ABC's vice president for programming, who worked as public relations director for Hollywood's Forest Lawn Cemetery before joining the network, argued that sports would bolster ABC's counterprogramming. "I made a pitch to them," Moore said. "Let's go all out for sports. Let's make this *the* sports network. The other two guys are underrating it."[28] He argued that sports had the unique potential to enhance the network's Woolworth-inspired efforts. "Advertisers find sports moves merchandise out of proportion to their ratings," he said. "They will pay more for a sports viewer than for any other."[29] He also reasoned that live sports' immediacy would prompt stations to clear space for ABC's broadcasts whether or not they were ABC affiliates. Though he found Moore's pitch persuasive, ABC News president John Daly had no interest in overseeing this additional content. Goldenson consequently put Moore in charge of the task. The already overextended Moore contracted Scherick's fledgling company Sports Programs Incorporated (SPI) to produce and package ABC's sports offerings.

The savvy and opportunistic Scherick had continued to build expertise in sports programming since handling ABC's professional football and baseball broadcasts earlier in the decade. After taking these packages from ABC and delivering them to CBS at a considerable rate increase, the Tiffany Network hired him in May 1956 as its "sports specialist in charge of all sports program sales." Just four months into his CBS tenure, Scherick noticed that his new employer was not planning to renew Big Ten college basketball. Scherick thought he could sell the basketball broadcasts on a regional basis like his Falstaff-sponsored midwestern baseball telecasts.[30] The salesman phoned Big Ten commissioner Tug Wilson and made his pitch: "You're getting cancelled by CBS," he said. "You'll never make it as a national vehicle but you can make it as a regional one and I can clear the regional network and sell it so that Big Ten basketball can have a very fruitful and long life."[31] Once the Big Ten agreed, Scherick left CBS to form SPI. He took with him CBS producer Jack Lubell and hired Chet Simmons as an assistant. Scherick rented a grimy two-room office on Manhattan's West Forty-Second Street where he and the hard-drinking Lubell, according to Simmons, "would fight like cats and dogs."[32] Simmons once walked into the office to find Lubell choking Scherick in a fit of blind rage. "Lubell literally lifted Scherick off the floor with his hands around Ed's neck," Simmons said. "I thought Jack was going to kill him, because all the while Scherick was making these gurgling noises with his tongue hanging out. Finally, Jack let him go. . . . I don't even recall what they were battling about because they were always scrapping, but it wouldn't have shocked me if a murder had been committed."[33]

Shortly after forming, SPI teamed with Dick Bailey's Sports Network Inc. (SNI), which also launched in 1956 and specialized in providing telephone lines for sports TV productions. SNI handled technical operations while SPI took care of sales. With SNI's assistance, SPI became ABC's de facto sports department. But even after Moore recruited Scherick and company, ABC's slate of sports content was lean. It programmed only seventy-six hours of sports in 1958, which placed it last among the networks.[34] ABC also reneged on the contracts to broadcast big-ticket events like the 1960 Winter Olympics and the Gator Bowl after deciding it would not be able to recoup its contract expenditures—decisions that lowered its credibility among potential clients.

The safety razor company Gillette, which was more closely associated with sports media than any other business at the time, paved the way for ABC's sustained entry into big-time sports. Gillette underwrote *Gillette Cavalcade of Sports*, a series of sports programming that started on the radio in 1941, and variations of it like *Friday Night Fights*, which NBC debuted in 1944. Lou Maxon—head of Gillette's advertising division—described *Friday Night Fights* as the "backbone" of his client's marketing efforts.[35] A combination of declining ratings and boxing's associations with the criminal underworld compelled NBC to cancel the program in 1960.[36] Left without a home for its prized program, Gillette offered to give ABC its $8 million annual sports advertising budget if the network attached Gillette to its Wednesday evening fight package and moved the program to Fridays. While Moore and Scherick badly wanted the capital, Alka-Seltzer and Kool cigarettes were already sponsoring the network's weekly boxing show. With the ABC board's blessing, the media executives hammered out a pact to move the sponsors to different programs so it could accept the Gillette payout. It was not, however, able to shift the fights to Friday evenings—an alteration Gillette believed would create continuity with its canceled NBC program—and instead scheduled it on Saturday nights. Outside of the boxing package, Gillette would let ABC use the money for any sports programming it saw fit except horse races and roller derby.[37] The infusion provided a war chest that empowered ABC to pursue broadcast contracts not previously possible given its limited budget.

The network made NCAA football its first target, a sport ABC had not carried since its disastrous experience in 1954. NBC held the NCAA contract at the time and had been renewing it for several years without competition from CBS, which was primarily committed to pro football in the fall. While the Gillette contract was substantial, ABC's suddenly enlarged budget was still not vast enough to survive a bidding war with its deep-pocketed rival. Scherick cannily reasoned that ABC would only be able to get the rights if it kept secret its intention to bid. After consulting a series of informants, he discovered that Tom Gallery, the NBC executive in charge of the network's sports activities at the time, typically brought two envelopes to blind biddings like those the NCAA held. One packet contained a low bid—typically 1 percent higher than the previous year's contract—and the other contained a higher offer. "If NBC got the slightest inkling that we were in the game," Scherick explained, "they'd come in with their high bid. We were pretty sure we could top their low bid. Their high bid would be way beyond us."[38] The stakes were particularly steep because 1960 marked the first time the NCAA would sell its rights for two seasons.

Scherick then conjured up a strategy that could have been lifted from a cheap spy thriller. He would scour ABC to locate "the most innocuous fellow we can find, someone who could melt into the wallpaper," and use this unassuming character as a Trojan horse to deliver the network's shocking bid.[39] He found Stanton Frankle, a self-effacing and bookish accountant of average height and build. Scherick carefully instructed Frankle that he would go to the bidding meeting at New York's Royal Manhattan Hotel with ABC's offer and a document that ABC's lawyers drew up to guarantee that the recently flush network could afford its bid. He told Frankle to keep a low profile at the meeting, and not to lie if anyone asked about his affiliation. Frankle's main assignment was to keep an eye on Gallery, make sure he had no competitors, and register ABC's bid only after the NBC executive submitted his network's presumably lower offer.

On the day of the bidding, Scherick sent Frankle by limousine to the Royal Manhattan. He was so concerned that the plan might go awry that he sent a backup in a separate limo should the accountant be intercepted or otherwise incapacitated. Scherick reportedly told the understudy that "if he should see Stanton Frankle fall injured in the streets, he should let Frankle lie where he fell and proceed to the consummation of the mission."[40] Frankle made it to the meeting unscathed and in time for NCAA director of TV programming Asa Bushnell to open the bidding. Just as Scherick predicted, Gallery scanned the room to check for competitors. When he did not see anyone familiar, he took one of two envelopes from his jacket pocket and submitted it to Bushnell. The bid was for $5.2 million, a predictable 10 percent higher than NBC was paying per season. Frankle made his move. "My name is Stanton Frankle," he said to Bushnell as he handed him an envelope. "I represent the American Broadcasting Company and here is our bid." ABC offered $6,251,114 for the two-year contract—a sizable chunk of the Gillette cash. When asked why he tacked on the extra $1,114 to the massive bid, Scherick flippantly claimed that he did not want to seem "chintzy."[41]

Gallery, who had begun to treat the annual bidding as a convivial formality en route to resuming his network's business with college football, was stunned. So was the NCAA, which was not thrilled about the prospect of giving its most coveted TV contract to the third-ranked network but could hardly turn down the extra million dollars ABC offered. "The NCAA would as soon as have had a Martian descend and bid as give their games to ABC," Scherick explained. "The NCAA was used to the crème de la crème, NBC, and viewed ABC as a guttersnipe organization." But the money was enough to motivate the NCAA to swallow its pride and sign with the Almost Broadcasting Company.[42]

As Moore proclaimed, "The acquisition by ABC-TV of NCAA rights marks a new era in the field of sports programming for ABC." Beyond college football, ABC used the Gillette funds for rights to produce baseball, additional boxing, and the bowling program *Make That Spare*—a non-live "accordion" show it would place before or after NCAA football to round out its Saturday schedule. *Los Angeles Times* sportswriter Don Page claimed that ABC's increased commitment to sports caused NBC "to shed its prize feathers" and suggested it might need to replace its peacock corporate mascot with a turkey as a result of this industrial power shift.[43] Based on its acquisition of the desirable NCAA football contract, ABC started receiving station clearances in non-ABC markets. As Moore explained, "My argument to the top brass was 'you let us get into college sports and we'll get the games cleared in markets where ABC has no affiliates because the public doesn't give a good goddamn about a station's loyalty to NBC or CBS.'"[44]

"THE MARK TWAIN OF TV SPORTS"

Concerned about ABC's ability to set its sports programming apart, Scherick and Moore sought to pair the network's contracts to air marquee sporting events with an engaging way of presenting them. To help develop this approach, Scherick hired Arledge, a twenty-nine-year-old NBC producer whose primary experience up to that point was in children's programming. Arledge was a stocky, redheaded, and bespectacled attorney's son from Forest Hills, Long Island.[45] The inquisitive and private-schooled youngster developed an eclectic body of interests that included drama, literature, politics, geography, and sports. He indulged these curiosities by pursuing a liberal arts degree at Columbia. "I wanted to be a writer," he recalled, "but I couldn't decide whether I wanted to write sports, government, philosophy, or theater."[46] Arledge took courses on the great works of literature with celebrity professors Mark Van Doren and Lionel Trilling, who instilled in him a keen appreciation of and ability to analyze narrative. The serial overachiever served as president of his Phi Gamma Delta fraternity and edited the school's yearbook, *The Columbian*, during his senior year. He wound up directing his interests toward a specialization in government and politics. Arledge also briefly did some graduate work at Columbia's School of International Affairs, where he focused on the Near East and Middle East and assisted with the scholarly journal it published.[47]

Upon graduation, Arledge decided the communications industry might best foster his catholic passions and writing-heavy skill set. He had a promising connection in DuMont programming chief James Caddigan, a former Paramount Pictures employee. Arledge met Caddigan while working as a headwaiter over the summer at the Wayside Inn in Chatham, Massachusetts. Caddigan and his family entered the restaurant just as it was about to close. Rather than turn them away—which would have been firmly within his rights—Arledge left the kitchen open so the family could dine. Caddigan remembered Arledge's generosity when the freshly minted college grad applied for a job at DuMont in December 1952 and hired him as an assistant to the associate director of programming and production.

Arledge barely had time to learn the ropes at DuMont before being drafted into the military in March 1953. Until December 1954, he served at Maryland's Aberdeen Proving Ground, where he ran the radio and television section of the base's Public Information Office and, as he noted in his résumé, was "responsible for the dissemination of information concerning the United States Army Ordnance Corps and its weapons, training and other features."[48] Though there were protections in place guaranteeing soldiers the jobs they left after being drafted, DuMont's broadcasting wing was practically defunct when Arledge was discharged, and the company had nothing for him. Arledge threatened legal action and sent an enraged letter to Caddigan. "I deserve better treatment than to be notified by your secretary that you had left word that was nothing available for me," he seethed to his unresponsive former boss. "It looks as if the whole DuMont policy has been to keep me hanging."[49]

But not regaining the DuMont job proved a blessing in disguise. Arledge shortly found work as a floor manager at NBC's New York City affiliate WRCA-TV, where his first wife, Joan, served as one David Sarnoff's secretaries. In his letter of application, Arledge suggested his "main field of interest and experience has always been in the area of public service programming. My educational background, combined with the experience I have gained in the actual staging of television programs could best be utilized in News and Special Events Television Programming." Though his entry-level position amounted to little more than grunt work, Arledge optimistically told professional colleague Orrin Dunlap that "advancement from this position is very good and that I will have a chance eventually to do some creative work."[50] Arledge quickly worked his way up to director, producer, and unit manager. He oversaw an assortment of programs, including the Rockefeller Center Christmas tree lighting ceremony featuring Olympic figure skater Dick Button, whom he eventually hired as an expert commentator for ABC Sports. But Arledge's primary job was producing ventriloquist Shari Lewis's morning children's puppet show *Hi Mom!*, which starred the precocious sock puppet Lamb Chop. Though *Hi Mom!* got Arledge his first Emmy Award, the high-minded Ivy Leaguer divulged "it would have been even nicer . . . had it been acquired for producing something meatier than a morning kids show."[51]

Arledge's diverse ambitions and hopes for rapid career advancement drove him to explore a variety of TV genres. He wrote a teleplay titled *Nothing to Hide* in 1955, sold an adaptation of Charles Dickens's *A Christmas Carol* to CBS, produced the informational program *Tax Party*, worked on a quiz show named *Opportunity Knocks*, and did freelance productions that ranged from promotional films for American Airlines to features for the Nassau, Bahamas, travel bureau.[52] Arledge teamed with his Columbia classmate Larry Grossman to write a proposal for *Masterpiece*, a ninety-minute program that would dramatize the "stories of the world's greatest masterworks of art, music and literature and the men who created them," such as Michelangelo's Sistine Chapel fresco, Beethoven's "Eroica," and Walt Whitman's "Drum Taps."[53] Grossman, who went on to run PBS and oversee the similar public television franchise *Masterpiece Theater*, claimed that he and Arledge conjured up the show in a noble effort "to save television from triviality."[54]

Arledge went in a different direction with *For Men Only*, a variety program geared toward urban male sophisticates that he described as a combination of *Playboy, True, Sport*, and *Field & Stream* magazines. He recruited the dapper NBC weatherman Pat Hernon to host a self-funded pilot, which featured *Sports Illustrated* artist Robert Riger sharing drawings of a Carmen Basilio prizefight, sportscaster Marty Glickman narrating a segment on track and field, a feature on jazz, and a shapely young woman periodically parading in front of the camera in a bathing suit. The production team extended *For Men Only*'s flagrantly macho subject matter behind the camera by passing around a bottle of scotch while filming the sample episode.

Hernon knew Scherick from previous jobs and slipped the sports packager a copy of Arledge's production in hopes that he might find *For Men Only* suitable for ABC or have recommendations for where else they might shop it. Scherick had no interest in *For Men Only*, but he thought it showed some potential. "I recognized the talent in Roone as soon as I saw that kinescope," he recalled. "It was another attempt to do a sports magazine show. . . . But it was done with nice flair and I liked its production."[55] He consequently took a meeting with Arledge at SPI's cramped and disheveled office, which Arledge later likened to a "bookie joint." During the meeting Scherick explained his arrangement with ABC and their joint efforts to make a push in sports. He then tested Arledge's sports knowledge by having the producer identify the athletes whose pictures hung crooked and dusty on the walls. Arledge knew all those Scherick asked him to name—and later expressed relief that Scherick did not quiz him on the several athletes he did not recognize. Scherick offered him a job on the spot to produce ABC's NCAA football games for an annual salary of $10,000. Arledge started on May 1, 1960—just in time to begin preparations for college football.

Though his new position was hardly a step up, Arledge was elated to leave his days at *Hi Mom!* behind. "I finally got my fill of early morning hours and puppets and decided to live like a gentleman," he wrote in a letter announcing his career change to the Leo Burnett advertising agency's Hooper White. "As you can see from the letterhead I have left NBC to go work in the field I have always preferred." He giddily concluded the note by gloating that his "first assignment is a rough one. I have to go to San Francisco this weekend to watch the Giants and Dodgers play baseball." "It's a pleasure," Arledge wrote to another colleague, "not to have to get up at 5am and look at puppets." The producer made clear that he was moving on to bigger and better things. But several of Arledge's associates warned that working in sports would harm his professional credibility. "There's nothing creative you can do in sports," he later said in mocking imitation of this unsolicited advice.[56] But, as he demonstrated with *For Men Only*, Arledge viewed sports as part of a cultural tapestry that included music, fashion, and cuisine and that deserved the comparatively dignified treatment these topics commonly received.

In fact, Arledge's main complaint with 1950s sports television was that it did not appreciate this richness. "When I got into it in 1960, televising sports amounted to going out on the road, opening three or four cameras, and trying not to blow any plays. They were barely documenting the game, but just the marvel of seeing a picture was enough to keep people glued to their sets."[57] He noticed sports TV's singular power after witnessing NBC's telecast of the Baltimore Colts' sudden death overtime victory over the New York Giants in the 1958 NFL Championship—a contest now commonly referred to as the "greatest game ever played"—enthrall a national audience. But Arledge thought these spectacles could be dramatized and personalized in ways that would increase their already vast viewership. They relied, he thought, too much on the events and not enough on the people, places, and circumstances that made them worth televising in the first place. For instance, Arledge recalled taking his wife to a Notre Dame–Army football game and being surprised to discover her engrossment. But he soon realized that she was not interested in the game so much as the marching band, cheerleaders, and fellow onlookers. This experience reminded Arledge of how *Sports Illustrated*'s photos and drawings highlighted sport's emotion-laden details and atmosphere. He thought he could do the same with television. "The action on the field is only half of what's going on," he told *TV Guide*. "The peripheral action is just as important. . . . There's something impersonal about 100,000 people, but if you can see the reaction of just one cheerleader when a touchdown is made or the look on the face of one fan when a player drops the ball, then you really know what's going on."[58] Arledge sought to emphasize the drama surrounding sporting events to amplify their spectacular status and to attract those, like his wife, who might not care about games but were interested in the stories and personalities they harbor.

While Arledge's new position in sports may not have impressed his more elitist peers, Scherick's decision to put the greenhorn producer in charge of ABC's highest-profile sports account was a big gamble. Scherick admitted that Arledge's "experience did not warrant" the position "at all."[59] Gillette and the NCAA were fretful when word leaked in the trade press that Arledge—with whom neither entity was familiar—was slated to oversee the autumn games. To soothe their anxieties, Scherick said that he, not Arledge, would personally helm the telecasts—a promise he had no intention of keeping.

Because of the brouhaha surrounding Arledge's hiring, Scherick asked his new employee to pen an internal memo explaining how he aimed to produce sports telecasts and how this approach would distinguish ABC's college football coverage. The document—which Arledge claimed to have typed out over a couple of beers on a Sunday afternoon—became a de facto mission statement for ABC's "up close and personal" aesthetic. In fact, the questionable new hire's manifesto was eventually distributed in pamphlet form to all new ABC Sports employees. "Heretofore," Arledge wrote, "television has done a remarkable job of bringing the game to the viewer—now we are going to take the viewer to the game." He maintained that ABC would achieve this transportation by filtering NCAA football games through story lines that introduce the campuses where contests occur and include profiles of the otherwise faceless competitors. It would adopt a battery of innovations (handheld cameras, slow motion, split screens, crane shots, etc.) to display games and explain the feelings competitors bring to and experience during them. For instance, he argued that the handheld camera, which he referred to as a "creepy peepy" and borrowed from NBC's coverage of the 1960 Republican National Convention, would "get the impact shots we cannot get from a fixed camera . . . all the excitement, wonder, jubilation and despair that make this America's Number One sports spectacle and a human drama to match bullfights and heavyweight championships in intensity." "In short," Arledge wrote, "we are going to add show business to sports!...In addition to the natural suspense and excitement of the actual game, we have a supply of human drama that would make the producer of a dramatic show drool." He closed his bombastic memorandum by promising that this style would install ABC as the leader in networks sports TV. "We will be setting the standards that everyone will be talking about and that others in the industry will spend years trying to equal."[60] The proclamation was enough to convince Gillette and the NCAA that Scherick hired a producer with vision, if not experience.

Arledge insisted that his ornate method would amount to more than eye-catching bells and whistles. Rather, it would probe—and even create—sport's meanings. "You've got to distinguish between a legitimate journalistic device and a gimmick," he said.[61] The producer prohibited ABC's partners from approving announcers or censoring coverage, affordances other networks permitted that he contended would compromise ABC's integrity. As Arledge asserted, "We have to insist in our reporting, just as our news departments do in covering a space shot, that we name our own reporters, that we cover what we want to cover, that leagues or organizations do not tell us how much we can cover or what we can cover."[62]

Arledge's innovations prompted *Film Comment*'s Bruce Berman to name him the "D. W. Griffith of sports TV." Along these lines, ESPN's Ralph Wiley called Arledge "the Mark Twain of TV sports. The greatest storyteller that ever was, at least in this country. The author of the book from which all other American sports TV are [*sic*] made."[63] The producer did not discourage the many designations of him as a savant. A ferociously competitive workaholic behind the scenes, Arledge affected a suave persona punctuated by the glamorous friends he kept, the pipes he smoked, and the pinky rings, safari jackets, and aviator glasses he donned. His carefully curated image—an embodiment of the postwar "good life" that *Playboy* curated for affluent male professionals—made it no surprise that this was the mind behind a repertoire eclectic enough to include *Masterpiece*, *For Men Only*, and NCAA football. When Arledge assumed control over ABC Sports in 1964, he had his name appended to the closing credits of all its productions—whether or not he directly participated in their creation. Like a signature on a painting, this uncommon sports television practice positioned ABC Sports' programming as polished artworks comparable to films and situated Arledge as an auteur rather than a technician.

But Arledge was not completely alone in authoring many of the advances for which he is credited. In 1926, radio personality Graham McNamee encouraged sportscasters "make each of your listeners, though miles away from the sport, feel that he or she, too, is there with you in that press stand."[64] Arledge's stated desire to "take the viewer to the game" was therefore in place for decades before he entered the profession. The producer's contemporaries were also using TV's expanding palette of technological tools to develop similarly stylized approaches. Arledge hired director Andy Sidaris in 1960 to work the NCAA games after Sidaris sent him a letter of application proposing to use a combination of handheld cameras, halftime highlights, and shots of the atmosphere surrounding the games to create "unusual and exciting" telecasts that would appeal to both men and women.[65] The practices Sidaris proposed mirror those Arledge laid out in his memo. Sidaris—who wound up working under Arledge for the next twenty-five years—also has the dubious distinction of developing the "honey shot," a titillating cut to an attractive female spectator designed to pique and sustain male viewers' interest that is also often credited to Arledge. "I'd rather see a great looking body than a touchdown anytime," Sidaris, a self-described "dirty old man" admitted. More specifically, Arledge took credit for pioneering the instant replay and slow motion, which NBC's Tony Verna and ABC's Robert Trachinger both claim to have conceived. "Roone is like the Russians," Verna sniped. "He likes to say he invented the hot dog and motherhood."[66] While Arledge never claimed to operate in a creative vacuum, he willingly allowed these myths to persist and clearly benefited from them.

Arledge paired his auteur persona with an evasive but looming management style. He was difficult to reach and sometimes would be inaccessible for days on end. Arledge did not like to deliver bad news and sometimes simply avoided conflicts in hopes that they would resolve without his intervention—a strategy that usually backfired. While generally evasive, he would reportedly give employees hours of undivided attention when they finally caught him. He also insisted on keeping a conspicuous red "Roone phone" at each production site that gave him a direct line to call in suggestions and, perhaps most important, to give the impression he was always scrutinizing his staff. "You knew dad was watching," ABC director Roger Goodman noted.[67] Despite these unorthodox practices, Arledge's staffers were fiercely loyal and many—such as Sidaris; directors Chet Forte and Doug Wilson; engineer Julius "Julie" Barnathan; and producers Chuck Howard, Dennis Lewin, Geoff Mason, and Jim Spence—remained in his employ for decades and became industry icons in their own right. Others, such as Dick Ebersol and Don Ohlmeyer, left ABC to become high-ranking media executives elsewhere after apprenticing under Arledge. As football player turned ABC Sports commentator Frank Gifford said, "Vince Lombardi and Roone Arledge are the two men I've known in my life who could make me go the extra yard."[68] Like Lombardi, Arledge was a merciless competitor. "The man is totally unscrupulous. A jackal," said a rival sports TV executive. "Beneath that Howdy Doody face lurks one of the most ruthless, opportunistic guys in the business." Arledge, who enjoyed toying with competitors and had a reputation for driving up prices for properties that he did not even want, responded to such charges by matter-of-factly acknowledging, "If you don't have the rights, you can't do the show."[69] The ends, the Machiavellian sports television executive calmly indicated, justified the means.

To lend credibility to ABC's NCAA broadcasts, Scherick hired established sportscaster Curt Gowdy as play-by-play announcer and former University of Missouri and NFL quarterback Paul Christman as color commentator. Upon Arledge's urging, Scherick also brought in Bob Neal to serve as network sports television's first sideline reporter—another innovation that stuck. The night before ABC's debut game, Arledge delivered a presentation that outlined the network's production plan to his staff as well as to Gillette and NCAA representatives. An apparently inspired Moore felt moved to join in on the speech: "We do not want a football game like NBC. I want to see the good-looking gals! The chrysanthemums! The cheerleaders! The fans! The players sitting on the bench! I want to see the apprehension of the guy about to go into the game! I want to see the head coach pacing! I want you to capture the story of the game!" "I sure hope in the middle of all this stuff that you get around to showing some football, too," interrupted Christman—a hardened industry veteran accustomed to more hemmed-in productions.[70]

ABC's first game featured Alabama and Georgia on September 17, 1960. Its coverage presented the game as a duel between Alabama's legendary coach Paul "Bear" Bryant and Georgia's flashy quarterback Fran Tarkenton. The narrative Arledge created of the wise veteran taking on and ultimately defeating the impetuous and gun-slinging young man reflected the popular westerns that ABC aired in prime time during the week. Arledge expanded on these cinematic practices later in the season by opening a Pittsburgh and Penn State game with a shot from a hospital rooftop near the University of Pittsburgh stadium. The aerial establishing shot emphasized the event's grandeur in a way that evokes so many epic Hollywood films' opening moments. ABC also strove to enhance coaches' and players' participation in its narratives by having them provide the now-standard halftime interviews—a request the NCAA initially denied. "Our coaches are just that," huffed NCAA television committee chair Rix Yard, "not actors."[71] While the coaches may not have been actors, they were quickly becoming characters in the Saturday afternoon sporting dramas ABC built.

ABC repeatedly made clear its responsibility for this stylized coverage. "The greatest contribution we can make," Arledge claimed, "is getting people aware of production."[72] ABC telecasts called deliberate attention to their inventively crafted status to ensure viewers knew they were not simply watching sports TV, but ABC productions. They would frequently showcase the network's many camera operators and control room to emphasize ABC's labors to offer a cutting-edge sports media experience. "It was important for people to understand that we're trying to do things differently," Lewin remarked. "If we had the latest slo-mo machine we would make a point of it, if we had the overhead crane we would tell people how high it was and show the guy dangling from it."[73] ABC also made sure that its brand and trademarks were prominent throughout broadcasts. During the first season of its NCAA football package, the network agreed to plug UCLA's marching band if it played songs and made halftime formations that celebrated ABC and its sponsors—a reflection of ABC's promotion-friendly deals with Disney and Warner Brothers.[74]

ABC purchased the contract to televise the upstart American Football League the same year it began broadcasting NCAA football. The AFL was formed by a cadre of millionaires who responded to the NFL's continual refusals to grant them expansion franchises by starting their own league. The fledgling operation needed television's revenues and exposure to get off the ground. As with *Disneyland*, ABC was the only network desperate enough to show interest in the new league. "They told me that if we would take them on they had a chance," Moore noted.[75] After negotiating with the AFL owners, who had far less bargaining power than the network's typical clients, ABC settled on a five-year deal for $2,125,000 annually, which provided the AFL with roughly $300,000 per game that aired. ABC tailored its weekly coverage to regional audiences by broadcasting one eastern and one western game. Moreover, the initial contract would escalate yearly only if the broadcasts met advertising targets, a condition that provided ABC with some insurance. The deal, according to sport historians David A. Klatell and Norman Marcus, gave ABC "the inexpensive programming it was seeking" and provided the AFL "a life-line, albeit a fragile one." By 1966—and with the aid of ABC's TV coverage—the AFL ate away at enough of its competitor's market share to force a merger.[76]

Because the AFL so urgently needed TV's money and publicity, it was amenable to ABC's efforts to combine coverage with "show business." *Variety* called the AFL "the league that television built," and *Broadcasting* reported that it was "organized with TV in mind."[77] The league eliminated the fair catch rule and instituted a two-point conversion after touchdowns to make its games more exciting. It also built familiarity with its lesser-known players by affixing names to the backs of jerseys so TV viewers could identify them, an implementation ABC's telecasts assisted by including graphics that introduced players and their statistics.

The AFL's reliance on TV made it relatively untroubled by its games' mostly low attendance. Rather than impose blackout policies to protect ticket sales, it wagered that ABC's dynamic coverage might lure fans to the stadium. But Arledge still thought it important to give the impression that AFL matchups took place in vibrant atmospheres like Notre Dame and Alabama. He bunched the scattered smattering of fans who did show near midfield to "provide the appearance of a reasonably full house" and avoided shots that tracked the ball through the air after kickoffs and punts, "because to do so would reveal endless rows of empty seats."[78] Instead, ABC cut directly from the kicker to the receiver or had camera operators pan along the ground. The network also took liberties to stage—and even restage—events. When a Dallas Texans game began before ABC's cameras were rolling, the volatile Jack Lubell thundered onto the field screaming at the lead official: "You cocksucker, never again kick off until I tell you you can kick off! Do you understand?"[79] Commentator Jack Buck smoothly described Lubell's disturbance as that of an irate fan who interrupted the game. The teams kicked off again, and ABC's cameras captured the game in its entirety. This brand of sports television—which those in the industry sarcastically called "AFL coverage"—treated the players as actors and the fans as extras in a methodically staged drama based on reality, but not entirely beholden to it. The AFL's agreeability toward television, according to Arledge, gave ABC "the freedom to try new things" and develop its style.[80]

Variety expressed amazement at how quickly ABC's AFL telecasts, which attracted roughly 80 percent of the ratings that CBS's NFL broadcasts achieved, sold out their advertising spots.[81] This success demonstrated that there was sufficient room on TV for the new league as well as for ABC's approach to covering sports. Fans may not have been buying tickets, but they were watching the games—at least ABC's version of them.

ABC's American Football League coverage reversed the logic that traditionally guided sports television. Rather than telecasting sports because they were popular, ABC would make sports popular by telecasting them. ABC posted an advertisement in *Broadcasting* to showcase its ability to create such striking made-for-TV spectacles. "Every Sunday, come September," it reads, "a conservatively estimated turnout of 15,000,000 fans will take their ABC-TV seats (on the 50-yard line) and follow the AFL's exciting brand of football." The ad reminds potential sponsors that "AFL football, with its razzle-dazzle, wide-open style of play that is made to order for home screens, delivers . . . responsive families in concentrated strength."[82] As ABC indicates, fan attendance at AFL games was irrelevant to their potential to deliver a reliable and diverse TV audience. It suggests the sport is better appreciated via ABC's virtual seats than a stadium's bleachers. The AFL's dependence on ABC illustrated the beginnings of a broader industrial shift in which television became sports organizations' primary revenue source and, as a result, increasingly dictated how events were staged in order to suit the medium's creative and economic motives.

Shortly after ABC began its NCAA football and AFL packages, *Broadcasting* reported that the network was for the first time "on the CBS-TV and NBC-TV level in sports billing." That same year, *Variety* declared ABC a "major sports network," and the *New York Times* observed that the network's heightened emphasis on sports "enhance[d] even more its varsity standing among the networks." But because ABC still had no coverage in a significant portion of the United States, it remained a distant third. While acknowledging this disadvantage, ABC insisted that "where viewers have a choice of three networks they choose ABC-TV first." It located its sports coverage as the key factor that attracted this relatively small but rising viewership.[83]

Though ABC soon lost the contracts to air both NCAA football and the AFL, its football coverage was promising enough to compel the network to acquire SPI from Scherick in March 1961 for a tax-free transfer of ten thousand shares (a value of roughly $500,000 that transformed Scherick into the network's second-largest individual stockholder) and to create ABC Sports, a programming banner and division that grew into a fully autonomous subsidiary by 1968.[84] While ABC's early sports offerings privileged autumn, the network needed year-round content to solidify its identification with the genre. *Wide World of Sports* would extend the AFL package's stylized efforts to draw viewers without featuring popular sports.

TWO

ABC's Wide World of Sports

"THE SEEDBED OF MODERN SPORTS
TELEVISION" AND THE COLD WAR

Wide World has given America a wider and more sophisticated view of the games people play than any other single mass media outlet.

JIM MCKAY, host, *Wide World of Sports*[1]

Everything we do at ABC Sports evolves from the *Wide World* philosophy.

DENNIS LEWIN, coordinating producer,
Wide World of Sports[2]

"I TOLD ABC WE NEEDED A SHOW that could go everywhere on the weekends, and that's how *Wide World of Sports* was born," Edgar Scherick reflected some twenty-five years after the flagship ABC Sports program's April 29, 1961, debut. "It wasn't some brilliant stroke of insight that caused me to come up with the idea for the show, but more a matter of economic necessity."[3] Although professional baseball was—by leaps and bounds—the United States' most popular spring and summer sport, Major League Baseball's inflexible blackout rules eliminated telecasts of its games in 30 percent of the country, including the largest cities. "Rather than simply lose those markets," Scherick noted, "we thought 'Why not get something else in that spot, some sporting events that don't necessarily get heavy television coverage?'"[4]

Wide World would focus on comparatively fringe sports that ABC could deliver to all affiliates no matter their location. The competitions' generally marginal profile ensured inexpensive broadcast rights and permitted ABC to air featured events retrospectively without most viewers being aware of, or likely even caring about, their results. The ninety-minute weekly anthology's mostly non-live format allowed ABC to schedule it in a consistent Saturday afternoon time slot that would strengthen the network's growing association with sports and foster a regular viewership. As Arledge explained, "Our purpose was to build, in effect, a franchise not dependent upon one type of sport."[5] If a particular event became prohibitively expensive or did not draw, *Wide World*'s built-in variety allowed it to move on to something else.

ABC wagered that *Wide World*'s approach would compensate for its subject matter's obscurity. "What we set out to do was get the audience involved emotionally," Arledge said. "If they didn't give a damn about the game, they might still enjoy the program."[6] *Wide World* fashioned this emotional involvement by combining the format of a sports show with a travelogue that emphasized the places where events occurred, the cultures surrounding them, and, above all, the people participating. It suggested featured events gained meaning from these geographic and humanistic circumstances. As the program's famous introductory lines—which Arledge claimed to have scribbled on the back of an airline ticket while on one of his many transcontinental expeditions to secure broadcast rights—announce: "Spanning the globe to bring you the constant variety of sport. The thrill of victory. The agony of defeat. The human drama of athletic competition. This is *ABC's Wide World of Sports*!"[7] *Wide World* privileged this variety, thrill, agony, and drama over the competitions it showcased and used these qualities to attract interest in often unfamiliar sports.

Launched the same year as the Bay of Pigs invasion and the Berlin Wall's construction, *Wide World* presented sporting competitions as activities that showcase, but ultimately transcend, geographic and cultural borders. "One of the original concepts of *Wide World of Sports*," commented Tom Moore, "was to mirror sports as the international language whereby people all over the world could better know and understand each other."[8] The Cold War, which historian Ban Wang calls a "narrative or moral drama," composed a familiar way to season many of *Wide World*'s obscurities with intrigue.[9] As Arledge observed, "If you had an American and a Russian, it didn't matter what they were doing, they could have been kayaking and people would watch it."[10] Cold War narratives propelled ABC Sports and *Wide World*'s entwined emergence and fashioned salable touchstones that the rapidly globalizing sports television industry used to dramatize international competitions.

Wide World established its popularity and renown by carrying a series of annual track meets between the United States and the Soviet Union from 1961 to 1965. The telecasts at once emphasized sport's capacity to cultivate cross-cultural harmony and reassured the program's American audience of the United States' superiority over its Cold War nemesis. Just as important, they advertised ABC Sports as a respectable and even educational cultural institution that mediates this fellowship and vocalizes this supremacy.

THE WASTELAND AND THE COLD WAR

By the time *Wide World* premiered, television had eclipsed radio to become the United States' most powerful mass medium—what media historian Thomas Doherty calls "the prized proscenium in American culture."[11] It was simultaneously facing criticism for using public airwaves to peddle gratuitous fare that blatantly put profits over edification. FCC chair Newton Minow's May 9, 1961, address to the National Association of Broadcasters (NAB)— delivered less than two weeks after *Wide World*'s debut—crystallized these plaints. "Your industry possesses the most powerful voice in America," Minow observed. "It has an inescapable duty to make that voice ring with intelligence and with leadership." He famously attacked the medium as a "vast wasteland" littered with "game shows, formula comedies about totally unbelievable families, blood and thunder, mayhem, violence, sadism, murder, western bad men, western good men, private eyes, gangsters, more violence, and cartoons.... And most of all, boredom." The resolute FCC chair cautioned that station license "renewal will not be *pro forma* in the future."[12] Minow caused such debate that the Associated Press annual poll of editors voted him 1961's top newsmaker in the field of entertainment.

Critics identified ABC as a leading perpetrator of television's apparent degradation. The network's youth-oriented counterprogramming compelled it to continue producing westerns and increasingly violent crime dramas like *The Naked City* (1958–63) and *The Untouchables* (1959–63) to attract and retain viewers. A December 1961 episode of ABC's short-lived series *Bus Stop* (1961–62), an adaptation of a William Inge play centered on the travelers who pass through the fictional town of Sunrise, Colorado, became a lightning rod for Minowesque charges against TV. Titled "A Lion Walks among Us," the episode starred teen idol Fabian and was directed by future "New Hollywood" auteur Robert Altman. Fabian played Luke Freeman, a handsome and charming sociopath who makes a pass at the woman who generously gives him a ride from the program's eponymous bus stop into Sunrise. After the woman rebukes his advances and kicks him out of her car, Freeman robs and murders an elderly shopkeeper. The killer casually sings the macabre ditty

"I Didn't Hear Nobody Pray" while exiting the store and continues to croon remorselessly while in jail awaiting trial. During the eventual hearing, Freeman's defense attorney discredits the testimony of the woman who gave Freeman a ride into town—who is also the principal witness against him and, coincidentally, the prosecuting attorney's wife—on account of her alcoholism and Freeman's claim that it was she, in fact, who attempted to seduce him. As a result, the young murderer is exonerated. The homicidal teen proceeds to kill his lawyer after the decidedly proficient attorney requests payment. On his way out of town, the disgraced woman again picks Freeman up and suggests they run away together. Instead, she drives off a cliff and kills them both. The unnerving episode closes biblically with 1 Peter 5:8 emblazoned on the screen: "Be sober, be vigilant. Because your adversary the devil, as a roaring lion, walketh about, seeking whom he may devour."

Two of *Bus Stop*'s sponsors, the Singer Sewing Machine Company and Brown & Williamson Tobacco, removed their advertisements from the bleak episode, and twenty-five ABC affiliates declined to clear it. Based on these concerns, the NAB Code Committee asked to prescreen the program—a request Ollie Treyz declined. The controversy provided "A Lion Walks among Us" with free publicity that got many to watch just to see what all the fuss was about.

New York Times media critic Jack Gould panned "A Lion Walks among Us" as "a commercial exploitation of sensationalism and savagery, a depiction of the ugliness of man to furnish cheap thrills for the large numbers of young people known to tune in *Bus Stop* and Fabian." The *Chicago Tribune*'s Larry Wolters added that "TV like this is a stimulant to crime and has no place in the living room," and the *Los Angeles Times*' Cecil Smith equated the program to "the worst in drug store fiction."[13] While Minow cited the twenty-five ABC affiliates' refusal to clear "A Lion Walks among Us" as a positive indication that stations were slowly improving standards, ABC's insistence on airing the program suggested "the Network of the Young" was uninterested in such high-minded pivots. "ABC for the last several years has been skirting the edge of acceptable programming in its concentration on so-called action drama," Gould declared. "Now it has gone over the line."[14]

Beyond the critics, "A Lion Walks among Us" garnered the attention of the Senate Juvenile Delinquency Subcommittee chaired by Connecticut senator Thomas J. Dodd. The committee explored the link between violent media—especially TV—and youth crime. Dodd's group located ABC as a principal cause of this epidemic. It claimed that Treyz, as well as CBS president James T. Aubrey and NBC head Robert E. Kinter—both of whom had previously worked at ABC—"learned to 'entice' an audience with crime and sex at the same school, ABC." The committee specifically accused ABC's opportunistic counterprogramming of fostering an industrial culture that would stop at nothing to secure an audience. Counterprogramming, Dodd charged, "is not a philosophy, but a hackneyed formula worn out by the pulp magazines years ago. The high regard it is given by the industry reflects a deep lack of imagination, but a deeper lack of responsibility."[15] The wave of progressively graphic programming against which the committee railed came to be known as the "Treyz trend" because of ABC's identification with it. Treyz wound up losing his job—a position Moore overtook—in 1962 partly because of the negative reaction *Bus Stop* provoked. These critiques suggested ABC stood among the vast wasteland's most desolate provinces.

Networks and affiliates responded to widespread attacks against television's quality—and threats to cancel licenses—by investing in and emphasizing documentary, a genre commonly identified as exceptionally thoughtful and educational.[16] Even before Minow's speech, ABC used documentary to balance its less respectable properties. In particular, *Bell & Howell Close Up!* (1960–63) aired a range of celebrated films, including several Drew Associates "direct cinema" productions that included the handheld camera work and synchronized sound that ABC Sports adopted and refined. Treyz, in fact, defended himself against those who decried the "Treyz trend" by arguing that documentary played as big a role on ABC as the network's youthful and violent content.[17]

A key way these network documentaries established interest was by engaging Cold War themes and promoting the United States' role in spreading democracy amid the proliferation of communism. As Michael Curtin observes, "This flourishing of documentary activity was part of an ambitious effort to awaken the public to its 'global responsibilities' and thereby consolidate popular support for decisive action overseas."[18] Many of the documentaries during *Close Up*'s first two seasons foregrounded foreign policy and warned against the perils of communism with titles like *Yanki No!* (1960), *Ninety Miles to Communism* (1961), *Our Durable Diplomats* (1961), and *The Remarkable Comrades* (1961). They demonstrated television's civic utility by tapping into Cold War anxieties and suggesting the medium, as well as the networks that filled it with content, "had an important role to play in the global struggle against communism."[19] *Wide World of Sports* enriched ABC's strategic involvement with documentary and Cold War nationalism.

"I thought it was the screwiest idea I'd ever heard," admitted Goldenson of his initial reaction to Scherick and Arledge's pitch to develop *Wide World*.[20] Though perhaps screwy, *Wide World*—originally titled *World of Sports*—was a low-risk experiment that would compose a serviceable twenty-week summer replacement to fill weekend hours during the sports calendar's slowest season. The program commanded relatively few resources and attracted advertisers simply because of its sporting focus. But *Wide World* was not unprecedented. CBS launched the similar Sunday afternoon sports anthology *CBS Sports Spectacular* in 1960. Moreover, the new ABC program borrowed its title from established media brands that included NBC's *Wide, Wide World* (1955–58) documentary travelogue program and *Sports Illustrated*'s "Wonderful World of Sport" column. Ever the salesman, Scherick tacked ABC onto the program's name so that *ABC's Wide World of Sports* would sell the network every time its title was uttered.

Neither Scherick nor Arledge knew precisely which events *Wide World* would cover, but only that they needed to be affordable and have no blackout policies. ABC did not have a research library at the time, but Arledge had kept the keys to NBC's reference collection, which was located on the same floor as his old office. Since he was still familiar to his former colleagues, Arledge sent production assistant Chuck Howard to use the rival network's facilities to research potential contracts. A legal pad in hand, Howard scoured rolls of microfilm to create a compendium of events to which Arledge could start purchasing rights, such as the Frontier Days Rodeo in Cheyenne, Wyoming, and the Hydroplane Championships in Seattle. The only parameter they initially set—one that quickly fell by the wayside—was that the events had to be competitions with winners and losers rather than exhibitions. As the *Philadelphia Inquirer*'s Lee Winfrey put it, "Arledge and ABC were forced to the task of making silk purses out of the sow's ears of sports."[21]

Wide World's first contract gave it rights to Amateur Athletic Union (AAU) competitions. Though hardly a marquee sports organization, the AAU was a recognizable institution with an identity steeped in patriotism and amateurism. While Scherick typically served as ABC Sports' main negotiator, he sent Arledge to deal with the AAU because he suspected the organization was anti-Semitic. "The AAU had all the power in amateur sports back then," he recalled, "and I figured we could get in on the ground floor on televising some of their events. But I'm a Jew, and, since there was still a great deal of prejudice at the time and since Arledge is a Gentile, I sent him in to do that negotiating."[22] Arledge struck a $50,000 deal for one year of the AAU's exclusive TV rights. *Wide World* devoted seven of its first season's twenty episodes in whole or part to AAU events and reinforced the alliance with its first client by adopting a logo that resembled the AAU shield (see appendix 1).

Even though it secured a promising menu of content, Treyz would not greenlight *Wide World* unless it presold 50 percent of its advertising spots—a policy the network enforced for most new programs at the time. If *Wide World* did not sell these spots by the close of business on March 31, 1961—less than a month before its scheduled premiere—Treyz would kill it. Gillette had already reserved one-quarter of *Wide World*'s rights, but the offbeat show was having a difficult time unloading the rest. ABC eventually found a sponsor not because of *Wide World*'s attractiveness but because of NCAA football's appeal. The network's college football coverage lost a quarter of its sponsorship after L&M Cigarettes changed ad agencies and moved away from sports. Though several advertisers were interested in the NCAA package, Scherick tied the advertising space remaining on its NCAA coverage to a quarter sponsorship of *Wide World*—which was considerably less costly than college football—to get the program on the air. Brown & Williamson, a stalwart of sports marketing at the time, offered to take one-eighth of the *Wide World* rights to get on ABC's NCAA football package. Even with Treyz's deadline fast approaching, Scherick refused and gambled that *Wide World* could find a sponsor to take the full quarter. Arledge readied himself for the disappointment of losing the show that would so neatly display his approach to sports TV, but Scherick remained hopeful. Mere minutes before Treyz's 5:00 p.m. deadline, R. J. Reynolds begrudgingly agreed to take the *Wide World* spots if it was the only way to be a part of the NCAA broadcasts.[23]

Wide World had content and sponsors, but no host. Scherick and Arledge sought a recognizable figure with the dexterity to handle the program's diversity and the creativity to transform its little-known events into captivating stories. They hired the avuncular and sincere Jim McKay, who, like Arledge, was a well-read Renaissance man whose sprawling interests drove him to pursue a career in media. Born James McManus, the native Philadelphian joined the *Baltimore Sun* after studying journalism at Baltimore's Loyola College— where he edited the school's paper and was class president—and serving as captain of a navy minesweeper that escorted convoys between Trinidad and Brazil during World War II. Though sports were McManus's main passion, he began his career as a police reporter and shortly thereafter transitioned into a television correspondent for a station the *Sun* owned. McManus, in fact, was the first person ever seen on Baltimore TV when he announced an October 1947 horse race from the city's Pimlico racetrack—a production that local tastemaker H. L. Mencken panned as "a very poor show." "I'd not give ten cents for an hour of such entertainment, even if it showed a massacre," Mencken grumbled in his diary.[24] Despite Mencken's grievances, McManus parlayed this initial assignment into a position hosting the three-hour weekday afternoon program *National Sports Parade*, a horse racing–focused rundown of sports news and analysis that McManus would occasionally sprinkle with a song during slow news days. He also emceed a range of daytime programming that the station used to fill out its schedule, including *Traffic Court*, *The Johns Hopkins Science Review*, *Know Your Sunpapers Route Owner*, and *Teenage Forum*.

In 1950, New York City's WCBS-TV took notice of and hired away the affable and multitalented TV reporter to host a daytime talk and variety program titled *The Real McKay*. At the time, networks owned names for their talent—a practice that allowed radio programs to continue using a familiar appellation after those who adopted the title left. CBS carried this practice over into TV and owned the name Jim McKay. Producers liked *The Real McKay*'s resemblance to "The Real McCoy" and asked McManus to use the snappier moniker, which became his permanent professional handle. *The Real McKay*, according to *Variety*, supplied a "homey atmosphere" that "makes for relaxed and pleasant viewing."[25] The program's introductory song emphasized its lighthearted focus: "Brighten your day with *The Real McKay*, here's a show just meant for you. / We're gonna chase all your blues away. Gonna make you feel just like *The Real McKay*." The show featured interviews, banter among McKay and his cohosts, and musical numbers. McKay sang "It Had to Be You" during *The Real McKay*'s premiere.

As in Baltimore, McKay was a utility player for CBS during *The Real McKay*'s short run and after its 1951 cancellation. Most notably, he served as a reporter for CBS's *Morning Show* opposite Walter Cronkite. He also moderated a public affairs program titled *Youth Takes a Stand* (1954–55), manned the quiz show *Make the Connection* (1955), and served as a reporter on the courtroom drama *The Verdict Is Yours* from 1957 until it relocated to Los Angeles and left him behind in 1960. Sports assignments were sprinkled throughout his duties, such as a short evening report called *Sports Spot*, horse races, the Little League World Series, and radio commentary on the 1956

Melbourne Olympics. McKay's most prominent early moment with CBS was securing an interview with English track star Roger Bannister for *The Morning Show* as the runner arrived unannounced in New York City just days after becoming the first person to clock a mile in under four minutes. Bannister was set to appear on the CBS game show *I've Got a Secret* later in the day. Despite resistance from the game show's producers, McKay intercepted the runner at the airport and conducted a live interview (without divulging the impending game show appearance). As it turned out, Bannister, a clean-living physician, refused to appear on *I've Got a Secret* after learning that a cigarette company sponsored it. McKay's furtive interview turned out to be the only footage of Bannister CBS was able to air.

McKay also freelanced for Sports Programs Inc.'s first production, the 1956 opening of Long Island's Roosevelt Raceway Harness Track. McKay's work so impressed Scherick that the SPI owner promised to find him a sports program that would complement his storytelling prowess and gentlemanly demeanor: "I used to say to him, 'Jim, sit tight. I'm gonna get a literate sports show for you.'" McKay, as Scherick identified, possessed the ability to situate sport within its cultural contexts that would come in handy when he joined ABC Sports. "I'm as interested in the front page as I am in the sports page," he told *Sports Illustrated*. Incidentally, McKay submitted a proposal to *Sports Illustrated* shortly after the magazine's 1954 launch to create and host a program like *Wide World*.[26]

McKay's most visible opportunity at CBS came in 1960 when the network assigned him to work its coverage of the Squaw Valley Winter Olympic Games, much of which aired prerecorded in prime time. The overworked television reporter, however, suffered a nervous breakdown and was forced to take a hiatus. Worried he might be fired if CBS discovered his malady involved mental health—still very much stigmatized at the time—McKay told the network he had pneumonia. "The [CBS] studio and New York itself began to feel like my enemies," he recollected. "Most of the time, all I could do was cry, for no apparent reason."[27] Sean McManus—McKay's son who eventually became president of CBS Sports—recalls that his father somberly puttered around the house and built model ships like those he once captained to pass the time during this difficult stretch.[28] McKay began to see a therapist and reorient. But he missed the Winter Olympics and feared that he may have ruined his career until CBS sports director Bill MacPhail asked him to participate in the network's coverage of the Rome Summer Olympics later that year. McKay posted up in a rented studio in Grand Central Terminal and reported on taped footage of events immediately after it arrived by jet from Italy.

Though his commentary on the Rome Olympics was successful, McKay worked only occasionally for CBS after *The Verdict Is Yours* left New York. He did nothing for the network, in fact, between the Olympics and the April 1961 Master's Golf Tournament. Meanwhile, Arledge and Scherick were scrambling to find a host for their recently approved program. Despite Scherick's long-standing affinity for McKay, the CBS sportscaster was not ABC's first choice. The network originally sought a better-known personality who would lend star power to the quirky program, such as Curt Gowdy or Chris Schenkel (both of whom eventually worked for ABC Sports). But Arledge noted that "most of the top announcers were tied up with baseball" during the spring.[29] Arledge phoned McKay with an offer while he was in Augusta, Georgia, covering the Master's. He explained that *Wide World* was a summer replacement that "would involve a fair amount of travel"—a description both Arledge and McKay later laughingly dismissed as a gross understatement. Given that he had no other prospects lined up, McKay was inclined to accept Arledge's offer. But he wanted to consult his wife, Margaret—also a respected journalist whom he met at the *Sun*—before making a commitment. Arledge, however, insisted that ABC needed an immediate answer. "We're having a press conference in a half an hour to announce who the host of the show is gonna be," he told McKay, "and if it's gonna be you we gotta have a deal."[30] McKay asked for $1,000 per show plus expenses. Arledge—who was not privy to McKay's dire job prospects and limited negotiating leverage—agreed, hung up, and began publicizing him as the program's host. "He was more than an announcer," Howard said of McKay. "He was articulate; he wrote his own stuff. Plus, he was available."[31]

McKay extensively researched the sport he would be covering and the place where he would travel for each *Wide World* installment. As Sean McManus recalled, "The first thing he'd do would be to go to the living room and pull out the *Encyclopedia Britannica* and read about the country he was going to. Then we'd go to the Westport [Connecticut] Public Library, take out books on the country and the sport and study some more." McKay created files on different sports and locations that he used throughout his career to pepper his commentary with historical and cultural factoids. "It was an educational process for him," Sean McManus explains of his father, "one that he took really seriously because he believed his role was more than a sports commentator, it was a travel guide."[32] McKay, as *Sports Illustrated*'s William

Taaffe put it, became "a homeroom teacher for a nation of eager learners," thoughtfully mediating their televised encounters with unfamiliar lands and peoples. The *Los Angeles Times* called McKay the "Marco Polo of sports" because of his endless journeys.[33] But his first trip for *Wide World*—just three weeks after joining ABC Sports—was back to his hometown for the University of Pennsylvania relay races.

Immediately capitalizing on its AAU contract, *Wide World*'s debut featured live coverage of the Penn relays and the Drake University relays in Des Moines, Iowa. McKay reported from Philadelphia alongside *New York Herald* track reporter Jesse Abramson and former Olympic pole vaulter Bob Richards, while *Wide World* correspondents Bill Flemming and Jim Simpson were on the scene in Des Moines. The inaugural broadcast was forced to be slightly less dynamic than Arledge would have preferred after a Philadelphia rainstorm damaged three of ABC's six cameras and waterlogged parts of the track. ABC built excitement by alternating between the two races. Segments focusing on the Penn relays ended by reminding viewers of an exciting upcoming event in Philadelphia just before cutting to Drake, and vice versa. This technique strove to create a lively pace and keep viewers for the program's duration. Though *Wide World*'s maiden voyage survived the rainfall, the program attracted little attention—positive or negative.

Wide World expanded on this tame debut with more adventurous sports like auto racing, demolition derbies, barrel jumping, and surfing—seemingly anything to which it could acquire reasonable rights. It also regularly broadcast women's sports during a time when they were rarely on national TV outside of the Olympics, roller derby, and novelty wrestling matches. "We did women's sports on a large scale right from the beginning," McKay bragged.[34] But *Wide World*'s coverage of women's athletics—most of which were initially AAU events—was first and foremost a consequence of its need for affordable content and paled in comparison to the frequency with which it aired men's sports. Moreover, the women's competitions it did feature overwhelmingly privileged stereotypically feminine sports like figure skating, gymnastics, and diving that did not upset gender norms. While *Wide World* lent women's sports visibility, it also tacitly reinforced assumptions regarding which types of women's sporting activities merited attention.

Arledge pointed out that *Wide World*'s mostly non-live format demanded heightened stylization. "There's just no comparison in the built-in excitement and tension of an event that is live, no matter who wins, because you just don't know what's going to happen," he said. "If the results are known . . .

then showmanship and creative ability is much more important."[35] *Wide World* highlighted its innovations to underscore the effort it put into production, such as the underwater camera it used to cover the 1961 AAU men's swimming and diving championships. The program introduced camera operator Dale Barringer and transformed his assignment into a subplot for the event coverage. "And here, our underwater cameraman Dale Barringer getting ready to go down by the deep six," McKay commented as Barringer collected his camera—an enormous cylindrical unit with waterproof casing and Plexiglas plates at either end—and disappeared below the surface. "There's his camera, a long metal object that was specially designed and perfected this week by Ralph Elmore, one of our engineers." As the broadcast cut from a bird's-eye view of the race to Barringer's camera, McKay announced, "That's the way it looks to frogman Dale Barringer on the bottom of the pool."[36] Similarly, the final episode of *Wide World*'s inaugural year covered a preseason AFL match between the Buffalo Bills and the San Diego Chargers. Reflecting CBS's renowned documentary *The Violent World of Sam Huff* (1960), *Wide World* increased the number of cameras beyond what was typically used for football broadcasts and placed wireless microphones inside several players' pads to provide an inside view of the already TV-friendly league's game. The segment, which publicized ABC's coverage of the upcoming AFL season, paid nearly as much attention to the network's cameras and microphones as it did to the featured event.[37]

Wide World's nomadic format added mystique to its technological prowess. It used the locations it visited—and the cultures that mark them—as characters that further dramatize and personalize events. The 1961 Le Mans auto race, for example, was not only an exciting competition but a glimpse into a quaint French community that is annually transformed by an exhilarating twenty-four-hour competition. "The first time we did the Grand Prix road race in Le Mans," Arledge noted, "we tried to handle it like *Moby Dick*, going for more than a race, for the soul of Le Mans. We filmed at great length a Mass that a priest said right on the course. We dramatized the prospect of death and the grueling effects of the race."[38] Similarly, *Wide World* presented the 1962 Southern 500 in Darlington, South Carolina, as a folksy affair that occurs in a "small town . . . a long way from any place." It characterized the race as "the southern version of the station wagon tailgate of the Ivy Leagues" that turns the isolated region into a festive tourist destination for a weekend. The program would also sometimes employ the far-off locations and marginal sports to comic effect, as when McKay cheerily opened coverage of the

World Lumberjack Championships in Hayward, Wisconsin, while balancing on a floating log (which ABC Sports crew members stabilized off camera) like a competitive logroller.

Though often playful, *Wide World* strove to treat its subject matter with dignity—a practice it developed after some regretful slipups. McKay recalled a case in which he treated a two-time demolition derby winner sarcastically during a postevent interview. "Well, Mr. Lucky," McKay said, "how do you account for winning the World Championship two years in a row?" The driver earnestly attributed his success to religious faith. "I had committed an unforgivable bit of gaucherie," McKay repentantly admitted, "looking down on this man in a condescending manner during what he considered the greatest moment of his life." "We don't go to an event in order to be big city sophisticates," Arledge added.[39] *Wide World* suggested that although not all cultures partake in the same sports, these varied activities hold the same significance for those who participate in them. In doing so, the educational show nurtured deeper understanding of and identification with people who—like the games they play—otherwise might seem odd.

Wide World basked in its commitment to sport's "constant variety"—however esoteric—in a tongue-in-cheek advertisement it placed in *Variety*: "If centaur racing should ever be revived in Greece, you'll see it on ABC television."[40] Like many news programs, it incorporated a flattened globe into its logo to assert that nothing stood beyond its ambit. It also suggested a spirit of humanism informed its globe-trotting. As Arledge explained, "If we could present these great spectacles to the American people in a meaningful way, we could provide attractive television entertainment, broaden the knowledge and perspective of the viewer, and maybe even make an occasional contribution to understanding among people of the world."[41] Though *Wide World* cast its cosmopolitanism as apolitical, the program was made from an unmistakably American point of view and built an audience through engaging dominant attitudes about the United States' place in the world during the Cold War. The annual US-Soviet track and field competitions, which Arledge called the "gem" of *Wide World*'s agreement with the AAU, embodied this tension.[42]

SPANNING THE IRON CURTAIN

The AAU-sponsored track meets began in 1958 as the product of the US-USSR Exchange Agreement signed by Soviet ambassador Georgi

Zarubin and William S. B. Lacy, President Dwight D. Eisenhower's special assistant on East-West exchanges. The pact instituted bilateral interactions spanning science, industry, art, and athletics.[43] Sport historian Joseph M. Turrini claims the meets, which alternated between the United States and the Soviet Union and ran intermittently through 1985, composed "the most important and visible of the Cold War sport competitions that emerged in the late 1950s and 1960s" aside from the Olympics.[44] Unlike the Olympics, which include dozens of competing countries, the meets "provided a direct and undiluted competition between the two countries that mirrored the bipolar perspective that pervaded the Cold War period."[45]

The meets also furnished a way for the United States to combat Soviet critiques that used America's endemic racial discrimination to undermine the country's democratic appeals. A National Security Council task force on international communism surmised that the United States could offset this propaganda by allowing nonwhites to represent it on the international stage. "We should make more extensive use of nonwhite American citizens," the group advised; "outstanding Negroes in all fields should be appealed to in terms of the higher patriotism to act as our representatives."[46] The coed events would also contrast Soviet charges that US women were unfairly fettered to the domestic sphere.

The US Information Agency (USIA) saw US-produced global TV broadcasts as potentially improving America's international repute.[47] *Wide World*'s track meet coverage contributed to these efforts. But ABC also knew the competitions' resonance with Cold War tensions would draw an unusually broad audience to the fledgling program. It leveraged the annual events' narrative potential to transform them into "the cornerstone of televised track in the United States."[48]

Wide World billed the 1961 US-USSR track meet from Moscow's Lenin Stadium as the peak of its first season and the culmination of three previous track meets it had featured up to that point. McKay opened the program by mentioning the broadcast's position as the first US-made sports TV production from the Soviet Union: "For the first time, an American television network has brought its own television cameras into the Soviet Union. The occasion: classic track and field competition between the United States and Russia." ABC transported fifty staff and twenty tons of equipment—including two Ampex videotape machines, five camera units, and a twenty-five-hundred-watt portable generator—to document the two-day event and edit it down to ninety minutes. It also spent $100,000 on the broadcast, an increase of about $60,000 over the typical cost of its international productions, to set the meet apart.[49]

"In those days," Arledge reminisced in a documentary commemorating *Wide World*'s fortieth anniversary, "you didn't fly into the Soviet Union with 20 tons of equipment and expect a friendly greeting. Lenin Stadium and the Soviet Union in 1961 was the inner center of the enemy." ABC's crew and equipment were almost unable to gain entry into Russia. The Russians were so slow to approve the network's travel that Arledge posted a staff member at the USSR's Washington, DC, embassy to wait for the decision and pressure the Russians to make it. When word did not come, Arledge gambled by sending the program's personnel and gear to Amsterdam, from where they would be able to arrive in Moscow quickly once the approval was levied, which eventually happened just in time to cover the meet.

McKay described invasive security protocols once they did get to Moscow and portrayed the city as a drab place devoid of the liveliness one might expect from a major international metropolis.[50] The ABC crew deplaned in an empty hangar and was transported into Moscow proper by army trucks. While driving into the city, they passed a World War II tank trap left intact to signal how close Nazi forces advanced toward Moscow before the Russian military defeated the invaders. In no uncertain terms, the monument signaled the communist center's unfriendliness to outsiders—a sentiment that was not lost on the ABC Sports crew. McKay likened their hotel—where authorities assigned him, Arledge, and another producer to share a single room—to "a great house that had been inherited by someone who didn't have the funds to keep it up."[51] Their bags arrived separately after being searched, and McKay suspected the KGB had tampered with his shoes, which mysteriously fell apart as he was leaving town. These portrayals paint Moscow as a peculiar and hostile locale—certainly the most foreign of the faraway locations *Wide World* had visited. "The only real signs of life and enthusiasm we found on that trip to Moscow were at the scenes of the event," McKay remembered.[52] He observed that Russian authorities went to great lengths to make Lenin Stadium appear state of the art and well maintained—in contrast to the otherwise unkempt city—since it would be on display for a US audience.

Capitalizing on this Cold War unease, ABC promoted the broadcast as both a political and a technological feat. "Russia & U.S. thaw down to a simple track," read an advertisement the network placed in the *New York Times*. "The first sports event ever to eventuate from Moscow over Yankee teevee!" (figure 1).[53]

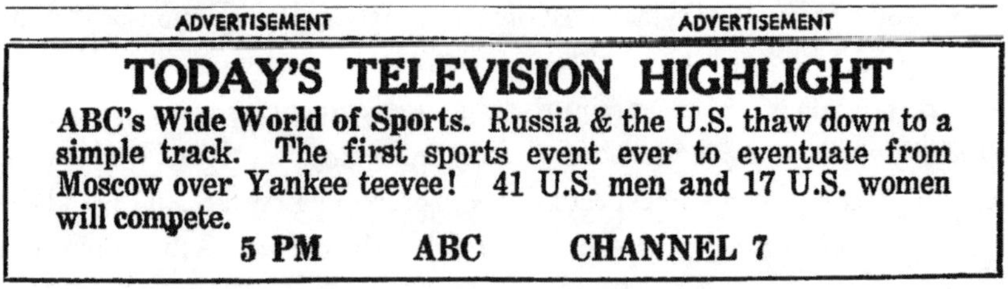

FIGURE 1. This *New York Times* advertisement for ABC's coverage of the 1961 US-USSR
track meet emphasizes the Cold War tensions that informed the event.

McKay set the scene at Lenin Stadium by explaining the differences that
separate how Soviet and US fans consume sport. "Inside are more than
70,000," he announced. "Most of them paid, some of them, however, are here
on an incentive basis. They put out a little more in their factory or their farm
this week, and thereby got free tickets." But the remainder of ABC's presentation stressed sport's potential to generate unity amid antagonistic dissimi-
larity. As is customary at international sporting events, the teams entered the
stadium side by side before their respective national anthems played. To
accent this pageantry's collaborative overtones, ABC camera operator Mike
Freedman lay on the field with a "creepy peepy" to showcase the US and
Soviet teams passing overhead. The low-angle shot, which framed the athletes
against the sky, emphasized the track meet's grandeur and echoed the diplomatic assurances that had been made in ABC's ad in the *New York Times*.

Complementing Freedman's camera work, ABC recast various potential
points of discord as opportunities for cross-cultural affinity. As the weather
soured toward the end of the meet, McKay cheerily noted the frequency with
which US events are similarly disrupted. "What started out as a beautiful day
with the temperature at 85 [degrees Fahrenheit] has turned into a real summer Sunday evening thunderstorm. It happens halfway around the world just
like it does in Kansas and Missouri," he said along with shots of rain-soaked
Russian spectators and ABC's tarp-covered equipment. The instance could
easily have been used to paint Moscow and Lenin Stadium in an unfriendly
light. Rather, ABC employed it to stress the similarities that united
Americans and Russians. The Soviet fans may procure their tickets differently, but they ultimately display the same passion for their games and face
the same obstacles common in Middle America.

ABC's telecast deliberately elided several disagreements surrounding the
competition. The AAU requested that the men's and women's events be

scored separately—as is customary in America. The Soviets, however, wanted the scores combined—as is routine in Russia. Possessing a superior men's team, the United States would win the men's and lose the women's meet with divided scoring. However, the Soviet women's team was so dominant—a point Western commentators often used to attack communism's deleteriously hardening impact on Russian women—that it would give the USSR an overall victory were the scores combined. Though the meet did officially score the men's and women's teams separately—ensuring victory for the American men and the Russian women—several Soviet newspapers persisted in reporting an overall USSR victory, which irked many US-based commentators and struck them as typical of the country's tendency to defame their homeland.[54] "I realized," Arledge said of the scoring quarrel, "I was experiencing the Cold War in microcosm, and that this kind of obdurate, uncompromising dispute, in which both sides in their own environment were right, characterized what went on in much more important spheres."[55] While the US and Soviet officials quibbled about how the event would be scored, ABC focused on the meet's capacity to transcend such comparatively petty trifles.

Instead, *Wide World* joined in the AAU's defense against Soviet critiques of US racism and gender relations by focusing in large part on sprinter Wilma Rudolph—already a star who earned a gold medal in the 1960 Rome Olympics—and broad jumper Ralph Boston. It had featured Rudolph and Boston, both of whom attended the track and field powerhouse Tennessee State University, as part of its coverage of the AAU's National Track and Field Championships in New York City earlier in the season. Both African American athletes delivered standout performances for the US team in Moscow: Rudolph tied her hundred-meter world record time of 11.3 seconds to win the event, and Boston set a new record with his jump of 27 feet, 1¾ inches. The coverage depicted them as national heroes during a time when the overall representation of African Americans on network TV was still limited. Its celebratory representations, however, unsurprisingly failed to mention the basic civil liberties these athletic stars were still denied in the country they represented so well. *Wide World* thus paired its depictions of cross-cultural unity with a similarly oversimplified vision of domestic harmony.

Though ABC isolated African Americans as the United States' best performers, it ultimately positioned Russian high jumper Valery Brumel's record-breaking victory over the United States' John Thomas—another African American and a previous record holder—as the show's climax. Brumel's jump occurred just two months after the Soviet space program made cosmonaut Yuri Gagarin the first human to orbit Earth, a signal moment in the US-Soviet "space race" that suggested the USSR held a decisive edge. *Wide World* explained Brumel's record—which he accomplished in dramatic fashion on his final attempt as the rain poured—by comparing it to Gagarin's feat. "Valery Brumel has set a new world's record in the high jump," McKay noted as ABC's cameras cut to cheering Russian fans. "At this moment," McKay continued, "Brumel rivals Yuri Gagarin as a national hero in the Soviet Union." Brumel's jump was indeed a point of immense national pride that convinced the Soviet government to give him the Merited Master of Sport Award—the nation's highest sports honor. McKay's commentary characterized Brumel's jump as an extension and confirmation of the USSR's rising superiority in the space race.

But *Wide World* also reassured its audience against such Cold War anxieties by appealing to ABC Sports' technological sophistication. Up to this point in *Wide World*'s inaugural year, ABC used mostly locally sourced equipment and labor when producing programming abroad. It insisted, however, on transporting its own equipment to Moscow—a decision that suggested Russia did not possess the resources and expertise to create, or even assist the creation of, a production of ABC Sports' caliber. For instance, the Russians did not have Ampex videotape recorders, which display the television video feed in a monitor as content is shot on location. Arledge claimed the Ampex Company was so worried that the Russians would steal the technology that it would only allow ABC to bring the machines if the network vowed to lock its recording heads in the US embassy's safe each evening.[56]

McKay notes that when ABC set up the machines in the bowels of Lenin Stadium, "several thousand" spectators gathered to marvel at the technology rather than watch the live event.[57] "For the Russians, who had no video machines," Arledge claimed of the awestruck spectators, "it was as if we'd invented fire."[58] McKay's and Arledge's comments represent the Russians as a primitive bunch when it comes to telecommunications and entertainment. Indeed, McKay claimed the Russian television crews were insecure about their deficiencies and tried to copy ABC's comparatively advanced practices. "Our every move was monitored very carefully," he wrote. "Roone requested a camera position at field level to get tight close-ups. . . . After a long wait, the cameras were okayed, but when we arrived the next day, Soviet cameras were right beside ours."[59] While the US space program may have been lagging, *Wide World* demonstrated that American television—and ABC in particular—was far ahead of the Soviets. The coverage and the discourses surrounding it combined to locate television as a facet of the space race that the United States was indisputably leading and to situate ABC as the organization that made evident this technological supremacy's nationalistic implications while propelling sports television's globalization.

Arledge described *Wide World*'s coverage of the 1961 US-USSR meet as a "turning point in our acceptance as a show." "That trip to Moscow really set up the whole odyssey of *ABC's Wide World of Sports*," McKay added.[60] At that point in the season, the program had not attracted considerable audience numbers and was facing potential cancellation. "We did receive a lot of favorable comments," McKay adds. "Not only for going to the Soviet Union, but also for bringing all of our own equipment. People began to talk about *Wide World* as a permanent fixture at ABC." Most important, the trip convinced Moore, who joined the *Wide World* crew in Moscow, to keep the program on the air despite its initially underwhelming ratings.[61] Shortly after the meet, ABC renewed *Wide World* for a full fifty-two-week run starting in January 1962. The program's extension into the autumn months would compensate for the absence of NCAA football broadcasts, which ABC lost after the 1961 season and did not regain until 1966.

By the end of *Wide World*'s first season, *Variety* reported that the program that almost did not secure enough advertisers to make it on ABC's weekend schedule had sponsors "backed up trying to get onto the show" for its sophomore season.[62] Its 1962 Emmy Award nomination in the category of Outstanding Achievement in Public Affairs was the first such recognition a sports program received and demonstrated *Wide World*'s rare ability to straddle the sport, news, and documentary genres. The *New York Times* expanded on this decoration by citing *Wide World* as "one of the programs adding prestige to the medium" as a whole.[63]

Wide World continued to bill itself as a site that mediates sport's global meaning after its debut season. It hired a collection of expert celebrity commentators, including the British Formula One racing driver Stirling Moss, figure skater Dick Button, and swimmer Lynn Burke, who became the first female TV sports commentator when *Wide World* recruited her to participate in its coverage of the 1961 AAU Women's Swimming and Diving Championships. As with its coverage of women's sports, ABC was ahead of its competitors when it came to hiring female commentators. Though not an official policy, it typically only allowed women to comment on women's sports—a form of segregation it did not impose on its male talent when covering women's events that remains commonplace in sports media.[64]

Wide World also started giving out an Athlete of the Year Award in 1962 (see appendix 2). Like *Sports Illustrated*'s Sportsman of the Year—which the magazine based on *Time*'s Man of the Year honor—*Wide World*'s Athlete of the Year suggests the TV program has the authority to organize and assess sport's significance. Its more inclusive title also advertises *Wide World*'s willingness to recognize both men and women athletes (though women received the honor infrequently) who participate in activities that *Sports Illustrated* often overlooked.

Wide World paired this cultivation of expertise with an amplification of its formal and technological daring. It created a floating TV studio on a sixty-foot fishing trawler named the *Whitestone* to cover the 1962 America's Cup yacht race off the coast of Rhode Island. "Equipment aboard included a fourteen-by-eight-foot control room, housing all necessary audio and video equipment and a video-tape recorder; two TV cameras, mounted on special platforms; and a micro-wave dish, set up on the *Whitestone*'s decks to pick up pictures from a camera in a helicopter, which also covered the race." After ABC recorded each segment of the race from the trawler, the helicopter gathered the tapes and delivered them to Newport, Rhode Island. They were then flown to Providence, where a video unit was set up to feed the tape over rented phone lines to New York, and then to the rest of the country.[65] As with the 1961 US-USSR track meet, *Wide World* made sure its audience was aware of this state-of-the-art and arduous production process.

In a different but similarly imaginative direction, *Wide World* hired Robert Riger to film, photograph, and sketch events. The de facto artist-in-residence humanized further the program's aspirations and showcased a different perspective from ABC's cameras. In particular, Riger developed a dual action camera that simultaneously shoots motion picture film and still pictures so scenes can be displayed in real time and later broken down into split-second intervals.

Wide World brought these intensified practices to bear for its return to Lenin Stadium to tape the 1963 US-USSR meet, for which it again used its own equipment. Less than one year removed from the Cuban Missile Crisis, relations between the competing nations were even icier than in 1961. At the time of the meet, W. Averell Harriman—ambassador at large for the Kennedy administration and a Kremlin expert—was in Moscow negotiating with Soviet leader Nikita Khrushchev the Partial Test Ban Treaty, an agreement designed to decelerate the US-Soviet arms race. In a gesture of goodwill, and despite their reportedly tense talks earlier in the week, Khrushchev invited Harriman to join him at the track meet in a private viewing box. Khrushchev opted to attend the meet with Harriman rather than see off a Chinese delegation that had been visiting Moscow. "Normally," McKay claimed, "Khrushchev would have been [at the airport] with school children and flowers and protestations of Socialist solidarity. . . . Instead, on this particular afternoon, he decided to go to a track meet with the American."[66]

In a dispatch to the United States, Harriman reported that "tears seemed to well up in" Khrushchev's eyes "when our two flags were being carried side by side around the track with the two teams walking arm-in-arm."[67] Khrushchev's emotions continued to run high as the politicians watched Brumel break his own high jump record, an achievement that moved an overwhelmed Khrushchev to embrace Harriman in euphoria. *Wide World*'s presentation announced Khrushchev's attendance and cut to his box immediately after Brumel's jump to show his reaction. The image it displayed was uncharacteristically hazy—the kind of shot that would normally end up on the carefully edited program's cutting-room floor. But it was indispensable to *Wide World*'s appeals to the track meet's ability to soothe tensions between states that were otherwise at odds. Arledge, in fact, later named the grainy shot "the single most important image I have ever broadcast."[68] "Their nations had come to the brink of annihilation," he added of Khrushchev and Harriman, "and it wasn't too much of an exaggeration to say that they'd had the fate of the world in their hands all that week. . . . But now because of the simple feat of a man jumping over a bar, they were hugging each other. That, for me, was *ABC's Wide World of Sports*."[69] Harriman claimed that Khrushchev's jolly mood continued after—and likely because of—Brumel's spectacular jump. The Soviet leader invited Harriman to join him for dinner. "He was most cordial throughout," Harriman reported, "and attempted to impress upon me his desire for closer collaboration in a wider field" and a "future shorn of much of the existing tension and suspicion" between the United States and Russia.[70] "Track races, [Khrushchev] commented, were far better than arms races."[71] Harriman reported that the meet accelerated these improved relations between the political adversaries—a diffusion ABC exhibited and indirectly aided.

ABC built on the peacekeeping the 1963 meet bespoke by naming Brumel *Wide World*'s second Athlete of the Year. Given *Wide World*'s American audience, the program's decision to recognize Brumel advertises its worldliness while suggesting it places athletic excellence over nationalism. It also promotes the annual US-USSR meets as key events on its schedule. The

Soviets were so flattered by Brumel's decoration that they permitted him passage to New York City for the ceremony ABC held in his honor. With USIA director Carl T. Rowan delivering the keynote address and Soviet ambassador Anatoly Dobrynin in attendance, the ABC-curated ceremony doubled as a conspicuous display of diplomacy that reinforced *Wide World's* position as an entity capable of mediating genial international exchanges. ABC Sports even produced a short commemoration of Brumel's honor that it aired on the following week's edition of *Wide World*.[72]

Wide World's 1965 US-USSR track meet from Kiev—the final US-USSR meet the program aired—continued this diplomacy, amplified the annual competition's status, and reinforced ABC Sports' reputation for pushing the aesthetic and technological envelope. It was the first live TV broadcast from the USSR—an achievement Arledge named "a milestone in television and quite possibly the most important advance in sports telecasting in history."[73] Because of the time difference, ABC displaced its regularly scheduled weekend morning lineup to make room for the historic telecast. It consequently expended the additional promotional resources necessary to alert viewers to the program's unusual time slot and banked on their being intrigued enough by the meet's established popularity and live presentation to watch the episode outside of *Wide World's* normal schedule. "The satellite will change people's viewing habits," Arledge wagered. "They won't care that the event is not coming over at 2pm Saturday; they'll rather watch a live track meet from Russia at 11am."[74] ABC publicized the global spectacle as the highlight of its 1965 season in an advertisement that claimed the unprecedented broadcast would "add a new dimension to imaginative sports coverage techniques."[75]

Wide World used the Early Bird satellite, which launched into orbit less than three months prior, for the July 31 telecast. It piloted the nascent technology with live coverage of the Le Mans and the Irish Derby Sweepstakes horse race earlier in the season. The Le Mans broadcast encountered glitches that temporarily blocked ABC's image feed and forced the network to put up a standby card and present only its audio commentary. ABC's broadcast of the Irish Sweepstakes the following week, however, went smoothly and allowed *Wide World* to work out what kinks remained before Kiev.

Wide World again planned to produce the meet with its own personnel and gear. But Arledge discovered that it could only be aired live if ABC agreed to share Russian equipment and relinquish some control over the production, even though, as he pointed out, it would not even be televised in Russia. "We knew we would rather cover the meet *live* without having complete control of production than tape it and fly it back," he recalled with a hint of lingering disappointment.[76] Arledge collaborated with Russian television authorities to guarantee the coverage would give equal attention to the American and Soviet competitors. He noted, however, that the Russians' inferior facilities made the already difficult production more challenging than it would have been were he given free rein to use his own equipment and staff. ABC initially planned to use an experimental Russian satellite, in addition to the Early Bird, that fed pictures from Moscow to Helsinki and then to the United states, but the Russian technicians were unable to tie the feed into a suitable foreign ground station. ABC instead devised a dual system of satellites and landlines that would be able to get around its host nation's limited facilities.

The process of building the collaborative, intercontinental live broadcast —which Arledge detailed in a *Wide World* yearbook ABC published in 1964 and 1965—was remarkably intricate. The image and sound tracks were shuttled via separate landlines from Kiev, where McKay was commenting live on the scene, to Rome, where ABC conscripted the assistance of Radiotelevisione Italiana. Bill Flemming contributed from a rented studio in Rome, where an ABC director had the sportscaster alternate between the live feed and taped segments to guarantee a seamless broadcast and fill in any gaps. Had they lost the audio from McKay but retained the video from Kiev, for instance, Flemming could still provide commentary from the Italian studio. From Rome, the program was delivered via satellite to Andover, Maine, then to New York City, where ABC had another standby studio and archived material ready in case it lost the picture. Finally, it was fed to the rest of the United States. "Technically there were about 100 different places where things could have gone wrong," Arledge wrote. "It was amazing that nothing did." ABC further advertised this unprecedented technological feat by including in its 1965 yearbook a map that traced the television feed's circuitous route from Kiev to American living rooms.

Alongside the map, it placed a Riger sketch of five-thousand-meter competitors Bob Shul and Pyotr Bolotnikov sharing a sportsmanlike embrace after Bolotnikov beat the favored American. Arledge indicated that ABC's collaboration with Soviet TV mirrored the runners' fellowship—a display he likened to Khrushchev and Harriman's unexpected hug two years prior. Despite their low-grade technology, "the Russians," he noted, "with a few exceptions of hometown enthusiasm, did very objective coverage and showed Americans as well as Russians, following all details of our plan."[77]

Arledge identified the live broadcast as "a forerunner of the direction international television must take."[78] More important, he claimed the achievement demonstrated sports television's sociopolitical utility. "It gives us an opportunity," he said, "to help the people of the world understand one another through the medium of television and through the medium of sports."[79] Arledge suggested the live broadcast fostered an even more intimate communion between the United States and the Soviet Union than *Wide World*'s previously tape-delayed presentations. "The world had really become a pearl in the broad hand of communication," he concluded.[80] As he made apparent, it was ABC Sports—not simply TV—that realized this political potential. The network braved Cold War anxieties to establish a global sports telecommunications grid that brought together geographically, culturally, and politically disparate groups with an unprecedented degree of intimacy.

Amid his utopian reverie, Arledge briefly mentioned that *Wide World* was publicizing the upcoming Thunderbird Golf Championship, which was scheduled to air on ABC after the track meet, from Kiev. The promotion further illustrates television's wondrous potential to transcend space, as American viewers received a reminder about an upcoming US-based program from a different continent. Arledge, however, also gestured toward the irony of advertising an event that took place at suburban New York City's posh Westchester Country Club—a locale he described as a "bastion of capitalism"—from a communist state. "It is undoubtedly the first time that a major golf championship has ever been promoted from the Soviet Union," he observed.[81] The live promo, Arledge implied, transformed the Soviet Union into an unwitting participant in US commercial television and the capitalist culture that supports it. While the US-Soviet collaboration heralded live television's potential to bond radically different groups, Arledge indicated that these technologized unions are ultimately driven by and serve US-based corporate interests. This ABC coverage assured viewers that TV's globalized "hand of communication" is a thoroughly American appendage.

By the time of its Kiev broadcast, critics had installed *Wide World* as a TV program of exceptional quality—a sophisticated contrast to since-canceled ABC programs like *The Untouchables* and *Bus Stop*. *Variety* claimed that even though ABC's network competitors held rights to "most of the 'marquee' sports," *Wide World* gave the younger and still less prominent network equal respectability. The program, *Variety* enthused, "lead[s] the field" of sports TV and stands "as a proving ground for technical innovation."[82] The globe-trotting show, according to *Sports Illustrated*'s Richard Hoffer, elevated the medium that Minow disparaged a little over one month after its debut. "The Saturday sloth," Hoffer wrote of sports TV's implied male viewer, "was often disturbed in his anticipation of the ski-flying championships by a historical travelogue on Oslo that was—how else can we say it?—literate." *Wide World* creates scenes, effused the *Los Angeles Times*, "that would make Michelangelo flip his easel."[83]

The anthology program, added TV critic Hal Humphrey, "has done a lot toward de-isolating Americans who cared for nothing but baseball or football."[84] Arledge, in fact, claimed *Wide World* was driven more by an effort to broaden sports fans' horizons than to generate revenues. He separated himself from his bottom line–oriented peers—a strategy he frequently employed to stress his comparative thoughtfulness and artistry—by boasting, "I can put stuff on the air I know isn't going to get a rating. We can do things just because we think they should be done."[85] Accordingly, ABC marketed the show as "not only entertaining, but educational" and referred specifically to the US-USSR track meets to make this claim.[86] France's Cannes Television News Festival recognized *Wide World*'s edifying cosmopolitanism by awarding the program its 1966 prize for live TV. The most prominent recognition of *Wide World*'s value came with the 1966 George Foster Peabody Award it received in the category of International Understanding. It was the first Peabody given to a sports program. The accolade—which *Wide World* collected shortly after its live broadcast from Kiev—suggests the US-USSR meets stimulated the program's acknowledgment as an exceptional representative of TV's capacity to foster global connections and cross-cultural affinity.

Wide World's US-USSR track meet coverage ended after Kiev. The Soviet Union boycotted the event from 1966 through 1968 in protest of the United States' military involvement in Vietnam.[87] When the meets resumed in 1969, CBS purchased away ABC's television rights.[88] The Cold War, however, continued to serve an important role on *Wide World*, which featured various other US-Soviet competitions and continued to visit locales that were off-limits to most Americans. The program made seventy trips to communist nations between its debut and the toppling of the Berlin Wall in 1989. In 1971 it sent a crew to Havana to cover a men's volleyball match between the United States and Cuba—the first sports broadcast from Havana to air on US television since the countries severed diplomatic ties ten years prior. Because Americans were not allowed passage to Cuba, ABC used a Canadian crew fronted by ABC News correspondent (and future star anchor) Peter Jennings. Like the

US-USSR track meets, the broadcast underlined Cuba's difference from the United States and gestured toward sport's potential to reconcile these politically unfriendly nations. Jennings secured an interview with Fidel Castro before and after the match, which Cuba won. Though Castro was typically presented as a menacing threat—the enemy face of the Bay of Pigs Invasion and Cuban Missile Crisis—Jennings's interview presented a good-humored statesman who graciously took time to speak with the American media outlet and even joked around after his translator bungled a question. While it humanized Cuba's enigmatic leader, the program also presented his beautiful island nation as frozen in time since the communist revolution. ABC Sports' state-of-the-art cameras and large crew constituted an unusually glitzy presence in the out-of-date country fit to attract the attention of its prime minister.

Shortly after ABC stopped carrying the US-USSR meets, Arledge expressed interest in "the opportunity to do a sports program from China. It might erase some of the barriers between our two peoples," he conjectured.[89] He finally received the chance in 1977 when *Wide World* became the first US-based sports TV program to visit communist China to cover a gymnastics meet in Peking. *Wide World*'s introduction to the country predictably opens with McKay in front of the Great Wall backed by traditional Chinese music. It transitions to a shot of Tiananmen Square, which McKay describes as the city's "nerve center" where residents congregate each morning to exercise. The image switches from early morning calisthenics to a mass of bicycles traveling through the square as McKay explains that the people of Peking "get more exercise by riding their bikes to work because there is no such thing as an automobile owned by a private citizen in the People's Republic." The introductory scene emphasizes Peking's contrast to the United States' car-heavy urban centers and, perhaps more pointedly, highlights the broader cultural differences between China's communist uniformity and America's capitalist individuality—a characteristic the automobile symbolizes. In fact, *Wide World* featured an auto race from Riverside, California, the previous weekend. Taken together, the consecutive installments show the vast cultural, economic, and technological differences that make cars largely forbidden in China and enable them to be used for sport in the United States.

McKay delivers his introduction to Tiananmen Square from a crowded street crammed with onlookers gazing curiously at the sportscaster and ABC's cameras. Their astonishment at the network's unfamiliar technology echoes the Russian spectators' fascination with ABC's Ampex machines in 1961 and similarly emphasizes the United States' dominant position in the global economy. His introduction then takes an abrupt and curious turn by outlining the densely populated city's readiness for war. "The holocaust that would be caused by an atom or hydrogen bomb in this city boggles the human mind," McKay notes. He uses this ominous factoid as an excuse to showcase the entrance to an underground air-raid shelter capable of housing "some 10,000 people for a day or two. It's Peking's way of saying, 'we're ready whatever happens,'" McKay explains with a stern gaze. The introduction depicts Peking's citizens as prepared for the hardships of modern warfare, but unfamiliar with the affordances of modern technology.

Ranging from friendly to wary, *Wide World*'s depictions of Cold War rivals like Russia, Cuba, and China created what Derek Gregory calls "imaginative geographies," or, politically interested ways of structuring understandings of spaces that cannot be directly experienced.[90] They promoted international exchange as they reinforced and capitalized on the host nations' mysteriousness. Simultaneously, *Wide World* reassured its American viewership of the United States' leading status in global hierarchies during politically uncertain Cold War conditions—a point it made in part through accentuating the United States' comparative technological advancement and situating ABC Sports as an exemplar of it.

WIDENING *WIDE WORLD*

By the time *Wide World* stopped carrying the US-USSR track meets, ABC Sports had firmly established itself as Arledge's creative domain. Arledge and Chet Simmons initially shared leadership duties after Scherick left ABC Sports. Arledge guided the creative activities, and Simmons oversaw the business arrangements. But Simmons grew disillusioned as Arledge's star rose and his partner demonstrated little interest in the increasingly unwieldy balance sheets Simmons had to manage. "We had a hard time running [ABC Sports] because we were always over budget," Simmons recalled. "And there was mostly an inclination to support the creative side and not care about the side that I was dealing with. And I began to feel that perhaps there was something more out there than arguing with Arledge over budgets."[91] Simmons left in 1964 to run sports programming at NBC, where he stayed until departing to become ESPN's first president in 1979. Though Arledge ran ABC Sports alone after Simmons quit, he was not formally named president until it became an official subsidiary in 1968.

ABC Sports created spin-offs of its signature show to broaden its audience. Extending *Wide World*'s third episode—which covered the Professional Bowlers Association World Championship in Paramus, New Jersey—ABC launched *Pro Bowlers Tour* in 1962. Described as a "Main Street and Midwest" counterpart to *Wide World*'s preoccupation with the unfamiliar, the slow-paced winter and spring program visited different bowling alleys each weekend to showcase one of North America's most popular "participant sports."[92] More exotically, *Wide World* expanded on a 1963 segment that featured Americans Joe Brooks and Curt Gowdy in a trout fishing competition against Argentinian fishermen in the Andes Mountains to create *American Sportsman* in 1965. Hosted by Gowdy, the program featured big-game hunting and fishing around the world with celebrity guests (who often had some business relationship with ABC that their appearances benefited). Gowdy fished for salmon in Iceland with Bing Crosby and hunted sable antelope in Zambia with Ted Williams. After critiques from animal rights activists, the program shifted focus from hunting to wildlife conservation.

Though their scopes varied drastically, *Pro Bowlers Tour* and *American Sportsman* both complemented *Wide World*'s globe-trotting, and they were less expensive to produce than the already economical program that inspired them. Confined to indoor alleys, bowling tournaments require fewer cameras and production staff to cover than most of *Wide World*'s events, and *American Sportsman*'s voyages into the wilderness did not demand broadcast licenses. As Gowdy put it, "We don't have to pay rights fees to fool will Mother Nature."[93] The shows rounded out a weekend programming block centered on *Wide World*.

ABC also created *Wide World*–related products that reached beyond television. Compiled by Riger, *Wide World*'s briefly published yearbooks commemorated the program's most interesting moments and elaborated on its production practices. Riger opened the 1964 yearbook by explaining that its combination of print, photographs, and drawings will allow readers to understand and appreciate moments that pass by quickly on television. The yearbooks emphasized *Wide World*'s sophistication and artistry. "The spontaneity of sports offers the greatest opportunity for television to express itself as a new, valid art form," wrote Robert Trachinger in a short essay. "What the stage and proscenium is to the theater, what film stock and the sound stage are to the movies, the remote and the sports remote, in particular, is to television."[94] *Wide World*, Trachinger contends, brings into focus and extends TV's inventiveness.

Along these lines, ABC Sports published *Wide World*–themed encyclopedias, record books, and quiz books that reinforced its educational value by suggesting the program organized public knowledge of sport and broadened viewers' intellectual horizons. "*Wide World* has also created its own generation of sports fans," the quiz book explains, "knowledgeable and intelligent, weaned on the penetrating, expert coverage of athletics, both amateur and professional that has become the trademark of this popular network series. . . . These are sophisticated sports fans."[95] The books indicate that this enlightened brand of sports fan—and the knowledge that makes it possible—would not exist apart from ABC Sports and *Wide World*.

"THE BACKBONE OF OUR WHOLE
SPORTS ACTIVITY"

ABC Sports' advertising billings increased twentyfold between 1960 and 1967.[96] *Wide World*'s year-round presence, accolades, and promotion of other ABC Sports properties spurred this growth. "We consider the show the backbone of our whole sports activity," Arledge asserted. "If we had the rights to every major sports event in the universe we would still consider *Wide World of Sports* our number one show."[97]

Wide World overshadowed CBS's and NBC's similar programs and forced the rival networks to define their sports offerings in contrast to its popular format. CBS Sports' Bill MacPhail claimed his network focused only on marquee sports. "We are only interested in quality sports," he said, "you won't find us carrying any of those barrel-jumping contests." NBC began marketing itself as "the Network of Live Sports." "I don't really consider them sports shows," NBC Sports executive Carl Lindemann said of *Wide World* and ABC's other taped programs. "We concentrate on live events because my management believes that the real drama is in live."[98] While ABC built its network identity through counterprogramming against CBS and NBC, the still third-place network's renowned sports coverage had competitors scrambling to find a niche in the genre it had come to dominate.

Aside from installing ABC atop sports television's industrial hierarchies, *Wide World* built interest in sports that previously garnered scant media attention. Its regular coverage of surfing, for example, anticipated and influenced Bruce Brown's documentary travelogue *Endless Summer* (1966), which similarly spanned the globe to showcase the world's best surfing spots.

Brown, in fact, parlayed his filmmaking experience into a gig as a *Wide World* cameraman. In 1971, Steve McQueen starred in *Le Mans*—an action film centered on the race that *Wide World*'s annual coverage put on American sports fans' radar. Three years later, German filmmaker Werner Herzog released *The Great Ecstasy of the Woodcarver Steiner*, a meditative documentary on prodigious Swiss ski jumper and erstwhile artist Walter Steiner. Ski jumping, with its combination of graceful aerial soaring and violent crashes, was a *Wide World* staple. Herzog's film, produced for German television, resembles *Wide World*'s humanistic format. But it contrasts the program's typical reliance on predictable athletic narratives by highlighting Steiner's inscrutability. At one point it calls attention to—and turns its nose up at— *Wide World*'s apparent comparative superficiality by including footage of an unprepared ABC Sports correspondent asking Steiner inane questions that ignore the artistic and philosophical concerns animating Herzog's documentary. Though very different, these films all demonstrate the awareness *Wide World* gave to previously fringe sports and the program's impact on media culture beyond US sports television.

The program also inflated broadcast rights fees and led sports promoters to presume that TV outlets would be willing to pay top dollar for nearly any event. While in Acapulco to cover the 1962 Water Ski Championships, ABC Sports producers sought out some local cliff divers whose jumps would make a compelling way to set the scene. When asked what price the divers required, a representative said the group sought $100,000 because it was planning its own television special. Arledge immediately rejected the outlandish demand. A few minutes after Arledge's rebuff, the spokesperson returned and said the group would perform for $10 per dive—including practice jumps.[99] ABC started receiving invitations to bid on rights to events that were beyond even *Wide World*'s ample range, such as the International Pro-Am Clam-Digging Championship in Ocean Shores, Washington. "The color comes not from the clams themselves, which are rather long and ugly," wrote the delegation from Ocean Shores, "but the contestants. Ocean Shores is in a very goofy area where many of the inhabitants are scruffy old beachcombers, or woodsmen, or Indians from the Quinault Reservation. Put these in harness with some nice young things in minimal bathing suits and we will have some interesting shots."[100] *Wide World* passed on the clam digging. But its coverage of events like log rolling and rattlesnake hunting created an environment where the prospect of televised clamming was imaginable, if not entirely feasible.

THREE

"The Network of the Olympics"

STARRING MUHAMMAD ALI AND
HOWARD COSELL

I wasn't sure if *Wide World* was a weekly Olympics or if the
Olympics was a two week *Wide World*.

DENNIS LEWIN, ABC Sports producer[1]

The Olympics is the biggest sports event on earth and it is worth
every penny—every single million bucks—you have to spend to
get it. Because then your network is "The Olympic Network"
and people see your image as something special.

ROONE ARLEDGE[2]

JUST AS IMPORTANT AS COMPOSING the "backbone" of ABC Sports'
practices and the "seedbed of modern sports television," *Wide World* formed
the basis from which ABC fashioned the Olympics into sports TV's biggest
spectacle. ABC became the first US network to gain exclusive Olympics
rights when it secured the contract to air the 1960 Winter Games from Squaw
Valley, California. It planned to make Squaw Valley the first nationally televised Olympiad and hoped to parlay the broadcast license into a deal to carry
the more popular Rome Summer Games later that year. But ABC's plans
suddenly swiveled when CBS purchased the Rome contract for $394,000.[3]
An infuriated Ollie Treyz wrote to Squaw Valley Olympic Organizing
Committee (OOC) chairperson Prentis Hale that the Rome rights "were very
much a part of our understanding in connection with the rights to your
Squaw Valley project." He threatened that ABC would "be forced to with-
draw from any participation in such winter Olympic Games" if it did not
also get Rome. Hale responded by maintaining that his committee simply
agreed to "use our best efforts to assist ABC in obtaining Rome TV" and
insisting that "our contract with you for Squaw TV included no provision"
for Rome and "remains in effect regardless."[4] ABC ultimately decided the

cost to telecast Squaw Valley—roughly $100,000 including rights and production costs—was too great without Rome and killed the deal, a move that reportedly made the Squaw Valley Committee "hoppin' mad."[5]

CBS paid $50,000 for Squaw Valley shortly after ABC dropped out. Its broadcasts, mostly brief taped highlights run late in the evening, yielded middling ratings. But CBS satisfied sponsors by attracting a disproportionately moneyed audience and generated goodwill by providing what *Variety* called a "noble public service." The network's modest but unprecedented Olympics coverage—according to sport historian Allen Guttmann—"proved that the games were marvelously telegenic."[6]

CBS's Olympics broadcasts profoundly inspired Arledge as he was moving into sports TV. "There was magic in seeing the divided world come together," he recalled. "It's like a whole nation sitting down to read a book together." Arledge wanted to bring the Olympics' singular aura to ABC, and he made it his mission to acquire rights for the 1964 Winter Olympics from Innsbruck, Austria. "Chet Simmons and I convinced Tom Moore that the future of ABC Sports—indeed, of the network itself—rested on a successful Olympic bid," he said. Arledge also reasoned that the 1964 Winter Games—for which ABC paid $597,000—would nicely complement *Wide World*. "We felt that the Winter Olympics from Innsbruck would give us the opportunity to utilize the techniques we had developed on *Wide World of Sports* during the previous three years and put them all into effect at one time."[7] He viewed the Olympics as a "logical culmination" of the global "kinship" *Wide World* showcased every Saturday. *Wide World* built personalities and story lines that led into and promoted the Olympics. Likewise, the higher-profile Olympics expanded the weekly anthology program's viewership. ABC called its Olympics broadcasts "the ultimate *Wide World of Sports*" and eventually branded itself as "the Network of the Olympics" to emphasize its relationship to the event that Arledge called his "child" and claimed defined him professionally.[8]

Howard Cosell and Muhammad Ali became *Wide World*'s biggest stars as ABC aligned with the Olympics. The program regularly featured Cosell's polarizing commentaries and interviews with Ali that showcased the boxer's controversial views on race, religion, and politics. Their on-air conversations exploited Ali's marketable divisiveness while giving the celebrity athlete a platform to share his resonant perspective with a national audience. ABC's coverage of the 1968 Mexico City Summer Olympics expanded on Cosell and Ali's sometimes-heated discussions by making one of its key plotlines the racism that the United States' African American athletes faced within the country they represented and the possibility that some—emboldened by the worldview Ali shared on *Wide World*—might use the Games to protest these inequities. Tommie Smith and John Carlos's iconic raised-fist demonstration on the medal stand became ABC's top story. Reflecting *Wide World*'s coverage of the US-USSR track meets, ABC's 1968 Olympics broadcasts at once used the racial controversy as a salable narrative device and to advertise Arledge's division as a uniquely enriching outlet that carefully reported on sport's cultural meanings.

INNSBRUCK '64

"Being as schooled as we were on a weekly anthology show made it easier for us to turn our attention to the Olympics," notes ABC Sports producer Geoff Mason. "When it came time to start working on the Olympics the territory was somewhat familiar." Gowdy likened each day of ABC's 1964 Innsbruck broadcast to "covering two or three *Wide World of Sports*."[9] The anthology constituted a veritable portfolio that ABC used to gain Olympic contracts by showing rights holders precisely how it would present featured sports and the locations where they took place. Regardless, the Innsbruck OOC knew of ABC's failure to honor its 1960 Squaw Valley deal and made the network post a bank guarantee before it would sign an agreement.

Immediately after securing Innsbruck, ABC Sports added the Olympics' five-ring logo to its internal stationery to ensure that each correspondence it sent would announce its prestigious new relationship. A two-page advertisement ABC placed in *Variety* shortly before Innsbruck promised the network would show the Olympics like never before. It claimed ABC would have "one of the greatest teams of technicians in television sports history" on the scene and reminded readers that "complex assignments" like the Olympics "are second nature for ABC Sports. Fifty-two weeks a year, viewers are treated to an ever-changing panorama of creative sports coverage."[10] ABC asserted that *Wide World* made it uniquely equipped to do justice to an event of the Olympics' magnitude.

Wide World had visited Innsbruck three times prior to the 1964 Games. ABC built further familiarity with the Austrian city through a series of thirty-minute previews that aired directly after *Wide World* for fourteen weeks preceding the festivities. Arledge claimed the series would deliver "a thorough understanding of every event to be seen on ABC-TV's exclusive coverage of the actual Winter Olympics," and an ABC press release promised it would offer "a motor tour of Innsbruck and the various sites around the beautiful Tyrolean city."[11] The publicity helped ABC to sell out its sponsorship well in advance of the games. "One of the key strengths of the Olympics," observes television scholar Douglas Battema, "was that it appealed both to traditional advertisers and to first time entrants." ABC groomed those old and new sponsors for future business by treating executives to a junket during the event.[12]

Despite ABC's experience in international sports broadcasting, *Variety* described Innsbruck as "the toughest logistical challenge the web [network] has ever faced." Arledge praised CBS's Squaw Valley coverage but explained that Innsbruck posed far more difficult obstacles. He also asserted that "heavy programming of winter sports" through programs like *Wide World* "has made the viewing audience far more sophisticated in its expectations" since the 1960 Games.[13] ABC described traversing perilous terrain—some of which was accessible only via helicopter—to prepare for the production. During a blizzard, the network conscripted the Austrian army's help transporting equipment up a mountainside where alpine events would be staged. "Two of the Austrian soldiers skied ahead and strung a lifeline," recalled Trachinger. "Then the whole crew of 12 men picked up the equipment and hauled it on their shoulders at least a mile with one hand on the lifeline because it was impossible to see ahead, and at times, impossible to see the man in front. Very easily a man could have been lost in those circumstances."[14] ABC developed new gear to get around the many hurdles Innsbruck presented. In particular, it partnered with the Sylvania Company to create the Newschief, a portable and lightweight camera that could be strapped to camera operators' backs for use in otherwise inaccessible spaces.

Overall, ABC aired 16.5 total hours from Innsbruck on tape delay for 1 hour each weeknight and 4 hours across the weekend days. Because nascent satellite technologies could relay signals only for brief intervals, ABC utilized the technology to transport just fifteen minutes of the opening ceremony and twelve minutes of the closing ceremonies to the United States. The rest of the footage was shuttled from Innsbruck to New York via land and air. ABC would complete the day's programming by 4:00 a.m. Innsbruck time— finishing what took a week to create for *Wide World* episodes in less than a day—and drive the tapes 3.5 hours to Munich. The tapes were then transmitted to Frankfurt, where technicians made dubs. Both the masters and copies were flown to New York City's JFK Airport from their separate locations and then transported to ABC's Manhattan studio, where Flemming was on hand to make any necessary changes prior to airtime. The network had a mobile unit at JFK in case the tapes did not arrive with enough time to reach Manhattan and had at the ready a backup program—a hockey game between the United States and Romania—in case they did not arrive at all. Though it never needed to run the hockey game, Jim Spence notes that ABC did have to "clean up" some of the tapes. One tape included what Arledge determined was a bad take of Jim McKay's commentary. "A revised version was flown to New York but did not arrive in time to make it to Manhattan," Spence recalls. "We aired the first tape from the studio, but switched to the second tape at JFK to avoid the commentary problem, and then returned to the studio recording" to ensure that Arledge's preferred version aired.[15]

Because of the Olympics' prime-time scheduling, ABC's coverage necessitated even greater dramatization than *Wide World*. "Most of the people in the audience for Olympic telecasts aren't even sports fans," McKay explained. "We can get them interested if we bring the athletes to life as individuals."[16] Like *Wide World*'s travelogue sequences, ABC stressed Innsbruck's natural beauty and used the city's quaint Old Town section as what Arledge called "the image we'd be sending home."[17] McKay introduced the town with a characteristically enthusiastic thumbnail sketch of its geography and history. "It is a city that has known plagues and wars and medieval grandeur," he announced. "Innsbruck means bridge over the river inn. Roman troops marched through the nearby Brenner Pass and encamped here one thousand years ago." The nightly coverage further followed the *Wide World* format by presenting segments focusing on single competitions rather than cutting among several events. Innsbruck was, for all intents and purposes, a magnified and sped-up adaptation of *Wide World*.

Among US homes with television sets, 68.3 percent watched at least part of ABC's coverage, which the *Atlanta Constitution* called "one of the visual highlights of the viewing year" that allowed viewers to "appreciate anew the miracle of television."[18] This success made a compelling case for ABC to deepen its association with the Olympics. To this end, shortly after Innsbruck, *Wide World* procured rights to cover several of the 1964 Summer Olympic Trials even though NBC would broadcast the Tokyo-based Summer Games. "This type of bidding just doesn't make sense," responded NBC's mystified Carl Lindemann. "All they are going to do is build up the audience for our coverage of the Summer Olympics from Tokyo."[19] Lindemann was correct in the short term; but the coverage was part of ABC's longer strategy to use *Wide World* to brand itself as the Olympics' television home.

THE FRED AND GINGER OF *WIDE WORLD*

ABC secured contracts to broadcast both the 1968 Winter Games in Grenoble, France, and the Summer Games in Mexico City. It more aggressively and deliberately used *Wide World* to publicize these events. Between 1964 and 1968, *Wide World* consistently covered Olympic sports and introduced viewers to the athletes—in particular the Americans—who would likely be competing in the Games it would eventually broadcast. "By the time the Olympics came around you had someone to cheer for," remarked associate producer Jack Gallivan.[20] For instance, *Wide World* used the interval between 1964 and 1968 to fashion figure skater Peggy Fleming into a marketable all-American girl next door like so many perky sitcom daughters of the time. When *Wide World* featured Fleming's 1964 national championship performance, former Olympian and ABC analyst Carol Heiss predicted the spritely athlete could win gold in 1968. *Wide World* traced Fleming's ascendancy, leading to its coverage of her eventual Olympic victory. Reinforcing figure skating's feminine appeal, *Wide World*'s coverage routinely called attention to Fleming's dainty beauty—a trope it did not use when covering men. It even produced a segment called "Girl Talk" in which Heiss interviewed Fleming about skating, school, and boys. Arledge later confessed that ABC partially bankrolled Fleming's training by paying a larger than normal fee to a Seattle ice skating club for TV rights to a competition it hosted. The club used the excess money—to which neither Fleming nor the International Olympic Committee was privy—to finance Olympics-caliber training that the skater's family could not afford.[21] ABC was investing in the athlete whom it was priming to be the profitable and conventionally feminine face of its 1968 Winter Olympics coverage.

But the sportscaster Howard Cosell and the boxer Muhammad Ali became the biggest *Wide World* celebrities between 1964 and 1968 and most clearly demonstrated the program's potential to grow salable personalities and promote big events. Cosell was born Howard Cohen in Winston-Salem, North Carolina, while his father served in the military. He grew up in the working-class neighborhood of Prospect Heights, Brooklyn, and made good by earning a law degree from New York University. The young barrister started practicing after a brief stint in the army during World War II, where he achieved the rank of major. Cohen changed his name to Cosell while in law school, a move that prompted his many critics to remark on the irony of a journalist who so often professed to "tell it like it is" needing to do so without his birth name and while wearing a conspicuous hairpiece. Cosell, however, claimed he was fulfilling his father's wish to restore the family's original surname, which had apparently been bastardized by a lackadaisical clerk when the family immigrated. While Cosell always loved sports and harbored aspirations to be a broadcaster, the legal profession offered a more reliable corridor to the financial stability that eluded his parents.

Cosell found a pathway into sports through his work at the Marro, Pomper, and Cosell Law Firm, where he began working for athletes, including New York Giants center fielder Willie Mays and Brooklyn Dodgers first baseman Gil Hodges. Cosell cast himself as an advocate who looked after athletes' best interests and helped them to navigate the convoluted contracts many often signed without giving them the scrutiny they deserved. The verbose and self-promoting attorney called himself a "voorlooper" who advised athletes faced with a "veldt of agents constantly besieging them with questionable propositions."[22] He turned this work into a connection to sports media by providing pro bono counsel to several ABC executives. After working with Little League Baseball to write the organization's charter, Cosell developed a concept for a short radio program he would host that featured Little Leaguers asking pro ballplayers questions (written by Cosell). ABC liked the idea—as well as Cosell's offer to host gratis—and launched *All League Clubhouse* in July 1953. The Sunday morning program, which Cosell described as a combination of *Meet the Press* and *Juvenile Jury*, started as a six-week trial and lasted through 1956. The unseasoned host particularly enjoyed how radio's immediacy contrasted the legal profession's frequent bouts of tedium.

All it took for Cosell to abandon his comfortable $30,000 yearly salary practicing law was ABC offering him $25 a show to host the ten-week summer replacement program *Speaking of Sports* in 1956. The introduction to *Speaking of Sports*—"The gifted one speaks here"—demonstrates the broadcaster's dual capacity for self-importance and self-awareness. It was a mixture he used to great commercial effect, but one the thin-skinned sportscaster sometimes struggled to keep in balance that often bewildered his coworkers. Cosell approached his broadcasting work as seriously as he took his legal practice and was confident he could turn the small opportunity into a full-time career. He spent $350 of his own money to purchase a bulky, seventeen-pound portable Magnemite tape recorder. He schlepped the machine to events and locker rooms and integrated the sound bites he gathered into his radio program—a state-of-the-art practice that distinguished him on the medium but alienated him from the notepad-toting sportswriters who surrounded him on his beat. "I must have looked like Edmund Hillary carrying his knapsack," the reporter later waxed nostalgic about his early days in radio. By most accounts, the lawyer turned journalist was a grating presence who did not abide by the traditionally cozy mores that characterized sports media practitioners' relationships to those they covered. Moreover, he cultivated sources with unusual persistence. Apparently worn down by Cosell's doggedness, New York Yankees catcher Ralph Houk once told him, "You're like shit. You're everywhere." Cosell also ruffled feathers among his more entrenched colleagues. The *New York Daily News'* Dick Young—a lifelong nemesis of Cosell's—would reportedly yell curse words while his foe gathered audio to render his tape unusable. Regardless, Cosell claims his interview-driven radio work was a hit at ABC because it "was the first time they have ever gotten personal, incisive actualities on the radio in sports."[23] His approach anticipated the "up-close" style Arledge would soon develop in TV and kept *Speaking of Sports* on the air until 1992.

The determined radio host expanded beyond his native medium by briefly penning a column for *Real* magazine titled "Cosell's Clubhouse" in 1957. That same year, Cosell began to appear on ABC-TV with a nightly report called *Sports Focus* that ran through September 1958. Despite his program's brief existence and unremarkable reception, Cosell trumpeted its originality to his ABC superiors by pointing out that "no network had ever before attempted a nightly network sports show." He then provided a bulleted list of *Sports Focus's* varied highlights that included interviews with star athletes like Bob Feller and his eventual *Monday Night Football* cohost Frank Gifford.[24]

Sports Focus was quickly canceled, but Cosell continued to appear on ABC-TV's sports programming in assorted capacities until unexpectedly being taken off the national airwaves in 1959. "For five years, beginning in 1959, I was locked out of television," he sourly recollected. "Five years stolen from a career that started late."[25] Arledge confirmed that Cosell was inexplicably "blackballed" because Tom Moore did not like his style. "Under no circumstances was I to hire Cosell," Scherick added. Some suspected that Moore's distaste for Cosell was veiled anti-Semitism, and others guessed that Moore was mistreating Cosell to get back at an enemy with whom the sportscaster was friendly. Whatever the reason, Cosell was off television until spring 1965. Moore denied taking Cosell off the air out of prejudice or spite, but he did confess that he "never expected Howard would make it" on TV.[26]

Frustrated but undeterred, Cosell established himself as the voice of ABC Radio's coverage of heavyweight championship boxing matches during his exile. He maintained a connection to television by founding Legend Productions to create sports documentaries. His company's first films—*Babe Ruth: A Look behind the Legend* (1963) and *Run to Daylight* (1964)— provided new takes on well-worn sports figures. *Run to Daylight*, which Cosell partially funded with his own money, adapted W. C. Heinz's book of the same title to provide an inside look at Green Bay Packers head coach Vince Lombardi's philosophy and preparations for the season while his team was at training camp. Cosell recruited Horace McMahon, who narrated the introduction to ABC's *Naked City*, to handle the documentary's voice-over duties, and ABC cleared an hour during prime time for the production's premiere. Lombardi biographer David Maraniss credits the documentary with both introducing Lombardi "to a larger television audience beyond those who watched the Packers on autumn Sundays" and marking the beginning of Cosell's "rise as the dominant mythmaker of the modern television sports era."[27] The Legend Productions titles complemented ABC's prestige-driven investment in the documentary genre during the 1960s.

Arledge respected Cosell's work and used the institutional clout he acquired after assuming control of ABC Sports to get the exiled broadcaster back in front of the camera. As he explained, "I was very impressed with the fact that, at a time when ABC didn't have the major events on the scale of CBS and NBC, Howard had more access to athletes than just about anybody." Through "stealth and slipperiness," Arledge assigned Cosell to do pregame interviews for ABC's Saturday afternoon Major League Baseball package in spring 1965.[28] The gig finally made Cosell a consistent presence on network television at the age of forty-seven. Beyond respecting Cosell's journalistic chops, Arledge recognized the nasally voiced, stooped-over, and opinionated announcer as "the sort of personality whose very attitude on the air seems to elicit a reaction." "This was still the time of the golden-throated announcer and the ex-jock," Arledge recalled. "Nobody ever criticized anything, nobody ever asked an athlete a difficult question. Howard stood all that on its head." Cosell responded to Arledge's decision to put him back on TV with his signature brand of irony-baked grandiosity. "Roone, we are today witnessing an occurrence on the scale of Philo T. Farnsworth's invention of the cathode ray tube: the television rebirth of an acknowledged genius. You are to be congratulated, young man, on your sagacity." Arledge told him to "cut the crap," the duo had a laugh, and Cosell set out to infiltrate ABC Sports' flagship program.[29]

Cosell—who once called sports TV a "horizontal ladder of mediocrity"— railed against the common practice of networks hiring well-known former athletes without broadcasting experience, an industrial norm he spitefully termed the "jockocracy." "I am a journalist," he insisted, "I am no house man, no shill and no pretty boy. I stand for frank, creative journalism in a business in which too many others are the essence of blandness."[30] He lamented sports television's tendency to kowtow to sponsors' whims rather than probe the organizations it covered and claimed this promotionally amenable approach typified "the kind of thinking that led Newton Minow to pen his 'Vast Wasteland' speech." Moreover, Cosell claimed that responsible sportscasters had a duty to look beyond box scores. "In sports today a truly good journalist must know the black movement, the labor movement, the law . . . we have an obligation to do more." Critics, however, liked to point out that Cosell's frequent and righteous diatribes against sports and television conflicted with his role as a handsomely compensated promoter and representative of them. ABC paid Cosell to draw attention to events on which the network endeavored to profit. Young, for instance, called him "Howie the Shill." The often contradictory Cosell at once decried what he dubbed "America's sports syndrome" and helped spread the epidemic. But the strident broadcaster contrasted the cheery Jim McKay and Chris Schenkel, an establishmentarian sportscaster ABC signed in 1964. The *Chicago Tribune* called the enthusiastic and midwestern Schenkel "Pollyanna with a microphone," and Arledge even once confessed that he "would like to see more journalism out of Chris." Schenkel, however, envisioned his role as "an adjunct to the pictures" ABC displayed rather than an interruption of them.[31] By adding Cosell and Schenkel, Arledge diversified his stable of broadcasters and ensured that ABC Sports would appeal to a range of audiences—rural and urban, milquetoast and edgy. ABC Sports created uniformity among its different personalities by outfitting them in yellow blazers, a sartorial relic as emblematic of the division as *Wide World*'s opening theme.

Muhammad Ali's rise to fame was simultaneous with and aided by Cosell's emergence. Like Cosell, Ali grew up in a working-class home, adopted a name other than the one he was assigned at birth, and boisterously refused to conform to dominant expectations. The fighter—who went by

Cassius Clay until 1964—won a gold medal in the 1960 Olympics as a light heavyweight. But the eighteen-year-old African American Olympian became disillusioned after returning to the United States to face the same prejudices he confronted before becoming a famous champion. Clay claimed to have thrown his medal—which he proudly wore around his hometown of Louisville—into the Ohio River when he was denied service at a local restaurant. Whether or not the disputed story is true, the young pugilist was most assuredly enraged by the cruel irony of the fact that he could win gold for his country and still be barred from a hometown eatery.

Clay grew into a heavyweight and was rising up the professional ranks when he first appeared on ABC in 1962. That same year, he visited Cosell's radio show, where he proceeded to throw barbs at then heavyweight champion Sonny Liston. The so-called Louisville Lip—who composed and recited witty rhymes predicting the round when he would finish opponents and had "The World's Most Colorful Fighter" painted on the side of his tour bus—made an excellent guest. Arledge even claimed that one of Cosell's early Ali interviews helped convince him to bring the sportscaster back on television. But neither Cosell nor his sports media colleagues believed the effervescent upstart stood a chance to beat Liston.

Cosell provided color commentary for the 7–1 underdog's shocking February 25, 1964, victory over Liston live on ABC Radio from Miami. The following day, Clay changed his name and announced his conversion to Islam—a decision that immediately transformed him from a plucky loudmouth into a mysterious threat. He accompanied his transformation with heightened political outspokenness. In an interview with *Playboy*'s Alex Haley published between his championship victory and May 1965 rematch with Liston, Ali shared his cutting views on the links between Christianity and US race relations. "The Christian religion has just been used to brainwash the black man here in America," he seethed. "It has just taught him to look for his heaven in the sky, in the hereafter, while the white man enjoys his heaven here on earth."[32] The boxer's religious conversion, name change, and comments alienated him from both white and black Americans. The National Boxing Association, in fact, unsuccessfully (and illegally) tried to revoke Ali's license after his turn to Islam. While ABC could not get rights to telecast Ali's initial title defenses—which were shown on a closed-circuit basis in movie theaters and other public spaces—it recognized the polarizing fighter's unique capacity to draw and began airing replays of his matches and having Cosell interview him before and after they occurred.

Cosell became "Ali's Boswell" through his *Wide World* interviews with the champion, and the sportscaster eventually named Ali "the dominant figure in my career" because of the symbiotic celebrity images their many televised encounters fashioned.[33] *Sports Illustrated*'s Myron Cope called Cosell's Ali interviews, which oscillated in tone between poignant and playful, "the Hope Diamond in *ABC's Wide World of Sports*," and the *Washington Post*'s Tony Kornheiser dubbed the pair *Wide World*'s "Fred [Astaire] and Ginger [Rogers]" on account of their palpable on-air chemistry.[34] Beyond Ali's star power, the boxer's many appearances—most of which took place in ABC's Manhattan studios—were inexpensive. They required no rights fees, necessitated less equipment, and demanded fewer staff than covering even the least complex sporting competitions. The interviews also hyped Ali's upcoming fights. The bouts, in turn, built an audience for the conversations ABC aired about them on *Wide World*.

In advance of Ali and Liston's rematch, *Wide World* showed a replay of their first encounter along with McKay's analysis and included a visit to Ali's Deer Lake, Pennsylvania, training camp, where Cosell asked the cocksure fighter to predict the round when he aimed to put Liston away. Following the advice of his similarly expressive trainer and hype man Drew Bundini Brown, Ali resisted the temptation to share his prediction on the grounds that it might hurt ticket sales (he knocked Liston out toward the end of the first round with a mysterious "phantom punch"). Cosell followed this question by asking Ali whether his exaggerated public persona was an elaborate act, a charge the champion patently rebuffed before wildly hollering into the microphone to leave a chuckling Cosell alone to wrap up the interview. "And with that final stage of the *act*," Cosell sarcastically announced, "we leave heavyweight champion of the world Muhammad Ali, or Cassius Clay if you will." Four days after Ali and Liston's short rematch, *Wide World* featured Cosell with a panel of experts—sportswriters Jimmy Cannon and W. C. Heinz and retired heavyweight champions Jack Dempsey and Rocky Marciano—analyzing film of the fight and assessing the suspicious punch that dropped Liston. The varied *Wide World* segments surrounding Ali and Liston's bout demonstrate the boxer's unusual potential to attract an audience outside of his fights and after their outcomes were decided. They also demonstrate ABC's indisputable role as an accomplice to and coproducer of whatever act Ali was performing.

Cosell and Ali's interplay intensified during a November 20, 1965, preview of Ali's fight against former champion Floyd Patterson. The older and comparatively conservative Patterson spoke out against Ali's religious conversion and—like many at the time—refused to call him by his Muslim name. He even cowrote a series of *Sports Illustrated* articles that critiqued Ali as un-American. "He's practically turning the title over to the Black Muslims," Patterson wrote. "Because of that I can't respect him as a champion or as a man."[35] Cosell asked Ali what he thought about Patterson's comments and the fact that the challenger had "become a kind of sentimental hero in this country" among the many who similarly took issue with the champion's perspective. "I want him to be the hero," Ali responded. "I want everyone to cheer him and everyone to boo me. . . . So he's the good American boy and I'm the bad boy." Cosell continued this line of inquiry—and emphasized his unique access to the champion—by reminding his guest that "once privately you confided that Patterson had become the 'white hope' of this country. Do you still believe that?" "That's what he is," Ali curtly replied. "He's the Technicolor white hope." Ali positioned his African American challenger as a naive instrument of the establishment. The boxer's tone then lightened, and he recited a poem that predicted his "beautiful swing" would "lift Floyd right out of the ring." "I want to tell our viewers, Muhammad," responded a visibly charmed Cosell, playing the straight man as he searched for words to match his counterpart's demonstrable wit, "that you shall never qualify as either John Keats or Percy Bysshe Shelley, but I look for a good fight."

While Cosell admired and respected Ali, he unyieldingly couched their interactions in journalistic terms: he was a professional reporter who asked the newsworthy athlete probing questions to which viewers sought answers. Moreover, the liberal-minded former attorney—who had a record of championing civil rights—explained his support for Ali's perspective in legal terms. Ali, as Cosell saw it, had a constitutional right to change his name, worship however he chose, and exercise his right to free speech. Denying or persecuting these rights, Cosell charged, was far more damnable than Ali's choice to enact them in an unpopular way.

Cosell most noticeably exhibited his support by calling the champion Ali during a time when many commentators and publications—including the *New York Times* and many African American newspapers—persisted in referring to him as Clay. "I understood, better than most," Cosell reflected, "that names are not necessarily engraved on marble tablets, never to be disturbed." Arledge supported Cosell's decision, though he rationalized this endorsement in less politicized terms: "Somebody with the name Roone has no right to tell anybody what they can be called," he cracked. "If he wants to be called Muhammad Ali, that's what we're going to call him."[36] But ABC and *Wide World* did not always caption Ali by his preferred name, and some of the network's commentators continued to call him Clay. When covering one of Ali's 1966 title defenses, Cosell referred to him as Ali, and Flemming called him Clay.[37] The decision, which the broadcast did not explicitly address, allowed ABC to accommodate the divided public it served. It also positioned Cosell as *Wide World*'s go-to progressive. But Cosell's conversations with Ali were perhaps most notable for giving the champion a chance to explain and defend his perspective during a time when many were content to speak for him. Commercial imperatives undoubtedly informed Ali's frequent presence on *Wide World*, but the program circulated his provocative voice to a national audience (figure 2).

Ali's controversy magnified after his punishing win over Patterson—a bout during which the champion taunted his outmatched and aging adversary. Shortly after the fight he famously spoke out against the Vietnam War when his draft status was reclassified from mentally unfit to eligible. While his religious principles forbade participation in Vietnam, Ali's comments echoed his long-held frustrations: Why should African Americans be forced to fight and die in the service of a nation that does not take adequate care of them? "Nothing alienated him from his detractors more than this," observes biographer Michael Arkush. "For the athletic and political establishment," sport historian Randy Roberts adds, "Muhammad Ali was the enemy." A revolted Red Smith, for example, wrote that "Cassius makes himself as sorry a spectacle as those unwashed punks who picket and demonstrate against the war." The World Boxing Association temporarily stripped Ali of his title for "conduct detrimental to the spirit of boxing," an ironic move considering the sport's rampant corruption.[38]

Cosell opened an interview with Ali before his April 1966 bout against George Chuvalo in Toronto—a match that provoked widespread protests at closed-circuit exhibition sites because of Ali's stance on Vietnam—by introducing his guest as "one of the most controversial personalities in this entire country."[39] "It remains," Cosell added, "coequally a fact that the heavyweight champion of the world is an integral part of the whole wide world of sport." The host's introduction stressed that legitimate journalistic goals guided *Wide World*'s inclusion of Ali. Cosell reiterated this point during his interview with Ali after the champion beat Chuvalo by unanimous decision. Ali thanked Cosell for defending him by remarking on low blows Chuvalo threw that the referee did not punish. "No," corrected Cosell, "that was a

FIGURE 2. LeRoy Neiman sketch of Muhammad Ali and Howard Cosell, 1970. Courtesy of the LeRoy Neiman Foundation.

reporter asking the questions that we felt had to be asked at the time." Cosell closed the dialogue by inquiring whether Ali planned to register for military service. "You a sports man," an unusually befuddled Ali responded to the unexpected inquest, "and we're here talking about sports." Cosell's approach underscored his apparent impartiality and showed that his public support of Ali's constitutional rights did not mean he would pull any journalistic punches.

The uproar Ali sparked pressured many closed-circuit venues to cancel their exhibitions of his Chuvalo bout. As a result, the match was a financial disaster—a fact the champion's detractors relished. Promoter Bob Arum declared Ali "a dead piece of merchandise" in the United States. "He's through as far as big-money closed-circuit is concerned."[40] Ali's management was forced to book his next three fights, all of which occurred in 1966, in Europe. While Ali's de facto exile limited his earning capacity, it allowed ABC—which had been priced out of live rights to heavyweight championship matches by the closed-circuit market—to carry his European bouts as special presentations of *Wide World*. "Our thinking after what happened when we put Clay-Chuvalo on closed-circuit TV is that it makes more sense to sell our rights to a network," said Main Bout Inc. vice president Michael Malitz.[41] Building on *Wide World*'s 1965 US-USSR track meet from Kiev, ABC transformed Ali's European fights into live transcontinental TV events.

Ali's first live *Wide World* bout pitted him against Henry Cooper in London on May 21. The network emphasized the fight's status with a twenty-five-minute introductory piece on Ali's time abroad that paired footage of the champion merrily gallivanting around London with Roger Miller's jaunty folk song "England Swings." Cosell narrated the piece, which extended his documentary work for Legend Productions while humanizing the misunderstood athlete for US audiences by demonstrating his markedly different reputation abroad. "People in London don't view him the way so many in America do," Cosell said. *Wide World*, however, was almost unable to use the segment because the undercard fights resolved earlier than expected. Cosell sprinted from ringside to Ali's dressing room in a harried attempt to get the boxer to stall so they could include it. "Muhammad," Cosell said to the champ as he warmed up, "remember the great footage we shot of you walking around London—the way the people here feel about you—how much you want the people in the United States to see it now, with all your troubles? . . . It's on the air right now. Just started. We won't be able to show it if you go out there now."[42] Ali consented and delayed the bout long enough for the sympathetic vignette to run.

ABC advertised Ali's next bout—also in London against Brian London on August 6—just as aggressively. It prefaced the bout with a promo in which Ali reminded viewers of his alliance with the network. "This is Muhammad Ali, the heavyweight champion of the world, inviting you to stay right here to watch and witness me defend my title against Brian London, in London, England, over *ABC's Wide World of Sports*." The network created another lighthearted introductory segment that showed Ali clowning around London's streets atop Frank Sinatra's love song "A Foggy Day (in London Town)." Director Doug Wilson played the segment for laughs by pairing Sinatra's romantic lyrics with footage of Ali and Brian London training. Wilson coupled shots of Ali being followed by hoards of autograph seekers with the melancholy lines "as I walk through the streets alone." He also alternated between shots of Ali and his opponent readying for the match along with Sinatra's lyrics about a couple falling in love. Like the introduction to Ali's fight against Cooper, the segment framed the bout as a happening that exceeded its status as a sporting competition.

Ali's final European fight that ABC carried in 1966—against Karl Mildenberger in Frankfurt on September 10—was the first live intercontinental sports event transmitted in color. Other than that technological feat, it was yet another in a string of decisive and unsurprising Ali victories over woefully outclassed opponents. However, these live transatlantic broadcasts solidified ABC's position as Ali's TV home, situated the star athlete within *Wide World*'s international scope, and demonstrated the program's ability to build exceptional TV events. ABC did not gain the rights to broadcast the three fights between Ali's European sojourn and his eventual suspension from boxing for refusing military induction in April 1967. However, it continued to find ways to associate with and profit from those contests through Ali's interviews with Cosell. It previewed Ali's November 1966 fight against Cleveland Williams and offered a recap of the easy victory that ended with the champion demonstrating the "Ali Shuffle," a stutter step—or, as Ali put it, "a dance that will make you scuffle"—designed to disorient opponents.

Ali's most heated *Wide World* appearances occurred leading up to and following his bout against Ernie Terrell—the penultimate match before his suspension. Like Patterson, Terrell persisted in calling Ali Clay and made public his disdain for the champion. ABC encouraged and exploited their grudge. Terrell, for instance, appeared on the ABC variety program *The Hollywood Palace*, where he tried to outwit Ali by performing a song he wrote that included the refrain "Ain't it a shame you changed your name / I'll change your features too."[43] The following week, *Wide World* had Ali and Terrell together on camera with Cosell. In an attempt to heighten the prefight tension, Cosell introduced Ali "as the author of a great new poem." Ali then recited his lyrical prognostication, which forecast, "At the sound of the bell, Terrell will catch hell," as ABC's cameras zoomed in on his opponent's irritated reaction. Terrell dismissed the poem by claiming that "Shakespeare would have turned over in his grave when he heard that" and proceeded to goad Ali by calling him Clay. Ali took exception and shoved his adversary. "Why don't you call me by my name, man? You're acting just like an old Uncle Tom, another Floyd Patterson," Ali hollered. "I'm going to punish you," he yelled as the two started to tussle with only a comparatively puny Cosell separating them until their trainers stepped in to defuse the conflict. Cosell continued commenting amid the ruckus and advised his camera operator to "keep shooting" as the fracas ensued to make sure *Wide World* captured the incident it no doubt provoked.

Ali delivered on his promise to punish Terrell—and then some. The press criticized the champion for taunting his dominated opponent for the match's full fifteen rounds rather than finishing him off earlier. *Sports Illustrated*'s Tex Maule described Ali's performance as "a wonderful demonstration of boxing skill and a barbarous display of cruelty."[44] Ali appeared on *Wide World* alongside Cosell five days after the match to explain himself. The conversation began with a split-screen phone call to Terrell, who was still wearing a patch over his left eye to conceal the damage Ali did. Cosell asked Terrell what Ali said during the match to taunt him—statements ABC's microphones did not pick up. "You're an Uncle Tom," Terrell replied in monotone. "He was shouting, 'What's my name?'" Continuing to stoke their conflict, Cosell asked Terrell Ali's name to see whether the pounding had changed his opinion. "His name is Cassius Clay as far as I'm concerned," Terrell responded as ABC cut to Ali snickering at his obstinate foe.

After finishing the phone conversation with Terrell, Cosell took Ali to task for his "pitiless taunting." Ali defended himself by claiming that Terrell "deliberately insulted me publicly and said my name is Cassius Clay," but he apologized for heckling his opponent during the match. Unsatisfied with Ali's explanation, Cosell continued to criticize the boxer's apparent "cruelty" and "malice" as they proceeded to watch the fight and questioned why Ali did not retire Terrell earlier. "I'm out to be cruel," Ali matter-of-factly responded. "That's what boxing is about. He's out to beat me, I'm out to beat him . . . the referee has the authority to stop it if it's so cruel, the judges have the authority to stop it if it's so cruel, and the doctor who was in his corner each round has the authority to stop it. . . . He would have won the fight if I stopped it. So it's my job to whip him." Ali persuasively defended his approach by suggesting that he was simply doing his job—and doing so in accordance with boxing's fundamentally violent rules. He suggested the charges that he acted with undue brutality were unfair and cloaked excuses to attack the controversial athlete because of his views on race, religion, and Vietnam. "If I'm going to be judged by the American press, which are white people," the champion asserted, "if I'm going to be judged for talking to a man then you would be awful, awful guilty if you were judged for the wrongs and things that you were doing every day and have been doing for 400 years to the so-called Negro in America." Ali succinctly located the sporting press that was so quick to disparage his behavior as a duplicitous instrument of white supremacy.

Ali softened his stance on the press after *Wide World* returned from a commercial break by clarifying that he did not intend to attack "all writers." In a somewhat cheap journalistic move—but one that again flaunted his privileged access to Ali—Cosell asked the fighter if he was backpedaling because of the advice of his manager Herbert Muhammad (Nation of Islam leader Elijah Muhammad's son), who approached him during the interval and whispered in his ear. After Ali denied the suggestion, Cosell proceeded to defend the journalistic establishment his guest castigated by pointing out that "there are people [in journalism] who do agree with you" and asserting that "the test of a reporter is not necessarily his willingness to support you." Cosell's retort does not defend those journalists who attacked Ali, but maintains that journalism is a noble public service that is not nearly as partial as Ali indicates. By implication, he billed *Wide World* as an outlet that practices the craft with integrity. The otherwise intense interview closed on a humorous note when Cosell pointed out that there seemed to be no suitable contenders left for Ali to fight since he so convincingly bested Terrell. Ali then playfully suggested he and Cosell might fight. "That may come about someday," Cosell smirked. Ali advised him to "stay in shape" as a chorus of off-camera laughs erupted. The interview—their last before Ali's suspension aside from the fighter's gimmicky appearance alongside the basketball player Wilt Chamberlain—alternates between fiery antagonism and affectionate ribbing. It demonstrates *Wide World*'s dual exploitation of Ali's image and role as a public forum for the fighter to explain his point of view.

Despite Cosell's defense of sports journalism, critics accused the broadcaster of shilling for his costar. Don Page called Cosell "the best public relations man in the media" because of his interviews with Ali and said *Wide World* amounted to an "instrument to satisfy [Ali's] ego and exploit the Muslim philosophy to the utter delight of his backers and partisans."[45] Others—particularly writers in African American papers—claimed Cosell's treatment of Ali after the Terrell bout was racist. "I was no longer a nigger-loving Jew bastard as I usually was in any adverse mail that reaches my office," a miffed Cosell recalled. "I was the black-hater. I actually got, for the first time in my life, a letter signed by a whole dormitory in Michigan State telling me I was anti-black."[46] Like Ali, Cosell drew flak from divergent audiences.

Ali was scheduled to report for military induction on April 28, 1967, in Houston—the same city where his fights against Williams and Terrell went down. The event became an antiwar and civil rights demonstration with Student Nonviolent Coordinating Committee chair H. Rap Brown in attendance and protesters chanting, "Hep! Hep! Don't take that step" while holding signs that read "Stay home, Muhammad Ali." As expected, Ali refused to take the step to signify his intention to enter the armed services. The New York State Athletic Commission immediately stripped his title and boxing license—a decision the United States' other commissions all followed. Less than one month later, a federal court made an example of Ali by judging the deposed heavyweight champion guilty of draft evasion, sentencing him to five years in prison, and fining him $10,000. Ali had the resources to stay out of jail through funding a protracted appeals process, but he was not reinstated into boxing until 1970. Like Cosell, the boxer was exiled from the profession at which he so prodigiously excelled during the height of his career.

ABC News produced a special report on Ali's induction refusal titled "The Champ: Count Me Out" for the public affairs program *ABC Scope*. Hosted by eventual US ambassador to the United Nations John Scali, the segment conscripted Cosell to explain the controversy. Cosell was without a doubt the ABC employee best suited to cover the story—he knew the topic and had the sources to report on it better than anyone at ABC News. The prime-time segment demonstrated the beginnings of increasing convergence between ABC's sports and news units.

Cosell continued to defend Ali through the boxer's suspension. "I am a lawyer," he claimed. "I studied Constitutional law. I had to recognize Ali's rights, just as I would recognize any other man's rights. If the ritualistic establishment hate [*sic*] me for it, alright."[47] Along more commercial lines, *Wide World* found ways to put Ali on camera despite his absence from the ring. Arledge hired Ali to serve as a special commentator with Cosell for an October 1969 boxing exhibition between the United States and Russia—yet another *Wide World* event mining Cold War frictions. "It did not relate to our wanting to put Ali on television to support his political position," Spence candidly recalled. "We hired Ali for his expertise, but also wanted a colorful superstar on the telecast to help our ratings."[48]

As anticipated, the event successfully drew attention—positive and negative. American boxer Jimmy Ellis criticized Ali's participation, and US representative Fletcher Thompson (R-GA) expressed to Congress his discontent with ABC. "Maybe the American Broadcasting System [*sic*] feels that they need to appeal more to the hippies and yippies of America for support than they do to loyal Americans," Thompson stated. He further called ABC's inclusion of Ali "an affront to all veterans and loyal Americans and an obvious attempt to build the image of Cassius Clay at the expense of those who build this country through the sacrifices they make."[49] Arledge refused to take Ali off the air but made the suspended boxer promise that he would stay away from politics and religion. Ali's presence was the *Wide World* episode's most notable feature and no doubt drew viewers who otherwise may not have watched. It further illustrates how the weekend anthology cultivated stars and used them to build events—a process ABC fully realized with its 1968 Winter and Summer Olympics coverage.

THE NETWORK OF THE OLYMPICS

By 1968, ABC Sports was generating 20 percent of the network's total earnings. As a result, ABC finally established it "as a full and separate division" of the network shortly before the Grenoble Olympics. The network also gave Arledge a hefty raise, named him president of the subsidiary, and signed him to a contract through 1971.[50] "ABC really started to understand the value of the Olympics with Grenoble and Mexico City," said Dennis Lewin. "ABC started to realize that the Olympics were more than two weeks' worth of summer or winter programming; that it was something that could translate to future success for the network itself."[51] One day after the Grenoble Games began, ABC announced itself as the Network of the Olympics in a full-page *Variety* ad that promised its event coverage would bring viewers "closer to the action than ever before. Close enough to sense and understand each athlete's personal drama—the thrill of victory, or the agony of defeat."[52] ABC pegged its entire network identity on the Olympics and advertised its approach to covering the global event by appealing to *Wide World*'s market-tested aesthetic.

ABC paid $7 million total for rights to the 1968 Winter and Summer Olympics—$2.5 million for Grenoble and $4.5 million for Mexico City. With production costs, the network invested over $15 million in the events. Desperate to maintain a foothold in sports broadcasting, NBC reportedly told the Mexico City OOC that it would top any bid ABC issued. The committee, however, was sold on ABC's experience and accepted Arledge's proposal anyway. "After watching us covering past Olympics, they just assumed we could do it best," Arledge remarked.[53]

Arledge called Grenoble "Innsbruck cubed: three times the effort, three times the crew, three times the programing hours." ABC punctuated the event's grandeur by adopting Leo Arnaud's stately "Bugler's Dream" as a theme song. The tune, which ABC used in all its subsequent Olympics packages, is now so identified with the event that it is known as the "Olympics Theme." ABC had 250 staff on site in Grenoble—more people than the US Olympic team sent to compete—and staked out three hundred different camera locations in places even less accessible than the Innsbruck mountaintops. The network aired twenty-seven total hours of Grenoble coverage, with eight in prime time. But it showcased only fragments live—including the opening and closing ceremonies and the women's figure skating finals with Fleming—because of the time difference separating the United States and France. ABC transmitted all its content to the United States via satellite—a process for which *Wide World*'s coverage of Ali's European fights provided valuable training.

Arledge also named Grenoble "the most extensive single color undertaking in the history of broadcasting." The network covered every event in color except the bobsled races, which took place during the evening under sodium vapor lights that were unfriendly to ABC's color cameras. ABC also utilized its nearly exhaustive camera positions to offer start-to-finish coverage of downhill skiing and used split-screen technology to compare skiers' performances to their competitors' earlier runs.[54] Instead of presenting single events each evening, Arledge cut among the studio commentators and several competitions. The format enabled ABC to create a livelier pace by focusing on events' most exciting moments—cutting to a competition that it otherwise may not have shown, for instance, if a record was about to be broken—and packing more action into its coverage.

ABC began publicizing Grenoble with a January 1967 special titled "1968 Olympics—One Year to Go" that outlined the preparations it was making in France and introduced a collection of Olympic hopefuls that *Wide World* would be following intermittently until the Games commenced. The network offered an incentive to affiliates with the ABC Daily Electronic Feed, which provided interviews with athletes and coaches, weather reports, and updates that those affiliates could integrate into their programming.[55] ABC's extravagant coverage went smoothly. It constructed an idyllic and harmonious international event highlighted by Fleming's elegant skating and French skier Jean-Claude Killy's spectacular downhill racing. As the *Chicago Tribune* effused, "ABC-TV itself has struck gold with its excellent coverage of the winter games."[56]

ABC called Mexico City the "most extensive and complicated coverage of any event in TV history," utilizing cameras in helicopters and on a 225-foot crane above the central stadium, and a microphone inside the Olympic flame to capture the whooshing sound of it being lit.[57] The network carried forty-four total hours of coverage, with ten in prime time. ABC also benefited from Mexico City's time zone—mountain time in the United States—which enabled the network to increase its live offerings. "The time differential between New York and France murdered us when it came to live coverage," Arledge grumbled about Grenoble. "But Mexico City's perfect, two hours behind New York."[58] The Mexico City Olympics were also the first to be held in a developing nation. NASA launched the Intelsat 3 satellite just before the event to ensure global coverage from Mexico City, which was previously a blind spot on the telecommunications satellite grid. Beyond the technological advances, ABC began using the Olympics to cross-promote with other network properties by scripting an episode of the sitcom *Bewitched* (1964–72) to take place in Mexico City during the Olympics and working the event into its plot.[59]

Even more than the technological and stylistic advances of ABC's Olympic coverage, the atmosphere in Mexico City was a striking political contrast to Grenoble's wintry tranquillity. Led by San Jose State University sociology professor and former college athlete Harry Edwards, the Olympic Project for Human Rights (OPHR) emerged to organize a boycott of the games by the United States' many participating African Americans. The OPHR's goal was to expose the exploitation of African American athletes for political and economic purposes by a state that denied them equal rights as citizens. The movement countered the vision of domestic accord that international events like the US-USSR track meets—as well as *Wide World's* coverage of them—so strategically built.[60] Threats of a boycott dated back to attempts by the athlete turned comedian Dick Gregory to organize black athletes for Rome and Tokyo. But the combination of Vietnam and intensified domestic strife helped the OPHR gain a critical mass of support leading to the Olympic Games in Mexico City. "If a boycott is deemed appropriate then I believe most of the black athletes will act in unison," Tommie Smith told a Japanese reporter in 1967.[61]

Ali's public defiance and willingness to sacrifice his lucrative career inspired and energized the OPHR. The group threatened to boycott unless three principal demands were met: (1) restore Ali's title; (2) remove Avery Brundage, a known racist who supported Adolf Hitler's 1936 Olympic campaign and owned a Santa Barbara, California, country club that did not allow blacks or Jews as members, as IOC chair; and (3) disinvite apartheid nations South Africa and Rhodesia from Mexico City. Only the third demand—for which other groups had also pushed—was met.

Eight months before Mexico City, the OPHR organized a boycott of the New York Athletic Club's (NYAC) February 16, 1968, track meet at Madison Square Garden because of the sponsoring organization's denial of membership to African Americans. Edwards triumphantly claimed the NYAC boycott marked "the end of an age when Afro-American athletes would compromise black dignity for a watch, a television set, a trophy, or merely the love of competition."[62] It also demonstrated African American athletes' power—because of their disproportionate presence in elite track and field—to delegitimize events in which they refused to participate.

Wide World contracted to televise the NYAC meet as part of its buildup to Mexico City. ABC briefly considered dropping the coverage on account of the controversy but eventually elected to honor its agreement. However, the network refused to ignore the conflicts surrounding the event. "We've told the NYAC that if anything should happen during the telecast that we're not going to shy away from it," Spence told the *New York Post*. "We'll cover it like a news story." Spence further noted that *Wide World* would not have televised the event had it banned African Americans from participating, and he maintained that ABC did not "condone the policies of the NYAC." *Wide World* wound up including only a brief mention of the boycott and protests during the episode's introduction. However, sport historian Amy Bass claims "the NYAC meet emerged as a formal coming out party for the politics of race within sport" and proved "that a large-scale boycott by African American athletes was feasible." One month after the NYAC meet, *Life* magazine published a survey of top black college athletes that found most would be willing to boycott the Olympics if doing so improved conditions for African Americans in the United States.[63] This racial tension composed a central plotline in ABC's Mexico City coverage.

But the OPHR's boycott plans fizzled for lack of organizational solidarity, leaving only the potential for individual action. Several basketball players—most notably University of California, Los Angeles, star Lew Alcindor (who later converted to Islam and changed his name to Kareem Abdul-Jabbar)—declined invitations to try out for the US team, but most of the athletes who earlier threatened to sit out decided they could better build awareness by participating. "The black athletes, who months ago threatened a boycott of the games, were smiling and waving and obviously eager," Don Page reported at the Games' outset. "Harry Edwards, leader of the abortive boycott, should have been embarrassed." Without the smugness, McKay reported "there is no organized thing" planned for the Games as they began.[64]

As the OPHR boycott effort lost steam, Mexico City became the site of varied protests that resonated with the US athletes' grievances. Though embroiled in civil turmoil, Mexico City was still attempting to solidify its status as part of the modern world and urgently wanted to appear unified and prosperous for the global audience the Olympics would attract. It consequently strove to suppress activities that might compromise this glossy image. Most notably, the Mexican government handled an October 2 protest in the capital city's Tlatelolco district, just ten days before the Olympics' opening ceremonies, with deadly force. Police and military—including members of the Olympic Battalion, a security force created expressly for the Games— opened fire on the roughly ten thousand protesters. The official report of what was later named the Tlatelolco Massacre listed 38 dead, but eyewitnesses estimated as many as 350 casualties. As historian Kevin B. Witherspoon writes, "There were rumors of dead bodies—even some living victims—being cremated by police to prevent the true extent of the slaughter from being known."[65] The Olympics proceeded on schedule despite the violence. "We have conferred with the Mexican authorities," Brundage stated, "and we have been assured that nothing will interfere with the peaceful entrance of the Olympic flame into the stadium on October 12, nor with the competition which follows." The intransigent executive further claimed Mexico had promised "that the Mexican people would remember the obligation they had assumed as hosts to the Games and there would be no further trouble."[66]

ABC reduced its live coverage because of anxieties regarding how its audience and sponsors might respond to any protests it aired. Arledge, however, planned for the possibility of dissidence and had no intention to shrink away from it. "My personal opinion is there's going to be trouble, what kind I don't know," he said. "We're going to be prepared, of course, as well as possible." Reflecting Spence's attitude toward the NYAC meet, Dennis Lewin added, "If it was going to happen and happen in front of us, we were going to talk about it. We weren't going to stick our head in the sand and pretend it wasn't there." Arledge assigned Cosell to work the angle of potential protests in addition to his primary assignment covering boxing—both of which extended the commentator's work with Ali on *Wide World*. "Do your thing," Arledge reportedly told Cosell. "I don't want any newsman beating us on any story." Were there a protest, the executive wanted to use the occasion to prove sports television's capacity to cover an important event with the rigor of a news unit. "I was psychologically buoyed," Cosell reminisced, "by the knowledge that I would be supported if there was a black protest situation that would require direct head-on reporting."[67] McKay joined in probing the story line by asking Tommie Smith about the potential boycott before the Games began—a question the runner skillfully dodged.

Four days into the competition—October 16—Smith and his teammate John Carlos waged the Games' most visible demonstration on the medal stand after their respective first- and third-place finishes in the two-hundred-meter dash. The shoeless sprinters wore black socks, bowed their heads, and raised black-gloved fists as "The Star-Spangled Banner" played. Both donned OPHR buttons—as did Australia's Peter Norman, who placed second and joined them on the platform. The IOC immediately banished the sprinters from the Olympic Village and forbade them from further participation in the Games. In his journal, Brundage resentfully wrote that Smith and Carlos "had deliberately violated the spirit of the Games." The IOC chair responded to the several letters he received complaining about their conduct by righteously asserting that "good manners and sportsmanship are more important than athletic ability." No less grudgingly, he reflected on the event in his unpublished memoir by dismissing Smith and Carlos as "feeble" and "warped."[68]

Despite Arledge's preparations, ABC's cameras almost missed Smith and Carlos's statement. "Get in there," Arledge hollered to his crew when he spied the demonstration from the production headquarters. "This is black power!"[69] ABC Sports hustled to edit together a short segment on the incident for ABC News to air that evening. The news division, however, was uninterested. "It turned out to be on the front page of every newspaper in America the very next day and here ABC News could have scooped everybody," remembered a mystified Don Ohlmeyer. "But they didn't want to pay for a telco [telecommunications] line from Mexico City to New York." Arledge claimed ABC News was "screaming and yelling" for more coverage of the demonstration the following day.[70] Cosell was already in tenacious pursuit of the story.

Smith and Carlos disappeared after their expulsion. Cosell stayed up all night working the phones, hounding sources, and chasing any leads that surfaced. With the help of ABC commentator and former Olympic sprinter Hayes Jones—an African American friendly with the runners and their

OPHR comrades—Cosell discovered that Smith was holed up with his wife not far from the Olympic Village at the Diplomat Hotel. The sleep-deprived reporter rushed over to interview the suddenly famous sprinter. While Smith was reluctant to talk with the press—which he believed had treated him unfairly—Cosell convinced the runner that he needed to make his perspective known. The journalist's on-air work with and publicly expressed sympathy for Ali eased Smith's trepidation and compelled him to join Cosell for a one-on-one conversation at ABC's Mexico City studio.[71]

ABC News aired Cosell and Smith's conversation later that day—the first TV interview with the athlete since the medal ceremony. Anchor Frank Reynolds introduced the segment by explaining the demonstration over the footage of Smith and Carlos that ABC News passed up the previous evening. "Before the Olympics there was a furor in this country over a threatened boycott by Negro athletes. Then most of them decided that participation in the Olympics would further the cause of Civil Rights in this country and abroad," Reynolds reported as Smith and Carlos were shown leaving the podium to scattered boos. The anchor then passes to Cosell, who asks Smith to "explain to the people of America" precisely what he did on the medal stand and why. "First of all," Smith replied, "I would like to say that I am very happy to have won the gold medal in Mexico City. . . . The right glove that I wore on my right hand signified the power within black America. The left glove my teammate John Carlos wore on his left hand made an arc with my right hand to his left hand to also signify black unity." He then noted that the scarf he wore was meant to signal blackness, and that his and Carlos's black socks referenced poverty. When Cosell asked Smith whether he believed he "represented all black athletes" with his demonstration, the runner claimed he "represented black America" and calmly reiterated that he was "proud to be a black man." ABC's short interview allowed Smith to clarify the motives behind a divisive gesture that many commentators were quick to judge and slow to comprehend. Future sports broadcasting star Brent Musburger, to list one particularly egregious example, called the runners "a couple of black-skinned storm troopers" in a column for *Chicago's American* published the day after their demonstration.[72] As with Ali, ABC at once profited on Smith's newfound infamy and gave the sprinter the space to share his viewpoint.

ABC News revisited the story the following evening by reporting that the US Olympic Committee had apologized for Smith's and Carlos's actions and asserting that "not all of the American black athletes were sympathetic to the demonstrators." ABC News correspondent Ray Falk interviewed a number of African American athletes from the Olympic Village who expressed their disagreement with the protest and promised they would not engage in similar behavior if they ended up on the victory stand. The report reassured viewers that a wholesale boycott was not in the works. After presenting this angle on the controversy, ABC News allowed Cosell to register his pointed opinions on the protest and the Olympic Committee's response:

> Doubtless the preponderant weight of public opinion will support the [Olympic] Committee, but nothing is solved really. The US Olympic Committee, in the manner of the fabled Village of Brigadoon, appears on the scene once every four years. It is in the main a group of pompous, arrogant, Medieval-minded men who regard the Games as a private social reserve for their tiny clique. They view participation in the Games as a privilege, not as a right earned by competition. They say the Games are sports, not politics; something separate and apart from the realities of life. But the black athlete says he is part of a revolution in America, a revolution designed to create dignity for the black man, and that he is a human being before he is an athlete. He says his life in America is filled with injustice, that he wants equality everywhere, not just in the arena. He says that he will not be used once every four years on behalf of a group that ignores what happens to him every day of all the years. He says he earns participation, wins fairly, and that he will use his participation in the arena to better his plight outside of it. He says, "Don't tell me about the rules, the US doesn't dip its flag in front of the reviewing stand and that's a rule all other nations follow." He's aware of backlash, but says he's had it for 400 years. And so the Olympic Games for the United States have become a kind of America in microcosm; a country torn apart. Where will it all end? Don't ask the US Olympic Committee. They've been too busy preparing for a VIP cocktail party next Monday night in the lush new Camino Real [Hotel]. Howard Cosell, reporting from Mexico City.[73]

The expert rhetorician's voice swelled to accentuate his points, and he grasped a pair of sunglasses in this right hand with which he delicately traced the cadence of his carefully prepared speech. The former attorney clearly savored the opportunity to speak truth to power on a national stage. He lucidly pointed out the Olympic establishment's hypocrisy and persuasively suggested its intolerant response to Smith and Carlos evidenced the very bigotry the athletes were challenging. When Brundage issued a complaint to Arledge that claimed the network should not have televised the protest, he said that ABC had added insult to injury by having Cosell cover the story. But Smith and Carlos thanked the reporter for his fair treatment.[74]

ABC continued reporting the story through the remainder of its Olympics coverage. Between Lee Evans's four-hundred-meter victory and the medal ceremony, Cosell asked the sprinter, who was closely allied with the OPHR, to share his plans for the ceremony. Evans avoided Cosell's question. But moments later he wore a black beret and raised his fist on the podium. He was joined by teammates Larry James and Ronald Freeman, who respectively placed second and third and also sported berets. Though Evans's gesture clearly expressed solidarity with Smith and Carlos, the runner contrasted their solemnity by waving and grinning because, as he explained later, "it's harder to shoot a guy who's smiling."[75] Unlike their predecessors, Evans, James, and Freeman removed their berets and stood at attention while the national anthem played. Cosell secured Evans's first on-camera interview after the demonstration and asked him to explain the "cause" motivating his actions. "Black people all over the world," the runner succinctly responded.

Cosell again appeared on ABC News two days after Evans's October 20 demonstration. He reminded viewers that although tensions had calmed, the issues for which Smith, Carlos, and Evans sought to raise awareness remained within and beyond the United States. Cosell claimed that the US Olympic Committee would "like to believe that the black athlete once and for all has backed down." But, the sportscaster continued, "I can tell you he has not backed down. . . . They're well aware of the fact that when they go back to the country that they begin all over again their fight for racial justice."[76] Cosell connected the athletic demonstrations to the larger struggle for racial equality in the United States and suggested they helped build momentum to that end.

Smith's, Carlos's, and Evans's "defiant actions became the defining moment of the XIXth Olympiad." This is in large part because of the concerted attention and explication ABC gave them across its sports and news coverage. *Variety*'s Bill Greeley, for instance, reported that Smith and Carlos's "gesture startlingly resembled a Fascist salute until Howard Cosell straightened out the matter in an interview." "I felt good about my role in the telecasts," Cosell later reflected. "I had helped to bring some journalism to the world of sports broadcast."[77] His work in Mexico City continued to explore the polarizing but vitally important perspectives his *Wide World* interviews with Ali inserted into network sports television.

But Cosell was not finished after the medal ceremony protests subsided. ABC News gave him a final opportunity to air his perspective on the Olympics—and Avery Brundage in particular—before the closing ceremonies. "It is false any longer to pretend that the Olympic Games are sports and not politics," Cosell declared. He proceeded to outline how Brundage—whom he labeled an "archaic curmudgeon"—had bastardized IOC founder Baron de Coubertin's utopian vision of an event devoid of nationalism and politics. The sportscaster mourned the degree to which Brundage enabled the Games to become an extension of nations' efforts to flex their might on an international stage. "The job is to make the games in the Olympic ideal," Cosell concluded. "One man seeking to prove that he is the best in the world at what he does. That's not the way the Games are now."[78] The IOC, Cosell's commentaries suggested, not only allowed politics to infiltrate the Games but hypocritically punished acts that defied the brand of political expression it preferred.

Critics, however, pointed out that ABC's commercially driven emphasis on US athletes simply perpetuated the Olympics' lamentable politicization. Recognizing the Olympics' visibility and patriotic overtones, Republican presidential candidate Richard Nixon purchased $500,000 worth of advertising spots for use during the Mexico City Games.[79] Like Smith and Carlos—though with a very different agenda—Nixon identified and exploited the nationally televised sporting event's status as a political platform.

ABC's lavish Olympics package operated on a scale that only TV coverage of political conventions and elections could rival. Throughout 1968, ABC used much of the same equipment—most of which it purchased with the funds from its outsized Olympics budgets—to cover the Winter Games (February 6–18), Republican National Convention (August 5–8), Democratic National Convention (August 26–29), Summer Games (October 12–27), and presidential election (November 5). It designed the gear so that it could be quickly dismantled and transported to each subsequent event.[80] But unlike the Olympics, no single network can purchase exclusive rights to cover conventions or elections. As a result, all three major networks, and any other credentialed entity, were present at the events and grasping for ways to attract viewers. ABC—still less reputable than CBS and NBC in news—distinguished its convention and election coverage by borrowing from its sports broadcasts. Along these lines, it hired the conservative William F. Buckley Jr. and the liberal Gore Vidal to debate issues pertaining to the upcoming election. Though far more antagonistic, their conversations extended Cosell and Ali's many encounters on *Wide World* while anticipating the rise of TV punditry.[81]

ABC's Mexico City coverage was even more gushingly reviewed than Grenoble. Though it did not generate substantial revenues, the production further secured ABC's status as the undisputed leader in sports television.

The *New York Times'* Jack Gould called it "a virtuoso display of television resourcefulness and artistry." Gould also pardoned ABC's commercially motivated flourishes as inevitabilities given the network's steep investment in broadcast rights and need to recoup at least some of those costs. The coverage, he enthused, was "a model of enlightened reconciliation of economic needs with good sports journalism." The Academy of Television Arts and Sciences agreed and awarded ABC two Emmys. Robert Lipsyte saw Mexico City as "a turning point for sports in general and the Olympics in particular. Something happened," he stated. "The Olympic Village became the global village and the scoreboard became the bulletin board for messages about products, ideas and ways of life."[82] This metamorphosis occurred as ABC was establishing itself as the Network of the Olympics and using the *Wide World* template to transform the Olympics into a mega media event that attested to sports media's globalized commercial and political import.

ABC Sports also at times avoided efforts to transform its coverage into an ideological soapbox. The University of Buffalo Marching Band planned a politically charged performance during the halftime of an October 31, 1970, football game against College of the Holy Cross that ABC broadcast on a regional basis to upstate New York and New England. Titled "Give Peace a Chance," the recital included sections that spoke out against war, racism, and pollution. The band formed a peace sign and spelled Martin Luther King Jr.'s initials (figure 3). "What we are doing is presenting a program of ideas and music voted on by students in the band as part of a non-violent Moratorium Day," explained band director Frank J. Cipolla.[83]

The band followed Smith and Carlos's lead by using the televised sporting event to make its point. In fact, the student group cynically predicted that it would be more likely to get the attention of President Nixon—a rabid football junkie—by making its statement during a game broadcast than through a more traditional channel of civic discourse. But ABC knew of the Buffalo band's plans before the game and refused to show its performance, which would no doubt irk the NCAA and potentially compromise the network's partnership with it. Instead, ABC displayed sterile shots of Buffalo's campus and cut to updates from its New York City studios during halftime.[84] As a result, Buffalo's students waged a separate protest—against ABC. The protesters chanted "Fuck ABC," took down a sign on campus welcoming the network, and displayed a new sign that used the network's initials to spell "American Big Brother Censors."[85] The network's cameras avoided this demonstration as well (figure 4).

FIGURE 3. The University of Buffalo marching band staged a politically loaded halftime performance during a 1970 football game televised by ABC. The network, however, refused to show the performance. University of Buffalo Archives.

FIGURE 4. University of Buffalo students protested against ABC on October 31, 1970, when the network declined to show its marching band's dissident halftime recital. University of Buffalo Archives.

The University of Buffalo Student Association filed an FCC grievance charging that ABC unfairly censored the protest. It also noted that the network had willingly aired a politically pointed halftime show during the army-navy game shortly after the Buffalo–Holy Cross match that celebrated US military operations in Vietnam. The student association requested that ABC broadcast some content similar to the halftime program or that it give the Buffalo students airtime to express their views.[86] When testifying before the FCC, Arledge argued that ABC chose not to televise the halftime performance "because it was an editorial to get out of Vietnam." ABC further claimed that the army-navy halftime content was appropriate because it simply extended the military pageantry traditionally associated with these very specific schools' athletic encounters. The majority ruled in ABC's favor. A dissenting opinion, however, pointed out that while ABC's decision to avoid the marching band's statement was not necessarily censorship, it did slant the coverage in a way that prioritized safeguarding the network's commercial interests over giving a faithful view of the event. The minority report gestured toward the dangers of ABC abusing the powerful forum its sports broadcasts had—for better or worse—indisputably become.

Though he was not part of ABC's broadcast team for the Buffalo–Holy Cross game, Cosell sympathized with the students' perspective. "I think that every time they run up the flag and fly the airplanes and everything else, they should also hold an antiwar demonstration on the field," he told *Playboy* in 1971. "I only take sports seriously in terms of the public interest," he added in a separate interview that same year. "For God's sake, young men are still getting killed in that cesspool in Southeast Asia. You can't breathe the air. Look at the racial situation, the housing situation, the employment situation."[87] Sports, Cosell argued, are principally worth considering insofar as they illumine the issues Buffalo's marching band, Ali, and Smith and Carlos sought to address. While it only selectively probed sport's political resonances, ABC's coverage unquestionably demonstrated television's potential to reveal them.

ON TO PRIME TIME

Television became the International Olympic Committee's primary income source after 1968. By 1974, the IOC drew over 98 percent of its income from TV and had effectively "mortgaged itself" to the medium.[88] This shift occurred alongside ABC's commitment to the Olympics. The Network of the Olympics covered seven of the next nine Games to which the United States sent teams after Mexico City and continued to promote them year-round on *Wide World*. Tellingly, a 1976 *Variety* article announced that *Wide World of Sports*—not ABC—purchased rights to "exclusive coverage of the games."[89] Though minor, the error instructively demonstrates the role *Wide World* played in building ABC's association with the Olympics and furthering the event's marquee status. Moreover, Dick Ebersol claims that ABC's intensified investment in the Olympics—in particular its prime-time coverage from Mexico City—"led to *Monday Night Football*, and those two things led to the true explosion of sports in this country."[90] The network's Olympic spectacles demonstrated that sports TV—if packaged properly—could compete in prime time against sitcoms and game shows.

FOUR

Monday Night Football, Brian's Song, *and the* Roots *of the Prime-Time TV Event*

Prime time wasn't Sunday afternoon. Everything was different: audience, habits, program content, choices. You turned on your set at night wanting to be entertained. If you weren't the channel got switched.

ROONE ARLEDGE[1]

Monday Night Football is unique because it isn't simply a game, but a game inside an event.

FRANK GIFFORD, *Monday Night Football* cohost[2]

PROFESSIONAL FOOTBALL'S RAPIDLY INCREASING POPULARITY on television during the early 1960s convinced enterprising NFL commissioner Pete Rozelle that football could succeed in prime time. In 1964 the young executive struck a deal with ABC to air games on Fridays.[3] The 1961 Sports Broadcasting Act, which awarded the NFL an antitrust exemption that allowed it to pool television revenues among its clubs, forbade the league from scheduling games on Saturdays while NCAA football was in season. Fridays emerged as the next best option. ABC secured Ford Motor Company as a sponsor and prepared to air five Friday night games starting in September. But NCAA executive director Walter Byers claimed this arrangement would overshadow high school football's Friday evening matches and violated the spirit—if not the letter—of the Sports Broadcasting Act. Byers, who was ultimately more interested in limiting the NFL's power than protecting high school football, rallied the support of the National Federation of State High School Athletics and persuaded Congress to pass a resolution banning the Friday games. "Congress descended on us like you cannot believe," Tom Moore remembered. "There had never been a clearer case," confirms historian Ronald A. Smith, "demonstrating the NCAA's fear of the pros and the commercial threat they posed."[4] Worried the deal might compromise its anti-trust exemption—the linchpin of its rising economic might—the NFL backed off.

With Friday and Saturday evenings off the table, Rozelle began experimenting with Mondays. The league scheduled an untelevised 1964 game in Detroit between the Lions and the Chicago Bears that set an attendance record at Lions Stadium.[5] It continued to book sporadic Monday evening matches and allow regional telecasts. The seven NFL contests that appeared on TV in 1967 and 1968 attracted between a 30 and 42 percent share on the affiliates that carried them.[6] The ratings convinced Rozelle—who had recently launched an aggressive promotional and licensing campaign to broaden the NFL's fan base—that a sizable national audience would welcome prime-time football were it available. Meanwhile, Arledge was confident that the approach he adopted so successfully in Mexico City could work consistently in prime time were it delivering the right attraction. The NFL and ABC consequently struck a deal to launch *Monday Night Football* in 1970.

ABC billed *Monday Night* as a prime-time event in which the football game was but a part of the overall attraction. "On Monday nights we're in the entertainment business competing against the other networks for prime-time ratings," explained Chuck Howard. "Here we work at pontificating less, particularly if the score is lopsided, because we're aware that, unlike Sunday afternoons, viewers can easily switch to other prime-time programming."[7] The new program adopted a souped-up version of Arledge's method to build what media scholar Victoria E. Johnson calls an "unusually consensual space" that spanned divergent audiences.[8] As part of these efforts *Monday Night* deliberately downplayed racial polarization that might fragment its crossover ambitions. While *Monday Night* grew out of the prime-time model that ABC's Mexico City broadcasts established, it suppressed the racial divisiveness that Tommie Smith and John Carlos's iconic demonstration enacted in an effort to attract and retain a consistent prime-time audience.

Monday Night stood among prime-time network TV's most racially integrated programs when representations of African Americans were still rare. But like contemporary productions that featured African Americans, *Monday Night* was created by whites, made for a primarily white audience, and fashioned a picture of racial harmony that did not challenge the status quo or the institutions—including professional football, network television, and the advertising industry—that construct and benefit from it. However, *Monday Night*—the second-longest-running prime-time program after

CBS's *60 Minutes*—is not commonly mentioned in scholarship that historicizes and critiques network television's representation of African Americans since 1970.[9]

ABC built on *Monday Night*'s popularity with prime-time TV events that expanded beyond sports but grew out of the programing flows it established and reflected its watered-down racial politics, most notably the 1971 melodrama *Brian's Song* and the 1977 miniseries *Roots*. Aside from transforming pro football into a prime-time spectacle, then, *Monday Night* established intersecting representational and programming conventions that informed the mediation of race on some of network television's most popular, celebrated, and influential TV events.

MONDAY NIGHT FOOTBALL

Don Ohlmeyer credits Pete Rozelle's "ingenious chicanery" with getting *Monday Night* on the air.[10] Like any savvy businessperson, Rozelle was attempting to grow his thriving company. With the help of Cleveland Browns owner and NFL television committee chair Art Modell, Rozelle reasoned that moving beyond Sundays would both protect against overexposure and get the attention of new consumers. "We can't expand our box office because our stadiums are filled," the commissioner explained. "Our lifeline is TV, and revenue-wise, we have gone about as far as we can on Sunday. Monday night means not only extra money, but opens exciting new possibilities for reaching people who haven't been in the habit of watching on Sunday."[11] The league was particularly interested in women. "Right now, our commercials are all for hard goods sold to men," observed NFL broadcast coordinator Bob Cochran. "Get more women interested and you might find Tide in there."[12] Persuading women to watch a sport that so prominently signals homosociality and manliness, however, was a separate task.

Neither NBC nor CBS—the NFL's network partners through the 1960s—was interested in replacing its already popular Monday evening lineup with football. They doubted the sport could attract women, no matter how it was displayed. "They told me we couldn't preempt *Doris Day*," CBS's Bill MacPhail said after he ran Rozelle's Monday night package past the network's brass. "The wives wouldn't stand for it." "All weekend long, the husband has had the TV, watching football," echoed NBC's Chet Simmons. "Now he wants it Monday night. The little lady has got to say 'Enough is enough!'" In 1968, NBC made tentative plans to air a collection of AFL games on Monday evenings. *Tonight Show* host Johnny Carson became so enraged upon learning of the proposed arrangement—which would delay his program on Mondays—that he threatened to quit. "I found out that somebody at NBC sold an AFL football game for Monday night and they want me to cut down on my show," Carson complained. "I won't do the show any night anymore unless it starts at 11:30. . . . It's not fair to treat my show like late-nite filler."[13] Unwilling to risk losing its biggest star, NBC canceled the 1968 agreement and, with this incident still fresh in mind, passed on Rozelle's continued efforts to schedule football on Monday evenings. "Monday night will always be a strong night for conventional shows," reckoned Simmons. "You're coming off the weekend and people want to stay home."[14]

Arledge coveted the NFL and wanted ABC Sports to make inroads into ABC's prime-time schedule beyond the quadrennial Olympics and scattered championship fights. In fact, when ABC regained the NCAA football contract in 1966, Arledge immediately proposed a slate of prime-time games. "We feel that in the future, sports attractions in prime time will become increasingly popular," he explained to the NCAA's television committee. The NCAA unreservedly shot down his request. Arledge tried again in 1967 and received the same response. Beyond Arledge's interest in moving to prime time, ABC—still in last place—did not have a popular Monday evening lineup that would need to be relocated. Regardless, the network's new president, Elton Rule, who replaced Moore in 1968, did not share his predecessor's enthusiasm for sport. Instead, he agreed with his competitors' assumption that Monday evening games would alienate women and fail as a result. The new executive said he "did not want football intruding on our prime-time schedule, no matter how dismal the ratings."[15]

After the networks all passed on the Monday night games, Rozelle revealed that billionaire Howard Hughes wanted them for his new Hughes Sports Network (HSN), which he established after purchasing Dick Bailey's Sports Network Incorporated in late 1968. The network planned to grow by luring affiliates who craved more sports.[16] Because of its popularity, NFL football would provide the best opportunity to gain these unfulfilled stations. "We're very interested in pro football," said Bailey, whom Hughes kept on as the outfit's president. "Mr. Hughes has the resources. All we have to have is the product."[17] In 1969, HSN began carrying NFL Films' syndicated weekly highlight program *This Week in Pro Football* to develop an association with the NFL that it hoped might lead to a contract for live games.

Arledge surmised that ABC's affiliates—given the network's relative unpopularity—would be among the most likely to join Hughes. He again pleaded his case to Rule, arguing that "if we don't get this football package, you can kiss a hundred affiliates goodbye on Monday nights. We'll be wiped out. We might as well go black."[18] Arledge's histrionic pitch worked, and Rule agreed to pursue the package. Though HSN bid higher than ABC, the NFL granted ABC the contract because of its broader affiliate base and experience in sports. Critics wondered whether the notoriously slick Rozelle was ever seriously considering HSN or simply using it to pressure one of the major networks into taking his games. "We did not bid lower than ABC," Bailey bitterly recalled. "There were other circumstances."[19] Rozelle's ingenious chicanery was chief among them.

The NFL and ABC initially settled on a three-year contract with an option for a fourth season that would give the network thirteen regular season games per year for $8.5 million annually. But after unofficially settling on these terms, Rozelle decided to give CBS and NBC another chance to acquire the NFL games. The decision riled Arledge—who thought the league was simply using ABC to inflate the contract's value. "But we made a deal," the ABC Sports president protested. "You can't just shop it!" The commissioner, however, did shop it and justified his seeming shiftiness by claiming he had an obligation to his long-standing network partners. When CBS and NBC passed again, ABC once and for all obtained the package. In a letter to Rozelle stating ABC's preferences for *Monday Night*, Arledge stipulated that "the Monday night games shall each be 'key' games insofar as your scheduling judgment can provide" and insisted that "the night games in our package shall be the only night games so scheduled by the league."[20] The network agreed to black out the games in the host city but requested that none be scheduled in New York City given its importance for ratings and advertising contracts.

ABC announced the deal during a May 27, 1969, affiliates meeting at San Francisco's Fairmount Hotel, which Arledge missed because of his protracted negotiations with Rozelle. A red light toward the back of the conference room interrupted the sports presentation ABC vice president and general manager I. Martin Pompadur was giving in Arledge's stead. Rule emerged to announce exultantly that ABC had closed the deal for Monday evening games—a development that did not excite the many station owners who shared Rule's initial skepticism. He called the contract "one more testimony to the enterprise and creativity of ABC Sports in making available to our television audiences during the nighttime hours the excitement of professional football." Rule then patched Arledge and Rozelle through to the meeting via telephone. Arledge expressed "great confidence" in what would become *Monday Night* and promised it would both "maintain ABC-TV's position as number one in sports" and be "the best football package on the air." Rule echoed Arledge's proclamations by suggesting *Monday Night* would finally make ABC competitive in prime time. "We believe our 1969–1970 schedule in entertainment programming as well as news and sports has great balance and unusual appeal as well as a strong contemporary look," he said. "It is a television schedule offering freshness and change-of-pace to all TV audiences."[21] ABC began advertising its new partnership with the NFL by having Rozelle appear on a January 1970 installment of *American Sportsman* along with Chicago Bears running back Gale Sayers to fish for striped marlin in Baja California's Sea of Cortez.

ABC's NFL deal dismayed the NCAA, which harbored such great antipathy toward professional football that it forbade CBS and NBC from promoting their NFL coverage or even running ads that featured NFL players during NCAA telecasts. ABC regained the right to cover NCAA football in 1966 based in large part on its status as the only major network without an NFL contract. Arledge eased Byers's worries by assuring him that "our first team is still on Saturday afternoon."[22] He promised his discontented partner that ABC would not use its college football announcers on *Monday Night* and guaranteed that the network would never mention its professional telecasts during its NCAA coverage. ABC would, however, promote its NCAA games on *Monday Night*. The network made other smaller concessions to remain in the NCAA's good graces, such as producing a *Wide World* segment on the dedication of the organization's new headquarters outside of Kansas City—a mundane event that stretched even *Wide World*'s scope.

In its attempts to attract women, *Monday Night* emphasized players' backstories and incorporated still images of their faces into its coverage—with a deliberate focus on the most handsome men. It also published a booklet for women on how to watch football that promised they would be able to understand and enjoy the stereotypically male spectacle.[23] But ABC primarily marketed the program to men and assumed women would eventually follow. It purchased a two-page *Variety* ad leading to *Monday Night*'s debut that stressed its distinctly male appeal. The first page read, "With apologies to the American housewife, ABC presents *Monday Night Football*" along with an image of a football player contritely holding a bouquet of flowers to offer the apparently distressed and lonesome women the show would produce. "It's not that we have anything against women," the ad continued. "In fact, we've had a very lively love affair going on with them (especially the under fifties) all season long. But we've also got our sights set on the male of the species."[24] Critics reinforced ABC's manly marketing campaign by surmising that "divorce rates may well increase" and claiming the program would "send a shudder down the spine of many a housewife."[25]

Arledge's strategy to retain football's mostly male audience and draw women centered on building an irreverent program that would entertain independent of—and in some cases despite—the featured game. "I'm tired of football being treated like a religion," he vented. "The games are not played in Westminster Abbey." His top priority was to hire a provocative broadcast team "so strong that people would be interested regardless of the game or score."[26] He first approached Cosell, an established star he thought "would add a touch of journalism, controversy, excitement, and interest." Arledge imagined Cosell's part to reflect the antiheroic role that journalist Dorothy Kilgallen played while serving as a panelist on the CBS game show *What's My Line?* "Howard's role is not unlike that of a newspaper sports columnist," Arledge explained. "He provides the kind of comments you normally get on the sports pages the day after the game. The big difference is that he is right there, live on camera."[27] Because Cosell was neither a play-by-play announcer nor an expert commentator, Arledge opted to use three broadcasters instead of the standard two—another point that would separate *Monday Night* from Sunday broadcasts.

Arledge hired former Dallas Cowboys quarterback Don Meredith to provide color commentary and play the foil to Cosell. Growing out of the tradition of Dizzy Dean, the charming and folksy southerner offered wry country wit that complemented Cosell's verbose elitism and appealed to the many who disliked his self-serious partner. When the inexperienced broadcaster voiced doubt that he would be able to handle the high-pressure *Monday Night* job, Cosell reminded Meredith of their potential marketability as a duo: "Middle America will love you. Southern America will love you. And there are at least forty sportswriters in the country who can't wait to get at me. . . . You'll wear the white hat, I'll wear the black hat."[28]

After acquiring two strong leads, Arledge sought a play-by-play announcer content to stay in the background and provide little more than scores and updates. But he still craved a market-tested star for this less prominent role. After unsuccessfully courting Gowdy, Los Angeles Dodgers announcer Vin Scully, and former New York Giants running back Frank Gifford—all of whom were under contract with competitors—Arledge settled on journey-man sportscaster Keith Jackson, an ex-marine who performed admirably on sundry ABC Sports assignments. Jackson appreciated the big break but ambivalently described his role as "the world's highest paid public address announcer" who kept the "river running" and did not "interfere with what-ever the other two guys were doing."[29]

Monday Night matched its increased slate of sportscasters with magnified production techniques. It used nine total cameras separated into two units helmed by ABC Sports' most accomplished staff. The A unit, run by Chet Forte, included five cameras and focused on the game. The B unit, which Ohlmeyer oversaw, handled isolated coverage. "It's the way the job should be done," Forte explained of the configuration. "It gives the producer more flex-ibility. . . . There are elements that we hope to add to our overall coverage concept that just wouldn't be possible without that second unit."[30] The first season's introduction put on display the program's high-tech practices by beginning with a production room filled with blinking lights, gadgets, and a group of frantic ABC Sports technicians rushing to bring the ornate spectacle to life. The hurried voice of an off-camera producer emerges to organize *Monday Night*'s ranks: "Fifteen seconds to air; standby all cameras." A differ-ent producer then surfaces to announce he is "ready with slow motion and isolated cameras" as the show begins along with its jazzy, organ-heavy theme song. The introduction further emphasizes the show's stylistic excess—and builds on Arledge's insistence that his name be appended to each ABC Sports creation—by including the captioned names of *Monday Night*'s key producers, much like a film's initial moments. These practices, unprecedented in sports television, announced *Monday Night* as a singularly lavish program driven by the meticulously coordinated vision of its many creators.

Because of his role on the NFL's television committee, Modell volunteered Cleveland to host the program's inaugural game, which pitted the New York Jets against his Browns. Jackson's opening remarks framed the contest as a historic battle between two exciting teams headed by charismatic stars. "Two powers in professional football meet for the first time ever as members of the new American Football Conference of the National Football League," Jackson announced atop a bird's-eye view shot of Cleveland's Municipal Stadium. "The New York Jets, led by the passing wizardry of Joe Namath, and the Cleveland Browns, led by the power running of LeRoy Kelley." The telecast cuts from Jackson's introductory comments to Cosell at midfield, who sets the "hot, sultry, almost windless" scene and conducts brief interviews with Namath and Jets middle linebacker Al Atkinson to stress the contest's import and provide insight into its key participants. *Monday Night* combines its emphasis on the game's excitement with a display of the program's style by wiping to a split-screen view with Cosell at midfield and Jackson in the main booth—a technique that communicated little about the game but said a lot about how the show would present it.

Cosell then establishes his and Meredith's playful antagonism by introducing his costar through a montage of the recently retired quarterback absorbing violent hits and committing fumbles during his career. *Monday Night*'s producers accentuated the prank by cutting to Meredith blushing after viewing the embarrassing footage. "Dandy Don Meredith," says Cosell, proud at having humbled his counterpart. "How does it feel to review the glories of yesteryear?" The program again wipes to a split screen with Meredith offering his take on the competing teams after recovering his composure and Cosell still chuckling at the well-executed gag. These first minutes unveil the announcers' characteristics and indicate how *Monday Night* will complement them. Jackson is the straight man, Cosell is the witty journalist with the inside scoop, and Meredith is the good-natured goof with the wisdom of a former player. It also clearly positions Cosell as the star—the "spice in the stew," as Arledge put it—who sets the weekly program's tone.[31]

The game coverage continued the introduction's conspicuous stylization by debuting a bevy of newfangled conventions. It featured cameras on either sideline gathering sound from the teams' respective benches and slow-motion replays from a variety of angles that incorporated split screens to demonstrate how single plays developed in different parts of the field. It punctuated this coverage after Browns linebacker Billy Andrews sealed the win by returning a Namath interception for a touchdown. Rather than showcase the Browns' victory celebrations, *Monday Night* director Chet Forte displayed the view from a B-unit camera trained on Namath. The shot lingered for several seconds on the disappointed quarterback alone at midfield as the Browns celebrated behind him. The image emphasized the tragic failure of the hero through which *Monday Night* framed its game coverage, bringing closure to the narrative it introduced before the event began. "There's a depressed Joe Namath," Jackson remarked as the quarterback hung his head in dejection. "That was a great shot," Cosell added. "It was like one taken by a great sports photographer as Namath walked off the field after the final loss to Kansas City last year—a shot entitled 'Namath Walks Alone.' We could call that last one 'Namath Stands Alone.'" *Monday Night*'s first episode thus took careful steps to bill the new show as dramatic, humorous, innovative, and artful. The premiere drew sixty million total viewers to capture 35 percent of the network audience.

The following day, Arledge sent Namath a thank-you note for his willingness to give Cosell an audience prior to the match. "I really appreciate your taking the time to go on with Howard before Monday night's game with the Browns. I know coming at the time that it did was an imposition and I just wanted you to know how much I appreciate it," Arledge wrote. "It is a tragedy that the Jets didn't win a game that you so clearly dominated, but it is a long season and I'm sure that you'll come out on top in the end."[32] The dispatch betrays Arledge's efforts to groom Namath into a resource the program could tap for future broadcasts. Arledge would, in fact, eventually recruit the quarterback to join *Monday Night*'s team in 1985, an unsuccessful one-season stint. The short note also demonstrates that the pregame interview, which quickly became a stock ingredient of sports broadcasts, was a practice *Monday Night* popularized that grew out of the program's focus on building a sports spectacle suitable for prime time.

Responses to *Monday Night*'s early weeks mirrored the polarization Cosell generally prompted. "I knew Dandy and Howard would be great, and they were," *Sports Illustrated*'s Dan Jenkins wrote to Arledge. "Here's hoping you keep 'em turned on, and let 'em go. They're guaranteed to become the Huntley-Brinkley of pro football, but far more lively, and a welcome breakthrough in the business of telecasting the pro game." Arledge thanked Jenkins—whose endorsement carried considerable industrial weight—but added that the broadcast team still had improvements to make. "Cosell was not as effective as he normally would be because of some logistical problems we had," Arledge divulged, "but I expect to be hearing some incisive and hopefully, intelligent commentary from him in the future." Arledge's reply indicated that he was anticipating the many Cosell-directed attacks that followed the debut, such as *Los Angeles Times* columnist Jim Murray's unforgiving and insensitive charges that Cosell "comes off as if he were reading the tablets of Sinai to a group of retarded children who are hard of hearing and unfamiliar with the language" and that the broadcaster "treats the game as if it were a pointless interruption of an otherwise brilliant monologue." Sharing Murray's reaction, Henry Ford II—the auto manufacturing scion who presided over *Monday Night*'s primary sponsor—thought Cosell overshadowed the games and expressed this complaint directly to Goldenson. "Take that Cosell guy off. He's hogging all the time."[33] Goldenson was inclined to indulge the powerful sponsor. But Arledge convinced his boss to give Cosell a month to prove himself—a negotiation he did not reveal to his touchy commentator for fear of rattling him.

The program found its stride a few weeks into the season when it showed the St. Louis Cardinals blow out the Cowboys 38–0. *Monday Night* turned its focus from the uninteresting game to Meredith's agonized reactions to his former team's folly as Cosell delightedly hassled him. The broadcast attracted *Monday Night*'s largest audience of the season and, as Arledge put it, "proved you could have an awful game and still have an audience watch."[34] Even Ford, who quickly came to appreciate Cosell and withdrew his complaint midway through the season, recognized *Monday Night* was a special type of broadcast designed to exceed the featured game. Ford, of course, realized that whether viewers tuned in to watch the game or just laugh at the hosts, all would see the advertisements his company used *Monday Night* to deliver.

As *Monday Night*'s inaugural season came to a close, ABC executive James Duffy proudly proclaimed that the new show had "restored event television to prime-time television."[35] It achieved an average audience share of 31 and ranked third among the prime-time programs that premiered in 1970. Striving to enhance his pet project's marketability, Arledge hired Frank Gifford to replace Jackson—who learned of his termination by reading of it in the newspaper because the conflict-averse Arledge delayed breaking the news. ABC moved Jackson to ABC's college football package, where he remained until retiring in 2006. Despite his soft landing, Jackson resentfully claimed, "An announcer's job is to amplify, clarify and define, not to do a song-and-dance act."[36] But this was not, of course, the *Monday Night* announcer's job. Gifford was an unpolished sportscaster who repeatedly butchered names and flubbed lines—shortcomings that prompted Cosell to assign him the ironic nickname "Faultless Frank." While not as talented as Jackson, Gifford was a handsome and high-profile former NFL star who had done some acting and endorsing, was beloved in the powerful New York City market, and tested well among women. When it came to *Monday Night*— especially given the limited role he envisioned for the play-by-play announcer—Arledge had no problem trading Jackson's technical polish for Gifford's glamour.

Gifford, Cosell, and Meredith constituted *Monday Night*'s "classic" lineup and—aside from Meredith's 1974–76 absence—shared announcing duties until Cosell left after the 1983 season. Ohlmeyer described the trio as "three distinct personalities with three different points of view. Frank thought everything was fantastic. Don thought the players were great and the owners were pirates. And Cosell thought they were all bums. You put those three points of view together and you're going to have a lively discussion."[37] In 1973, *Monday Night* rebooted its introduction to emphasize these featured characters. It combined the original introduction's focus on *Monday Night*'s innovation with individual shots of the stars that—like a sitcom's introductory sequence—gestured toward their divergent but complementary dispositions. More important, the introduction suggests *Monday Night* shares aesthetic ground with the sitcoms that surrounded it in prime time. Cosell frequently boasted that the program had become "bigger than the game"—a conceit the *Sporting News* substantiated by reporting that "fewer persons turned off one-sided Monday night telecasts than similar games on Sunday" and crediting this retention to the announcers' ability to entertain as well as cover the game.[38]

Monday Night augmented its broadcast team with accoutrements designed to draw and hold a crossover viewership. "What you wanted to do was get people to talk about *Monday Night Football* on Tuesday in the office," Ohlmeyer said.[39] Building on NBC's *Tonight Show*, *Monday Night* invited celebrity guests to visit the booth, many of whom had an ABC property to promote. William Shatner, for instance, dropped by to plug his ABC series *Barbary Coast. Monday Night* referenced Shatner's work as Captain Kirk on *Star Trek* by using an effect that made it look as if he was "beaming" into the broadcast booth from the deck of the starship *Enterprise*. During a single 1974 game from San Francisco, actors John Wayne and Michael Douglas, musician Andy Williams, and boxing trainer Dick Sadler made appearances. Burt Reynolds opened another 1974 broadcast by mouthing Cosell's introductory monologue while the sportscaster spoke off camera—a stunt that played on the dashing actor's dramatic contrast to Cosell's physical appearance and strident persona (figure 5).

Solidifying the program's crossover ambitions, a December 9, 1974, contest from Los Angeles featured appearances by then California governor Ronald Reagan and former Beatle John Lennon. Cosell—who was strangely obsequious around nonsports celebrities—was originally slated to interview Reagan. He passed those duties to Gifford when he learned Lennon was joining. "You take the governor," he told Gifford. "I'll take the Beatle." Besides capitalizing on Lennon's and Reagan's celebrity and filling time during the game's lulls, the dual appearance demonstrates *Monday Night*'s unique ability to traverse and unite seemingly disparate demographics—from the more traditional viewers who allied with Reagan to the countercultural fans who identified

FIGURE 5. Actor Burt Reynolds appears on a 1974 installment of *Monday Night Football*.

with Lennon. Most important, such celebrity appearances—and the Tuesday morning watercooler chatter they provoked—worked to motivate viewers to stay tuned through the program's duration lest they miss a surprise visitor.

Perhaps *Monday Night*'s most popular extra feature was its NFL Films–edited halftime highlights that recapped the previous day's games—a complement on which Arledge insisted from the start of his talks with Rozelle. Matching *Monday Night*'s stylish presentation, the highlights featured NFL Films' signature use of ground-level slow-motion shots and rousing scores. But ABC claimed these packages as the province of *Monday Night* by trading NFL Films' deep baritone narration by John "The Voice of God" Facenda for Cosell, who recorded his often-extemporaneous voice-overs on Monday afternoons shortly after NFL Films delivered its highlights to the site of the weekly game. While NFL Films had crews at every league match, ABC's promotionally minded producers requested footage for its *Monday Night* halftime highlights package based on which contests were most important to league standings and the teams slated to appear on the program later in the season. The highlights provided the only venue to see footage of the NFL's weekly games outside of brief Sunday evening news recaps or NFL Films' syndicated programs, which aired later in the week but not in every market and often only at unusual times. They became an event within ABC's prime-time TV event that retained audiences at least through the program's midway point. "Even when it's not a good game," the *Washington Post*'s Leonard Shapiro observed, "people stay tuned through halftime."[40]

An array of anecdotes emerged to explain how *Monday Night* displaced viewing habits and routines—tidbits ABC was happy to recirculate. These stories suggested fewer people were going to the movies on Mondays, bowling leagues were avoiding the day, and water pressure dropped in major cities during the show's commercial breaks because so many were waiting until those gaps to use the restroom. Bars and restaurants began installing television sets to win back the clientele who were staying home to watch football on Mondays. A tavern in Denver sweetened the deal by holding a raffle that allowed the winner to toss a brick through a TV set when Cosell appeared on-screen, and the same city's ABC affiliate gave customers foam bricks so they could (less destructively) share in the ritual at home. ABC Sports accommodated the shifts *Monday Night* prompted by increasing the use of graphics to allow those viewers watching in noisy bars to understand more clearly what was happening. "There was an expansion of what people's viewing habits were," noted ABC producer Dorrance Smith of the spike in public TV watching *Monday Night* stimulated, "that made it all the more important for what you were seeing to complement what was on the screen."[41] *Monday Night* ushered and exploited these changes in sport media's presentation and consumption.

Soon after *Monday Night* established itself as a prime-time sensation, the networks that originally passed on the program started taking shots at it. They complained that the NFL was giving ABC the league's best games and suggested the irreverent program was cheapening professional football—a sentiment epitomized by the sarcastic title of Edwin "Bud" Shrake's 1971 *Sports Illustrated* feature, "What Are They Doing with the Sacred Game of Pro Football?" As Bill MacPhail carped, "ABC has lost sight of the fact that pro football is a game, not a show for three stars. What should we do, follow them with a team of Don Rickles, Milton Berle, and Mickey Rooney?" MacPhail continued by charging that ABC had "lessened the game a little with this star approach. Which is bigger, the game or the announcers?"[42] Cosell, of course, had voiced his perspective on this matter.

Monday Night's flustered competitors were eventually forced to adapt to the industrial norms the program established. In 1971, NBC began airing its weekday World Series games in prime time. Two years later, the network debuted *Monday Night Baseball*, a series of prime-time games that mimicked *Monday Night Football*'s title and aesthetic recipe by including a rotating weekly guest commentator from sports or entertainment—baseball player Satchel Paige, singer Dinah Shore, actor and director Woody Allen, and so forth. Cosell even appeared as a *Monday Night Baseball* guest host in 1973. Beyond NBC's sports offerings, Johnny Carson began taking Monday evenings off in 1972 to let his *Tonight Show* guest hosts go toe-to-toe with the show that provided him with his stiffest competition of the week. NBC also sporadically aired blockbuster movies against *Monday Night*. Its 1974 presentation of Francis Ford Coppola's *The Godfather* (1972) outrated *Monday Night* 9–1, and its 1976 scheduling of Victor Fleming's *Gone with the Wind* (1939)—which it presented across a Sunday and Monday evening—became the highest-rated TV broadcast ever. The network, however, could not program marquee Hollywood films every week, and those viewers who skipped *Monday Night* to view *The Godfather* or *Gone with the Wind* typically returned to ABC.

CBS took a different tack to competing with *Monday Night* by counter-programming with a block of women-centered sitcoms. In 1974, it moved *Maude*—a spin-off of Norman Lear's *All in the Family* about an opinionated and progressive middle-aged woman on her fourth marriage—to Monday evenings alongside the *Mary Tyler Moore Show* spin-off *Rhoda*, another series about an independent woman making her way in the modern world. The programs provided an alternative for viewers—especially women—who found *Monday Night*'s macho world tiresome, or just uninteresting. CBS magnified this effort the following season by launching *Phyllis*, another female-driven *Mary Tyler Moore Show* offshoot, on Monday nights and moving *All in the Family*—network television's highest-rated program at the time—to Mondays from Saturday night. Starting at 8:00, *Rhoda* and *Phyllis* led in to *All in the Family*, which began at *Monday Night*'s 9:00 start time. *Maude* followed the legendary sitcom at 9:30. It was both clever and ironic that CBS programmed the show starring Archie Bunker—a loudmouthed sexist who enjoyed nothing more than watching sports and drinking beer—alongside a group of freethinking women to challenge *Monday Night Football*. The high-stakes ratings battles *Monday Night* set off were, in the words of *Boston Globe* reporter Percy Shain, "as savage as the line play in those pro games."[43] Beyond its impact on bowling leagues and bar patronage, then, *Monday Night* changed the programming practices of prime-time network television and—albeit inadvertently—precipitated a swell of important shows starring and geared toward women.

Monday Night's greatest industrial impact, of course, was on sports programming, which quickly became standard in prime time. Even the NCAA took advantage of the viewing habits *Monday Night* established by scheduling Monday evening games before the program's 1975 and 1976 seasons began.[44] While CBS mostly competed with *Monday Night* via its sitcoms, the network's radio division teamed with the media company Westwood One to provide national broadcasts of the games ABC televised. Hosted by Jack Buck and former Kansas City Chiefs coach Hank Stram, the CBS broadcasts billed themselves as an alternative—marketed with the slogan "television should be seen and not heard"—to *Monday Night* for the many who bristled at the program's Cosell-dominated soundscape.[45]

The vitriol on which CBS's radio package traded often appealed to Cosell's relationship with and publicly expressed support for Muhammad Ali. The sportscaster, in fact, claimed that most of the letters he received after *Monday Night's* premiere began with racist attacks on his Jewish heritage and willingness to defend a rebellious Black Muslim. Cosell's relationship with Meredith on *Monday Night* mirrored—and to some degree adapted—his banter with Ali on *Wide World*. Ali reportedly grew concerned that Meredith was usurping his role as Cosell's primary TV sidekick. "And this guy who works with you," Ali told Cosell shortly after *Monday Night* took off. "What's his name, Dandy? I think you're making too much of him. You gotta remember, we're the number one act in sports."[46] But rather than playing counterpart to a militant African American on a prerecorded Saturday afternoon program, *Monday Night* had Cosell serve as antagonist to a jovial white country boy in prime time. "From a political bent," observes Cosell biographer Mark Ribowsky, "the act was defanged" when Cosell teamed with Meredith on Mondays.[47]

Moreover, Cosell and his cohosts conspicuously avoided interrogating the NFL's racist underbelly on *Monday Night*. In October 1970—the month after *Monday Night's* premiere—the US Commission on Civil Rights reported "a major breakdown in the enforcement of laws against racial discrimination." The NFL reflected these conditions. Alongside *Monday Night's* emergence, exposés like *Sports Illustrated* reporter Jack Olsen's article "The Black Athlete—A Shameful Story" and memoirs from retired players including Jim Brown's *Off My Chest* (1964), Dave Meggyesy's *Out of Their League* (1970), Chip Oliver's *High for the Game* (1971), Bernie Parrish's *They Call It a Game* (1971), and Johnny Sample's *Confessions of a Dirty Ballplayer* (1970) detailed the NFL's inequitable treatment of African Americans through unofficial racial quotas, de facto segregation, and the paucity of blacks in leadership positions like quarterback and middle linebacker. A group of African American players even called for Rozelle's resignation as a result of his unwillingness to address racism in the NFL.[48] These perspectives, however, never found their way onto *Monday Night*. Cosell later admitted that his work on the show lacked the critical edge and political import he strove to achieve in his regular reporting. "Looking back on it, my work on *Monday Night Football* is a matter of monumental indifference to me," he said in 1985. "My real fulfillment in broadcasting has always come from crusading journalism, fighting for the rights of people such as Jackie Robinson, Muhammad Ali, and Curt Flood, and obviously there was none of that on *Monday Night Football*."[49] The program overlooked the NFL's troubling racial politics en route to engineering and sustaining a comfortable experience for its prime-time audience.

BRIAN'S SONG

ABC supplemented *Monday Night's* mainstream aspirations with *Brian's Song*, a melodramatic installment of *ABC's Movie of the Week* that premiered November 30, 1971. Based on a chapter in Gale Sayers's memoir, the film tells the story of Sayers's friendship with Chicago Bears teammate Brian Piccolo. Initially competing for the same job, the reserved African American Sayers (played by Billy Dee Williams) and the gregarious Italian American Piccolo (played by James Caan) composed an unlikely pair and were the NFL's first interracial roommates in training camp and on the road. But Piccolo was suddenly diagnosed with lung cancer and died shortly thereafter. *Brian's Song* celebrates the teammates' friendship and mourns Piccolo's untimely passing. It extends the made-for-TV movie's tendency to package current events into prime-time entertainment by combining the true story of Piccolo's death, the social currency of race relations at the time, and the popularity of pro football.

The opening lines of *Brian's Song*, delivered by the actor who played Chicago Bears owner and coach George Halas, guarantee the tale's authenticity and pathos: "Ernest Hemingway said every true story ends in death," he mournfully intones. "Well, this is a true story." The film's melodramatic format and tragic themes built on the massive popularity of *Love Story* (1970), another film about a young couple cruelly torn apart by grave illness. Director Buzz Kulik imagined it as a variation of Hollywood director Howard Hawks's love stories between men such as *A Girl in Every Port* (1928) and *Rio Bravo* (1959).[50] The telefilm reaches its emotional apex with a heartrending speech Sayers gives while dedicating an award for his ability to come back after injury—a recovery Piccolo aided—to his dying friend. "I love Brian Piccolo," he sobs. "And I'd like all of you to love him too. And tonight, when you hit your knees, please ask God to love him." *Brian's Song* ends with another Halas voice-over atop the production's doleful score: "Brian Piccolo died of cancer at the age of twenty-six. He left a wife and three daughters. He also left a great many loving friends who think of him often. But when they think of him, it's not how he died that they remember. But rather, how he lived. How he did live."

ABC programmed *Brian's Song* to complement *Monday Night* by premiering it one night after the show carried a Bears game in Chicago. Screenwriter William Blinn sought to create connections between the film and *Monday Night* by noting in his stage directions that Don Meredith would serve as an ideal narrator.[51] Beyond taking advantage of *Monday Night*'s renown, *Brian's Song* reflected the prime-time football broadcast's emphasis on building story lines by stressing the "human drama" that the NFL harbors beyond the field. The film's story resembled the often pathos-laden human interest segments ABC used to introduce athletes prior to event coverage.[52]

Also like *Monday Night*, *Brian's Song* was produced by white men and directed primarily to a white viewership. It provides a similarly uncritical perspective on race relations and locates the NFL as an organization that fosters interracial understanding. The film depicts race as a barrier that Sayers and Piccolo's friendship effortlessly transcended. Though he and Piccolo were the NFL's first interracial teammates, Sayers did not find the arrangement remarkable. "Friends like to room with friends," he matter-of-factly wrote, "it has nothing to do with segregation."[53] In the film, the Bears leadership summons Sayers to Halas's office to propose the trailblazing rooming assignment. Sayers expresses relief once they explain why he was called in. "I thought it was something serious," he dismissively remarks in response to their proposed arrangement. Veteran African American player J. C. Caroline (played by former NFL receiver Bernie Casey) interjects to assure Sayers that he will be judged harshly for sharing a room with Piccolo. "You're going to be called a Tom by some blacks and an uppity nigger by some whites," he says. "You're going to rock the boat, Sayers. And there's plenty of people around who are already seasick." Sayers, however, accepts the rooming assignment without hesitation. In *Out of Their League*, Meggyesy locates segregated rooming as a key indicator of the NFL's institutional racism. *Brian's Song*, however, presents the Bears franchise—and, by extension, the NFL—as an open-minded organization that welcomes and even initiates the integration that provoked discord in the world beyond pro football.

Throughout the film, Sayers and Piccolo make light of the racial differences that spark such enmity outside of their team and friendship. "The best thing about our relationship as it developed was that we could kid each other all the time about race," Sayers wrote.[54] They joke about hate mail they received because of their rooming arrangement—letters similar to those sent to Cosell because of his rapport with Ali. In another instance, Piccolo calls Sayers a nigger in an attempt to provoke his exhausted buddy when lifting weights to rebuild his injured knee. Rather than becoming enraged and lifting the weight, Sayers bursts into laughter at his friend's foolish effort to use a racist epithet as a motivator. Toward the end of the film, Sayers provides his dying pal with much-needed blood. Piccolo acknowledges the generous gift by claiming he had developed a craving for chitlins ever since receiving the infusion—a wisecrack that brings some levity to the grave conversation. Sayers and Piccolo's friendship, the film suggests, renders these would-be insults impotent. Their jests about racism, in fact, affirm and strengthen their bond.

Critics praised *Brian's Song* as a powerful film that "left no possible manipulation of the emotions unmanipulated." The *Washington Post* claimed "tears would be falling nationwide," and the *Los Angeles Times* credited the telefilm with leaving "a trail of soggy Kleenex from one end of the country to another."[55] Critics also lauded its unique ability to attract both men and women by combining melodrama and sports in the style of studio era "male weepies" like *Knute Rockne—All American* (1940) and *Pride of the Yankees* (1941). "It became socially acceptable for even the most rugged and taciturn man to shed a tear while watching this movie," explains media scholar Michael McKenna. "I can't tell you how many times guys have said to me, 'That's the first time I cried around other guys,'" added screenwriter William Blinn.[56] The production's appeal across gender divisions mirrors *Monday Night*'s capacious demographic objectives. Moreover, while women play only a peripheral role in *Brian's Song* through Sayers's and Piccolo's wives, these characters are depicted as devoted fans who passionately watch, understand, and enjoy pro football. They demonstrate the brand of female follower *Monday Night* strove to build and attract.

The critical success of *Brian's Song* was partly a consequence of the film's depiction of interracial affection and collaboration during racially turbulent times. "The characters have a universal appeal," effused the *Atlanta Constitution's* Howell Raines. "You stop seeing color on the screen." "It makes race relations look so simple and uncomplicated and so right that you wonder what the fuss is about," echoed Don Page. Adding to the chorus, Jim Murray named *Brian's Song* "a television movie of extraordinary poignancy and importance in this day when the rhetoric of hate is otherwise drowning out the microwaves. I hope it gets a bigger rating than the Super Bowl." He added, "It's for sure it'll be remembered a lot longer."[57] The African American press registered similarly glowing praise. "Television should produce more stories like *Brian's Song*," wrote the *Chicago Defender's* A.S. "Doc" Young. "That's what the world needs now." The *New York Amsterdam News* cited Sayers and Piccolo's friendship as a "human reminder that a black man and a white man could compete for the same job, yet develop a friendship that was envied by every member of the Bears organization."[58]

Brian's Song became the highest-rated made-for-TV movie ever after its premiere and the most honored title of 1971.[59] As a result, the telefilm had a brief theatrical run in Chicago, precipitated a string of ancillary products, and became a mainstay in syndication. Its accolades included five Emmys, a Peabody, commendations from the NAACP, and a citation in the *Congressional Record* as "one of the truly moving television and screen achievements in recent years." As Illinois representative L.C. Arends said, "We see and hear so much about hate on television. . . . It is time a few stories about love and friendship were told, too. Perhaps *Brian's Song* will encourage more young people to realize that there is love and compassion in America, if you seek it." The film, as the *New York Times'* John J. O'Connor reported, was viewed as "an effective tool for bettering race relations in this country" and, as a result, was requested for exhibition at schools, prisons, and even the Pentagon.[60]

Brian Gomery observes that *Brian's Song*—though formally generic—transformed the made-for-TV movie into a respectable and lucrative practice.[61] It established a market-tested prototype that paved the way for iconic productions like *Roots* as well as exploitative "Disease of the Week" telefilms that traded on tragic current events. The pay cable channel HBO, for instance, first tried its hand at original productions with *The Terry Fox Story* (1983), which mimicked the formula of *Brian's Song* by detailing the life of a charismatic athlete who perishes before his time.

But Gomery also argues that the 1971 racial melodrama's success resulted in part from its failure to interrogate the structural circumstances that nurture and perpetuate racism.[62] The film's depiction of Sayers as a gifted natural athlete and Piccolo as an underdog who excels through his wits and work ethic mirrors long-standing stereotypes about black and white athletes. More forcefully, its celebration of Sayers and Piccolo's friendship presents what media scholar Herman Gray calls an assimilationist perspective that elides long-standing inequalities in favor of building a harmoniously salable vision of the United States that will not alienate the production's principally white audience.[63] *Brian's Song* depicts racism as an individual problem that can be overcome if people—like Sayers and Piccolo—simply take the time to get to know and understand one another. It reduces the nuances of racism to a single friendship and encourages viewers to mimic Sayers and Piccolo's openheartedness rather than critique or attempt to change the social institutions—including professional football and network television—that foster the persistence of racial inequity. As O'Connor pointed out, "While football is being pounded with allegations about racism, drugs, and unethical business practices, *Brian's Song* focuses on friendship and racial harmony."[64] The production emphasized its veracity by using NFL Films footage for game sequences and casting a number of NFL players and coaches—including linebacker Dick Butkus and quarterback Jack Concannon—to appear as themselves. These practices strategically aligned the carefully fashioned world of *Brian's Song* with the actual NFL.

Williams strengthened the film's assimilationist sentiment through his celebrity persona. He contrasted the more defiant African American blaxploitation stars emerging at the time as well as rebellious athletes like Ali, Smith, and Carlos. "Blacks respect Williams for trying to change the stereotypes that exploitative films only reinforce," wrote the *Chicago Tribune*. "Whites have been impressed by the seemingly biracial nature of his sensitivity." Williams called *Brian's Song* "the kind of thing I'm interested in doing" and added, "I'm not interested in those exploitative-type situations where you're pitting blacks against whites. I don't think it serves any purpose except to polarize people more and create less understanding.... So I've concentrated on doing positive, productive things, and I've seemed to find myself in situations that deal with unity." "Last year it was the whole militant thing," Williams told the *Chicago Defender*, "but this year it's graduated, and I'm happy about that."[65] Williams and *Brian's Song* complement *Monday Night's* efforts to create a crossover event that situates the NFL as a unifying institution.

Don Meredith left *Monday Night* after the 1973 season to join NBC, which mainly hired him to work its Sunday afternoon NFL games but promised him the chance to explore his burgeoning interest in acting. "This is a once-in-a-lifetime opportunity for me to move into some entirely new areas of show business," said Meredith, an intelligent and creative man who was growing tired of playing the buffoon on *Monday Night*. "I'm more interested in pursuing the dramatic area than I am in the sports area."[66]

At this point, *Monday Night* was outrating the other networks' Sunday afternoon NFL broadcasts by 50 percent. Arledge sought a replacement with comparable star power and ability to spar with Cosell. He initially tried to hire Namath—still an active player at the time—but the Jets blocked the deal. He then considered Buffalo Bills running back O. J. Simpson—another active player who had done some work for ABC during the off-season—before settling on Fred Williamson, an outspoken African American former NFL defensive back. Williamson nicknamed himself "The Hammer" because of his (now illegal) signature tackling style of striking opponents with his forearm, which he proudly described to *Life* as "a blow delivered with great velocity perpendicular to the earth's latitudes." "It's like running through a yard at night and running into a clothesline," he crowed.[67] Arledge hoped Williamson would maintain *Monday Night*'s widespread appeal while forging inroads with black audiences.

The media-savvy former athlete called himself the "Muhammad Ali of football" and, like Ali, was not averse to playing the heel to drum up publicity. Williamson, for instance, took it upon himself to improve attendance at Kansas City Chiefs home games while on the team. As he reflected, "I called a press conference and said 'Kansas City is the worst town I've ever been in. Bunch of crackers. Hicks. I don't know why they traded me here. The broads are ugly. I don't want to be here.' Two weeks later 48,000 showed up for our game and they all stood and booed Fred Williamson."[68] After retiring, Williamson earned a master's degree in architecture and started a firm in Montreal, where he briefly played on the city's Canadian Football League team. But he missed the spotlight and moved to Los Angeles in hopes of following in the footsteps of Jim Brown by transforming his brash persona and good looks into an acting career. He played the role of Spearchucker in Robert Altman's *M*A*S*H* (1970), appeared in the TV sitcom *Julia* (1968–71), and, like Brown, starred in blaxploitation films such as *The Legend of*

Nigger Charley (1972), *The Hammer* (1972), *Black Caesar* (1973), and *Hell Up in Harlem* (1973). Williamson had three stipulations prior to accepting a role: his character would never be killed, won every fight, and always got the girl. In October 1973, the celebrity became *Playgirl*'s first African American centerfold. One image from the *Playgirl* photo spread displayed Williamson smirking along with a strategically placed white kitten. Another had him in an athletic pose with a leg raised to obscure his genitals. The Hammer brought this sexualized swagger to *Monday Night*. "Seeing as how I'm bringing much needed class to TV," he said before his job began, "I don't see how I can miss. I'll even take pressure off Howard because I'll be another target to throw rocks at."[69]

Williamson's *Monday Night* gig, which the *New York Amsterdam Times* praised as a "broadcast breakthrough," was the highest-profile sportscasting position an African American had achieved in US television.[70] As part of Williamson's contract, ABC agreed to let him produce, direct, and star in two made-for-TV movies. "Fred's football ability and expertise are obvious," Arledge commented. "His acting talent has made him one of the most sought-after personalities in Hollywood. He is an interesting, articulate, and charismatic personality who will work well with Howard and Frank to bring a new perspective and excitement to *Monday Night Football*." Shortly after hiring Williamson, ABC sent its re-formed *Monday Night* lineup on a tour of southern cities with large African American populations—the so-called chitlin circuit—to see how he would play. "They were excited," Williamson said of their trip, "because they knew I would talk back and be as witty as Howard.... The black press especially was very happy that I was there because they knew that my personality, my character, would not take 'caca' from Howard without fighting back."[71]

Though African American audiences met Williamson's addition enthusiastically, his edgy demeanor contrasted with the prime-time program's mainstream aspirations. Williamson showed up to one preseason press conference wearing two gold chains. Dangling from one was a charm of a clenched fist like those Smith and Carlos raised in Mexico City. Attached to the other was a golden penis and testicles. Williamson also joked that he was hired to "bring color" to *Monday Night*'s previously all-white cast and claimed he was preparing for the season not by studying but with "a lot of bedroom exercises." Like Ali, Williamson questioned Cosell's ability to match his wit. "I'm a street cat, man. My gift of rap and wit is much quicker and sharper than Howard's. This cat is all book learning, book knowledge, throwing them heavy words at me. Don't mean nothing to me."[72] Williamson appealed directly to his blackness and sexuality to construct his broadcasting persona and stress its difference from his cohosts.

While he shared their racial identity, Williamson represented a contrast to Gale Sayers and Billy Dee Williams's crossover appeal. The *Chicago Tribune*, in fact, praised Williams by welcoming the African American actor as a nonthreatening alternative to the "Jim Brown or Fred Williamson type."[73] Williamson, by comparison, refused to wear the standard necktie while working for ABC. "I'll wear your ABC yellow jacket," he said to producers. "I ain't wearing no fucking tie." He explained this nonconformity along racial lines. "I'm not going to change my image; I'm going to be me," he told *The Sporting News*. "If white people can't relate to me that's going to be their problem, not mine." He embodied the racial dissension *Monday Night* and *Brian's Song* suppressed. The Hammer's defiance prompted Arledge to assure viewers and potential sponsors that his new commentator's persona was a harmless act. "The real Williamson is very easy to like. He's a helluva guy to sit and talk to, once you get all the cockiness out of the way. He's a very warm, nice guy. He's got interesting ideas. He tells funny stories. And he can laugh at himself and his football career."[74] The real Williamson, Arledge promised, was more or less a black Meredith.

But after only three preseason games, ABC fired Williamson and paid off his contract without making the movies that accompanied it. Arledge called it a mutual decision and cited Williamson's lack of chemistry with Cosell as the main reason behind his termination. Indeed, Cosell found Williamson's braggadocio irksome and refused to facilitate the mischievous banter that made his on-air relationship with Meredith so winning. Williamson claims that Cosell was simply upset that he could not joust with The Hammer. "I was too edgy for Howard. When he would say something to me, I would say something back quicker, faster. So that made him stop talking to me." Williamson claims he tore off Cosell's toupee at the end of their final preseason game, threw it on the ground, and did the Mexican Hat Dance on it—an uncorroborated incident, but one that speaks to their strained relationship.[75]

Days after ABC's agreement with Williamson, Arledge hired former Lions defensive lineman Alex Karras, another athlete turned actor who starred in *The 500 Pound Jerk* (1973) and played the memorable role of Mongo in Mel Brooks's *Blazing Saddles* (1974). *Monday Night* introduced Karras with a montage of clips from his films—a primer that privileged the new cohost's comedic chops over his football experience or acumen. Extending his oafish movie roles, Karras composed a goofy and mostly deferential contrast to Williamson's rebellious tough guy. He hosted with Cosell and Gifford until Meredith returned in 1977.[76]

Though not as outwardly defiant or combative as Williamson, Karras was also controversial. He was suspended for one year during his playing career for gambling on games, a grave offense in professional sports. Despite his checkered past, *Monday Night* deemed Karras a more suitable complement to the prime-time TV event than Williamson. It was acceptable to feature a white man who gambled on professional football, but not a black man who refused to wear a tie, openly flaunted his sexuality, and did not care whether white audiences liked him.

THE RACIAL *ROOTS* OF THE PRIME-TIME TV EVENT

Monday Night maintained its exceptional popularity despite the personnel changes. ABC built on the program's success and brand recognition by adding *Monday Night Baseball* in 1976.[77] The network's original deal for *Monday Night Baseball* spanned four years and featured sixteen regular season games, which ABC split into a primary and secondary match to avoid blackouts, as well as the divisional playoffs, All Star Game, and alternating World Series. The program included three commentators—with Warner Wolf, Bob Prince, and Bob Uecker composing its primary crew—who strove to reproduce *Monday Night Football*'s in-booth antics.

When the new program's debut season disappointed, ABC gave it a jolt by inviting Cosell to join its principal squad. The sportscaster had long challenged baseball's mythic status as America's national pastime. He described it as a "laborious and tedious game played by dull people who take a painfully long time to perform this awful function." The addition peeved Major League Baseball commissioner Bowie Kuhn, who attempted to block the assignment by claiming it was a breach of contract. Arledge—who needed the ratings bump Cosell's controversial presence (including his rift with Kuhn) offered—would not budge. He righteously claimed his decision "came down to journalism, Bowie Kuhn's version or our version."[78] But as with his work on *Monday Night Football*, Cosell softened his stance on pro baseball while commenting on ABC's prime-time coverage of it.

ABC's addition of *Monday Night Baseball* gave the network Monday evening sports throughout the year.[79] It also reflected the broader trend of spin-offs in the network's prime-time entertainment programming. *Monday Night Baseball*, in fact, launched three months after ABC debuted *Laverne & Shirley*, a spin-off of the prime-time sitcom *Happy Days*. As ABC wagered that those viewers who enjoyed *Happy Days* would sample *Laverne & Shirley*, it figured *Monday Night Football* fans would watch a program that used a similar approach to showcase a different sport.

ABC also used *Monday Night Football*'s identification of the network's Monday evenings with outsized TV events to launch a collection of big-budget miniseries branded as *ABC Novels for Television*. The network's first miniseries, an adaptation of Leon Uris's courtroom drama *QBVII*, premiered on a Monday evening in 1974 just after *Monday Night*'s season ended. Two years later, ABC debuted the nine-part and twelve-hour miniseries *Rich Man, Poor Man*—an epic melodrama that depicts the working-class German American Jordache brothers' divergent paths in the post–World War II United States—on a Sunday night between *Monday Night Football* and *Monday Night Baseball*'s seasons. The eight subsequent episodes aired on Monday evenings.

Most notably, in 1977 ABC premiered *Roots* on eight consecutive evenings between *Monday Night Football* and *Monday Night Baseball*'s seasons. The twelve-hour melodramatic adaptation of Alex Haley's best-selling 1976 book about his ancestors' lives in Africa, enslavement in the United States, and eventual emancipation became network television's biggest-ever hit. The miniseries was, in Helen Taylor's words, "the film trade's dream 'crossover': a feature which appealed to the urban black mass market as well as the majority white audiences." Anecdotes flourished about dips in restaurant and bar patronage while the program aired that mirrored the stories illustrating *Monday Night*'s event status. As *Monday Night* lured viewers who did not normally consume TV football, *Broadcasting* reported that *Roots* attracted "people who don't normally watch television."[80] It also briefly evoked televised football by giving O. J. Simpson a cameo as Kadi Touray, who chases down *Roots* protagonist Kunta Kinte (played by LeVar Burton) after he clumsily runs through his camp during a manhood training ritual. The scene displays a panning long shot of Touray easily outrunning Kinte in an open field that reflects and evokes footage of one of Simpson's touchdown runs.

Roots achieved its event status in part through its consecutive nightly presentation at 10:00, which enabled it to dominate the network schedule for eight straight nights. "We've done something in making this that no one has ever done before," bragged ABC Entertainment executive Fred Silverman. "Let's show it in a way that no one else has ever shown television before!"[81]

Silverman, however, was not entirely motivated by an effort to pioneer new programming practices. He worried, in fact, that *Roots* would not sustain an audience over eight weeks. Scheduling *Roots* at 10:00 over a single week starting in late January would not disrupt ABC's plans for February's sweeps week, which sets quarterly local advertising rates, or displace its regularly scheduled prime-time programs. In the event that *Roots* failed, Silverman ensured that it would be over quickly and have minimal impact on ABC's industrial standing. Instead, the initial run of *Roots* captured eight of the top thirteen largest-ever TV audiences, with 85 percent of American TV households watching at least some part of it. The other five slots belonged to NBC's 1976 airing of *Gone with the Wind* and Super Bowl broadcasts (see appendix 3). Television executive Neil Kuvin likened *Roots* to a "Super Bowl every night" because it so dominated TV schedules, and fifty cities declared "*Roots* weeks" to commemorate it.[82]

The *Atlanta Constitution* speculated that *Roots*' staggering audience numbers "might never be topped unless the professional football teams decide" to move the Super Bowl "to a night game." Inspired by the success of *Monday Night* and *Roots*, the NFL began scheduling prime-time Super Bowls in 1978. NBC's Carl Lindemann began advocating for a prime-time Super Bowl in 1976. "Our feeling is that the Super Bowl would do somewhat better in the ratings at night than in the afternoon," he said. "It certainly would be desirable from our standpoint to have the game at night."[83] The NFL, however, did not approve the change until after *Roots*. Super Bowl broadcasts steadily eclipsed *Roots*' record viewing numbers in large part because of this scheduling shift, which the miniseries inspired.

Beyond its connection to *Monday Night*, *Roots*' consecutive nightly model adapted the format of ABC's Olympics coverage, in which the network reserved a block of time for the sporting event's duration over successive evenings. "If any evidence was needed as to the growing appeal of 'event' programming," observed the *Los Angeles Times*, "*Roots* supplied it." The program solidified ABC's first-ever achievement of top ranking among the networks in fall 1976, a feat gained in part through its coverage of both the Winter and Summer Olympics that year.[84] Thus, in addition to the context in which its importance is usually noted, *Roots* grew out of and re-formed the economy of network sports television. ABC Sports capitalized on *Roots*' renown one year after the miniseries' premiere with an *American Sportsman* segment that featured LeVar Burton traveling to Suriname to visit a group descended from rebel slaves.

Roots was ABC's most widely acclaimed program since *Brian's Song*, gathering 145 total awards, including 9 Emmys and a Peabody. And, as with *Brian's Song*, many critics located *Roots* as an important work with the potential to improve racial understanding. The miniseries was "credited with reviving and strengthening the black history offerings in schools and colleges, with enlightening whites about black heritage, and with improving the quality of television programming." It also "led to the expectation among some observers that the days of serious African American drama had finally arrived in American television." Silverman proudly called *Roots* "one of the most important television events of the last 15 or 20 years," and the one-time communications graduate student predicted, "There will be Ph.D. dissertations written on the TV production of *Roots*." Colleges started offering courses based on *Roots*, and the program sparked a renewed interest in genealogy.[85]

Also like *Brian's Song*, *Roots* was produced mostly by whites and made with a primarily white audience in mind. *Brian's Song* screenwriter William Blinn, in fact, served as its script supervisor. Gilbert Moses, who directed part VI, was the only African American hired to oversee one of *Roots'* eight segments—a decision made only after the production was denounced for its lack of diversity behind the camera.[86] Critics correctly charged that the miniseries sanitized Haley's book to appease mainstream expectations and make the story more uplifting. The TV adaptation's revision of Haley's subtitle from *The Saga of an American Family* to *The Triumph of an American Family* evinces this effort to enhance the program's mainstream salability. *Black Scholar's* Chuck Stone panned *Roots* as an "electronic *Uncle Tom's Cabin*," and the *Los Angeles Times'* Stanley O. Williford decried it as "pablum." *Time's* Richard Schickel said *Roots* offered "almost no new insight, factual or emotional," on slavery in the United States. Instead, he unpityingly continued, "The entire dramatization was trash melodrama and degrading to what should have been a seriously-taken historical and psychological study."[87]

In particular, critics suggested that *Roots* filters African American history through a familiar narrative of immigration that "invites white audience members to identify with the struggles" of the main characters "while relieving them of the responsibility to acknowledge the social and political contradictions underlying race relations in the United States." *Film Comment's* Stuart Byron called it "a profoundly conservative piece of work" primarily because of its "unyielding defense of the family."[88] Indeed, *Roots* presents the story of Haley's kin through a framework similar to the one *Rich Man, Poor Man* uses to narrate the Jordaches, but without giving proper treatment to the vast differences separating black and white experiences in the United States.

The creators of *Roots* candidly admitted to taking measures to guarantee the miniseries would attract white viewers and justified this decision by appealing to prime-time television's commercial exigencies. "You have to remember," explained executive producer David Wolper, "that the TV audience is mostly white, middle-class whites. We were trying to reach the maximum white audience." Blinn added that it would be foolhardy "to do four hours of television without showing a white person with whom we could identify."[89] Though widely recognized as groundbreaking and educational, *Roots* was geared toward the presumed interests of the white audiences it needed to become a successful prime-time TV event.

Roots' efforts to appease white audiences have been trenchantly critiqued as evidence of network television's tendency to prize satisfying dominant expectations over furnishing equitable, responsible, or accurate depictions of African American culture. But these representations emerged in part from the unlikely genre of sports television. Growing out of ABC's 1968 Olympics coverage, *Monday Night Football* established audience expectations, production practices, and programming flows ABC used to launch TV events that ventured far beyond sport but extended the popular prime-time show's racial politics.

FIVE

The News from Munich on the "Arledge Broadcasting Company"

For one very long day ABC Sports operated as if it were ABC News, and no one could have done it better.

FRED PIERCE, ABC-TV president[1]

As the only person at any network with two live TV divisions, Arledge is the virtual czar of live television.

HUNTINGTON WILLIAMS, *Beyond Control: ABC and the Fate of the Networks*[2]

ABC'S COVERAGE OF BOTH 1968 OLYMPICS and its creation of *Monday Night Football* sparked unprecedented increases in sports television's aesthetic scope, cultural prestige, and visibility leading to the next Olympic year of 1972. "Given the current trend in television, it is possible to conceive a schedule completely dominated by sport," wrote *Sports Illustrated*'s Gwilym S. Brown. The networks planned a combined 1,052 hours of sports coverage in 1972—with ABC providing nearly half of the total.[3] NBC's presentation of the Winter Olympics in Sapporo, Japan, and ABC's coverage of the Summer Games in Munich accounted for more than 100 of those hours. The Olympics coverage was as prominent as it was copious. NBC preempted the morning program *Today* for a week and nine installments of Johnny Carson's *Tonight Show*—a program whose influential star blocked the network from carrying pro football four years prior. By 1972, not even the "King of Late Night" dared challenge the Olympics.

ABC used Munich to cement its place as "the Network of the Olympics." But its coverage was interrupted and overwhelmed when the Palestinian Liberation Organization group Black September took as hostage and ultimately killed eleven Israeli Olympians. Utilizing its position as the media outlet with the most equipment, personnel, and resources present at the Games, ABC Sports transformed into an ad hoc news unit and became the primary source for TV coverage of the crisis. The network's reportage was immediately hailed as a milestone in live TV news and indicated that ABC Sports could produce such content as rigorously as—and perhaps more inventively than—conventional network news units. Based in large part on ABC Sports' work in Munich, ABC hired Arledge to revive its long-struggling news department in 1977. By the end of the decade, ABC Sports had infiltrated and was a driving force in both the network's prime-time entertainment and its news programming.

MUNICH

ABC gained the Munich contract in April 1969 after an exceptionally acrimonious rights battle with NBC, which attempted to gain an edge in the negotiations by planting stories in the German trade press that suggested ABC could not cover its debts. ABC countered by presenting the Olympic Organizing Committee with a dossier of unenthusiastic reviews of NBC's coverage of the 1964 Tokyo Summer Olympics along with glowing reports on its own work in Mexico City.[4] ABC eventually outbid NBC after the price escalated to $13.5 million—$9 million more than it took to win Mexico City. ABC structured the bid in a way that devoted $7.5 million to rights and $6 million for the use of German TV production facilities. This arrangement made its offer particularly appealing because it lowered the amount the OOC had to pay the International Olympic Committee, which demands a percentage of the rights fees but not the costs gathered for facilities and installations. ABC using its own equipment further reduced OOC expenditures and increased the Games' profitability.[5]

An ABC official called the network's acquisition of unilateral coverage "the most important factor to us in our negotiating." As an ABC promotional guidebook boasted, "This summer, a video feed for the world will be provided by a hundred cameras of the Deutsches Olympic Zentrum (DOZ), a special joint effort between the two West German networks. Of the foreign networks, only ABC will be permitted to supplement German video with coverage of its own." NBC's Sapporo coverage, by contrast, was cribbed from pooled video shot mostly by Japan's NHK. The unilateral coverage granted ABC flexibility that would better showcase its distinct style—"to Americanize our coverage," as Chuck Howard put it. The international relationships ABC established through *Wide World*'s many visits to Germany aided the deal.[6] ABC stealthily found a way to use even more cameras than its contract permitted by bargaining with David Wolper, who was producing the Olympics documentary *Visions of Eight*, to allow several of its camera operators to pose as his employees. The undercover workers wore David Wolper Productions jackets as they did ABC's bidding. The network later repaid Wolper by purchasing rights to air *Visions of Eight*. The deal solidified the relationship that led to ABC and Wolper's collaboration on *Roots*.

ABC planned 66.5 total hours of coverage, with 52 in prime time. These ambitions were hindered by the FCC's 1970 Prime Time Access Rule (PTAR), which endeavored to limit network power over local stations. It barred stations in the top fifty markets from carrying more than 3 hours of network-produced content during prime time. The rule effectively narrowed the network prime-time window from 7:00–11:00 to 8:00–11:00. As the FCC explained, "Our objective is to provide opportunity—now lacking in television—for the competitive development of alternate sources of television programs so that television licensees can exercise something more than a nominal choice of selecting the programs which they present."[7] But the FCC promised to grant waivers to network programming that it determined served the public interest, and it encouraged ABC—which secured the Munich rights prior to the PTAR's passage—to apply for an exemption.

ABC requested a waiver by appealing to the Olympics' unique status as "the single most important international sports competition," noting the financial losses it would incur because of the PTAR limitations and citing exemptions NBC already received for the 1972 Orange Bowl. But the FCC denied ABC's request by a 4–3 vote. The commission argued that granting ABC a waiver "would amount to an expansion of network control of prime time" and pointed out that the network could easily adjust its plans since so little of the Olympics would be presented live. As FCC commissioner Nicholas Johnson charged, "ABC wants to drive home its rating victory over CBS and NBC by getting a half-hour lead at the starting line—beginning at 7:30 p.m., when its competitors do not begin until 8pm." Johnson extended his sports metaphor by insisting that "such behavior would scarcely be tolerated by sports fans in an Olympics race, and I don't think it should be accepted by them in a rating race either."[8]

ABC contested the FCC ruling—again by billing Olympic broadcasts as public services. "We at ABC feel that it is important to every individual in America to be part of the Olympics right in his living room," said ABC PR director Eli Henry. "Another reason our production of the Olympics is important, is because most Americans want to know what is happening to their fellow countryman whether he wins or loses." Limiting this coverage, Henry implied, would deny Americans this inspirational and important information.[9] The FCC, however, did not budge. As a result, ABC still planned 66.5 total hours of coverage but reduced its prime-time hours to 47 by scheduling select content after 11:00 p.m.

ABC producer John Martin described the Olympics as "a big buffet" where the network "could go and try everything possible."[10] Munich was the most plentiful yet. Among ABC's 330-person staff were the celebrity artist LeRoy Neiman—*Playboy* magazine's artist-in-residence who had previously sketched events on camera for *Wide World*—and Erich Segal, the author of the best-selling romance novel *Love Story* (1970). Hired to humanize further ABC's humanistic coverage, Neiman drew the Games and Segal lent his writerly perspective. "I tried to take a look at the things the TV cameras were not zooming in on," claimed Neiman, whose sketches reflected Robert Riger's early labors for ABC Sports but possessed the conspicuous celebrity artist's splashy and colorful style. He captured US gold medal–winning swimmer Mark Spitz under a locker room hair dryer (figure 6), drew Russian gymnast Olga Korbut practicing in solitary, and—ironically building on his work for *Playboy*—rendered four-hundred-pound American wrestler Chris Taylor in a "cheesecake" pose like a pinup girl. "I felt like I was on a special mission," Neiman added. "I was the artist and everything else was the cameras."[11] An avid distance runner, Segal conducted a revealing interview with American Jim Ryun while they jogged through the West German countryside. Complementing the fresh creative dimensions they brought to ABC's coverage, Neiman and Segal were populist artists familiar among the mainstream audience the network's mostly prime-time Olympics coverage courted.

ABC began publishing the monthly *Olympic Journal* newsletter in advance of Munich and formed a research team to gather information on key athletes and story lines. The researchers deposited their findings into a bank of computers that producers and announcers could access to prepare and invigorate coverage. As with Grenoble and Mexico City, ABC used *Wide World* to establish familiarity with the sports and personalities it would eventually showcase in Munich. It extended *Wide World* by tasking a Special Projects Unit led by Brice Weisman to produce a collection of two- to five-minute *Up Close and Personal* profiles on notable athletes that would be

FIGURE 6. LeRoy Neiman sketch of the charismatic American swimmer Mark Spitz drying his hair during the 1972 Munich Olympics. Courtesy of the LeRoy Neiman Foundation.

interspersed with its coverage. "The approach," Weisman explained, "was based on Roone Arledge's very accurate forecast that our audience was going to need more background information" to appreciate Munich. As Arledge added, "For the past several months, we've been sending crews around the world to film Olympians at home, in training and at work."[12] Aside from using *Wide World* as a formal template for the *Up Close and Personal* vignettes, ABC crews would often shoot the profiles while *Wide World* was covering an event near an athlete of interest.

The *Up Close and Personal* pieces on Spitz and his teammate Mark Chatfield present an Olympian odd couple. McKay asked each of these swimmers how he occupied his mind while swimming. "I picture a different beautiful girl I know at the end of the pool. A different one on each lap," the fetching and magnetic Spitz confidently divulged. The more reserved Chatfield, an accomplished cellist, said he imagined a favorite composition being performed flawlessly from beginning to end. The profiles constructed characters for viewers to monitor as the Games progressed. Don Ohlmeyer described the vignettes as "a codification of what our whole approach to sports broadcasting was about," and Weisman claimed they eventually became "the middle initial of our Olympic signature." "Come to Munich with us for Olympic action," read an advertisement published just before the Games began. "Up Close and Personal . . . The ABC way."[13]

By the time Munich kicked off, ABC Sports had a vast storehouse of archetypes and narratives ready to season its coverage with excitement. Its depictions of Spitz adapted *Monday Night*'s glamorous treatment of Joe Namath. Neiman's sketch of the swimmer punctuated the *Up Close and Personal* by emphasizing his status as an image-conscious sex symbol. The background of the sketch includes a female swimmer whose slight yet curvy physique shares more in common with a model than an Olympic athlete. Simultaneously, placing Spitz drying his hair alongside an attractive woman accentuates his pretty boy persona and sex appeal by putting him in proximity to the kind of girl he claims to fantasize about while swimming.

ABC's depiction of Korbut—Munich's biggest breakout star—combined the network's treatment of the cute and identifiable Peggy Fleming in 1968 with its long-standing exploitation of Cold War tensions. Korbut was all the more exciting because she entered the Games as an obscure alternate who secured a spot on the Russian squad only after a teammate's injury. ABC had not bothered to produce an *Up Close and Personal* profile on her, and its researchers overlooked the gymnast while collecting data. But ABC's staffers witnessed Korbut practicing a spectacular maneuver on the uneven bars—later named "The Korbut Flip"—and opted to give her special attention during the coverage. When Korbut delivered a nearly perfect performance, ABC was ready with close-ups of the elated underdog. And after Korbut fell during the same event later in the Games, ABC captured close-ups of the budding star weeping. This disappointment made its subsequent coverage of Korbut's eventual gold medal performance on the balance beam and in the floor exercise all the more triumphant. The young Russian became the embodiment of the "thrill of victory" and "agony of defeat" and a powerful expression of ABC Sports' diplomatic pretensions and gender politics. But ABC balanced its affectionate portrait of Korbut with a more predictably adversarial depiction of the Russians when it covered the Cold War rivals' suspicious win over the United States in the basketball finals—a contested victory (and the United States' first ever Olympic loss in basketball) that many suggested would have been overturned were it not for a mostly communist appeals committee.[14]

ABC also picked up on story lines it began tracing in Mexico City. For instance, its coverage of African American four-hundred-meter runners Wayne Collett and Vince Matthews's refusal to stand at attention during the medal ceremony reflected its reportage on Tommie Smith and John Carlos in 1968. Though their demonstration—which consisted of the sprinters chatting idly and twirling their medals as the national anthem played—was less direct than Smith's and Carlos's militant raised fists, they too were banished from the Olympic Village. Again, Cosell secured an interview and gave the runners a chance to explain themselves. While Matthews initially denied that he intended to protest, Collett claimed he could not stand in observance "with a clear conscience." When Cosell asked him whether he would stand at attention were he "in the same situation again," Collett replied, "Probably not. . . . I feel that my actions on the victory stand probably mirror the attitude of white America toward blacks—ignoring them. As long as we're not embarrassing you we're OK," he continued. "I can't go along with the words [of the national anthem] because I don't think they're true. I wish they were. We have the potential to have a beautiful country, but I don't think that we do." As in 1968, ABC offered a visible platform from which the athletes could clarify their actions and motives. It also utilized the controversy as a story line that evidenced the persistence of racial tensions in sport since 1968.

Variety reported that "virtually half of all viewing households were tuned to ABC's first week of primetime Olympic coverage," which the *New York Times* praised as an "electronic marathon" of "superb" television." ABC's opening week had the added benefit of airing mostly against reruns on CBS and NBC, which gave it a jump start heading into the fall season.[15]

The Munich OOC's efforts to brand the 1972 Olympiad as the "Serene Games" (*heitere Spiele*) aided the telecasts' great success. As Mexico City sought to assert its place among the developed world in 1968, Munich yearned to erase the memory of the 1936 Games in Berlin—when Adolf Hitler and the Nazi Party used the event to assert their ideology of Aryan racial superiority—and the Holocaust that followed. Munich in particular was the Nazi movement's main hub. "We know only too well what crimes have been committed in the German name," remarked OOC president Willi Daume. "From this particular historical experience we drew the conclusion that these Olympic Games should be what they are supposed to be—the great meeting of the youth of the world, of the new hopefully enlightened generation and thus a small contribution to world peace."[16] An OOC-produced promotional video opened with a beautiful young woman waking peacefully in a canopied bed atop a tranquil Bavarian mountain. "Munich is a kind of German paradise," a narrator announced. "We're sure that you'll agree." McKay described the carefully staged host city as "more Hansel and Gretel than Hitler and Goering." The West Germans eschewed military symbolism and had purposefully lax security to distance the Olympics from the nation's not-so-distant fascist past. Security guards were armed only with walkie-talkies and outfitted in light blue uniforms designed to evoke the "azure skies of Bavaria" and contrast the Nazi Party's severe red and black palette.[17] Munich ensured its skies would be as azure as possible by shutting down local industry for the two weeks leading up to the Games.

A key signal of Germany's apparent transformation was the participation of Israel's team and the warm welcome it received. McKay pointed this out while hosting ABC's coverage of the opening ceremonies. "There was a great applause when the nation of Israel walked in here. And of course, you couldn't be in Germany and not remember we're just about fifteen miles here from the concentration camp of Dachau. But it is perhaps a measure of the fact that people and times change and nations do change that Israel is here. The

Germans are cheering for Jewish athletes." ABC highlighted this harmonious environment and Germany's attendant metamorphosis by working Burt Bacharach's syrupy ballad "What the World Needs Now Is Love" into its pre-Olympics coverage.

Disguised as athletes, the eight Black September commandos took advantage of Munich's slack security to creep into the Olympic Village early in the morning of September 5. They broke into the Israeli quarters on the second floor of Building 31, killed wrestling coach Moshe Weinberg and weight lifter Yossef Romano, and took nine Israelis hostage. After making their presence known—and displaying Weinberg's body outside the building to show their seriousness—the group demanded the release of 234 prisoners in Israeli custody. The terrorists identified and sought to exploit the Olympics' status as a globally visible platform. "Sport is the modern religion of the western world," a Black September spokesperson later explained. "So we decided to use the Olympics, the most sacred ceremony of this religion, to make the world pay attention to us."[18] The presence of so many media outlets in Munich guaranteed that Black September would reach a maximum audience.

CBS was the first US network to report on the hostage situation. But Arledge pounced on the story shortly thereafter with his massive battery of resources. "I'll need the network," he told an obliging Leonard Goldenson. The producer vowed to stay with the hostage crisis live until it ended. He remembered how NBC had been the only network live on air when Jack Ruby shot Lee Harvey Oswald in 1963 and swore that ABC would not miss out on the opportunity to document a similarly important occasion. "The cardinal error is to be there with the only live camera then miss whatever might happen," he said.[19] ABC's Marvin Bader and Geoff Mason placed a camera on a berm just outside the network studio against the border of the Olympic Village, which offered a clear view of Building 31. ABC's only other live images of the scene were taken from a camera in an eight-hundred-foot transmitting tower nearby that had been gathering overhead shots of the Village throughout the Games.

Chris Schenkel ably served as ABC's main studio host during its first week of Olympics coverage. But Arledge thought McKay, the former police reporter, would be better able to report on the crisis with the accuracy and delicacy it demanded. "There's a steadiness there," Arledge remarked. "Jim has a depth and a sense of the moment."[20] September 5 was McKay's day off, and he planned to spend it touring the nearby Alps with his wife, Margaret. The sportscaster was taking a morning swim in the hotel pool when Mason feverishly summoned him to the studio.

ABC originally had a lineup of basketball, boxing, volleyball, weight lifting, and yachting booked for the day. The network turned its attention mostly to the hostage situation until focusing on it entirely once the Games were suspended that afternoon—a stoppage that Brundage instituted retroactively only after Israeli prime minister Golda Meir publicly shamed him. A somber McKay opened his studio commentary by announcing: "The peace of what have been called the Serene Olympics was shattered just before dawn this morning, about five o'clock, when Arab terrorists, armed with submachine guns, faces blackened, a couple of them disguised as guards or trash men in the Olympic Village, climbed the fence, went to the headquarters of the Israeli team, and immediately killed one man—Moshe Weinberg, a coach, two shots in the head, one in the stomach. They've been holding fourteen others hostage since then and the latest report is that one more has been killed." ABC Sports continued gathering information to correct, update, and expand upon this initial and inaccurate report. Though ABC News had reporters in West Germany and other nearby European bureaus, ABC Sports had the infrastructure in place to do a far more thorough job. "Quite frankly, the news department wasn't well equipped to come on the air with the story," Dennis Lewin explained. "We already had cameras everywhere."[21]

With almost eerie prescience, Arledge had recruited ABC News' Middle East correspondent Peter Jennings to work the Olympics as insurance in case something occurred that warranted his expertise. Arledge presented the assignment to Jennings—who helped with *Wide World*'s trip to Havana the previous year—as a sort of working holiday from the reporter's volatile home base in Beirut. The assignment initially brought more frustration than relaxation to the hard-charging reporter, who was reduced to commenting on facile tidbits like Neiman's sketches for lack of any worthwhile news. September 5, however, found the correspondent in the middle of a conflict that grew out of the geopolitical strife he covered daily. Jennings sneaked into the Italian headquarters just down the road from Building 31. He hid in the washroom while police swept the building and proceeded to offer updates via telephone and walkie-talkie. The reporter's expertise paid off handsomely when he rightly identified the terrorists as part of Black September, a connection no one at ABC Sports was equipped to make. Jennings also provided his ABC Sports colleagues with editorial guidance—such as saying "Arab" rather than "A-rab"—that ensured the division was reporting with the credibility, accuracy, and cultural awareness of a professional news unit.

Though not a trained journalist, ABC film producer John Wilcox also slinked into the Olympic Village by borrowing an athlete's uniform. He brought a gym bag filled with a film camera, still camera, and walkie-talkie and made his way into the Burmese soccer team's lodgings, which were across from the Building 31 balcony where members of Black September would sporadically peer outside. Meanwhile, temporary ABC employee Gary Slaughter was shuttling supplies into and out of the Village while posing as a member of the US track team, and several of the network's technicians sneaked in a remote truck by purchasing the signage from an ice cream van and pasting it over the vehicle's company logos. "We went from *Wide World of Sports* to *Mission Impossible*," recalled Bader.[22]

Not to be excluded from the mayhem, Cosell gained entry into the Village by posing as a Puma shoe salesperson. He sidled up near ABC's camera, provided reports, ran tape into and out of the studio, and secured an interview with Weinberg's friend. The sportscaster—who later described Munich as the "worst time of my life"—reportedly returned to the studio distraught and inebriated demanding that Arledge put him on the air. "I'm the only one who can tell it," he exclaimed. "Dirty bastards! They already killed six million of us. What's a few more?" Arledge refused to let him on camera—a decision for which Cosell reportedly never forgave his longtime boss.[23]

ABC's live reportage mirrored its multipronged Olympics coverage. As the Olympics broadcasts oscillated between the studio and competitions to keep track of simultaneously unfolding events, the hostage coverage transitioned from McKay's in-studio updates to the network's various reporters covering different facets of the event in the "field." Arledge continually reminded McKay to stress that ABC was reporting live from the scene to emphasize the subject matter's urgency and the network's access. ABC's producers and McKay collaborated to offer up-close views of the occasion through interviews with experts like Willi Daume; ABC's Bonn, West Germany, correspondent Lou Cioffi; and, most poignantly, an Israeli coach who escaped the Black September invasion by bounding out a window. They conveyed the confusion, tension, and helplessness permeating the Olympic Village as the day wore on and the terrorists negotiated with German authorities. McKay, for instance, pointed out a masked commando who kept peeking out onto the Building 31 balcony to keep watch. "You might wonder," said the war veteran, "why doesn't a sniper take off that head right now? Well, presumably his colleagues are inside and they would execute the hostages if that was done. Therein lies the problem.... There's that head at the door again," he continued. "What's going on inside that head? In that mind?" In another instance, McKay registered the unsettling tableau of athletes lounging at a pond near Building 31. "They're out there sunning themselves, they're swimming, talking about technique with athletes from other countries. And yet this grim, terrible thing is taking place inside the Village," he said as the tower camera showed the relaxing athletes' proximity to the invaded Israeli quarters.

The German police worried that Black September could monitor their tactical operations by watching TV coverage in Building 31, which had access to closed-circuit broadcasts of the event. Indeed, ABC's tower camera showcased German forces dressed as athletes and scaling nearby rooftops to set up sniper positions. Police seized the German cameras and asked ABC to turn off its cameras as well. The network, however, was allowed to continue after promising to transmit its signal only to the United States. Had it not negotiated the unilateral coverage, ABC's footage of the Village would have ceased at that point.

Recognizing the story's import as global breaking news, CBS requested access to ABC's satellite feed to augment its reportage—a standard practice in such situations. But a low-level ABC employee unfamiliar with these protocols denied the entreaty. CBS exacted revenge once its turn to control the satellite arrived at 6:00 p.m. Munich time. It declined ABC's request to remain on the satellite even though it had no facilities for live coverage in Munich. Moreover, a Brazilian network had booked the satellite after CBS to broadcast a basketball game but opted not to use it once the Games were suspended. In these cases, the international rules governing satellite usage gave the most recent customer first right of refusal. CBS spitefully took the extra time and aired a prerecorded soccer game. ABC switched to radio coverage once it lost the satellite, with McKay offering updates from the network's various vantage points and relaying whatever bulletins came across the wire. Shortly thereafter, ABC and CBS worked out a deal to pool coverage. "It's a news event and anybody in the world should be able to have it," Arledge recalled of the misunderstanding. "This is not sports anymore."[24] The tragedy's indisputable newsworthiness also allowed ABC to skirt the PTAR restrictions that prohibited network content between 7:00 and 8:00 p.m.

While CBS and NBC also reported on the hostage crisis, ABC "owned" the story because of its more extensive coverage and identification with the Olympics. ABC Sports, *Variety* commented, "was more than equal to the task" of serving reliable news.[25] When the Black September commandos and

FIGURE 7. LeRoy Neiman sketch of ABC cameras covering the 1972 Munich hostage crisis. Courtesy of the LeRoy Neiman Foundation.

hostages were transported from Building 31 to Fürstenfeldbruck Air Base just outside of Munich—where the Germans told the terrorists they would receive transport out of the country but had instead set an ill-conceived trap—ABC was the only network that covered it live. "The others could have had it," an ABC spokesperson told *Broadcasting*, "but they didn't carry it."[26] Neiman's sketches reinforced ABC's ownership of the story by capturing the network steadfastly covering the conflict in the Olympic Village as police patrolled and athletes milled about (figure 7). While his drawings render the police, athletes, and camera operators without markers of national origin or distinct facial features, they conspicuously include ABC logos on the cameras. The borderline product placements stress ABC's centrality to the global event and its reportage.

The hostage incident ended with a bloody and botched shootout at Fürstenfeldbruck—which barred cameras and reporters—that left all the

Israelis, one German police officer, and five of the terrorists dead. Historian Simon Reeve called the German ambush a "criminally shambolic failure" that grossly miscalculated the measures needed to save the hostages.[27] Since cameras were forbidden, ABC could only provide studio updates of whatever news came across the wire or from Bader, who was with Munich press chief Hans "Johnny" Klein. At one point, a false report surfaced that claimed the hostages had been freed—an update several outlets unquestioningly relayed. Given Arledge's hope to continue leading coverage of the story and prove his capacity to produce quality TV news, he exercised remarkable restraint by resisting the tantalizing but incorrect bulletin. "Roone would remind us five or six times that we had to be careful of every word we said because one of the Israeli athletes' [weight lifter David Berger] parents were in Shaker Heights, Ohio, and this was their only connection," Ohlmeyer recalled. "And so we had to be cautious. No loose reports; everything has to be confirmed."[28]

ABC, in fact, learned of the hostages' fate well before Arledge let McKay announce it. In the interim he advised his studio host to temper viewers' expectations. McKay sprinkled his commentary with somber primers like "we keep hearing that the indications are not good" before Arledge received final confirmation and allowed him to break the grim news. The sportscaster turned news anchor—who had been on the air for nearly sixteen hours—softened his voice and gazed solemnly into the camera to deliver what would be the most famous lines of his distinguished career: "When I was a kid my father always told me that our greatest hopes and our worst fears are seldom realized. Tonight our worst fears have been realized. Two were killed this morning—yesterday morning—in their rooms. The others were killed at the airport tonight. They're all gone. It's all over. What will happen to the Games of the XXth Olympiad? None of us knows. What will happen in the course of world history? . . . I have nothing else today." The exhausted anchor let his announcement linger in silence and his cast his eyes downward before ABC resumed coverage.

The network's crew was just as drained. "Once I knew they were dead," Ohlmeyer reflected, "I said to Roone, 'I gotta get out of here, I can't go anymore.' [Sportswriter] Pete Axthelm and I proceeded to get shitfaced talking about how fucked-up is this world where here we are at the Olympics, which is supposed to be celebrating some of the best and brightest of the youth around the globe, and we're killing them."[29] Schenkel, who joined McKay in the studio toward the end of the day, closed ABC's coverage with a tone-deaf sign-off. "We'll be back tomorrow with the memorial services," he wearily announced. "I know you'll enjoy them." The normally smooth Schenkel's gaffe was more a consequence of fatigue and resignation than wooden insensitivity, but it made Arledge confident that he had assigned the day's hosting duties to the right person.

When the frazzled McKay finally retired to his hotel room, he realized he was still wearing his swimming trunks under his work clothes. After catching a few hours' sleep, he returned to host the memorial service. A telegram was waiting for him in his office mailbox from his old CBS colleague Walter Cronkite. "You are a credit to your network, to your medium, and to yourself," it read. The compliment gave the drowsy host a needed jolt.[30]

The Olympics continued after the brief memorial, which was tarnished by both Brundage's insistence that the Games continue and his likening of the Black September attack to Rhodesia's banishment from the competitions because of its apartheid regime—a measure the IOC president believed defied the Games' apolitical principles. "The Games of the XXth Olympiad have been subject to two savage attacks," he said. "We lost the Rhodesian battle against naked political blackmail. We have only the strength of a great ideal. I am sure the public will agree that we cannot allow a handful of terrorists to destroy this nucleus of international cooperation and goodwill." Jim Murray likened the Games' continuation to a "dance at Dachau." "This time surely, some thought, they would cover the sandbox and put the blocks aside," agreed Red Smith. "But no. 'The Games must go on,' said Avery Brundage, high priest of the playground." "For me, the Olympics died with the Israelis," Cosell wrote in a memoir he published the following year.[31]

The next day's installment of *ABC Evening News* included Jennings reporting on the memorial service, Cioffi discussing the calamity at Fürstenfeldbruck, and State Department correspondent Ted Koppel outlining an initiative on international terrorism aimed at preventing such crises from recurring. The report featured only ABC News personnel. Arledge believed the crisis deserved additional attention and had his staff produce a forty-minute documentary that reflected upon and contextualized it. ABC News passed on the special in favor of its own brief reportage. Arledge consequently rearranged that evening's scheduled Olympics programming—and the commercials slated to air during it—so he could present the documentary uninterrupted during prime time. For the second consecutive day, ABC Sports gave the massacre greater and more careful attention than ABC News was able or willing to offer.

The Olympic events that continued after September 5 did so in the ominous shadow cast by Black September. No longer a news unit, ABC Sports returned its focus to the competitions. "Our mandate from Arledge was to get back to the business of covering the Olympics," Mason explained, "but to be mindful of the context in which we were doing that coverage."[32] Schenkel briefly mentioned the killings during Frank Shorter's gold medal–winning marathon run on the Olympics' final day. "It's a friendly city," Schenkel remarked as Shorter strode through Munich's downtown district during the long race. "They believe in live and let live. That's sort of the motto of all the Bavarians and it's been, for the most part, that type of Games. Except for the misfortunes, the mistakes, the tragedy." The killings most explicitly arose in ABC's coverage of the closing ceremonies later that day when McKay recited A. E. Housman's poem "To an Athlete Dying Young" (1896) to honor the slain Israelis. His voice quaked as he read: "Smart lad, to slip betimes away / From fields where glory does not stay, / And early though the laurel grows / It withers quicker than the rose."

Along with ABC's additional reportage on the hostage crisis, the network wound up providing slightly more coverage than it had originally planned. The broadcasts garnered ABC Sports' most enthusiastic and widespread acclaim yet. *Variety* called Munich "the video hit of the summer" that marked ABC "coming into flower" as "a full-fledged third network force." "It's a pro job that will put the other networks on their mettle hereinafter," the trade publication continued, "a standard against which all future Olympic coverage of anything like it will be measured." One week after the Olympics ended, Alaska representative Ted Stevens commended the network's broadcast "as the magnum opus of sports." He also applauded ABC Sports' "journalistic expertise" and claimed its work marked a turning point in global telecommunications. "Just as my generation may recall superb radio reporting in another era 'from the rooftops of London,' today's generation will recall superb TV reporting from 'the stadia in Munich.'"[33] ABC gathered a handful of Emmys that spanned the sports and news categories as well as a citation from the National Association of Broadcasters and the University of Missouri's Honor Medal for Distinguished Service in Journalism.

McKay in particular received a wave of decorations for his steadfast work in the studio, including the George Polk Memorial Award for journalism and the West German government's Officers Cross of the Legion of Merit. *Time* christened him the "Walter Cronkite of sports."[34] In fact, McKay won an Emmy for "Outstanding Achievement in Coverage of Special Events" against Cronkite. "I won Emmys before, in 1968 and 1970, and did not think it would matter that much to win again," he said after gathering the honor.

"But it does. Tuesday night turned out to be the climax of my career—just to be nominated with guys like Harry Reasoner, and Howard K. Smith, and David Brinkley, and Walter Cronkite. There was only one prize in the division and I won."[35] The Academy of Television Arts and Sciences did not merely view McKay as the Cronkite of sports in 1972, but as outperforming the iconic newsman on his own turf.

Given the fact that ABC Sports formed by separating from ABC News, it is ironic that the division's most revered achievement resulted from its momentary transformation into a news unit. Munich, *Variety* pointed out, "gave ABC an extraordinary opportunity to demonstrate its news prowess" and, as a result, marked a "turning point in the no. 3 network's acceptance as an equal in communications to NBC and CBS, beyond ratings, in the truest sense of parity." More broadly, the event ushered in a transformation in the production of live TV news and audience expectations surrounding it. "From then on," explain Marc Gunther and Bill Carter, "whenever a catastrophe struck, viewers no longer were content to wait for film at eleven." It composed a precedent to collective TV news events like the explosion of the space shuttle *Challenger* in 1986 and the terrorist attacks of September 11, 2001. It also, Reeve argues, marked the "beginning of the modern era of international terrorism," when terrorists increasingly took into account the media attention their acts would receive when plotting them. Accordingly, the Olympics became even more newsworthy and their broadcasts rights even more coveted. Arledge likened an Olympics contract to "having exclusive rights to a Presidential election or a visit of a Pope."[36]

FRED AND FRED

ABC used the gap between Munich and the 1976 Olympics to revitalize its prime-time entertainment programming. The network promoted Fred Pierce to ABC-TV president in 1974 and devoted greater capital to researching viewing habits across audience groups. Pierce and his team found that viewers—frustrated by Vietnam, Watergate, and other social upheavals of the time—sought "a return to traditional values. They wanted television to reassure them that life was still essentially good."[37] Extending the light-hearted "Network of the Young" ethos ABC instituted two decades prior, Pierce invested in innocuous comedies like *Happy Days* (1974–84) and *Welcome Back Kotter* (1975–79). He was also quicker to reschedule, cancel, or reimagine programs that started off slowly rather than let them waste valuable prime-time slots. Pierce infamously augmented his research by contracting a psychic to help him assess scripts and pitches. The research—whether culled from surveys or the cosmos—ultimately compelled Pierce to follow his predecessors' lead by sacrificing substance for ratings. He justified this approach by appealing to the same commercial realities Goldenson cited in the 1950s. "We're as dedicated as anyone to uplifting what's on TV," he said. "But we also have a responsibility to our stockholders and local stations. We can do the good shows that don't make money only if we have a base of support from the rest of the programs."[38]

Pierce's highest-profile decision was poaching CBS programming whiz kid Fred Silverman in 1975. While at CBS, Silverman developed popular *All in the Family* spin-offs like *Maude* and *The Jeffersons*, whose creators assumed that viewers wanted content that did not depart too markedly from the familiar. TV critic Sally Bedell observed that Silverman possessed "a strange umbilical relation to the viewer" that, much like Arledge, enabled him to tell almost instinctively which programs would succeed. As a result, he became known around the industry as "the man with the golden gut." The programmer's reputation so preceded him that ABC's stock rose by five dollars the week after it recruited him.[39]

The new hire intensified Pierce's focus on audience research and was even more committed to ratings over quality. This manifested in prime time through content that, as TV scholar Elana Levine points out, "would help to solidify ABC's already-burgeoning reputation as the network willing to pander to young audiences with sexual appeals." Silverman began raiding other networks for talent and adapted the spin-off formula he began at CBS with the *Happy Days* offshoot *Laverne & Shirley* (1976–83) and *The Six Million Dollar Man* (1974–78) derivative *The Bionic Woman* (1976–78). When the ratings for *Happy Days* slid, Silverman oversaw and approved a simplified reinvention of it centered on the popular character Fonzie.[40]

Many at ABC worried the 1976 Winter Olympics in Innsbruck—a less popular event than the Summer Games, with fewer American stars to promote—might slow the momentum Pierce and Silverman had been amassing in prime time. But Arledge saw its lower profile as an opportunity to exercise greater artistic flexibility. He planned to "send a postcard back to the United States" that emphasized Austria's mountainous beauty. "So little had been expected of them, I said 'We'll do *The Sound of Music* in the Alps and we'll make the Olympics into something,'" he explained to David Frost. "In many respects, we made it out of whole cloth." Arledge's evocation of *The Sound of Music* was not entirely metaphorical. ABC licensed the film's theme song for use during the opening ceremonies and even programmed it to air on the network shortly after the Olympics finished.[41] ABC Sports punctuated further the event's cinematic splendor by accompanying Innsbruck's closing ceremonies with Beethoven's "Ode to Joy"—a tradition it continued for each subsequent Olympics it carried.

The Innsbruck coverage—which comprised 43.5 total hours, with 30.5 in prime time—augmented *Monday Night*, *Rich Man, Poor Man*, and Pierce and Silverman's creations to propel ABC to a number one prime-time ranking for the first time in the network's twenty-four-year history. Arledge later described Innsbruck as "one of the turning points in ABC's growth" that lifted the entire network through an increasing interdependence between its sports and entertainment programming.[42]

When ABC priced advertising for its presentation of the Montreal Games—which sold out three years in advance—it used *Monday Night* to set rates for the mostly live and prime-time coverage. It added to Montreal's spectacular status by producing more than fifty *Up Close and Personal* profiles, rehiring Neiman to paint an eight-by-twelve-foot mural of the Games as they proceeded, and commissioning former White House press secretary Pierre Salinger to offer "sidebar" stories like those Jennings fashioned in Munich. ABC Sports also utilized the network's radio services to supplement its telecasts, which allowed simultaneous live coverage of events and created room for additional commentary beyond the 74.5 hours ABC planned to televise.[43]

ABC's Montreal coverage used security as a subplot to stress the Games' legacy, import, and newsworthiness. Salinger, for instance, offered a special report that explored the precautions Canadian officials were taking to ensure athletes' safety. Earlier in the year, ABC produced the feature-length and Cosell-narrated documentary *Triumph and Tragedy: The Olympic Experience*. Aired in prime time, the film publicized the upcoming Olympics coverage and described how the Munich tragedy changed the event's cultural meanings. As Cosell explained in his introduction, "The use of the Olympic Games as a forum for protest, which really gained international attention in 1968, grew even further in 1972 to what some might regard as the genesis for the most horrible thing that's ever happened at any Olympiad: the grotesque massacre of eleven Israelis." Aside from recounting the Games' irrevocably altered history, the Emmy-winning documentary inflected the Olympics with macabre intrigue by implicitly questioning whether such atrocities could recur in 1976.[44]

Continuing the stylistic and technological escalation that had become as predictable an ingredient of ABC's Olympics packages as "Bugler's Theme," the network's prime-time and multiplatform Montreal coverage made Innsbruck look austere. *Sports Illustrated*'s Frank Deford identified a parallel between ABC's Montreal broadcasts and the programming philosophy that drove Pierce and Silverman's deliberately formulaic work in prime time. "In TV parlance," he wrote, "[gymnast] Nadia Comaneci was nothing more than a spin-off of the Olga Korbut show." "We figured Comaneci would be big for us," Arledge said when outlining his approach to Montreal. "People may be discovering her for the first time, but we've been working her into *Wide World* for a year or more now. And in the second week, [Frank] Shorter is attractive enough to be big again. And Bruce Jenner, of course. He could really come out of this hot. He's charismatic. I think he could be another Dorothy Hamill."[45] Like Pierce and Silverman's sitcoms, Arledge's Olympics did not swerve too dramatically from the popular plotlines and character types they had established.

Additionally, Montreal composed a visible platform from which ABC built excitement for *Monday Night's* upcoming season and publicized the launch of new series like *The Captain & Tenielle* (1976–77) and the far more successful *Charlie's Angels* (1976–81). The Summer Olympics worked in concert with ABC's other sports and entertainment programming to strengthen the network's number one ranking in prime time—with seven of the season's top ten programs—and to cultivate the record-breaking viewership *Roots* attracted the following winter.[46] Furthermore, the prime-time Olympics reflected *Monday Night's* representational politics by elevating as its featured stars mostly white men and women who did not challenge conventional gender norms with their body types or the events they played.

By 1977, ABC was both the United States' top network and held the largest lead of any TV network ever. It achieved these distinctions during the peak of network television's visibility—a time when 92 percent of prime-time viewers were watching ABC, CBS, or NBC. "The only comparison was back in the early days of CBS," Pierce said of ABC's ascent. "There is no parallel in the history of broadcasting—and few in any well-established industries to ABC's sudden rise," added *Time*.[47] ABC Sports—and the Olympics in particular—sparked, maintained, and enhanced this dominance. To be sure, Pierce and Silverman gained their success through methods similar to the strategies that guided ABC in the 1950s. But these programmers had the added benefit of a robust sports division promoting their prime-time content—an infrastructure that was not in place during the network's early and less fruitful years.

ROONE-ING THE NEWS

The boost Innsbruck and Montreal gave ABC did not help its news department, which perpetually trailed CBS and NBC. Pierce wagered that Arledge, who had an unimpeachable record in sports and proved able to produce award-winning live news coverage in Munich, could invigorate the moribund division. He moved ABC News president William Sheehan to the newly created position of senior vice president of news—a transition that amounted to little more than a "kick upstairs" for the outmoded executive—and hired Arledge to run the division effective June 1, 1977. Arledge accepted the job on the condition that he could continue overseeing ABC Sports. "These two major broadcast divisions, ABC News and ABC Sports, present similar challenges in that both require instant transmission of current events with uncompromising integrity," Pierce said when announcing the change. "Placing both of these highly important operations under the direction of Roone Arledge enables us to take fuller advantage of this imaginative and talented executive."[48]

The network also reasonably worried that Arledge, whose profile had climbed higher than ever after 1976, might pursue more lucrative opportunities elsewhere. Arledge was well aware of his broadening prospects and chose to work without a contract since 1976 so he could give them full consideration. NBC, for instance, offered him a hefty deal to be a sports consultant and entertainment producer. Arledge also contemplated starting his own production company. But the self-described news junky found the possibility of running ABC News a noble challenge. "The choice is as simple as this," he said. "Riches beyond what anyone could want, as opposed to making a contribution to American life." "I would much rather have it on my tombstone that I did something important," Arledge concluded before accepting the position. Beyond indulging his intellectual and professional aspirations, Arledge believed his experience made him a well-qualified candidate. "I felt that my whole emphasis in sports has been to elevate it," he told the *Los Angeles Times*, "getting rid of announcer approval, introducing journalism into it."[49]

While Arledge's journalistic know-how was important, Pierce mainly hired him to infuse ABC News with the show business techniques he used to revamp the sports division. "He was coming in to make News the equivalent of ABC Sports," commented Dorrance Smith. Pierce's strategy, however, struck many in the notoriously unadventurous TV news industry as a considerable gamble. "Making Roone president of ABC News was like throwing the deed to the family farm on the casino table," recalled Goldenson. "I couldn't be sure we'd win—but if we did, I thought we would win big." The hire put Arledge in charge of more than thirteen hundred annual programming hours and prompted some in the business to nickname ABC the "Arledge Broadcasting Company" because of the far-reaching influence he suddenly acquired.[50]

ABC News had little to lose in viewership or repute. Goldenson admitted that his network "put development of our news department on the back burner" as it was struggling to establish itself during the 1950s and 1960s.[51] As part of these efforts to build market share, it scheduled popular youth-oriented shows like *Disneyland* during early prime-time hours against CBS's and NBC's evening news programs. The network's counterprogramming success drove competitors to move their news programs earlier in favor of similar entertainment shows. ABC thus effectively lowered the audience for network news during the 1950s and, as a result, hastened the medium's movement toward the condition Minow bemoaned in 1961. And ABC News changed little even after Minow's castigation. But this stagnation was as much a result of the network's meager news budget as its overall quest for profits. In 1962, the division had a $3.5 million annual allowance compared with the approximately $30 million CBS and NBC each possessed. While its competitors transitioned from fifteen-minute to thirty-minute evening news programs in 1963, ABC did not shift until 1967 and considered dropping the evening news altogether as late as 1968. "ABC's reputation in the past has been to provide coverage, but as little as they could get away with," remarked legendary CBS producer Fred Friendly. "They do a lousy, chintzy job."[52]

ABC Sports was sometimes left to pick up the slack on stories ABC News did not have the resources to cover. In March 1977, less than two months prior to Friendly's disparaging assessment, Lewin was overseeing ABC's weekly Saturday afternoon sports package when he got news of the airline disaster on Tenerife, one of the Canary Islands—the deadliest airline catastrophe ever, in which two 747 jets collided on the runway. Lewin immediately phoned Sheehan at home to ask whether ABC News wanted to break into the sports programming with a report. Sheehan declined by noting that his division did not have the available personnel in place. Consequently, Lewin fed Frank Gifford—who was doing studio wraparounds from New York between the featured programming—updates on the disaster throughout the day. "Never once did ABC News report it," Lewin recalls. "We were on the air for four hours breaking in and out. That's how sad ABC News was at the time."[53] Reflecting Munich, Arledge's staff evidenced greater interest in and ability to cover Tenerife than their colleagues who were paid to report on such events.

Instances like these left no doubt among those at ABC Sports that Arledge would succeed in news. The main downfall, producer John Martin points out, was that the already elusive executive became even less available once he started dividing his time between the departments. "Once Roone gravitated to News, he was impossible to deal with on the sports side. You couldn't find him," Martin recalls.[54] Those at ABC News—despite its poor standing—were far more skeptical. "The news department in those days thought they were the Holy Gail," says Martin. "They saw Roone as a showman." ABC's Washington correspondent Charles Gibson claimed Arledge's hire "was considered to be the single biggest insult that management could inflict" on ABC News. "I thought he would be a disaster for the news division," added Koppel. "I thought he would be doing *Wide World of News*." Koppel and Jennings—both of whom eventually converted into staunch Arledge devotees—even confronted Pierce and asked him to reconsider the hire.[55]

Critics from beyond ABC judged Arledge's transition most harshly. *New Times* magazine published a cover depicting Howard Cosell interviewing Egyptian president Anwar Sadat, who was outfitted in a boxing robe. Beneath the title "Wide World of News," Cosell's likeness asked the politician, "Tell us, Anwar, do you want a rematch?" The cover bluntly suggested that ABC threatened to trivialize news by treating it like sports and entrusting its division to the executive responsible for making Cosell a star. Along these lines, commentators saw the transformation of ABC News as an alarming step toward the dystopian television landscape depicted in Sidney Lumet's satirical film *Network* (1976), in which a TV network replaces its languishing news programming with salacious, ratings-grabbing, and ultimately disastrous (but also dishearteningly prescient) gimmicks. "He could be setting the stage for one of the biggest catastrophes of all time," remarked the *New Leader*'s Marvin Kitman, "called 'Roone-ing the News.'"[56]

But Pierce had begun the process of infusing ABC News with entertainment well before hiring Arledge. "ABC's current news management believe that a news show can be loosened up," reported the *New York Times* in early 1977. Producer Av Westin said the division, inspired by eye-catching advances in local news, was attempting to "reach viewers at their level" by accompanying traditional reportage with more features, commentary, and human interest stories.[57] ABC's splashiest move in this direction was hiring NBC's Barbara Walters in October 1976 to coanchor *ABC Evening News* alongside Harry Reasoner. Walters's record $1 million salary was split between ABC's news and entertainment divisions—a sharing of expenses that illustrated the network's hope that the celebrity would give its news programming a new and larger audience. While Walters's hiring attracted considerable attention, the arrangement with Reasoner was ruinous. Reasoner found her approach shallow and resented her inflated salary while Walters thought her coanchor a stuffy, sexist bully. "It was like a scene out of *Who's Afraid of Virginia Woolf?*," Arledge recalled of the pair's open discord. "Harry was bitter and sour and they couldn't even face each other anymore." The network sought leadership that could nurture its investment in Walters and the stylistic transformation it signaled. Arledge disclosed his perspective on the course ABC News was taking shortly before the network announced his new position. "Harry has been on the program for six years, and the show has been steadily going nowhere," he said.[58] Well accustomed to managing high-maintenance stars like Cosell, Arledge offered a hint as to which anchor's needs he would prioritize.

The key difference to which Arledge had to adjust was news content's lack of exclusivity. Since all networks cover most of the same stories, viewers and critics can more easily compare editorial judgment and style. "Anytime you buy something exclusively, as you do in sports or entertainment, you can turn things around," he explained. "But in news, you more or less have the same thing on all three networks, which makes building much harder. And building from the bottom, like we were at ABC, makes it a real bitch."[59] One way Arledge created distinction was by hiring recognizable talent—who, unlike stories, were limited to whichever network paid them. With the help of lieutenants David Burke, Rick Kaplan, and Dick Wald, Arledge began luring his competitors' staff with mammoth contracts. CBS and NBC were forced either to match these offers or let their talent join Arledge's growing ranks. "Roone collects scalps," commented an employee. "He likes to put his scalps on the shelf and admire them. He may not use them very much, but once he has them, nobody else can get them." Burke admitted that the raids by ABC News were "crass," but he acknowledged that the network "was just trying to do what we had to do to bring credibility to the division."[60] Arledge was just as aggressive about removing those who were not performing up to his expectations. "We operated on the assumption that any time we can replace somebody with someone better, we're going to do it," he explained. Much as he inflated sports television rights fees during the 1960s, Arledge's princely offers changed the economy of network television news and made ABC a far more popular destination for its stars. "I want everybody in the news business to think of ABC before they go any place else," he said. "If it costs us an extra few thousand dollars to do that, what does it mean?" Arledge incurred $7 million in losses after his first year running ABC News. But he also secured financial support that evaded his predecessors by persuading the network to invest the extra revenues it was gathering from sports and entertainment into news. By 1980, ABC News' budget was finally on a par with those of CBS and NBC.[61]

"Roone is being described in exactly the same way I was, as show biz," remarked Walters—an Arledge supporter who later named the executive her professional "savior." "I'm afraid he'll bend over backward too far the other way, just as I did." Arledge made various public appeals to prove his credentials and standards. He invested heavily in the documentary series *Close-Up* and established partnerships with PBS.[62] Arledge even planned to produce an investigative documentary on "the state of journalism in the country. I think there is a legacy that came from Watergate that elevated journalism to an exalted position," he said, "and I think that a lot of that legacy is being squandered by the kinds of things that I guess people are afraid I'm going to do." Adding to this, he continually advocated for the elimination of ratings as the basis for judging news programming—a practice he believed intensified the decay his proposed documentary would interrogate.[63] Contrary to the critiques he absorbed, Arledge cast himself as a rare champion of rigorous journalism in a commercial environment that devalued it.

One month after joining ABC News, Arledge penned a memo to his ABC Sports staff announcing new restrictions to their participation in advertisements and outside commercial work. Star personalities like Cosell, Gifford, Meredith, McKay, and Schenkel had handsomely padded their incomes by taking advantage of such opportunities. "I hope you will be very careful of any advertising claims that you front for," Arledge wrote. "We expect to be somewhat more thorough in our perusal of commercial copy before we approve your involvement." The memo appealed specifically to the threat this work might pose to employees' perceived journalistic compunction. "Because of the possibilities of your objectivity as a reporter being questioned, henceforth any ABC Sports announcers must receive prior approval before acting as a commentator or narrator or participating in the production of official films or other public relations presentations for any sports organizing bodies or organizations acting on their behalf for any commercial ventures." Arledge later regretfully cited his decision to let ABC sportscasters do commercial work "as the worst mistake I ever made" because of the doubt it cast on his commitment to journalism. This anxiety perhaps informed his unwillingness to give Cosell, who had done more outside commercial work than any ABC Sports staffer, the opportunity to move over to ABC News despite the sportscaster's repeated requests. Along these lines, Arledge made it plain that he would not allow sports programming to interfere with news by referencing a 1976 incident when ABC aired a baseball game instead of parts of the Republican National Convention. "Believe it or not, I was the person who was arguing not to put the baseball game on. I said it would be embarrassing."[64]

Though he distanced himself from sports TV's commercialism, Arledge repeatedly used sports lingo to explain the challenges ABC News confronted and the strategies by which it would tackle them. "When you inherit a team without a lot of home run hitters, you try to be fast on your feet, to win by outhustling."[65] Despite his idealistic protestations that news ratings should be eradicated, Arledge freely exploited the profit-driven rules to which he was subject. The executive drew ire for leading the August 16, 1977, *ABC Evening News* broadcast with a report on Elvis Presley's death rather than an update on the Panama Canal Treaty. He justified the decision by noting that Presley's death was a surprise while the treaty had been dragging on for weeks without much change. But Arledge also recognized that Presley's death would attract more and different viewers. "One of the reasons why when Elvis dies or the Son of Sam is captured ABC News' ratings go up is because people who don't normally watch news are watching then. The question is, do you want to attract people who don't watch network news or fight over the people who do?"[66] Arledge designed ABC News to lure younger viewers who had not yet decided which nightly newscast they preferred—a counterprogramming tactic cribbed from his network's history of youth-oriented strategies.

Arledge also adapted techniques he developed at ABC Sports, such as placing the ABC News brand front and center and investing in high-tech graphics that would both explain and enliven reports. Adding to this, he instituted a production process like that used for live sporting events in which directors and producers sit alongside each other rather than in separate locations. "You both work off each other," explained Roger Goodman,

FIGURE 8. A 1977 ABC Sports holiday card designed by LeRoy Neiman emphasizes the alliance between ABC Sports and ABC News that occurred once Roone Arledge took over the network's news division earlier that year. Courtesy of the LeRoy Neiman Foundation.

who followed Arledge from ABC Sports to ABC News. "You're doing surgery; you're creating a live script."[67] This practice, Goodman explains, fostered news broadcasts that possessed the liveliness and dynamism of a sporting event. A 1977 holiday card Arledge commissioned Neiman to create—a tradition he started at ABC Sports in 1971—reinforced the new union between ABC Sports and ABC News by portraying Santa Claus decorating a Christmas tree. Neiman placed ABC News and ABC Sports ornaments alongside each other to emphasize their Arledge-driven alliance and to suggest the network's news received the creative treatment that made its sports so notable (figure 8).

But institutional turmoil simmered amid the transition. The acrimony between Reasoner and Walters continued to escalate—tension Av Westin attempted to skirt by minimizing the screen time the bickering costars shared. But Reasoner eventually deemed their differences irreconcilable and left for CBS in June 1978. Arledge viewed Reasoner's departure as an opportunity "to make a virtue of not having a star anchorman." "I recognized that short of Walters we had no stars," he recalled. "So I decided to do what we did with *Wide World of Sports*. We would make the presentation of the news the essence of our program, instead of building it around personalities, as the other networks did."[68] The month after Reasoner left, Arledge reinvented *ABC Nightly News* as *World News Tonight*. The program discarded the traditional single-desk format for a decentralized model featuring three anchors in different locations: Frank Reynolds reported national news from Washington, DC, Max Robinson covered domestic news in Chicago, and Jennings handled international news out of London. Based in New York, Walters contributed special reports and interviews—her professional forte. Anchors reported from the field as well as their desks to provide the broadcast greater proximity to the action than was possible with conventional nightly news programs.

"The evening news began to look more than a little like *Wide World of Sports*," commented *Horizon* magazine's Tom Buckley of *World News Tonight*. This resemblance, of course, was intentional. "All the production devices are designed to get viewers inside the game and to help them experience what it's like," Arledge said of his sports broadcasts. "And to the degree that it is possible, we try to do that in news as well."[69] *World News Tonight*'s three-anchor format reflected *Monday Night*; its global focus and frequent cuts among disparate reporters echoed *Wide World* and the Olympics; and the program's on-location reports and interviews extended ABC Sports' up-close and personal aesthetic. "We want our news people as close to their stories as possible, so that our viewers will benefit from a greater sense of immediacy," wrote Arledge in a press release announcing *World News Tonight*'s launch.[70]

Reynolds opened *World News Tonight*'s first installment on July 10, 1978, by promising viewers the rebooted program was no mere ploy: "Speaking for all the men and women of ABC News, I promise you an accurate, responsible and meaningful report on events at home and abroad." Arledge added to these introductory comments by asserting that the program's innovations would produce news more effectively than the traditional formats to which CBS and

NBC still clung: "I don't think we necessarily use anchor people's talents best by having them sit in a studio reading introductions from a teleprompter and not getting out from behind the desk to cover things, which was why they were promoted [to anchors] in the first place."[71] He also claimed *World News Tonight*'s elimination of a central desk would allow the program to cover additional content. As Arledge remarked of its competition, "Before they'd go into a commercial they'd sit on a wide shot of the two of them for 4 or 5 seconds, which was dead air. You add up a few of those in a show and it's costing you a story." By jettisoning this fluff, *World News Tonight* made room for stories that would otherwise go uncovered. Far from a stunt, then, ABC claimed *World News Tonight*'s lively style would generate more efficient coverage than the news its comparatively antiquated competitors delivered.[72]

Despite these journalistic rationalizations, TV critic Tom Shales joked that *World News Tonight*'s frenetic pace would work better as "a commercial for Dramamine" than a news report.[73] *Doonesbury* cartoonist Garry Trudeau repeatedly lampooned Arledge's approach as overly stylized. In a November 1977 comic strip, radio host Mark Slackmeyer asks an ABC producer how he will utilize the network's "tag-team format" to cover a story. "Well, it works like this," replied the producer. "The super anchor teases the story from New York. Then he throws it to the regional mini-anchor in Boston, who does the lead-in. We then feed my in-depth mini-documentary along with two follow-up micro-documentaries, and then whip around for the wrap-up and mini-commentary by the backup co-super-anchor."[74] Less lightheartedly, veteran ABC reporter Howard K. Smith called *World News Tonight*'s fast-paced cuts among reporters a "Punch and Judy show" and resigned shortly thereafter because of these changes. The equally establishmentarian Cronkite published an ABC-directed open memo that claimed "one of our competitors in particular now seems to have substituted a policy that publicity and personality promotion are the first considerations.... I hope for the good of broadcast news that those who lean more toward the values of Broadway than those of journalism will eventually put behind them the unseemly, undignified and unprofessional scramble for self-promotion."[75]

Arledge did not deny ABC News' focus on entertainment, but insisted that it was good journalism. "I don't think you have to be dull to have integrity," he commented. "If I can put together a solid professional news organization that has the confidence of viewers and then package it in an interesting format, I don't think there's anything wrong with that."[76] ABC did, however, eventually pare down *World News Tonight*'s roaming format—which would open from different locations depending on the lead story—by making Reynolds's Washington desk the customary starting point after viewers complained of being disoriented.

Arledge used the November 1979 Iran hostage crisis—in which a group of Iranian students invaded the US embassy in Tehran and took fifty-two American diplomats and citizens prisoner—to make his strongest statement about the new journalistic era he was ushering. As in Munich, he sprang on the story with all of ABC's available resources by immediately sending the London-based correspondent Bob Dyk to Tehran. Dyk and his crew captured the first footage of the conflict just before the country closed its borders to Americans. Producer Rick Kaplan recalls that ABC gained entry to Iran in part through a fortunate misunderstanding. Iranian officials thought the American Broadcasting Company "was the official network of the United States"—a mistake the network did not correct that made its access exclusive for a week. "We were alone because they thought that the American Broadcasting Company was the *American* broadcasting company and there was no need to have anyone else," Kaplan explained.[77] Dyk and company produced *The Iran Crisis: America Held Hostage*. The Reynolds-hosted special aired at 11:30 p.m. on November 8, four days after the hostages were taken, and leveraged ABC's exclusivity to furnish an inside view of the situation that explained its key figures and the political circumstances that gave rise to it.

Arledge was in Lake Placid, New York, after the special aired preparing for the 1980 Winter Olympics. He observed that those he encountered—from reporters to hotel staff—took even more interest in the hostage news than the impending Olympics. When he returned to Manhattan, he insisted that ABC News produce a special every night until the event resolved. "I didn't feel there was enough information coming out on the regular evening newscasts, which were giving it seven or eight minutes."[78] As in Munich, Arledge aimed to "own" the story and to make ABC the destination for updates on it. *America Held Hostage* went nightly on November 15—the eleventh day of the crisis. It appended the day of the saga to each installment's title (*The Iran Hostage Crisis: America Held Hostage, Day 20*, etc.) to underscore the event's protracted length and the nightly program's currency. The specials adopted Arledge's up-close template by giving background on the event, those embroiled in it, and the varied factors informing it. The shrewd ABC News president secured the continuation of *America Held Hostage* by promising Pierce—who was fielding complaints from affiliates that preferred to air more lucrative fare during the 11:30 slot—that he would continue the program only "as long as the situation remains critical." Unbeknownst to Pierce, Arledge harbored a broad definition of critical. When Kaplan asked his boss precisely what he meant, Arledge replied, "That means as long as they hold the hostages we're doing these specials because if they are holding Americans hostage, the situation is critical by definition."[79] The hostages were in captivity for 444 days. Shortly after acquiring the indefinite time slot, Arledge assigned Koppel to serve as the twenty-minute specials' regular host.

In addition to the role Lake Placid played in inspiring Arledge to create *America Held Hostage*, ABC used the ensuing Olympics broadcast to fan the nationalistic flames the crisis ignited and publicize the news program. Lake Placid was the first Olympics, in fact, to which ABC News assigned reporters—an illustration of the divisions' intermingling since Arledge's promotion. As ABC Sports covered the opening ceremonies, ABC News interjected a bulletin about the hostage situation that promoted the department's ongoing reportage. Moreover, ABC's Olympics broadcasts positioned America's athletic triumphs—namely, the hockey team's shocking and Cold War–laden victory over the heavily favored Soviet Union and subsequent gold medal—as important morale boosts during a vulnerable time. ABC's Lake Placid coverage celebrated the triumphs while the Iran specials reported on the challenges. To this end, ABC scheduled nightly Olympics recaps as lead-ins to *America Held Hostage* so the sports and news programming could directly feed off each other.[80]

But the hostage situation showed no signs of resolving as the Olympics ended. After more than three months on the air, *America Held Hostage* had covered most of the conflict's pertinent details. Arledge, however, did not want to relinquish the valuable 11:30 time slot he secured for ABC News. He proposed broadening the program's focus to offer similar features on current news. Still hosted by Koppel, *Nightline* premiered in March 1980 and maintained *America Held Hostage*'s twenty-minute format until expanding to a half hour in January 1981. The program served as an alternative to *The Tonight Show* that attracted more-affluent viewers. It also proved to be Arledge's most acclaimed news innovation and escaped—despite its similar approach—the critiques that beleaguered *World News Tonight*. *Newsweek* hailed it "the industry's great leap forward since the networks extended their evening newscasts to 30 minutes in 1963."[81] The network slowest to adopt the thirty-minute format ironically propelled the eventual expansion of TV news into late night and created a market for the flood of cable news programs that emerged during the 1980s. By 1981, ABC News was regularly outrating is competitors through continuing to adapt practices Arledge developed in sports. Just as significant, those competitors increasingly adjusted to this shift by appropriating the division's sports-inspired conventions. TV news practices that grew out of sports programming—and initially attracted industrial and critical wrath because of their ancestry—eventually became the norm.

"TAKING THE FEELING FROM SPORTS"

The cross-pollination between Arledge's two divisions continued at the levels of personnel, infrastructure, and aesthetics. In fact, Arledge preferred that those versed in his approach to sports handle some of the highest-profile assignments during his early years helming News. When he was planning to cover the 1980 Democratic and Republican National Conventions—the first conventions ABC News televised under his leadership—he assigned Chet Forte to the job. The director seamlessly transferred skills he perfected at *Wide World*, *Monday Night*, and the Olympics to realize the newscast Arledge envisaged. Amid ABC's live coverage of Ronald Reagan's 1981 inauguration, Arledge wanted to intercut footage of the Iran hostages finally arriving to freedom in Frankfurt—which coincidentally took place the same day—along with inspirational music to emphasize the new political era the jingoistic president's ascendancy marked. When the ABC News producer overseeing the program resisted for fear that such an approach would be unduly gauche, Arledge found someone from sports to perform the task. "They were basically doing 'The Thrill of Victory'" and "taking that feeling from sports," commented Goodman of ABC News' inauguration telecast.[82]

One month before the inauguration, *Monday Night* was live on the air when news of John Lennon's murder reached ABC. The tragic death of such a celebrity would warrant an ABC News report to disrupt the sports broadcast—particularly given the modifications Arledge had instituted. Moreover, and unlike the 1977 Tenerife disaster, ABC News had staff available to handle the report. *Nightline* directly followed *Monday Night*, and its crew was in ABC's studios—just blocks from where the murder occurred— when the report arrived. However, Arledge opted to have Cosell announce the bulletin during *Monday Night*. "An unspeakable tragedy, confirmed to us by ABC News in New York City," Cosell sorrowfully intoned during a break in the game action. "John Lennon, outside of his apartment building on the west side of New York City, the most famous perhaps of all the Beatles, shot twice in the back, rushed to Roosevelt hospital, dead . . . on . . . arrival." Cosell repeated the update several times during *Monday Night*'s remaining minutes and reminded viewers that *Nightline* would offer details directly afterward. Toward the end of the game, he memorialized his former *Monday Night* halftime guest by reading the opening lines of John Keats's "Ode to a Nightingale" (1819): "My heart aches, and drowsy numbness pains my sense." Cosell's slow and uncharacteristically muted delivery of "dead . . . on . . . arrival" reflected McKay's mournfully terse report that the Munich hostages were "all gone," and his recitation of Keats echoed his colleague's use of Housman to remember the fallen Israelis. In both cases, ABC Sports reported news. It did so by necessity in Munich, but by design on *Monday Night*.

SIX

"What in the Wide, Wide World of Sports Is Going On Here?"

TRASHSPORTS AND SCANDAL

The nonevent is a pseudosports happening that parodies the thrill of victory and eliminates the agony of defeat.

JOAN RYAN, *Washington Post*[1]

I wish somebody would define what TrashSports means.... Just because it's made for television? Does that mean the Super Bowl is TrashSports, too?

DICK BUTTON, ABC Sports commentator[2]

ONE OF THE MOST QUOTABLE MOMENTS in Mel Brooks's eminently quotable *Blazing Saddles* (1974) occurs midway through the western spoof when the bumbling thug Taggart (played by Slim Pickens) catches a handful of his underlings singing and dancing on the job. "What in the wide, wide world of sports is going on here," Taggart furiously howls as his embarrassed minions snap to attention. The comic line works through anachronistic nonsense. Neither *Wide World* nor television existed in the Old West *Blazing Saddles* depicts. But Brooks successfully banked that his audience would know the reference, identify its misplacement, and get the joke. The brief scene demonstrates ABC Sports' position as part of the popular lexicon by the 1970s.

Like Brooks, ABC Sports recognized the familiarity it had achieved and exploited this notoriety by moving beyond sports television. The increasingly renowned division licensed merchandise, created nonsports programming, and, most notoriously, built made-for-TV sports specials. Such manufactured spectacles attracted broad TV audiences and enthusiastic sponsors but generated critical dismissal as "TrashSports" that compromised the respectability ABC Sports had gained. As *Monday Night Football* and coverage of the

Munich Olympics took sports TV to new aesthetic and critical heights, ABC's lucrative made-for-TV programs brought the sports division unprecedented denunciation.

A contract dispute with the National Basketball Association sparked ABC Sports' move into TrashSports. ABC added the NBA to its expanding menu in 1965 with a five-year contract that gave it sixteen Sunday afternoon games from January through April. The NBA had been off national TV entirely since 1963.[3] Supported by ABC's other programming, the NBA telecasts steadily raised the still relatively marginal league's profile. As a result, the partners signed a new four-year contract in 1969 that gave ABC first right of refusal on future NBA TV deals.

By 1973, NBA commissioner Walter Kennedy believed his growing organization warranted the same resources and promotion ABC offered NCAA football, its most valuable partner. CBS offered the NBA $27 million for a three-year contract—a slight increase over the amount ABC was paying—and promised to give it privileged status. Worried that Arledge would match the bid, CBS and the NBA devised a way to keep the contract out of ABC's hands. "Let's think of all the ways we can to fuck ABC," said NBA attorney Alan Rothenberg as they schemed.[4] They demanded telecasts on Saturday afternoons from October through December in addition to the winter and spring coverage. These Saturday games interfered with ABC's NCAA football package, which the network clearly would not displace. ABC was forced to decline the proposal, and CBS captured pro basketball.

Arledge felt betrayed given the role ABC had played in helping the NBA enter the pantheon of major American sports. He believed Kennedy—whom he later described as "the most difficult man I have ever dealt with"—had "acted deceitfully in his negotiations."[5] Arledge consequently filed a lawsuit in the New York County Supreme Court charging that the NBA and CBS conspired to make it impossible for ABC to acquire the contract. The suit, however, was quickly dismissed. Despite the new deal's presumed benefits, Boston Celtics president Red Auerbach predicted that angering the most powerful person in sports media would be a losing proposition. As he asked his colleagues, "You don't really think a man like Roone Arledge is going to take this lying down, do you?"[6]

Arledge indeed was devising ways to fuck the NBA and CBS. He started by promoting the Saturday afternoon NCAA games more aggressively than ever. He also created a Sunday programming block scheduled against CBS's NBA coverage, the centerpiece of which was an additional installment of *Wide World* that began in January 1974 and ran through the basketball season. Arledge filled out the new Sunday schedule with *The Superstars*, an "unapologetic ratings grabber" that had varied athletes competing in different sports to determine the best all-around talent.[7] The program was a three-way production between ABC Sports, Dick Button's Candid Productions, and Trans World International, the sports producing arm of International Management Group run by former Arledge acolyte Barry Frank, who incidentally advised the NBA while it was plotting against ABC. Like *Wide World*, *Superstars* adopted a prerecorded format, featured a range of sporting competitions, and focused on humanizing competing athletes by showing them outside of their native environments. As McKay announced during the introduction to the show's first episode: "If you think you're pretty good at some of these sports, why don't you keep your own point total? See how you could have done against some of the greatest athletes in the world." Boxer Joe Frazier, for instance, lifted shockingly less weight than one might expect of a heavyweight champion boxer, and Baltimore Colts quarterback Johnny Unitas was not very fast.

With *Superstars* leading the charge, ABC's new Sunday lineup outrated CBS's NBA broadcasts within four weeks. The programming coup became known as "Roone's Revenge" and stunted the NBA's growth until its resurgence in the early 1980s fueled by Larry Bird and Magic Johnson.[8] In addition to evidencing Arledge's cunning vengefulness, *Superstars* propelled the rise of TrashSports and spawned a collection of offshoots (*Superteams*, *Women Superstars*, and *World Superstars*) and competitors. The TrashSports trend also infiltrated established sports like boxing, tennis, and golf in the form of made-for-TV tournaments and matches.[9]

ABC SPORTS BEYOND SPORTS

ABC supplemented made-for-TV sports programs like *Superstars* with an array of licensed items—from sporting goods to key chains—designed to expand its revenue streams and audience while hyping the broadcasts that composed its main focus. The products shared in the construction of ABC

Sports' brand, provided new entry points into it, and offered consumers ways to engage with ABC Sports outside of viewing TV.

Many of these items stress the beautiful and thrilling images ABC Sports captures by adopting the forms of stickers, puzzles, and slides that display snapshots from its cameras' action videography. They complement books that recounted ABC Sports' best moments and an LP that relayed its most memorable sounds to emphasize ABC's role as a curator of sport's visual culture and a producer of images that merit admiration independent of the programs they constitute. Other products focused on grooming children into lifelong viewers. Packages of stickers manufactured by the Topps trading card company directed purchasers to "just peel off the backing and slap 'em on your books, walls, lockers, brief cases, friends, or any other clean, dry surface." Like trading cards, the stickers were meant to circulate among kids and in the places they roam. Similarly, a die-cast production truck and a *Monday Night Football* board game extended the experience of watching ABC Sports programming. They facilitated experiences rooted in, but not confined to, ABC Sports—branded starting points from which kids could imagine their own televised sporting spectacles—and simultaneously expanded the division's efforts to bill itself as innovative. The truck included decals of the gadgetry ABC utilizes to create its broadcasts, and the *Monday Night* game adopted the technologized image on which the prime-time event trades by branding itself as "Realistic. Computerized. Electronic."

ABC Sports suggested it furthered athletic activity by partnering with Crown Recreation to license a collection of *Wide World* sporting goods. A 1977 catalog for the items reminded retailers that "since 1961, ABC's *Wide World of Sports* has not only enriched family life with the spectacle of sport, but has fostered new participation in it. . . . ABC's *Wide World of Sports* sporting goods will make that participation even more complete." Like the toys, the sporting goods allowed consumers to create their own "human drama of athletic competition" outside episodes of *Wide World* by playing some of the same sports the program features with gear it endorsed.

Alongside these brand extensions, ABC Sports' most famous personalities published memoirs, made cameos in feature films, and served as spokespeople—a practice Arledge hemmed in once he took over News. Gifford sold Planters peanuts, McKay fronted for Post Cereals, Meredith shopped Lipton Tea, and Cosell endorsed Fruit of the Loom underwear. The attention-hungry Cosell became one of the most pervasive celebrities of any type during the 1970s by augmenting his already diversified work across ABC with guest spots on *The*

Dean Martin Show, The Flip Wilson Show, Rowan & Martin's Laugh-In, Sonny & Cher, various Bob Hope specials, and seemingly any other program that invited him.

Cosell's visibility and distinctiveness made him an easy target for parody. *Mad Magazine* published an April 1972 article titled "When TV Makes Full Use of Howard Cosell" that poked fun at his grandstanding promises to tell it "like it is." It featured Cosell delivering a series of harsh put-downs to athletes that he presents as sincere journalistic inquests: "I want you to tell me, once and for all," *Mad*'s insensitive caricature says to a dejected quarterback, "exactly why you stink as a passer." The article then imagined how Cosell's style would translate to other familiar TV programs. When on *Sesame Street* to teach the alphabet, *Mad*'s Cosell could not resist lapsing into a convoluted discussion of the letter *T*'s marginalization at the hands of a corrupt alphabetical establishment. Another scenario has Cosell as a weatherman who criticizes his meteorological subject as if it were an underachieving team. "And to think that there are people who still have faith in the weather," he concludes while gesturing toward a weather map marked up like a bungled football play. "I'll be back again at 11:00 p.m. to humiliate the Jet Stream!"[10]

Filmmaker Woody Allen treated Cosell similarly by casting him in the 1971 comedy *Bananas* to play a role the sportscaster gamely described as "a parody of myself and *Wide World*."[11] *Bananas* centers on the misadventures of Fielding Mellish, a timid New Yorker played by Allen who joins a Latin American revolution in the fictional country of San Marcos to impress his activist girlfriend Nancy. The film opens with the assassination of San Marcos's president—a job Mellish would eventually assume through a bizarre series of events. Cosell, wearing his ABC Sports blazer, is on hand to announce the incident in the style of a prizefight. "The assassin's bullet rings out," he excitedly hollers, "the crowd is going wild. And down! It's over, all over for El Presidente!" He weaves through the mob to interview the dying politician before turning his attention to the rebel leader who orchestrated the coup. Cosell appears again at the end of *Bananas* to announce the consummation of Mellish's marriage to Nancy. The newlyweds enter their bedroom surrounded by handlers like warmed-up fighters ready to spar. Cosell narrates their romantic bout at bedside and conducts interviews when they finish to discuss their technique and plans for a rematch.

Allen again parodied Cosell two years later in the dystopian comedy *Sleeper*, which focuses on the hapless jazz musician Miles Monroe (also played by Allen), who awakens in a futuristic police state after being cryogenically frozen for two hundred years. In an effort to learn more about Monroe's time, researchers show and ask him to explain footage of Cosell from *Wide World* that somehow survived. "At first we didn't know exactly what this was," says a researcher of the content, "but we developed a theory. We feel that citizens in your society, guilty of a crime against the state, were forced to watch this." "Yes, that's exactly what that was," Monroe replies in deadpan. Beyond poking fun at Cosell, the parodies recognize him as a sports television authority who is familiar well beyond the medium. The sportscaster understood the spoofs would only broaden his fame. But even Cosell had limits. He refused, for instance, to play the role of a sex fiend in Allen's *Everything You Ever Wanted to Know about Sex* (*But Were Afraid to Ask)*.

ABC began using Cosell's mobile image to enliven its other programming. In 1971 alone, Cosell appeared on *Nanny and the Professor* (1970–71), *The Partridge Family* (1970–74), and *The Odd Couple* (1970–75). He featured most prominently in an *Odd Couple* episode titled "Big Mouth" to complement his persona. The program's eponymous couple—the neat-freak photographer Felix and the boorish sportswriter Oscar—becomes the object of Cosell's polysyllabic scorn when he discovers that Oscar penned a scathing critique of him. Reflecting Dick Young's frequent jabs in his *New York Daily News* column, Oscar called the sportscaster the "Duke of Drivel." Cosell retaliated by refusing to do a scheduled photo shoot with Felix. Cosell again appeared on *The Odd Couple* in 1975 with Arledge—in the only TV cameo of the producer's career—for an episode in which Oscar was hired to substitute for Alex Karras in the *Monday Night* booth. The cameos built a synergistic relationship between ABC properties; Cosell's presence distinguished the episodes, which promoted the ABC Sports programming on which he appeared.

ABC further exploited ABC Sports' renown by using it to brand non-sports content. In 1973, it launched a block of late night programming called *Wide World of Entertainment*. The following year, it debuted a similar series called *Wide World of Mystery* and began presenting *Wide World Specials*. The programs compiled an eclectic range of material—from live concerts to telefilms—none of which concerned sports. The *Wide World* banner signaled the content's diversity while associating it with one of ABC's best-known and most admired properties.

The singer Frank Sinatra identified ABC Sports' value beyond sports TV and hired the division to produce a live concert from Madison Square Garden in October 1974—part of a series of comeback performances following a hiatus. Sinatra and his management handpicked Arledge to transform the concert, conspicuously titled *Sinatra: The Main Event*, into a prime-time spectacle on a par with the championship bouts that regularly occur in the Garden.[12] Arledge tackled his first nonsports assignment since *Hi, Mom!* by applying his approach to *Monday Night*. He placed eleven cameras under Chet Forte's direction and tasked Cosell—a friend of Sinatra's who the singer personally requested—with hosting duties.

The Main Event predictably opens with a shot of New York's skyline. "Live from New York City, the city whose landmarks are familiar all over the world," Cosell, in a tuxedo befitting the concert's big-ticket status, grandly states. "And in the heart of the metropolis, the great arena—Madison Square Garden, which has created and housed so many champions. Which is why tonight, from the Garden, the most enduring champion of them all, Frank Sinatra, comes to the entire Western Hemisphere live with *The Main Event*." Cosell continues to accentuate the concert's import by noting the twenty thousand spectators gathered to witness the singer and spotlighting the many celebrities in attendance—a group that included Carol Channing, Walter Cronkite, and Robert Redford. The performance, he suggests, can only be compared to a sporting spectacle. "I've been here so many times," he comments, "and in a curious way this event, live with the King of Entertainment, carries with it the breathless excitement and anticipation of a heavyweight championship fight." The stage, in fact, was placed in the center of Madison Square Garden and painted to resemble a boxing ring. Sinatra entered through the crowd and alongside security like a fighter approaching the ring with his team. The singer reinforced this sporting theme throughout his banter between songs. At one point, he told the audience how pleased he was to be in New York—a city where he had some of his "greatest fights." Later on, the aging crooner self-deprecatingly reminisced about his earlier days by saying, "Of course, back then I was a featherweight."

The Main Event and Cosell's rising celebrity inspired ABC to create an Arledge-produced Saturday evening variety show that would extend the sportscaster's act in the *Monday Night* booth. "He's familiar to most people and he has a great sense of showmanship," Fred Pierce noted of Cosell. "Besides, he's a personality who has been developed by ABC and is associated with us."[13] Cosell appeared frequently on talk shows and had guest hosted for Dick Cavett, Mike Douglas, David Frost, and Merv Griffin. Launched in September 1975, *Saturday Night Live with Howard Cosell* would indulge the star's broadening interests and, just as important, discourage him from seeking such opportunities elsewhere, as Meredith did after catching the acting bug. ABC sacrificed little by scheduling the show on Saturdays at 8:00. "We were having trouble on Saturday night anyway so why not give it a shot," Pierce commented. The show would "put a little bread on the water with very little risk." Moreover, ABC surmised that it might take advantage of the void left after *All in the Family* moved from Saturdays to Monday evenings to compete with *Monday Night Football*. "With weaker competition there, and with our ability to promote Cosell and his guests through all the sports programming we carry on Saturday afternoons, we felt that we might be able to build a variety series into the kinds of unpredictable weekly events that the football games are," Pierce said.[14]

The restless Cosell—who had seriously considered running for US Senate in 1974—claimed *Saturday Night Live* would allow him to explore new and presumably more important topics. "I'm ready for the new challenge," he said. "You can't live your life in the dugout."[15] The variety show's grand ambitions reflected Cosell's distended ego. For instance, it was staged in the Ed Sullivan Theater—a landmark of TV entertainment. Cosell even asked John Lennon to reunite The Beatles on his program and re-create their historic 1964 appearance on *The Ed Sullivan Show*. Lennon politely declined.

Arledge staffed *Saturday Night Live* with industry veterans like director Don Mischer and writers Walter Kempley and David Axelrod, who had written, respectively, for Johnny Carson and Dean Martin. Kempley and Axelrod were joined by the *New York Times* sportswriter and Cosell apologist Robert Lipsyte, who described himself as "the number three writer on a two-man team."[16] Perhaps most notably, the program featured a group of up-and-coming comedians billed as the Prime-Time Players that included Christopher Guest, Bill Murray, and Brian Doyle Murray.

A promotional spot teasing *Saturday Night Live*'s premiere combined Cosell's boastfulness and willingness to engage in self-parody. It opens with a collection of his celebrity chums—Woody Allen, Mike Wallace, and Barbara Walters—throwing lighthearted insults in his direction. "The people you have just heard are throwing spitballs at a battleship," Cosell says. "In my time, I have sparred with Rickles, parried with Carson, quipped with Hope, and flipped with Wilson. You talk about Woody Allen: I made a star of him in *Bananas*." (The promo immediately cut to Allen shaking his head in annoyed disagreement.) "I have invaded prime time and won with *Monday Night Football*," Cosell continued. "We're going to translate to the world of entertainment the very same techniques that we have brought to *Wide World of Sports*, where

ABC is an unchallenged number one." The promo emphasizes Cosell's provocative image and previews the types of A-list celebrities his show would feature.

Despite the ad's playfulness, Cosell sincerely vowed that the new program would push the variety show format in productive new directions through his dogged reporting and immense network of connections. "I'm after stars and personalities who have steadfastly refused to go on television. I'll invade every avenue of the world," he said. "My interviews will be direct and succinct," the neophyte talk show host pledged. "Television desperately needs the bite it used to have."[17]

Saturday Night Live staged a star-studded debut that opened with a performance by the cast of the Broadway musical *The Wiz*. It continued with appearances by Paul Anka, Jimmy Connors, John Denver, Ted Kennedy, and Frank Sinatra—who was repaying Cosell for hosting *The Main Event*. *Saturday Night Live* also borrowed from sports coverage by including live remotes of Siegfried and Roy's Las Vegas magic act and a performance by the Scottish rock group the Bay City Rollers—whom Cosell dubbed "the next Beatles"—from London. Several weeks later, it featured a live interview with Ali and Frazier prior to their championship match in Manila. Such live performances and interviews were rare in the variety show genre. As with *The Main Event*, Arledge employed the ABC Sports recipe to distinguish Cosell's variety show.

Despite these efforts, *Saturday Night Live with Howard Cosell* was a flop that attracted almost universal denunciation and was mercifully put to rest in January 1976 after eighteen episodes. *TV Guide* described *Saturday Night Live* as "dead on arrival," and Sally Bedell identified it as "the most ill-conceived variety show of the decade." ABC saved face and guarded Cosell's fragile ego by blaming the time slot. "You could have Elizabeth Taylor doing a striptease and it wouldn't get a fifteen share," said Arledge.[18]

Others claimed the program was sloppy and would not have succeeded at any time. In particular, and despite his preseason promises, Cosell shied away from the cutting commentary and extemporization that made him so notable in sports. "He was doing a bad Ed Sullivan," observes Lipsyte.[19] Cosell fawned over celebrity guests, avoided thorny questions, and relied on cue cards—practices that stiffened his performance. "The Horrible Howard monster is now being marketed as the Cozy Cosell doll," wrote the *New York Times* of the confusing transformation. "Howard was unwilling to really be Howard," Arledge admitted. "He tried to be a nice guy all the time. The thing that made him Howard on *Monday Night Football* was his fearless, outspoken, brash, opinionated approach to things. And on this program he was being just the opposite." Arledge also made a series of rare creative missteps. "Roone was not the Roone I had seen in sports—quiet, authoritative, sure of what his next move would be," recalled ABC producer Jim Feeney. "He seemed to be a guy who lost his confidence." Arledge regularly scratched comic sketches that might have improved the languishing program. "He wouldn't allow Bill Murray, Brian Doyle Murray, and Christopher Guest to do what they could do," Lipsyte claims. "He didn't like the scripts that were being written. Everyone was afraid to do their job because it would be canceled Saturday morning." Lipsyte also speculated that Arledge was never particularly invested in *Saturday Night Live*'s success and simply wanted to get the experience "out of Howard's system" so he could return his full attention to sports.[20]

Mischer described the aborted variety show as "one of the great disasters in the history of television."[21] But the canceled program created an opportunity for a new NBC sketch comedy program titled *Saturday Night* that debuted during its short run and was developed by Arledge protégé Dick Ebersol. The comparatively hip NBC show even gently mocked Cosell's program by naming its featured comics the Not Ready for Prime-Time Players. In fact, each member of Cosell's comic troupe eventually joined Ebersol's program, which purchased the *Saturday Night Live* name in 1976 and adopted it the following year. While the most important legacy of *Saturday Night Live with Howard Cosell* might be its loose connection to NBC's groundbreaking program, the ill-conceived experiment also demonstrates ABC Sports' perhaps hubristic belief that its practices and personalities could find an audience beyond sports coverage.

MADE-FOR-TV SPORTS

As ABC Sports ventured into entertainment, its sports content relied increasingly on manufactured gimmicks. In 1970, *Wide World* aired Woroner Productions' *Super Fight*, a film that depicted a computerized bout that pitted the long-retired Rocky Marciano against Ali to determine the greatest ever heavyweight champion. The hypothetical fight, which Marciano won by knockout in the thirteenth round, premiered as a theatrical release. *Wide World* aired it one week before Ali's return from suspension to fight Jerry Quarry. *Super Fight*'s interracial drama mirrored much of the publicity surrounding the Ali-Quarry match, which Ali won by TKO, and gathered *Wide World*'s highest rating ever.[22]

The following year, *Wide World* carried prerecorded coverage of a decidedly poor bout between Ali and Buster Mathis. Critics accused the fighters of being out of shape and charged that Ali had carried his outmatched opponent for twelve rounds until finally knocking him out. After the bout Ali admitted to Cosell that he held back for fear of seriously hurting Mathis and blamed the referee for not stopping the match. Rather than air the entire fight—which Cosell tellingly called "trash"—ABC edited the footage into a blooper reel that made light of the lackluster contest. It combined the overweight fighters' tentative dancing with the show tune "Shuffle Off to Buffalo" and added Johnny Mathis's "Help Me Make It through the Night" to sequences of Buster Mathis stumbling dazedly through the ring before finally succumbing. Mathis threatened to sue ABC for the embarrassing depiction. His attorney claimed *Wide World* "deliberately made a sham and farce out of the fight" that damaged his client's reputation. Arledge defended the coverage by arguing that the bout fell beneath *Wide World*'s expectations. "ABC is standing both on its presentation of the fight telecast and on Cosell's comments during it," he said. "[T]he fight itself, in our judgment, did not meet professional standards. We chose not to run the fight in its entirety because of this reason and that is still our position." The match, Arledge suggested, was not good enough for television. *Wide World* remade it into something that warranted airtime.[23]

The Ali-Mathis fight, of course, was not the first time ABC Sports spiced up footage to make it suitable for TV. But it betrayed an intensifying trajectory that culminated with Arledge's department opting to create—often in alliance with independent production companies—sporting events made for the express purpose of being televised. It tested this approach with *Superstars*. Emboldened by this program's success, it partnered with promoter Jerry Perenchio seven months later to fashion Battle of the Sexes, a prime-time tennis match between the twenty-nine-year-old Billie Jean King and the fifty-five-year-old Bobby Riggs.

Aside from her professional accomplishments—which included victories in nine Majors—King gained renown and sparked debate by advocating for women's rights in and beyond sports. She founded the Women's Tennis Association in 1973 and secured equal prize money for women at the US Open the same year. Retired from professional competition since 1959, Riggs reinvented himself as a fast-talking hustler who challenged women to matches in the name of male supremacy. "I want the girls to prove they're worth all the prize money they're getting now," he taunted. "I'm giving them a chance to beat an old man. I don't think they can." The self-proclaimed "chauvinist pig" promised to "send women's tennis back 20 years."[24] Riggs—who played with a crafty lobbing style that complemented his wily personality—beat the Australian Margaret Court on Mother's Day 1973. The gloating victor dubbed the contest, which Perenchio promoted and CBS televised live, "The Mother's Day Massacre."

Perenchio—who rose to fame after putting together Muhammad Ali and Joe Frazier's 1971 "Fight of the Century"—made Battle of the Sexes into a prime-time spectacle by building on the controversy generated by Riggs and Court's duel and recruiting the higher-profile King, who more powerfully symbolized the women's movement and would raise the match's sociopolitical stakes. He staged the September 20 event in Houston's massive Astrodome and, like Sinatra, targeted ABC as the broadcast partner best equipped to realize his vision. The network paid $825,000 for domestic and foreign TV rights and $300,000 to carry Battle of the Sexes via radio. Under the assumption that it had first right of refusal for subsequent Riggs matches after televising the Mother's Day Massacre, CBS sued Perenchio and ABC. The network, in fact, filed suit just one week after ABC's grievance claiming that CBS and the NBA conspired to hijack pro basketball broadcasts was rejected. CBS's lawsuit was likewise dismissed. The industrial acrimony prompted *Variety* to claim that the networks' enmity was more heated than the animosity King and Riggs performed while promoting their match.[25]

But ABC hyped the made-for-TV duel like a championship fight. Riggs appeared on *The Reasoner Report* and visited the *Monday Night* booth during a preseason game to plug the contest and incite King. The network also staged a Cosell-hosted closed-circuit press conference for affiliates at which Riggs proclaimed that "women's tennis is for the birds" and quipped that Henry VIII "really knew how to handle his women." He even offered to wear a dress during the match to give his opponent a fair shot—a concession he made in previous events. The more reserved King shot back that Riggs's trainers would have "to scrape him off the court" once she was finished with the old man. The press conference served the same symbiotic promotional and political purposes that marked Cosell and Ali's conversations on *Wide World*. It publicized the upcoming competition while offering a forum to discuss the gender relations that composed its major plotline.

Stoking the buildup while advancing her feminist cause, King demanded that ABC include a female commentator. She also vowed not to participate unless the network replaced Jack Kramer—whom it hired on a freelance basis for the event—because of his intolerant views on women's tennis. "I have fought Kramer for what he stands against—women's tennis—all my life, and

I wasn't going to have him up there on my coattails," she later wrote. "I didn't care if the whole human race had bet on the match, I was not going to play if Kramer was up there with Cosell." Removing Kramer, however, would undermine ABC Sports' announcer approval policies—the cornerstone of its appeals to journalistic rectitude. Arledge considered dropping the coverage altogether rather than cave to King's ultimatum. "It's a damned irony that this comes up over Jack Kramer, who isn't even an ABC performer," he said. "But that doesn't matter. The principle does. We've got to back him up."[26]

Arledge devised a compromise by asking King's husband and manager, Larry, to tape an account of her perspective. He also asked Kramer to recuse himself from the assignment and go on record to assure viewers the decision was voluntary. ABC aired Larry King's and Kramer's taped segments just prior to the event. Fidgety and soft-spoken, King explained that his wife "feels her performance will be adversely affected by having Jack Kramer share this quorum with her today." The broadcast cut to Cosell, who claimed ABC initially dismissed King's request to remove Kramer as gamesmanship and promised the network left the final decision entirely up to him. "We wanted Jack Kramer, we respected him," Cosell said. "But Jack's his own man, he had his own ideas." Kramer appeared on camera and admitted he was "completely opposed to what [King is] trying to do in tennis" and waged several critiques against her character before registering his support for Riggs. "When I realized I was perhaps a problem for Billie Jean, I thought that she might want to use me as an excuse for losing to Bobby Riggs. To ABC's credit, they said, 'You call the shots, Jack, we'll go along with you.' But I'm withdrawing voluntarily and I wish 100 percent good luck to my pal Bobby Riggs." Larry King's and Kramer's prematch testimonies built further anticipation for the competition while guaranteeing viewers that ABC had not compromised its standards.

ABC's prime-time broadcast opened with an aerial shot of the Astrodome, whose 30,492 spectators composed the largest crowd ever to watch a tennis match. "It's like *Monday Night Football*," boomed Cosell when welcoming viewers. "It's not the usual tennis atmosphere, and not the usual tennis event. It's a happening!" Arledge ensured that Battle of the Sexes would share as much as possible with *Monday Night* by assigning Forte to direct and Chuck Howard to produce. Like *Monday Night*, the broadcast emphasized the marching bands, fans, and pageantry that made the event exceptional. Adding to the spectacle, ABC hired Neiman to sketch the scene (figure 9) and had Gifford conduct sideline interviews with the competitors and the many celebrities in attendance.

FIGURE 9. LeRoy Neiman sketch of Billie Jean King and Bobby Riggs prior to Battle of the Sexes. Courtesy of the LeRoy Neiman Foundation.

The broadcast spent most of its time milking Battle of the Sexes' man-versus-woman story line. The prematch coverage featured interviews with male and female celebrities speculating on who would win and culminated with a rendition of Irving Berlin's "Anything You Can Do I Can Do Better" that adapted its lyrics to complement the game with passages like "any ball you can hit, I can hit harder." ABC used an instrumental version of the tune as a leitmotif leading into and out of commercial breaks along with a title card that placed King and Riggs inside Venus and Mars symbols.

The athletes' entrances imitated the theatrics of a championship fight and accented their opposing interests. Riggs arrived on a rickshaw guided by a group of attractive young women dubbed "Bobby's Bosom Buddies" and wearing tight-fitting items brandishing the Sugar Daddy logo—a sponsor that used Riggs's sexism as a marketing ploy. King appeared in the style of Cleopatra on a litter carried by shirtless young men resembling Egyptian slaves. Riggs presented King an oversized Sugar Daddy lollipop—a suggestion that his victory would make her a sucker. King handed Riggs a live piglet. "One cannot describe it as primarily a sports contest," observed the *Atlanta Constitution*. "It is show business, liberally sprinkled with Hollywood gimmickry."[27]

ABC integrated King and Riggs's rivalry into its broadcast team by hiring the tennis players Eugene Scott and Rosie Casals to join Cosell. ABC directed the duo to play up the gender battle through their commentary. It outfitted Casals—a King compatriot—in a Billie Jean T-shirt and fed her lines that critiqued Riggs.[28] Cosell baited Casals throughout the match by asking her to share her opinions on Riggs; Casals called Riggs "bad news" and claimed he "walked like a duck." More perceptively, she observed that the match's officiating crew included seven linesmen and only four lineswomen and posited that the gender imbalance might result in an unfair Riggs advantage—a point Scott disputed as partisan bluster.

The broadcast further extended the man-versus-woman theme by having Gifford interview the costars of ABC's sitcom *Adam's Rib*—whom the network planted in the stands. The program, which lasted only one season, centered on a husband and wife's competitive professional relationship in the changing workplace environment the women's movement created. Battle of the Sexes provided a natural tie-in for the new ABC property.[29] CBS even engaged the theme to counterprogram against ABC by airing Arthur Penn's *Bonnie and Clyde* (1967) during Battle of the Sexes. "They tell us there's a big movie on against us," Cosell said at one point during the broadcast, "but you can see a movie anytime." The King-Riggs match, he suggested, was a one-of-a-kind live experience

As with *Monday Night*, then, ABC transformed Battle of the Sexes into a spectacle that people would watch regardless of the contest that composed its focal point. The match itself, which King controlled from start to finish, was lopsided and mostly uninteresting. Regardless, ABC's broadcast attracted more than fifty million viewers—nearly twice the typical audience for *Monday Night* and far more than *Bonnie and Clyde* gathered on CBS.[30] *The Sporting News* called Battle of the Sexes "the most magnificent sports hoax of the century." "Barnum would have loved it," chimed in the *Los Angeles Times*.[31] Such comments locate Battle of the Sexes as a tacky stunt that

FIGURE 10. LeRoy Neiman sketch of Billie Jean King tending to her appearance before Battle of the Sexes. Courtesy of the LeRoy Neiman Foundation.

exploitatively combined the tensions surrounding the women's movement and the popularity of sports to attract a prime-time audience.

Cosell praised King's victory as an inspiring boon for women in and beyond sports. "It became a cause célèbre, equality for women," he said after the match. "All the women in America—or at least most of them—seemed caught up with the anticipation of this match. Billie Jean King was perfectly ready. Not only ready, but willing and able." But amid this praise, the broadcast intermittently demonstrated reluctance to take seriously King or the point of view she represented. As King entered the arena, Cosell called her a "very attractive young lady." "You get the feeling," he continued, "that if she ever let her hair grow down to her shoulders, took her glasses off, you'd have somebody vying for a Hollywood screen test." In a prematch interview, retired football player Rosie Grier voiced his support for King on the grounds that "she's a beautiful lady, and I like beautiful ladies." Neiman's sketches focused on women. He drew King scrutinizing her appearance in a 180-degree mirror before the match (figure 10), a female photographer, King's mother sitting in the stands, and, most tellingly, the backside of a curvy lineswoman who caught his eye. These moments indicate the ABC broadcast privileges women athletes' looks over their skills—a long-standing tradition in sports media that suggests only those women deemed desirable warrant attention and the benefits it yields.

The broadcast also subtly diminished King's decisive performance by calling attention to her insistence that Kramer be removed and noting that she picked both the playing surface and the balls used in the match. "Billie Jean has had her way on almost everything leading into this match," Cosell said. Such comments painted King as a petulant diva who would only play if her many terms were met. Moreover, both Cosell and Scott continually rejected Casals's observations as overly emotional and prejudicial. "Your testimony on Bobby is disqualified on the grounds of bias," Cosell glibly retorted after one of her remarks. ABC producers, however, directed Casals's contributions. The broadcast deliberately situated the female commentator as irrational and even unprofessional. ABC thus protected Battle of the Sexes' crossover audience by combining its reportage on and praise for King's victory with subtle assurances that it did not too severely disturb traditional gender hierarchies.

ABC deepened its investment in made-for-TV events shortly after Battle of the Sexes by airing stunts featuring motorcycle daredevil "Evel" Knievel, whose seventeen *Wide World* appearances made him the program's biggest star since Ali. Like Ali, Knievel was a genius of ballyhoo. He first appeared on *Wide World* in March 1967 as a sideshow act jumping over fifteen cars at the National Tourist Motorcycle Championship in Gardena, California—a program successful enough for ABC to replay later in the season. *Wide World*'s Bill Flemming asked Knievel—who had not yet adopted his garishly patriotic getup of red, white, and blue leathers and was dressed in a comparatively understated yellow and black jumpsuit—to gauge his confidence prior to the feat. Knievel replied that he had never before jumped fifteen cars and disclosed, "I missed a jump in the northwest part of the United States over thirteen, and I was hospitalized and laid up for over five months. And I sure hope that doesn't happen today." Though affecting a tone of unpretentious candor, the Butte, Montana, showman slyly dangled the possibility of doom in front of viewers—a key ingredient in the ratings his jumps so reliably drew.

Later that year, Knievel used *Wide World* to secure a contract to jump the Caesar's Palace fountain in Las Vegas. Acting as his own manager, Knievel phoned Dennis Lewin to ask whether *Wide World* might be interested in televising the jump. Lewin replied that *Wide World* did not have room for it at the time but that he would consider footage after the fact. "I made him only one promise," Lewin said. "You do the jump and have it filmed or videotaped, and I'll at least take a look at it."[32] Knievel, however, told Caesar's Palace that *Wide World* expressed interest and used the exaggeration to strike a deal. He miscalculated the jump and spent twenty-nine days in the hospital with a concussion and breaks in his pelvis, femur, wrist, hip, and ankles. But the slow-motion footage of him flying through the air and tumbling limply across the pavement with his bike errantly trailing transformed Knievel into a celebrity who became the inspiration for toys, folk songs like "The Ballad of Evel Knievel," and a 1971 biopic starring George Hamilton. This swell of interest convinced *Wide World* that Knievel could be a feature attraction.

Wide World began regularly featuring Knievel—mostly on tape delay—shortly after Battle of the Sexes. It included six of his jumps in the two years after the King-Riggs match. *The Sporting News* even identified Knievel as "the legitimate successor to Bobby Riggs as a TV hustler."[33] Knievel's macho persona, blatant sexism, and traditionalist politics reflected Riggs's image. The self-described "conservative wildman" contrasted the progressive attitudes that *Wide World* fixtures like Ali and King embodied. He wore a number 1 on the shoulder of his patriotic outfit and continually warned his principal audience of kids to avoid drugs and alcohol—an ironic move considering his penchant for painkillers and tendency to amble about with a cane that doubled as a whiskey flask. "Everything was anti-establishment at the time," said Lewin. "Evel was a reaction to that."[34] Beyond helping ABC Sports to reach children, Knievel attracted many whom Ali alienated. Though their politics differed tremendously, the boxer and daredevil admired each other's promotional virtuosity. "You know who you are," Ali reportedly told Knievel during one of their few encounters. "You're the white Muhammad Ali." "Then you're the black Evel Knievel," the daredevil countered in amusement at his kindred spirit. *Wide World* was happy to showcase these equally charismatic athletes and capitalize on the differing messages they represented and the overlapping audiences they drew. Knievel and Ali account for six of *Wide World*'s ten highest-rated episodes (see appendix 4).

As with Ali, ABC Sports promoted Knievel's jumps with interviews and profiles. Prior to a February 1974 jump in North Richland Hills, Texas, *Wide*

World aired the short documentary *Portrait of a Daredevil*—part of an irregular series of *Wide World* profiles. "One has to admire this man," said Gifford in voice-over, "who, in a society that seeks more and more conformity and the elimination of risk, remains a free spirit. Perhaps we all have a little Evel Knievel inside of us. But unlike Robert Craig Knievel, that's where it stays—inside of us." Knievel's televised jumps offered viewers the chance to live vicariously through the singular rebel.

ABC used this image to help build an audience for Knievel's jump over Idaho's Snake River Canyon on Sunday, September 8, 1974—the most infamous of his career. Knievel endeavored to leap over the canyon in a steam-powered rocket he called a Skycycle. Top Rank Productions organized the event, which would be exhibited live on a closed-circuit basis across the country. ABC shared the expenses and assisted Top Rank with the intent to broadcast the feat a week after it occurred. The network also aired a documentary titled *One Man, One Canyon* and programmed the George Hamilton biopic in the week leading to the event. Hosted by ABC News science editor Jules Bergman to offer a whiff of credibility, the documentary explored the physics behind Knievel's Skycycle and the probability that he would make it. "Evel Knievel will either be a national hero or a dead screwball," Bergman gravely proclaimed. "There is no in between."

Though ABC helped Top Rank stage, promote, and cover the jump, the network agreed to keep secret its eventual plans to carry the feat on *Wide World*. Knievel aided the promotional blitz with a thirty-nine-city publicity tour. Upon learning that Ali and George Foreman were each set to receive $5 million for their "Rumble in the Jungle" fight the month after his Snake River jump, Knievel told audiences he would be receiving $6 million for the feat. The actual figure was $225,000. Ali, in turn, used Knievel's jump to promote the upcoming fight in Zaire by telling reporters, "If Evel Knievel can make that jump, I can whip Foreman's rump."[35]

Top Rank hired Don Branker to oversee the event. Branker had impressed earlier in the year when he staged the California Jam concert—a Woodstock-inspired festival ABC televised that drew 250,000 people with performances by Black Sabbath; Earth, Wind, and Fire; and Deep Purple. The Snake River jump aimed to be similarly raucous. "There were a bunch of spaced out idiots there with knives," observed ABC unit manager Bill Farrell. "They cut wires, smashed equipment, ripped off headsets. Our guys had to abandon the site."[36] The little security present was provided by a group of head-cracking Hell's Angels who agreed to be paid in beer.

British television personality David Frost hosted Top Rank's presentation with the astronaut Jim Lovell (a sort of heroic daredevil in his own right after commanding the perilous Apollo 13 mission), who offered expert commentary. The promoters packed the event—whose main attraction would take but a few seconds—with pomp to extend the occasion and ensure live and closed-circuit spectators would get their money's worth. The Butte High School marching band performed, and Bobby Riggs—whose sponsor Sugar Daddy was owned by the same company as Knievel's sponsor Chuckles candy—roamed the scene to puff the jump and support his and Evel's shared interests. Immediately before the stunt, the event's public address system presented a rendition of "The Ballad of Evel Knievel," a recording of Knievel reading a poem about his life and legacy, and a benediction by Father Jerry Sullivan, a cousin of the daredevil. The jump was disastrous, but not deadly. Knievel's parachute opened early, and he landed in the brush between the Snake River's shores and the canyon's rocky face. He likely would have perished had he wound up in the river or hit the rocks. Though the mission failed, his attempt was valorous enough to appease spectators.

Concealing its agreement with ABC, Top Rank told *Variety* that it had originally planned to continue exhibiting Knievel's Snake River jump theatrically but decided otherwise when the mission flopped.[37] *Wide World* presented its coverage the Saturday after the jump, which achieved the program's second-highest rating to that point. Knievel broke *Wide World*'s ratings record one year later when ABC secured live broadcast rights to air his leap over fourteen Greyhound buses at King's Island amusement park in Ohio. The October 1974 event, promoted in part by Knievel's appearance on *Saturday Night Live with Howard Cosell*, attracted thirty-two million TV viewers. Despite the unprecedented ratings, critics claimed the spectacles denigrated the reputation *Wide World* and ABC Sports had worked so hard to mold. *The Sporting News* called the stunts "a blemish upon the standards of *Wide World of Sports*."[38]

New York congressional representative John Murphy charged that ABC's Knievel telecasts were not simply absurd but also a danger to children who might try to emulate the daredevil. He enlisted twenty colleagues to call for ABC to cancel a scheduled replay of the Snake River jump. "Failure to do so," he contended, "would be obscene."[39] Murphy again protested ABC's use of Knievel the following year when the network aired *Portrait of a Daredevil* during the 8:00 to 9:00 family viewing hour that networks, under FCC pressure, had reserved for wholesome content in 1975. "At a time when we should all be striving to reduce the level of violence in American life, ABC had held up a program clearly devoted to violence as a model for use," he said. ABC defended itself by noting that the documentary continually warns Knievel's juvenile fans not to "try this at home," or at all without the proper training, supervision, and equipment. Unmoved, Murphy called ABC's Knievel broadcasts "one more indication that self-regulation by the industry will never eliminate violence from the home screen." He concluded by arguing that ABC's "fitness to own and operate a television station in New York" ought to be reevaluated.[40]

ABC persisted despite the complaints and threats. *Variety* even referred to *Wide World* as "*Wide World of Evel*" to highlight the program's reliance on the star-spangled biker.[41] *Wide World* expanded on its popular Knievel broadcasts by booking other daredevils like "Human Fly" George Willig and the high-wire artist Philippe Petit. It also used Knievel as the inspiration for a two-part *Happy Days* episode from 1975 in which Fonzie—adopting the moniker Fearless Fonzarelli—jumps fourteen garbage cans. Fonzie opted to hurdle fourteen because he believed thirteen would be unlucky. This was the same reasoning Knievel presented when choosing to jump fourteen buses at King's Island after failing to clear thirteen at London's Wembley Stadium five months prior—a proclamation that called attention to the guts it took to attempt fourteen after failing to pass thirteen. Fonzie wore white leathers, and his jump was covered by a local sports TV show similar to *Wide World*. The prime-time program exploited Knievel's popularity on *Wide World* to build a plotline worthy of a two-episode special.

ABC did not carry Knievel's last and most ludicrous televised stunt—a January 1977 leap over a pool full of "man-eating killer sharks" in Chicago that shamelessly fed off the popularity of Steven Spielberg's *Jaws* (1975). CBS contracted to air *Evel Knievel's Death Defiers* live in prime time on a Monday evening. But Knievel was injured during a practice run and was unable to perform. CBS filled the time by showcasing the program's undercard, such as free-fall artist Joe Gerlach and "Human Bomb" Orval Kisselberg. Knievel survived once again, but most of the sharks—nondeadly and heavily tranquilized lemon sharks—died in transit between Chicago and Florida. While ABC did not air *Evel Knievel's Death Defiers*, it continued its association with Knievel by presenting an interview from his hospital bed on the following week's *Wide World*. It also again used the daredevil as the basis for a *Happy Days* episode later that year in which Fonzie gallantly water-skis over a shark. The phrase "jumping the shark" is now industry shorthand for a program using desperate ploys to boost viewership. Such gimmicks and terminology have their roots in ABC's TrashSports.

ABC and *Wide World* aired separate made-for-TV gambits amid Knievel's jumps. *Wide World* broadcast a 1975 event in Toronto featuring George Foreman fighting five obscure challengers over the course of a single afternoon. Critics rejected the opponents as glass-jawed palookas who did not stand a chance against the elite heavyweight. One of the combatants—Alonzo Johnson—had not fought professionally in more than a decade. Cosell even questioned the exhibition's value in his ringside commentary by noting that Foreman had little to gain from beating stiffs and much to lose in the event that one of them landed a lucky punch. Ali joined Cosell as a commentator and spent most of his time taunting the fighter he had beaten in Zaire the previous year. Ali's showmanship and ringside banter with Cosell were easily the broadcast's most compelling features, which ABC highlighted by placing him in split screen with the dull fight coverage. Echoing his disgusted commentary on Ali's 1971 bout against Mathis, Cosell dismissed the fight as a "carnival." "Such an event may outrage boxing purists," pointed out *Sports Illustrated*, "but it is so bizarre that it may be a 'must-see' piece of electronic trivia."[42] This is precisely what ABC wagered.

Beyond sharing in the creation of made-for-TV sports events, *Wide World* agreed to promote Norman Jewison's dystopian sports film *Rollerball* (1975). It aired a short segment billing Rollerball as the "Sport of the Future" that shared clips from the film and interview footage with its lead, James Caan, who was still cashing in on the stardom spawned by his performance in *Brian's Song*.[43] The segment shows that ABC Sports was not simply willing to create made-for-TV sports but prepared to hype wholly fictional content. Unsurprisingly, the network arranged to program *Rollerball* after its theatrical run.

ABC intensified the relationship between its made-for-TV sports and other programming in 1976 with *Battle of the Network Stars*. The *Superstars* spin-off featured teams of the three networks' stars competing in Olympics-style competitions. For instance, Ron Howard of *Happy Days* might race against Jimmie Walker of CBS's *Good Times* and Robert Conrad from NBC's *Baa Baa Black Sheep*. The program aired as a biannual prime-time special and borrowed from ABC Sports' approach. A press release guaranteed viewers "a unique glimpse into the lives of celebrities" and a chance "to see their favorite stars in unguarded moments as they go all out to compete for honors in the field of play." In a letter to Arledge, Doug Wilson explained that the program's glamorous contestants enabled ABC "to minimize the electronic gimmickry and maximize the focus on the stars."[44] The inexpensive program capitalized on competitors' star power while advertising the shows that made them celebrities. An introduction to *Battle* emphasizes participants' allure by showing them arriving in limousines as they might when attending an awards gala. Cosell announced the lighthearted events with ironic seriousness that called attention to the celebrities' obvious athletic deficits compared with the elite performers he usually narrated.

Battle also demonstrated a persistent focus on the stars' bodies and sexuality. "The whole concept of method acting is that actors look upon their bodies as instruments they use in their performance," explained Don Ohlmeyer. "What makes most personalities stars is the way they look, how they move. They must take good care of their bodies because well-conditioned bodies are what fans admire." *Battle* paid particular attention to female bodies. Cosell regularly and explicitly commented on the female celebrities' desirability. In one episode he described Joyce Dewitt of *Three's Company* as "a diminutive bundle of instant sexuality" and called Belinda Montgomery of NBC's *The Man from Atlantis* a "lissome lass with a limber body."[45] The program reinforced his smarmy comments with slow-motion shots of buxom starlets like *Wonder Woman*'s Lynda Carter and *Charlie's Angels*' Farrah Fawcett performing in short shorts and T-shirts, often without bras. *Battle*'s dunk tank event—a decidedly slow-paced competition—composed little more than an excuse to show competitors in bathing suits. The program, made up almost entirely of honey shots, stretched Arledge's up-close aesthetic in titillating and exploitative new directions.

Battle built on ABC's Silverman-driven efforts to boost ratings and court younger viewers by focusing on sex. "It used to be when the set jiggled you called a TV repairman," cracked *Happy Days* creator Garry Marshall. "Now when the set doesn't jiggle you turn it off." But like Silverman's purposefully lowbrow programming, *Battle* sold well. "The premise was wonderfully simple," observed the *Los Angeles Times*. "If men will sit for six hours to watch other men in shoulder pads certainly they will linger for at least an hour over semi-nude starlets bounding about in slow motion replay."[46] The twice-yearly special attained higher ratings than *Monday Night*'s most popular telecasts. Moreover, it confirmed and advertised ABC's role as sports television's standard-bearer. While *Battle*'s inclusion of CBS and NBC stars surely promoted the ABC competitors, these networks' willingness to place their most popular personalities on an ABC Sports show conceded the network's position as the first stop for sports.

ABC's rival networks imitated its made for-TV programming in many forms—from NBC's *US against the World* and *Skins Game* golf matches to CBS's *Cheerleader Classic* and *Celebrity Challenge of the Sexes*—and used these productions to counterprogram. The airwaves were soon overflowing with TrashSports. "We've reached a point where there are too many manufactured sporting events on network television," Jim Spence candidly remarked. "There are so many manufactured things on the air that personally I feel we're at the point of saturation."[47]

But ABC continued and even took made-for-TV sports to what might have been their most asinine heights with *Almost Anything Goes*, a program like *Superteams* and *Battle* that placed squads representing small towns into an Olympics-style competition consisting of goofy events. The "Ri-bit, Ri-bit Relay" had contestants dressed as frogs do a hopping relay race through a wading pool. "Getting the Sack" costumed contestants as farmers, spun them around, and had them topple wooden pigs. The offbeat program launched in summer 1975 and was successful enough to inherit the *Saturday Night Live with Howard Cosell* time slot after that show's cancellation. It also encapsulated ABC's apparent philosophy toward made-for-TV sports during the 1970s: almost anything went—from motorcycle jumps to dunk tanks to costumed relay races—so long as it drew.

SPORTS TELEVISION'S WATERGATE

Though not as obvious in its gimmickry as Battle of the Sexes or Knievel's jumps, the 1977 US Boxing Championships became ABC Sports' most controversial made-for-TV spectacle. The animated promoter Don King proposed a tournament through his company Don King Productions (DKP) that would ride the popularity boxing enjoyed in the 1976 Montreal Olympics and the patriotism it inspired to create American champions. "The post-Ali era was nearing," Spence explains, "and we thought this tournament as proposed by King had the potential to create a spark in the various weight divisions and hopefully arouse new interest in boxing overall." The event also capitalized on the massive success of the boxing film *Rocky* (1976) by providing real-life opportunities for relatively obscure fighters to live out the film's underdog narrative. Cosell called the tournament "a dream come true for many faceless hardworking fighters who toiled in backwater arenas for a couple hundred bucks and the use of a locker." Sportswriter Jack Newfield charged that the Championships built further on *Rocky*—which appealed to mainstream audiences in large part because of its presentation of a white heavyweight fighter succeeding in what had become a largely black sport—by controlling the event's racial makeup to ensure that a disproportionate number of white fighters would participate.[48] ABC Sports liked the concept and paid King $2,035,000 to organize it.

King invited New York State Athletic Commission chair Jim Farley to serve as an unpaid consultant who would select the tournament's referees and oversee its rules committee. He then hired Al Braverman and Paddy Flood—both of whom had business connections to DKP—as matchmakers. Finally, the promoter designated *Ring Magazine*—the self-titled "Bible of Boxing" and leading authority on the sport—to provide the rankings that would govern which fighters were invited and decide their seeding. In particular, DKP paid *Ring* associate editor John Ort $5,000 to handle the rankings. The tournament's organization, however, included a contract clause that gave DKP future rights to participants. This suspicious—but not illegal—practice was commonplace in professional boxing. Nevertheless, it discouraged several well-qualified athletes from participating.

Alex Wallau, a twenty-seven-year-old ABC associate producer and head of on-air promotions, noticed problems with the tournament that exceeded boxing's baked-in crookedness. In particular, the ardent boxing fan found *Ring*'s rankings dubious. Several of the fighters had not competed recently, a disproportionate number had business ties to DKP, and many were simply not very good. Wallau teamed with Malcolm "Flash" Gordon—an eccentric prizefighting nut who published an underground bulletin for die-hard fans—to investigate the rankings' validity. "We were two schmucks trying to pretend we were Woodward and Bernstein," Wallau reminisced. The duo called sources and did newspaper research to piece together the fighters' records, which was particularly challenging since many of the fights *Ring* listed took place in states without official boxing commissions. After gathering enough information to conclude the rankings were unreliable—a case they mapped out with hundreds of three-by-five index cards on Wallau's living room floor—Wallau sent a memo to Spence, who was overseeing the tournament for ABC Sports.[49] The unsolicited assessment, delivered to Spence more than a month before the Championships began, deemed 31 of the tournament's 56 total boxers unqualified. Of these 31, Wallau dubbed 11 "marginal," 6 "distant," and 14 "disgraces." Wallau—later lauded by Newfield as the "Serpico of the Sweet Science"—cited potential damage to ABC's reputation and recommended that the tournament be suspended pending further investigation. "I was really incensed," he says. "What they were doing was obscene."[50]

Wallau's overture initially fell on deaf ears among ABC superiors who appreciated the young employee's tenacity but did not take him seriously. They certainly did not value his word above *Ring*. Similarly, while Flash knew boxing, he was an awkward and asocial character who lived with his mother, wore a frizzy ponytail, and spent his free time sketching train cars—quirks that cast doubt on his credibility. Spence, however, did confront King about the suspicions. "I imagined it at the time as a piece of programming that would have staying power," he said of the Championships. "We would be doing it year after year after year. And I told King that too when we heard these rumors and innuendos. He acted all affronted that I would insinuate there were any problems." Despite King's resolute denial, ABC had everyone involved in the tournament sign affidavits guaranteeing the event was on the level. It was the first time ABC Sports requested sworn affidavits from a business partner. "We did it more to reinforce the idea that this would be an honest tournament and that if anyone acted otherwise, he would be subject to criminal procedure," Spence explained.[51] Just as important, the affidavits insulated ABC from potential misconduct.

Voices within and beyond ABC worked to discredit Wallau amid the controversy he unleashed. Cosell, who butted heads with the young whistleblower, represented Wallau as selfishly drumming up scandal to improve his position at ABC. Moreover, *Sports Illustrated*'s Mark Kram published an article praising the Championships. "There are champions to be made—honestly," Kram wrote. "The last word is so important; the champions cannot be made in the back room, they must be made in the ring." "The *Sports Illustrated* article destroyed my credibility inside ABC," Wallau said. "I was just a kid. How could I know more than the most respected sports publication in the country?"[52] Tensions reached their peak when Braverman threatened Wallau at a production meeting before the first telecast. No news of the alleged wrongdoing had broken yet, but Braverman had caught wind that Wallau was snooping around. "In the old days we knew what to do with guys like you," Braverman said along with a throat-cutting gesture.[53] Arledge gave Wallau a $10,000 bonus for his careful work but reassigned him to different projects—a move designed in part to protect him from the shady characters he had rankled.

ABC programmed the Championships as special live events leading into *Wide World*. But suspicions about the tournament resurfaced after a second-round fight between Scott LeDoux and Johnny Boudreaux held at the US Naval Academy in Annapolis, Maryland—one of several staging techniques ABC and DKP used to infuse the event with Olympics-like patriotism. LeDoux lost by decision even though he registered a knockdown and seemed to have the upper hand throughout the match. The defeated boxer launched into a tirade and rushed his victorious opponent during his postfight interview with Cosell. He wildly kicked Boudreaux and screamed that the match was fixed. "You tell is like it is, Howard!" LeDoux hollered while his trainers held him back. "You tell the truth!" The sportscaster was busy collecting and reattaching his toupee, which had been knocked off during the melee.

ABC cut short the postfight fracas to begin *Wide World*'s presentation of speed skiing from Italy. However, Arledge took to the Roone Phone and directed *Wide World*'s producers to carve out space for Cosell to conduct live interviews with LeDoux and anyone else who might shed light on the curious match and the fighter's accusations. LeDoux had calmed down, but he still insisted the contest was rigged. "When I was up in Montreal a month ago working out for this fight, they told me not to take it," he told Cosell. "King's people, they own Boudreaux.... I said if I beat the guy bad enough on national television, they can't steal it from me. They did it, they stole it from me."[54] Cosell then interviewed the referee, who contended that Boudreaux had won in a close but fair match and that LeDoux was being a spoilsport. Cosell also talked with King, who rejected the charges and reminded Cosell that Jim Farley was in charge of the officiating and that the fighters were selected based on *Ring*'s rankings rather than their management affiliations.

Arledge sought to mollify the mounting suspicions by promising that ABC would investigate the event further. He also "invited any fighter who thought he hadn't gotten a fair chance to get into the tournament to call ABC if he thought he was getting the runaround from Don King." Several fighters did call and were made alternates. "Far from covering up or shilling," said Arledge in defense of ABC, "we put the story on the air on our own."[55] The Championships continued in the absence of definitive evidence and gathered some of ABC's highest weekend ratings of early 1977.

Soon after the LeDoux-Boudreaux kerfuffle, ABC producer Jeff Ruhe informed Ike Fluellen of Bellaire, Texas, that he was being dropped from the event because of his unimpressive résumé. Fluellen, a policeman by day, immediately divulged that *Ring* and his manager conspired to fabricate his record so he could enter the Championships. Fluellen had not fought since October 1975—when he lost by a unanimous decision in Mobile, Alabama.

However, *Ring's* 1977 Record Book listed two victories in 1976, which earned him a number three national ranking among junior middleweights and the magazine's Progress Award. "Almost immediately I got an invitation from King," Fluellen said of the fraudulent rankings. Fluellen's admission precipitated an ABC investigation into *Ring's* standings that found eleven fighters in the tournament were listed as having thirty matches that never occurred. As ABC announced, "The record of numerous fighters in the tournament as listed in the 1977 *Ring Record Book* are, in fact, inaccurate and contain many fights which apparently never took place."[56] *Ring* admitted to the inaccuracies but maintained it had not knowingly fabricated rankings.

Much of the blame was directed at King, an ex-convict who staged one round of the US Boxing Championships at Ohio's Marion Correctional Facility, where he served four years for manslaughter in the late 1960s. King vociferously persisted in denying any involvement. "We are trying to save the US Boxing Championships by trying to stop the wrongdoers," he exclaimed. "I am the essence of the American Dream and I am not about to let something like this tarnish my reputation." King blamed *Ring* and expressed amazement that the publication abused his trust. "I am absolutely appalled, shocked, and saddened to discover that *Ring Magazine*, for more than 50 years the 'Bible of Boxing,' has completely violated the tradition of rating boxers."[57]

Faced with the biggest crisis of his career, Arledge was also desperately searching for someone to blame—preferably somebody unaffiliated with ABC. The *Boston Globe* likened the Boxing Championships to "Watergate," and the *Chicago Tribune* called it "the worst television scandal since the quiz show frauds of the 1950s."[58] The indignity threatened to derail Arledge's imminent promotion as ABC News president. He suspended the Championships pending an investigation on April 16, 1977—two weeks before ABC announced his position at ABC News.

Arledge retained Michael Armstrong to head an inquiry into the tournament. Armstrong had gained national attention while working for the Knapp Commission, which exposed police corruption in New York City. The prominent lawyer assembled a team of three attorneys with "extensive investigative and law enforcement experience," as well as seven other lawyers, five law students, one legal assistant, and a private detective. Armstrong's team questioned two hundred people—from ABC executives to participating boxers to sportswriters who covered the Championships—and spent ten hours interviewing Arledge alone.[59] ABC commissioned Phillip Forlenza to conduct a separate review to determine whether the $10,000 bonus Arledge gave

Wallau was hush money. The inquiries publicly signaled the seriousness with which ABC took the allegations.

The network, in fact, planned to continue the Championships after Armstrong's team exposed the transgressors and reaffirmed its trustworthiness. "We hope the investigation will result in a system of tighter controls that will re-establish the tournament's credibility and allow resumption of the telecasts," read an ABC Sports press release.[60] It initially targeted June 1 for the Championships' continuation. The protracted inquiry, however, eventually compelled the network to suspend the tournament indefinitely. King wrote Arledge a menacing letter full of bizarre metaphors to indicate his disappointment that the tournament had been postponed and to register his dismay that so much of the blame had been directed at DKP. "I am deeply saddened and hurt to see that you have been stricken with two of the most deadly and feared diseases known to man: those of vacillation and insecurity." King continued by asserting that Arledge's actions had ensured that both ABC and DKP would suffer. "The ghosts of innuendo, suspicion and doubt will frighten both the public and the boxers away from Don King, and from his twin, Roone Arledge. I cannot fight these ghosts alone. They are impossible to grasp, to define. They drift around me, and therefore you, and taint our every move." King then accused Arledge of betrayal on account of ABC's insistence that it have an escape clause in all future agreements with DKP. "This hardly demonstrates that ABC Sports is ready to stand behind Don King," the promoter accurately observed. "Rather it suggests that I am not worthy of your confidence." King closed the manic correspondence on a baleful note. "When you release the monster of destruction, you must be careful that monster doesn't turn and destroy its creator. The ominous nature of suspicion and doubt—the ghost I cannot fight—will not rest with the elimination of Don King. It will then turn and seek Roone Arledge." Despite this friction, ABC was again in business with DKP the following month—before Armstrong and Forlenza had even finished their investigations—to broadcast a fight between Ken Norton and Jimmy Young. The network indicated that it was content to continue working with King as long as it did not have to trust him.[61]

Around this same time, CBS was embroiled in its own scandal surrounding a series of made-for-TV tennis matches billed as the Heavyweight Championship of Tennis. In particular, CBS falsely marketed four matches between 1975 and 1977 as winner-take-all when both participants were actually compensated (though the victors received more). It scheduled the first of these contests—which featured Jimmy Connors versus John Newcombe—against ABC's broadcast of George Foreman's Toronto exhibition. In combination with ABC's aborted Boxing Championships, CBS's winner-take-all matches suggested networks had betrayed the public's trust in their scramble to create popular and competitive made-for-TV sports.

After four months of work, Armstrong and his team delivered a 327-page report that praised the concept of the Championships but determined that the event was run irresponsibly. The report asserted that the tournament "does not, in our view, establish conduct which would warrant criminal prosecution. We did find, however, a good deal of unethical behavior by individuals involved with the administration and organization of the tournament." The investigation found "no basis to believe that ABC personnel engaged in any conscious wrongdoing." It also absolved King of any misconduct other than failure to properly supervise the operation and providing Ort payment for *Ring*'s rankings, which "seriously compromised the selection process."[62] Though Ort became the primary scapegoat, Farley was forced to resign as the head of New York's Athletic Commission for negligence. Neither faced criminal charges, and Ort retained his job at *Ring*. Like the Armstrong Report, Forlenza's investigation "failed to reveal any attempt by ABC Sports to influence Wallau's statements and conduct by the payment of the $10,000 fee he received or any of the other sums he received."[63] As Arledge had hoped, the commissioned probes cleared ABC of any transgression other than naïveté.

The fallout surrounding ABC's Boxing Championships and CBS's winner-take-all matches catalyzed a broader inquest into television's impact on and influence over sports by a congressional subcommittee on communications. Headed by California representative Lionel Van Deerlin, the hearings spanned three days across October and November 1977 and questioned personnel from each network—including Arledge, Cosell, Spence, and Wallau. "In general, we will try to determine whether the networks have become so involved with the arranging, promoting and scheduling of sports events that they, in effect, have come to control the event," explained Van Deerlin. "In other words, is the public seeing an independent event covered by electronic journalists or an event staged for and controlled by the television?" Previous congressional inquiries had considered sports organizations, but the 1977 meetings were the first to focus specifically on television. Massachusetts representative Ed Markey even claimed the hearings could provide a basis from which to consider the conditions under which networks as a whole gain and retain FCC licensure. "When the subcommittee began this investigation four months ago, we felt that the focus of our attention would be on the winner-take-all tennis and United States Boxing Championships," Van Deerlin explained. "But as we got into it, other practices in the television sports industry claimed our attention. We have found practices bordering on—if not actually—deceptive and anticompetitive."[64]

While the expansive hearings covered a broad range of issues, the subcommittee directed its most aggressive attention toward ABC and CBS. Spence, in particular, was chastised for his failure to stop the Boxing Championships after Wallau's entreaties. The producer defended himself by asserting that "we trusted *Ring* as all of the written press around this country had for years" and admitting that Wallau had not yet established himself as a credible voice at ABC. Regardless, Illinois representative Marty Russo castigated Spence for failing to do "his homework" after Wallau's warning. "Unfortunately you had your own people there telling you [about *Ring*'s dubious rankings] and nobody listened to them," Russo continued. "I think they did a tremendous job in trying to point out the problems ahead of time, and I think the industry is probably set up pretty well, except that down the line nobody was watching as all the signs were being given."[65] The subcommittee used these careless instances to question whether networks possessed the scruples to self-regulate despite the seductive economic gains presented by made-for-TV spectacles like the US Boxing Championships and Heavyweight Championship of Tennis matches.

With no direct legal or regulatory authority, the subcommittee hearings amounted to little more than a reminder that Congress would be keeping a close eye on sports television. The FCC intensified this scolding by officially admonishing CBS and ABC the following year. It presented a letter of admonition to CBS in March 1978 that imposed a short-term license renewal to one of the network's owned stations. "A short term renewal will be issued to whichever of CBS's stations that comes before us first," the FCC wrote. "We have chosen to issue a short-term renewal since it affords the Commission an early opportunity, in the context of a renewal application proceeding, to assure ourselves that there has been no recurrence of deceptive practices found." The renewal restriction was the strictest punishment the FCC had ever imposed.[66]

CBS showed its penitence by replacing CBS Sports president Barry Frank—an executive long associated with made-for-TV sports who helped launch *Superstars* before joining CBS and who oversaw the winner-take-all matches—and having network president Gene Jankowski apologize on the air. "For more than 50 years, CBS has tried to adhere to the principle that a CBS broadcast must be what it purports to be. I regret to say that in four tennis broadcasts between February 1975 and March 1977 this was not the case," Jankowski confessed. "The matches were described by CBS as 'winner-take-all'—and they weren't."[67] Ironically, the CBS president made this apology during a break in *Challenge of the Sexes*—the very brand of TrashSport programming that led to deceptive spectacles like the US Boxing Championships and the Heavyweight Championship of Tennis.

The FCC issued ABC a less severe—but still humbling—admonition in April 1978 for dropping "below the standard expected of a broadcast licensee." "ABC is strongly admonished for negligence and carelessness with respect to its telecasts of a boxing championship tournament," the FCC decreed. It gave ABC thirty days to file a report outlining "steps the network would take to prevent a recurrence of such events."[68] ABC demonstrated its reformation by instituting new regulations on boxing telecasts "to avoid our involvement as a broadcaster with boxing events shown to have problem areas like those found to have existed in the United States Boxing Championships." The changes called for multisourced verifications of every participating fighter's rankings and records. They also required ABC's legal department to fill out a checklist vetting each participating boxer. "In this manner we can best achieve our goal of continuing to assure our viewers of boxing programs of the highest degree of accuracy, objectivity, and professionalism," read ABC's new policy statement.[69]

These implementations satisfied the FCC, but ABC Sports remained tainted into the next decade. "The scandal of 1977 still haunts the halls of ABC Sports," wrote the *Chicago Tribune* in 1984. That same year, ABC, DKP, and *Ring* reached a settlement with a group of boxers who claimed the corrupted and canceled tournament deprived them of opportunities to earn money. ABC arranged to pay the plaintiffs in a way that would minimize the negative publicity the resolution might conjure. "To distance ourselves as much as possible from the settlement," wrote ABC attorney Charles Stanford, "we have arranged for the payment to be made to the plaintiffs by DKP's attorneys. Also, the plaintiffs (and DKP/*Ring*) have agreed to keep all terms of the settlement confidential."[70] This effort to protect ABC Sports' integrity was particularly urgent in 1984—an Olympic year when the department would be under more scrutiny than usual by broadcasting both the Winter and the Summer Olympics.

The 1970s saw ABC Sports simultaneously garner Emmys for its excellence and FCC admonitions for its negligence. But these conflicting achievements combined to fuel the division's expansion into news, entertainment programming, licensed products, and made-for-TV content, as well as the network's overall ascendancy during the decade. For instance, ABC Sports hired Billie Jean King as an analyst in 1974 to capitalize on Battle of the Sexes and retain the female audience it attracted. Arledge envisioned King as a female Cosell. "She will be given a lot of freedom. We want her to do magazine-type, in-depth reporting, tell it like it is," he said. King promised to use the opportunity to expand her activism. "I don't think I am like Gloria Steinem," she explained. "Gloria doesn't care about sports. She is more intellectual and sophisticated than I am. She may reach five percent of the women. I want to reach 100 percent—tired housewives with a lot of kids, the average, down-to-earth people."[71] Though short-lived, King's presence as a rare and accessible feminist voice on sports television grew out of her role in one of TV TrashSports' foundational events.

Perhaps more than anyone else at the network, Cosell personified ABC Sports' oscillation between seriousness and frivolity. In 1976, for instance, his activities ranged from hosting Battle of the Network Stars to fronting a special Wide World installment that featured the Harlem Globetrotters playing inside the Attica Correctional Facility—the site of deadly riots five years prior. The poignant special offered a rare glimpse inside the infamous prison, and Cosell peppered his commentary with observations about Attica, interviews with both inmates and guards, and meditations on the politics of incarceration more generally. The same year, Cosell taught a course at Yale titled Big-Time Sports in Contemporary America. The seminar offered a critical investigation of sport's cultural, political, economic, and legal contours. It promised to "take a hard look at the essential contradiction at the heart of all of this: that which exists between sports as an American ideal . . . and the more concrete and tarnished reality of big-time sports as they actually exist."[72] Readings included Harry Edwards's Sociology of Sport, Dave Meggyesy's Out of Their League, and Jack Scott's The Athletic Revolution. Cosell's course also devoted special attention to exploring television's impact on sport and critiquing the profit-thirsty trajectory that led to the made-for-TV programming on which the erstwhile professor so often appeared.

Along these lines, a January 1978 segment of *ABC Sports Magazine*—a fleeting fifteen-minute Cosell-hosted report that aired during ABC Sports' weekend programming block—explored the place of women in sports journalism. The story focused on *Sports Illustrated*'s Melissa Ludtke, who sued the New York Yankees for barring female sportswriters from its locker rooms. Cosell conducted a series of interviews to explore whether this controversial prohibition ought to be considered gender discrimination or simply a protection of players' privacy. Though he did not take a stand on the matter, he ended the piece by likening Ludtke's suit to *Brown v. Board of Education* and questioning whether segregation under any circumstances can ever foster genuine equality. Ironically, ABC led into this incisive report with a themed installment of *Superstars* that exclusively featured professional baseball players. Embodying the essential contradiction Cosell's course explored, ABC promoted an investigative report on Major League Baseball's discriminatory practices with a lighthearted made-for-TV event that celebrated the same institution.

ABC Sports' personnel bristled at the term *TrashSports*. Arledge dismissed it as "a glib word that sportswriters have invented."[73] He also pointed out that ABC Sports helped to popularize and legitimize a number of sports that were little more than curios on a par with Knievel's jumps before the network started giving them attention. So-called TrashSports, he argued, simply extended ABC Sports' established and renowned commitment to "add show business to sports." This mission—a promise both to display events and to present them in ways that complement television's aesthetic and commercial demands—suggests that all televised sports are, to varying degrees, made for TV.

SEVEN

"No More Sacred Cows"

THE END OF ABC SPORTS' GOLDEN AGE

Gradually, with hardly any viewers realizing it, the golden age of network sports has come to a close.

WILLIAM TAAFFE, *Sports Illustrated*[1]

If you lose money, what better way to lose money than on something that captivates a global audience?

ROONE ARLEDGE[2]

ABC SPORTS' RENOWN BECAME SO FAR-REACHING during the 1970s that it launched a syndication arm in 1977 to package versions of *Wide World of Sports* and *American Sportsman* (retitled *World Sportsman*) for global audiences.[3] The new subsidiary gave ABC Sports distributional range that matched *Wide World*'s cosmopolitan scope. Mexico's Canal 13 and Australia's Nine Network each paid homage to *Wide World* by launching similar programs that borrowed its title. These developments institutionalized ABC as the template for global sports television.

ABC Sports' sweeping notoriety bred greater competition at home. *CBS Sports Spectacular* and NBC's *Sportsworld* were vying for *Wide World*'s weekend audience, and syndicated programs like NFL Films' highlight shows and Major League Baseball's *This Week in Baseball* were appearing throughout the week in most major markets. Rights fees inflated apace. The $87 million NBC paid to air the 1980 Summer Olympics in Moscow—which the United States wound up boycotting in opposition to the Soviet Union's invasion of Afghanistan—was more than three times the amount ABC spent for Montreal. The $225 million ABC committed for the 1984 Los Angeles Summer Games was greater than the sum paid for the rights to televise every Olympics up to that point combined.

Additionally, cable television was rapidly evolving from a regional service for areas that had difficulty receiving over-the-air signals to a satellite-distributed technology with national range. It presented more options for consumers and allowed telecommunications speculators to build outlets devoted to narrower demographics. Adjusting to these shifts, ABC purchased a controlling stake in ESPN, the first and most prominent all-sports cable entity. But ABC Sports stalwarts like *Wide World* and *Monday Night* struggled as the sports TV ecosystem broadened. Moreover, Capital Cities Communications bought ABC in 1985 and instituted an array of economic and infrastructural modifications that resulted in ABC Sports losing Arledge and relinquishing its vaunted status as the Network of the Olympics.

CABLE SPORTS

Sports programing offered a handy way for nascent cable outlets to establish themselves during the 1970s. The second program Home Box Office (HBO) aired after its 1972 launch was a National Hockey League game between the New York Rangers and the Vancouver Canucks. Three years later, HBO contracted with Don King Productions to augment closed-circuit broadcasts of Muhammad Ali and Joe Frazier's "Thrilla in Manila" fight with a live satellite feed to three affiliates. HBO used the Thrilla in Manila to debut its transition to a continual satellite model and to promote its increased investment in sports.[4] The channel's subscriber numbers doubled within a year of carrying the bout. Ted Turner followed HBO's lead by using his Atlanta-based sports franchises to get his WTCG "Superstation" off the ground. Sports programing's capacity to guarantee at least modest audiences—a lesson these cable outlets learned from ABC—made it a fixture on the emerging medium. The 1977 *Home Box Office v. FCC* case, which eliminated network-friendly antisiphoning regulations on the types of sporting events cable outlets could offer, amplified this surge in cable sports programming.[5]

Sports' early viability on cable motivated the Entertainment Sports Programming Network (ESPN), headquartered in Bristol, Connecticut, to devote an entire channel to it. Initially led by Bill Rasmussen and a small group of collaborators, the upstart caught the attention of Getty Oil's Division of Diversified Operations, which purchased the channel and hired Chet Simmons away from NBC to oversee its development. ESPN attracted early partnerships by appealing to audiences' willingness to watch obscure, prerecorded sports on ABC and wagered that they would consume even more given the opportunity. It struck a deal with the NCAA to cover the many college sports that seldom received national attention and convinced Anheuser Busch to ink the biggest advertising contract in the history of cable to capitalize on the new network's potential to attract its target market of adult men.[6]

ABC Sports producer John Martin—who left in 1983 to join Don Ohlmeyer's Ohlmeyer Communications Company—says "ABC was totally against cable television" when it emerged. Despite these biases, Martin notes, "The top people at ABC saw cable as something we should not ignore."[7] The network established ABC Video Enterprises in 1980 to get ahead of the seemingly inevitable and fast-approaching curve. Run by Herb Granath, the subsidiary focused on cable and home video. It developed ventures like the fine arts–oriented ARTS cable channel in partnership with Hearst Corporation in 1981 (ARTS became A&E in 1984) and struck a deal with two airlines to show ABC Sports videos on flights. Slowly, ABC forged limited partnerships with ESPN. On Christmas Day 1981, ABC let ESPN air its tapes of the US hockey team's win against the Soviet Union at Lake Placid from the previous year. When ABC telecast the Sugar Bowl one week later, the network permitted ESPN to replay the event the following day, but made the cable channel use its own announcers and graphics. The prerecorded content gave ESPN access to high-profile games that it could not afford to carry live while reinforcing ABC's authoritative position as the outlet that originally aired these prestigious events. In addition to sharing select materials, ABC and ESPN planned an eventually aborted joint pay cable venture to carry boxing and other big events.[8]

By 1983, ESPN was cable television's most popular channel and an "anchor" property that drove subscriber rates. But it had yet to make a profit. The outlet generated returns from advertising revenue, and it paid cable providers a nominal fee to carry it. ESPN quickly realized that it could leverage its anchor status by demanding that providers pay it ten cents per subscriber. Providers were forced to oblige for fear that subscribers would disappear if they dropped ESPN. The arrangement, which quickly became the industry standard, gave ESPN a dual revenue stream and enabled it to pursue contracts that initially eluded its limited budgetary grasp. Nothing was more important to the channel's subsequently rapid ascendance.

ESPN's rising success and ABC's increasing investment in cable—which included A&E and Lifetime—motivated the network to purchase 15 percent of the all-sports channel in January 1984. The deal carried an additional option to acquire the remainder at a later date—an opportunity that arose sooner than expected after Texaco bought Getty Oil that same month for $10.1 billion. Texaco offset its gargantuan procurement by unloading Getty's non-oil assets. It consequently sold ABC ESPN's remaining 80 percent and its satellite transmission facilities for $202 million.[9] The May 1984 deal made ABC the United States' largest supplier of basic cable programming.

Since ESPN was still a money-losing venture, ABC mitigated the investment's riskiness by selling 20 percent to RJR Nabisco, which had partnered with and partially funded Ohlmeyer Communications. Ohlmeyer and Martin represented Nabisco on the ESPN board and lent their expertise to the still-budding media outlet. They saw in ESPN's dual revenue streams growth potential that surpassed even ABC. "To me, they [ABC] didn't recognize what they had," Ohlmeyer explained. "To me, it was not about advertising, it was about cents per subscriber. I looked at this thing [ESPN] and I said 'we can fix this thing pretty quickly and it's worth a lot more than they think it is.'" Ohlmeyer's original impulses proved remarkably prescient. But ABC approached the new acquisition gingerly and maintained only an "arm's length" relationship to it that allowed limited overlap.[10]

ESPN's potential profitability and profile increased shortly after the ABC acquisition when the Supreme Court ruled the NCAA's television deal for football to be anticompetitive in June 1984. The NCAA controlled individual schools' ability to negotiate TV contracts—a power it justified by claiming to protect ticket sales that served schools' educational missions. *NCAA v. The Board of Regents of the University of Oklahoma* overturned the organization's right to limit the market for broadcasts of its most popular sport. The Supreme Court ruled 7–2 that the NCAA restrictions restrained trade and unfairly inflated rights fees. "The NCAA's argument," Justice John Paul Stevens wrote in the majority opinion, "that its television plan is necessary to protect live attendance is not based on a desire to maintain the integrity of college football as a distinct and attractive product, but rather on a fear that the product will not prove sufficiently attractive to draw live attendance when faced with competition from televised games."[11] The ruling opened the door for previously exiled broadcasters.

"Once the dust settled," football historian Michael Oriard explains of the ruling, "three times as many football games were televised in 1984 as in 1983, but for $25 million less in total revenue."[12] ABC maintained its long-standing relationship with NCAA football, but its market share on Saturday afternoons dwindled. ESPN, however, benefited tremendously. The cable network's original NCAA agreement only allowed it to showcase football games infrequently and always on tape delay. When Jim Spence renegotiated with the NCAA after the 1984 Supreme Court ruling, he encouraged it to sell

ESPN games as well—a provision he could not legally include in writing.[13] The live college football matches composed ESPN's first big-ticket item.

Four months after the NCAA ruling, Congress passed the Cable Communications Policy Act of 1984, which cut regulations and gave outlets like ESPN greater freedom to set rates to whatever the market could handle.[14] ESPN increased subscriber fees from ten to thirteen cents in 1984 and boosted them to nineteen cents in 1985—a spike it justified in part because of the college football games it added. Cable operators passed those increases along to subscribers. Not coincidentally, ABC's newest cable property finally turned a profit in 1985.

College football primed ABC and ESPN to explore the many synergistic possibilities their relationship presented. "Roone would always say we could use ESPN as a sort of farm system to develop people, try programs we couldn't do for *Wide World*," Martin explained. But the collaborations were slow-going—a sluggishness that was partly a consequence of views within ABC that ESPN was an "ugly stepchild" that did not deserve to intermingle with the Network of the Olympics. "For a long time there were people at our place who sort of resented the attention being given to ESPN," Lewin explains. Many at ESPN "resented the way ABC Sports treated them."[15] For the more entrenched, even an arm's length was too close.

ABC's labor agreement with the North American Broadcasters Association (NABA) and ESPN's reliance on nonunion work prohibited certain collaborations at the level of production and intensified the enmity many at the network—particularly "below-the-line" workers—felt toward their new kin. Ohlmeyer and Martin recognized that ESPN's avoidance of union labor allowed the outlet to operate at lower costs. As a result, they encouraged ABC to abandon sports altogether and use ESPN to produce its programming. "The first thing Ohlmeyer and I did," Martin says, "is we told ABC, 'You guys should get out of the sports business. We'll [ESPN] just do everything for you and avoid the unions.'" While Ohlmeyer recognized "a lot of great reasons for unions," he argued that the NABA produced

an awful lot of featherbedding and an awful lot of "don't work so fast," and so the costs were really extreme for production. If you wanted to have a guy hold a microphone on the fifteenth tee of a golf tournament, you would have to fly that guy out from New York or Los Angeles, get a hotel room for him, rent a car . . . because of the union contracts. The reality is that you can hire some kid for fifty dollars a day from the college in the city where you're in. You can teach him in five minutes how to hold the microphone.[16]

ABC did not take Ohlmeyer and Martin up on their offer. However, the business-friendly logic informing their proposition—much like the Cable Communications Policy Act—reflected the deregulatory trends that would inform ABC's transformation as the 1980s wore on.

"THE MOST EXCITING YEAR IN OUR HISTORY"

Without even mentioning the ESPN purchase, ABC described 1984 as the "most exciting year in our history" that included the Winter Olympics in Sarajevo, the Summer Games in Los Angeles, and the presidential election.[17] It would conclude with the network's first Super Bowl in January 1985. ABC planned 63.5 hours of coverage from Yugoslavia and made room for them by convincing the IOC to expand the event from twelve to fifteen days, which gave it a valuable third weekend of coverage. The network was so committed to and confident in the Olympics that it contracted to televise the 1988 Calgary Winter Games for $309 million before Sarajevo even began.

ABC's Sarajevo coverage borrowed from its idyllic portrayal of Innsbruck eight years prior. It hired folk singer John Denver to serve as a special correspondent and cultural ambassador similar to LeRoy Neiman and Pierre Salinger. Denver composed an uplifting theme song for the event, titled "The Gold and Beyond," and ABC produced segments that followed the friendly troubadour as he explored Sarajevo and mingled with its people. In one, he taught a group of schoolchildren to sing his well-known tune "Country Roads, Take Me Home."

Denver took immense pride in his work for ABC and wrote Arledge a note requesting that the network continue using his song—which he described as "one of my best"—for the upcoming Summer Olympics. Sarajevo's ratings, however, disappointed. The US hockey team that so captivated in Lake Placid finished in a disappointing seventh place, and there were no American standouts in more popular sports like figure skating. Though the Games held fewer points of interest for American audiences, ABC could only recoup its costs by offering more coverage—a decision that diluted an already thin event. "An unfortunate trend is emerging in Olympics coverage," Spence admitted. "To justify the huge rights payments, we have to schedule so many hours of coverage that we risk overexposure. Our financial commitment makes it more difficult to render judgment about how much coverage each event really deserves."[18] This investment also made ABC extraprotective of its coverage. With the IOC's blessing, ABC prohibited competitors from taking cameras into Olympic venues. It also banned news outlets from showing ABC footage of events until after it appeared on the network. ABC limited that usage to a maximum of three-minute segments up to three times daily separated by at least three hours. This "3-3-3 Rule" also applied to radio. NBC futilely critiqued the policy as "draconian" and complained that it "wipes out stories about the Olympics on our local or network broadcasts." ABC demonstrated its seriousness when it sued NBC after the rival used less than ten seconds of seemingly innocuous footage of flags billowing above a medal ceremony during an evening news report.[19]

ABC's coverage—all of which was presented on tape delay except for a single US versus Norway hockey game—proved less valuable than the network predicted. Sarajevo was the first time ABC aired a mostly prerecorded Olympics since Innsbruck in 1976. But the dramatic increase in sports media—particularly cable—guaranteed that interested viewers would receive game results and news before ABC's event coverage, which put a severe dent in ratings. Even ESPN—also subject to 3-3-3 restrictions despite its ownership—regularly scooped ABC. "The old formulas don't work anymore," wrote *Sports Illustrated* of ABC's naive gamble that its non-live Sarajevo coverage could attract the same ratings Innsbruck had achieved.[20] ABC's viewership so disappointed that the network had to issue compensations to forty-five advertisers. Chuck Howard speculated that ABC would have an easier time filling 187.5 hours from Los Angeles than Sarajevo's 63.5 hours, since the Summer Games would be covered live and US athletes would likely have greater success.

Not content to continue simply outdoing past Olympic achievements, ABC promised the Los Angeles Games would be "the biggest show in the history of television." Beyond its domestic coverage, ABC provided the world feed that foreign media outlets used as the raw material to construct their coverage. As a result, the network bragged its broadcasts would reach "some 2½ billion people, more than half the world's population."[21] This spectacle was threatened, however, when a group of Eastern bloc nations led by Russia boycotted the Games. The decision was both retribution for the United States' 1980 boycott and a statement against what the group viewed as America's "chauvinistic sentiments and anti-Soviet hysteria." "It is known that from the very first days of the preparations for the present Olympics that the American Administration has sought to set course at using its Games for its political aims," wrote Russian representatives. A clause in ABC's contract with the IOC entitled it to a fee reduction in the event that certain countries boycotted, and the network purchased a $200 million insurance policy to insulate itself further against this possibility. Arledge, however, saw the boycott as a potential benefit because it would result in more American medalists and justify greater focus on US athletes.[22]

Unsurprisingly, Cold War–style patriotism composed the dominant theme from the start of the lavish Opening Ceremonies in the Los Angeles Coliseum. Hosted by Jim McKay and Peter Jennings, the ceremonies were bathed in American flags and anthems. They included the conspicuous presence of President Ronald Reagan and First Lady Nancy Reagan watching from a viewing box, not unlike the one Khrushchev and Harriman occupied during the 1963 US-USSR track meet in Lenin Stadium. Echoing *Wide World*'s coverage of twenty-one years prior, ABC frequently cut to Reagan watching with approval as "America the Beautiful" was performed and the US team entered the stadium. After Reagan declared the Games open from his box, he joined Jennings for a short conversation.

"Did I hear a rumor earlier," Jennings asked, "that you said you have never seen the spirit of America expressed so well?" Reagan responded by praising "a great patriotic feeling that is sweeping this country and that bodes well for our future." With his characteristic folksiness, the president extolled the Opening Ceremonies' embodiment of the Olympics' diplomatic ideals. "I just thought looking down there at all those wonderful young people on that field representing 140 countries, 'I bet if we turn some of the problems of international relations to them they'd solve them before tomorrow.'" Jennings then asked Reagan if he was "sad" the Soviets did not attend. "Yes," Reagan replied. "I think it would be far better for the world if they were [at the Games]. But I think they're the losers." Reagan identified the Russians as opponents of the Olympics' fellowship whose boycott demonstrated a self-centered lack of concern for the Games' larger diplomatic purpose. The brief appearance, journalist Marc Gunther argues, "provided the perfect lead-in for Reagan and his 'Morning in America' reelection campaign" that same year.[23] Reagan lent ABC's coverage gravitas, while the network gave the president a chance to engage a large segment of the voting public with a broadly appealing message that complemented his nationalistic campaign promises.

ABC's coverage of the competitions that ensued gathered the highest ratings of any Olympics to that point, and the $437,350,000 the network grossed from advertising made its $225 million rights expenditure seem like a steal. Julie Barnathan, head of ABC's Broadcast Operations and Engineering

Department, described Los Angeles as "the best covered Olympics" in a praiseful letter to the network's staff. "We covered more events for more hours and we broadcast more hours than ever before," he beamed. "The technical effort, the logistical effort, the physical effort and the mental effort are beyond comprehension."[24]

As Arledge predicted, the absence of boycotting countries allowed the United States to dominate the medal count with 174. Romania came in a distant second place with 53. ABC's coverage reveled in the United States' overwhelming success. Frank Beermann of *Variety* described the broadcast's tone as "frenzied patriotism" that was "filled with near-hysterical reaction to impending and final US victories."[25] Broadcasts—from both ABC and its affiliates—routinely used terms like "our" and "we" to describe American performances and omitted many foreign successes. In certain instances, ABC would announce that an American team did not prevail in an event without bothering to mention which nation did win. The coverage frustrated visiting athletes, who only had access to ABC's American feed via Los Angeles affiliate KABC. "It looks like it did in Moscow except now we're in America," remarked Yugoslavian shooter Rajmond Debevec. "There's an overemphasis that it's America's Games, and that the rest of the world is invited," added Australian race walker David Smith. "All they [ABC] are worried about is the medal count, and to me that's the worst thing about the Olympics." During his victory lap, British decathlon winner Daley Thompson wore a custom-made T-shirt with "Thanks, America for a good games and a great time" printed on the front. The back read "But what about the TV coverage?" to call out ABC's blatantly preferential depictions.[26]

The IOC registered a formal complaint about ABC's coverage to Los Angeles OOC president Peter Ueberroth. Arledge, however, maintained that the visiting athletes were supposed to receive the feed that appeared in their native lands. "The athletes from 139 nations thought—mistakenly—that this was what their fellow citizens were being subject to at home," he wrote of the blunder. Instead, Arledge claimed that Ueberroth had arranged for the athletes to receive only the American feed from KABC—an affiliate that deliberately played up the nationalism in its news coverage—because it would save money. Regardless of Arledge's explanation, "the network was declared the villain." David Wolper came to ABC's defense against the IOC, which he thought had no right to govern the network's coverage. "I said, 'You paid $225 fucking million for these Games. You put on what the fuck you want, Roone.'"[27] Though frustrated with Ueberroth and KABC, Arledge made no changes to ABC's approach. The audience certainly approved. ABC Sports made more money in 1984 than ever before—a year when the Los Angeles Olympics was its featured presentation.

ABC's opportunistic coverage marked an increasingly commercial logic guiding the Olympics that began to gain steam in 1976. Refining and streamlining this business model, the Los Angeles Olympics were financed mostly through the private sector, relied heavily on volunteer labor, and welcomed corporate sponsorship that enabled a bevy of products and services to become the "Official X of the Olympics" for the right price. These practices ensured the Games' profitability but also gave commercial interests more power to influence them. In this spirit, 24 percent of ABC's Los Angeles coverage was commercials—in contrast to the 10 percent typically devoted to ads during prime-time programming that same year. "The commercialization doesn't seem all that intrusive," argued Robert Lindsey of the *New York Times*, "and merely reflects the reality of the growing commercialization of sports as a result of the influence of television."[28] The foreign athletes clearly disagreed. But ABC's representations betrayed an ever-cozier relationship between capitalism and jingoism that suggested a deregulated and corporate-friendly approach to sports and communications can bolster their civic utility. It reflected the connection between free-market capitalism and patriotism that Reagan rode to an overwhelming victory in his reelection that November.

ABC Sports began 1985 by broadcasting its first Super Bowl. The coverage built on the division's approach to *Monday Night* and was used to celebrate the program's fifteenth anniversary. ABC also integrated the spirit of *Wide World* and the Olympics into the broadcast by situating the Super Bowl as a patriotic ritual with global appeal. The coverage's cuts to fans watching in London and US troops holding viewing parties in South Korea provoked Marc Gunther and Bill Carter to call it the "Wide World of Super Bowls."[29] ABC integrated the game into its regular Sunday programming block and reinforced its patriotic overtones by scheduling it after a *Wide World* installment that featured American boxers who competed in the Los Angeles Olympics the previous summer. Gifford opened the Super Bowl broadcast by preemptively dismissing the "elitist critics" who would inevitably berate its extravagance. Gifford suggested the Super Bowl—like the Olympics—merits its outsized status.

Echoing his role in the Los Angeles Opening Ceremonies, Reagan did the coin toss via satellite from the White House. Coincidentally, the Super Bowl was scheduled on January 20—the same day that Reagan's second-term inauguration was originally set to take place. Reagan, however, moved his inauguration ceremony to the following day. Previous presidents had pushed the event to Monday when January 20 fell on a Sunday because of the day's religious significance. But the media-savvy Reagan rescheduled the inauguration to avoid competing with and to benefit from the Super Bowl. His Super Bowl appearance publicized the next day's inauguration, and the broadcast hyped ABC News' coverage of it. Reagan, in turn, lent star power to the coin toss. As with the Opening Ceremonies, the network and the president created a cross-promotional opportunity.

Despite the success of ABC's Olympics and Super Bowl coverage, *Monday Night* began to sag in 1984. The ratings dipped 24 percent since peaking in 1981, and it lost money for the first time. The losses provoked several sponsors to request refunds and forced ABC to lower its ad rates. Concerned about these drops, the NFL commissioned a survey on viewer preferences. It found that 67 percent were dissatisfied with games' expanding duration, which had increased by an average of twenty-one minutes in ten years, and identified commercials as the main source of irritation. The survey recommended that the NFL cut telecasts' length or institute rule changes that would trim the games.[30] These suggestions put ABC in a difficult position: fans wanted shorter broadcasts, but the network had to include more commercials to recoup its escalating rights fees and could not charge more for those ads unless viewership increased. But perhaps *Monday Night*'s biggest challenge was Howard Cosell's decision to leave the program after the 1983 season.

COSELL'S LOUD EXIT

The sportscaster had grown increasingly bored at ABC Sports—where little of his work resembled the journalism that sparked his decision to abandon law. Cosell found an invigorating outlet in *SportsBeat*, an investigative weekend sports program that debuted as a monthly show in 1981 and went weekly in 1982. Conceptualized as a sports-themed *60 Minutes*, *SportsBeat* reflected Cosell's teaching at Yale and harkened back to his documentaries with Legends Productions. Biographer John Bloom identifies *SportsBeat* as "a concession to [Cosell] from the executives at ABC," who were hoping to placate the restless star. Cosell maintained control over *SportsBeat*'s staff and content. The program, in fact, did not officially fall under ABC Sports' purview, and its offices were on a different floor of the network's headquarters—an effort to ensure impartiality that also symbolically reflected Cosell's growing estrangement from his employer. Cosell trumpeted the *SportsBeat* group as crusading "adversaries of the sports establishment in the finest tradition of journalism." The program's highlights included a feature on cocaine in the NFL and repeated endorsements of Oakland Raiders owner Al Davis's effort to move his franchise to Los Angeles—topics that contrasted with *Monday Night*'s promotional tone and provoked a furious Rozelle to call for the job Cosell would soon leave.[31] *SportsBeat*'s aggressive reportage garnered widespread critical plaudits and gathered three Emmys. But like many critical darlings, its ratings were dreadful.

In a letter to Pierce, Arledge cautioned that *SportsBeat* was "hurting the programs that follow it." But Cosell blamed these problems on the many ABC affiliates that declined to clear the show. "I am taking the liberty of writing you directly because I feel so strongly about ABC *SportsBeat* and its importance to this company," he wrote to Pierce. "It is in no sense intended as a self serving statement, but only as a factual recital," he continued before proceeding to praise his "remarkable" show and urge Pierce to pressure affiliates to carry it. "It is my hope that someday all our affiliates are made aware of this so that the company, in terms of clearances, can reap the harvest from the show that both the company and the show deserve." Aside from skipping several levels of management to register his complaints directly to Pierce, Cosell copied Spence, Arledge, Leonard Goldenson, and ABC Broadcast Group president Tony Thomopoulos to make sure the entire network was privy to his dismay.[32]

Cosell's disaffection became more pronounced after he worked a November 26, 1982, boxing match between heavyweight champion Larry Holmes and Randall "Tex" Cobb. Holmes dominated Cobb—who absorbed brutal punishment for fifteen rounds but did not go down. At one point Holmes delivered twenty-six unanswered punches and reduced Cobb's face to what Cosell wincingly described as "hamburger meat." The sportscaster was outraged by the referee's unwillingness to end an obvious mismatch that devolved into "an assault on the senses of any civilized human being." Cosell was particularly aghast given the fact that lightweight boxer Kim Duk-Koo had died one week earlier from injuries sustained in a match with Ray "Boom Boom" Mancini. "Doesn't he know," Cosell asked of the referee, "that he is constructing an advertisement for the abolition of boxing?" Cosell ended his commentary by refusing to "dignify this fight with any interviews." The following day, he announced that he would no longer work professional boxing.[33] Critics pointed out the irony of Cosell's turning his back on boxing only after making a fortune on the sport. Cosell, however, insisted that he had been calling for regulations that would protect endangered fighters like Cobb and Kim since the 1970s and could simply take no more.

Cosell and ABC's fraught relationship intensified after a *Monday Night* broadcast the following September when he described the slippery Washington receiver Alvin Garrett as a "little monkey" after he broke several tackles. It was an irresponsible metaphor from a sportscaster intelligent enough to recognize its troubling implications when applied to African Americans like Garrett and who would not have hesitated to disparage a colleague demonstrating similar carelessness. Cosell had publicly bashed Gifford and Meredith for far less. The Southern Christian Leadership Conference's Reverend Joseph Lowery called for a boycott of *Monday Night* and demanded that Cosell apologize. Cosell eventually expressed his regrets and claimed that he meant to compliment Garrett's "ability to be so elusive despite the smallness of his size."[34]

There was overwhelming evidence to suggest that Cosell was egotistical, boorish, and cantankerous. There was little proof, however, to indicate that he was racist. He had certainly used black athletes to advance his career. But he had also risked that career defending their civil rights. A group of prominent African Americans including Ralph Abernathy, Harry Edwards, and Jesse Jackson voiced their support for Cosell, and the controversy cooled. Lowery later admitted that while he took issue with Cosell's words, he was mostly using the occasion to pressure ABC Sports to hire more African Americans into production positions.[35] Cosell returned to the program and finished out the season after a three-week hiatus. But the embarrassment marked "the beginning of the end of his career at *Monday Night Football*." After the Los Angeles Games, he informed Arledge that he would quit *Monday Night*. Cosell had made such pronouncements before—most of which amounted to little more than attention-getting ploys—and was willing to be coaxed into staying. But this time Arledge did not try to change his mind. Quite simply, Cosell's "penchant for generating controversy was no longer seen as an asset."[36] He had instead become a liability. ABC Sports was willing to lose its most famous voice on one of its signature shows as both faded from prominence.

Cosell presented his departure from *Monday Night* as a positive development that would allow him to turn his full attention to more consequential assignments like *SportsBeat*. "I'll work what I want to work," he said, "when a man gets into his mid-60s, it's time to cut back." Cosell could not resist, however, speculating that his absence contributed to *Monday Night*'s historically low 1984 ratings. *Monday Night* absorbed another blow when Meredith left for good one year after Cosell. "It's a different ball of wax now," said Forte. "The game is of utmost importance now. We are a slave to the game."[37] The program's "bigger than the game" event status dissipated along with Cosell's withdrawal.

Despite his professed happiness, Cosell continued to rankle his ABC coworkers. When asked what it takes to be a sportscaster he replied, "become a guttural illiterate and learn how to catch a football"—a shot at the former jocks with whom he shared duties. The year after quitting *Monday Night*, Cosell backhandedly hinted at ABC Sports' general shoddiness by calling *Battle of the Network Stars* "the purest show I ever did. No pretense about it—a prime-time entertainment show. No Mickey Mousing, no falsified transcripts, no under-the-table payments."[38] The combustible semiretiree's vitriol found an even larger platform when he published an excerpt of *I Never Played the Game*, his third memoir that he coauthored with *SportsBeat* staffer Peter Bonventre, in *TV Guide*'s September 1985 issue. The book savaged his ABC colleagues, including Arledge, whom he cast as a power-hungry narcissist. "He takes the title of executive producer of telecasts he has little or nothing to do with," Cosell charged. "The more people Arledge controls, the better he feels about himself and the world."[39]

ABC announced *SportsBeat*'s cancellation the month after Cosell's excerpt hit newsstands. From a financial standpoint, the cancellation was long overdue. In April 1985, Arledge wrote an urgent note to Spence and Vice President Irwin Weiner about *SportsBeat* that said, "Something *must* be done. We are currently at more than a million $ loss." But he struck a diplomatic tone after the program's cancellation, which he blamed squarely on its woeful ratings. "I believed in it and wanted it to stay on. We stayed with it several years beyond any rational reason for doing so. But it costs a lot of money in a period of tight money, and the audiences are just so small that it's just not possible to justify keeping it on."[40] Though *SportsBeat*'s fate was imminent, Cosell's comments made the easy decision even easier.

Cosell quit ABC-TV altogether after *SportsBeat*'s season. The sportscaster refused a role ABC offered him on its pregame World Series coverage—a task he thought was beneath him—and opted not to work the event at all. Al Michaels, a frequent Cosell collaborator slated to work the World Series with the disgruntled broadcaster, could not contain his satisfaction. "When the

Cosell decision was made I was certain a new atmosphere would exist but only after the fact can it be fairly assessed," he wrote to Arledge. "The production meetings became an honest exchange of thoughts and ideas and it was so refreshing for all of us to concentrate on the task at hand and not on any individual's whim and self-interests."[41] Beyond his difficult personality, Cosell was ABC Sports' most expensive talent. The network decided the cost was no longer worth the trouble. After *SportsBeat* finally ended in December 1985, Cosell transitioned entirely to radio, where he continued his daily program *Speaking of Sports* and his weekly program *Speaking of Everything*. He remembered *SportsBeat* as his finest contribution to television, but was bemused that his proudest achievement also stood among his least popular. "If I had to choose one show that I'd like to stand as my legacy in this business," he wrote, "*SportsBeat* would be it."[42] Cosell continued to speak truth to power on radio, but fewer people sought out or heard his clamorous voice.

"A CONQUERED NATION"

Aside from being the year when it lost Cosell, 1985 was the first year ABC Sports failed to make money. The division attributed these losses primarily to rights fees, which accounted for 82 percent of its total costs by 1986. Its contracts with the National Football League and Major League Baseball represented 81 percent of those expenditures. ABC Sports projected $40 million in losses over the life span of its 1982–86 deal with the NFL and $79 million from its 1984–89 agreement with Major League Baseball.[43] Alongside the sports division's struggles, ABC slipped back into third place for the first time since the 1970s.

The network's financial woes made it vulnerable to a hostile takeover in a Wall Street–friendly media market that nurtured rampant mergers and acquisitions. Analysts indicated that ABC might be more valuable were it split up and sold off as parts. This prospect horrified Goldenson. Rather than watch his company be swiped up and peddled for scrap, Goldenson proactively sought to join up with a friendly entity.[44] His first choice was IBM, a deep-pocketed potential partner that eventually lost interest. He then began talks with Capital Cities Communications, a relatively small but efficiently run company that owned seven TV stations, twelve AM and FM radio stations, ten newspapers, and various other properties. Though only one-quarter of ABC's size, the "lean and mean" Cap Cities had far greater profit margins than the network because of the thriftiness that CEO Tom Murphy and COO Dan Burke demanded. The low-profile company's "reputation among broadcasters," Huntington Williams wrote of Cap Cities, "was that of an impeccably managed, public-spirited enterprise." The company's annual report for 1984 bragged that it had achieved its "thirtieth consecutive year of record financial performance." Even more telling, the cover page to the company's yearly reports emphasized that Cap Cities expected employees "to be forever cost-conscious." These efforts stretched beyond garden-variety penny-pinching. Cap Cities refused to install air-conditioning in its Albany, New York, headquarters. When the building needed a paint job, Cap Cities coated only the sides that could be seen from the parking lot and road. Stockholders loved Capital Cities. Employees were another story. When staff at the *Times Leader* of Wilkes Barre, Pennsylvania, went on strike shortly after Cap Cities purchased it, the company locked them out and carried on publishing.[45]

ABC and Capital Cities had discussed the possibility of a merger years earlier with the expectation that ABC would acquire Cap Cities. As it turned out, Cap Cities was better suited to procure the larger company. The two already enjoyed a cooperative and generally amicable relationship. Four of Cap Cities' TV stations were ABC affiliates (Philadelphia, Houston, Buffalo, Hartford/New Haven) that delivered 7 percent of the network's total audience. Moreover, those affiliates rarely preempted network programming to air syndicated material—an expression of allegiance ABC appreciated.[46]

Slackened media ownership regulations made the eventual merger possible. Prior to 1984, a single company could own a maximum of seven television stations, seven FM radio stations, and seven AM stations. ABC's five stations and Cap Cities' seven would put the combined entity well over the limit. However, the FCC overturned the thirty-one-year-old law to allow twelve TV, FM, and AM stations as long as a company's total properties in a single format reached no more than 25 percent of the nation's households. The merger-friendly 12-12-12 rule opened to door for ABC and Cap Cities— which had exactly twelve TV stations between them—to unite. Business magnate Warren Buffett, an admirer of Murphy and Burke's corporate acumen, underwrote the deal with a $517 million investment that allowed Cap Cities to get the credit necessary to complete the purchase. "I feel that the company I built from scratch is in good hands and that it will be carried on and that's important to me," a soothed Goldenson remarked after the deal.[47]

Capital Cities' $3.6 billion purchase, which the FCC approved in early 1986, was the most expensive acquisition ever outside of the oil industry.

Williams described the ABC sale as "the 'shot heard round the world' in a communication revolution" that would see both NBC and CBS fall under the respective ownership of the multinational corporations General Electric and Westinghouse within a decade. As the 1948 *United States v. Paramount Picture Inc.* case—a ruling that limited vertical integration—sparked ABC's birth, deregulations that welcomed such consolidation initiated its takeover. Furthermore, Cap Cities reflected the profit-driven philosophy that Goldenson used to establish an audience for ABC during the network's infancy. Its news programming, for instance, had a reputation for the "if it bleeds, it leads" brand of sensationalism at which ABC News' finally respectable producers and journalists would scoff. "We are giving the American people what they want," Murphy said in response to critiques against Cap Cities' lowbrow fare. "If you want to give the people what you think they need, go into public broadcasting."[48]

In a statement to ABC employees announcing the merger, Goldenson and Pierce presented the change as cause for celebration. "Each company brings substantial strengths to the combination," they wrote, "and we feel the new company, to be known as Capital Cities Communications/ABC Inc., will be the premier communications, information and entertainment company in the world."[49] Goldenson and Pierce concluded by emphasizing the greater creative and economic opportunities the merger would offer employees. Despite the memo's rosy tone, the Cap Cities acquisition seemed to result in demotions for both Goldenson and Pierce—developments that ABC employees could not have interpreted as good signs. While Murphy and Burke retained their respective CEO and COO duties over the newly combined company, Goldenson, closing in on retirement, became the ABC chairperson and moved out of active management. Pierce was moved from ABC chair and CEO to vice chairman of Cap Cities/ABC. He resigned six days after the merger became official.[50]

The Capital Cities takeover may have been friendly on paper, but the transition was tempestuous in practice. Cap Cities' management viewed ABC as wasteful, complacent, and undisciplined. Murphy lamented that ABC's programming too often put high-profile money losers over less showy but reliably profitable properties. "We cannot—and will not—let ABC get out of shape in the future just because it can afford a richer diet," he declared. "This is how Capital Cities has run its business for 31 years—and the philosophy we have followed is one we will adhere to at ABC from now on."[51] According to Arledge, Cap Cities "looked at anyone who was in the network with suspicion." The new ownership eliminated the executive dining room, prohibited the use of limousines, and threatened to institute drug tests. "Suddenly," wrote journalist Ken Auletta, "ABC felt like a conquered nation."[52]

Capital Cities viewed ABC Sports as the principal contributor to the network's extravagant culture. The Calgary Games—partly because of market forces ABC could not have predicted when buying the rights—were projected to lose $100 million. As ABC Sports' figurehead, Arledge symbolized the improvidence that so offended his new superiors. "He hated budgets," Martin remembered of Arledge. "He hated the bureaucracy of how it was done."[53] "I don't think they quite ever understood Roone," Rick Kaplan adds of Cap Cities' wariness toward the mysterious executive. Kaplan claims that Arledge was actually quite sensitive to the network's financial interests and carefully took them into account when doing business. "Roone wasn't that way," Kaplan insists of his former supervisor's profligate repute, "but he loved that people thought he was that way. It spooked the other networks into wasting money. The Cap Cities guys didn't understand that. I think they bought into the reputation of Roone."[54]

Capital Cities immediately reassigned Arledge as group president of news and sports—a position that included no direct oversight of ABC Sports. The executive, however, retained his $2 million annual salary by agreeing to oversee the Calgary Games (he also somehow managed to keep his chauffeured company-owned Jaguar). Cap Cities presented Arledge's new position as a collaborative decision that would allow him to spend more time running ABC News. "News is just too important, it's the unique element for a network," said Pierce's successor, John B. Sias. "The news part of Roone's responsibility had grown so, and at the same time, his sports duties were not getting any easier. We felt that having Roone full time at News was very important to us." Arledge voiced his agreement with Cap Cities and even called the change "a move I've wanted to make for a long time." "If I had been opposed, it would have been a different situation," he explained. Arledge even endorsed the new management's thriftiness. "You manage according to the needs of your company," he explained. "There's a lot of people at all three networks who have grown up expecting the golden ring to always be there, and that's not a fact in this economy."[55] The executive suggested he and his new supervisors—despite their seeming differences—were on the same page.

Whether or not Arledge fell in line, Cap Cities sought a wholesale shift away from the era and practices he represented. The company did not even bother give Spence—who had run ABC Sports' day-to-day operations since

Arledge took over News—an interview. Instead, it hired Dennis Swanson, president of ABC's Owned and Operated Television Stations Division. Swanson joined ABC in 1976 as an executive producer of local news at KABC in Los Angeles. He quickly built a reputation as a smart administrator in Los Angeles and worked his way up to general manager of Chicago's WLS-TV, where he gave Oprah Winfrey her first TV show, before taking over the Owned and Operated Division. A former marine who initially studied engineering, Swanson was a straight-laced and often unbending executive whose values neatly aligned with Murphy and Burke's style. He expected his staff to wear ties, refrain from cursing, and show up on time. "My priorities are to maintain the standards set by Roone Arledge but make the red ink go away," he matter-of-factly explained after taking the job.[56]

Arledge liked Swanson but identified him as "somewhat of a martinet"—not the type of urbane sophisticate Roone would invite over to sip martinis and shoot pool while talking art and politics. "If you walked out on the street and tried for six months to find a guy more different from Arledge, you would have been hard pressed to come up with somebody any more different than Swanson," Howard explained.[57] Arledge, though, respected Swanson's work ethic and devotion to ABC. For instance, he once sent Swanson tickets to the 1978 National League Championship series between the Los Angeles Dodgers and the Philadelphia Phillies, which ABC was broadcasting. The Dodgers won the series 3–1, leaving Swanson with tickets for a fifth game that would not occur. Not the type to let money go to waste, Swanson returned the tickets to Arledge in case he was entitled to a refund. On the letter Swanson included with the returned tickets, an Arledge staff member reminded him that Swanson recently declined a job offer from NBC that would have increased his annual salary by $30,000.[58] Swanson, the note indicates, was a responsible and loyal company man. But his stinginess also irked Arledge when he conspired with Ueberroth during the 1984 Los Angeles Games to save money by providing foreign athletes access only to KABC's nationalistic feed. Arledge viewed his successor as a reliable administrator, but one who was perhaps too willing to sacrifice quality to keep costs down. This made Swanson a perfect fit for Cap Cities.

Swanson fully realized that he had impossible shoes to fill. "I'm not going to try to out-Roone Roone," he declared.[59] But his superiors saw serious problems at ABC that they hired Swanson to fix. They were confident that the former marine, if anything, would follow orders. Lacking Arledge's suave demeanor, Swanson inelegantly presented his mission to reform ABC Sports in a way that characterized his inherited staff as reckless—a tactic that did not win him many admirers among a group that took pride in its acclaimed, if pricey, work. "I could turn more of a profit if I took the money across the street and put it in the bank," the new ABC Sports boss said of the resources his division was evidently squandering.[60]

Swanson affirmed his authority and divergence from the Arledge school in a staff meeting shortly after assuming control. "I didn't go to an Ivy League school," he huffed. "I went to a land-grant college in Illinois because my family didn't have the money to send me to an Ivy League school. I had to get into the Marines to go through graduate school. I worked my way up." Swanson implied that Arledge and his top lieutenants—almost all of whom attended elite private universities—were entitled brats incapable of making sacrifices for the greater good. "There's a fine line between professional pride and arrogance," he continued before ending his presentation on an authoritarian note. "Everyone does not have a vote here. This place is going to be run like a dictatorship. And I am the dictator." Though Swanson embraced his role as a stern representative of the changes Cap Cities would institute, Lewin claims the new ABC Sports president simply doled out the executions and did not issue the sentences. Swanson, Lewin explains, "had one arm tied behind his back the entire time."[61] The executive did care about sports programming, but he lacked the resources to maintain the quality for which ABC Sports was known as well as the diplomatic tact to explain these constraints gracefully.

Among ABC Sports' first moves under Swanson's watch was a series of layoffs followed by a group of resignations from high-profile Arledge acolytes. Though Cap Cities did not consider Spence for Arledge's position, it invited him to retain his job, title, and salary. But the slighted sports TV veteran opted to leave and start his own company, Sports Television International. "I had a contract that gave me the right to resign at any point in time if Roone Arledge left the ABC Sports presidency, and I was not named president after he departed," Spence explained. "Once I learned that Swanson was named president, I exercised that right and I resigned."[62] Spence was obviously far more qualified than Swanson. But Cap Cities viewed him as an extension of the Arledge administration. Giving him the position would have been perceived as a continuation of the status quo Cap Cities was working to annul. Forte, Howard, and Jeff Ruhe followed Spence shortly thereafter. Though these respected figures would be difficult to replace, Cap Cities was happy to remove their hefty salaries from its books.

The migrations made it easier for Capital Cities to set about changing the culture at ABC Sports to one that avoided loss leaders and put the commercial bottom line above all. As Lewin explains, "Every meeting it was the same basic message: 'If we can cut this much of the cost and add this much in revenue look what it will do to the price of the stock.' That was their mantra." These shifts created escalating tension between ABC Sports' efforts to produce quality programming and meet budgets. Doug Wilson fondly remembered that "management serviced production" before the merger. "We would go out and do a survey and decide what we needed to cover a particular event. Then we would go back and tell them what we needed and the budgetary folks figured out a way to supply those needs. After Capital Cities took charge, production serviced the money guys."[63] Aside from the layoffs, ABC Sports created no new positions in 1986, elected not to pursue rights to several events it had previously carried, and prioritized adding those "events that incorporate commercial names in their titles in an effort to add profit to our bottom lines," such as the Budweiser Boxing Series. It also dropped money-losing programs including *SportsBeat, The Superstars, Battle of the Network Stars*, and even *American Sportsman*—which had been on the air since 1965. As one member of ABC's management put it, "There are no more sacred cows."[64]

Before Spence left he negotiated a deal to acquire NBA basketball, which ABC had not carried since before "Roone's Revenge." By all accounts, the agreement was a bargain. But ABC Sports' new bosses refused to approve the agreement on the assumption that it might lead the NFL to believe it could renegotiate its contract for a higher rate. "We have to try to come to grips with what people who control these sporting events expect in return for our right to televise them. There are some difficult days ahead," Swanson said.[65] By declining the NBA pact, ABC aimed to show sports organizations that it would not be pushed around. "I couldn't help wondering," wrote a perplexed Arledge of Cap Cities' curious negotiation tactics, "if a premier event like the NBA could be turned down for 'message sending,' why not the Kentucky Derby next? And the World Series, the US Open, then the Olympics? Didn't they know it was crazy to give away events to the competition? Didn't they realize that we'd spent years striving for a position of dominance and how valuable that was to the entire company?"[66] If Capital Cities knew this, it showed little signs of caring. It deliberately avoided bidding high enough to acquire rights to the 1988 Summer Olympics in Seoul, which NBC secured for $300 million.

While ABC passed on the NBA and Seoul, Swanson emphasized that *Monday Night* remained a top priority. But he reiterated that ABC would not simply pay anything to keep it. "Dropping *Monday Night Football* is an extreme position, but we can't continue to lose money," he told the *Los Angeles Times*. "We recognize the value, in terms of programming, of *Monday Night Football* to the entire network," he said in a separate interview. "But we're not the government. We can't operate losing money every year."[67] ABC kept *Monday Night* but implemented a smattering of money-saving shifts. First, it used Cosell's and Meredith's departures as excuses to pare the booth down to two commentators. It hired Al Michaels to do play-by-play and moved Gifford to color commentary—an abrupt transition that tempted the even-keeled sportscaster to quit. ABC producer Ken Wolfe argued that the change, which lasted only one season, would clarify broadcasts. "When you have three people in the booth, your telecast goes in a lot of different directions," he said. "We think the telecasts will be cleaner, crisper, and more focused than in the past." But ABC also reduced the number of cameras used for the program, a shift that indicates the modifications were more economic than aesthetic. Furthermore, the network integrated a three-minute window during *Monday Night*'s halftime segment—which had diminished in popularity along with Cosell's departure and the rise of cable highlight shows—for local newscasts from affiliates that had been complaining about losing money when the program regularly cut into their 11:00 p.m. news programs. The changes made *Monday Night* less expensive but also less distinctive. "Swanson performed a function for Cap Cities, but he's not a production guy," said Forte after leaving ABC. "Dennis was brought in to chop heads and he did what he had to do. But you lose creativity."[68]

One of Swanson's rare early triumphs at ABC Sports surrounded a deal to carry the 1987 Citrus Bowl. He agreed to pay the Citrus Bowl $200,000 for television rights—a typical fee at the time. He then sold the Citrus Bowl ten of the game's fifty-four commercial spots for $200,000, which the Bowl could resell at whatever price it could gather. The contract guaranteed that ABC would make significant money on the event. Tellingly, the Citrus Bowl attracted interest throughout the industry because of Swanson's "creative financing," not how ABC covered it.[69]

Though it did not pose anything near the budgetary strain of the Olympics or *Monday Night*, *Wide World* was also struggling as Capital Cities took over. "For years, we could get a good rating on *Wide World of Sports* no matter who we really put on," opined ABC Sports' Bob Iger, who went on to helm Capital Cities/ABC and the Walt Disney Company. "But people tend to be far more event driven these days. . . . If they want to watch something in particular, they'll go and find it."[70] In 1987, *Wide World* cut its Sunday edition—which could no longer compete with all the sports programming surrounding it. McKay also scaled back his appearances. The beloved host's decision to reduce his workload was not a direct response to the shifts Cap Cities instituted; however, it coincided with the sports media sea change that produced so many fissures within ABC. *Wide World* moved to salvage its audience by integrating a younger crop of hosts and developing "a whole new look" to revive what Swanson called ABC Sports' "cornerstone program."[71] It further adjusted to the sports media landscape that seemed to be passing it by with more timely segments like "ABC Sportswatch" and "Athlete of the Week."

ABC Sports instituted broader stylistic and marketing adjustments to make its programming seem current. A 1987 commercial titled "Reaching New Heights," for instance, adapted the hit song "Everybody Have Fun Tonight" by the new wave group Wang Chung and featured two kids who stow away in a basket of sports laundry and are taken into a fantastical locker room filled with the gripping events and personalities that ABC Sports features. That same summer ABC Sports launched *SportsNite*—a lighthearted Monday evening sports news program that followed *Nightline*. *SportsNite* lasted only fourteen episodes, but its humorous focus demonstrated ABC Sports' efforts to adjust to a changing market and compete with ESPN's increasingly popular *SportsCenter*.

ABC Sports extended its attempts to stay relevant beyond TV by creating home videos—from instructional programs and commemorations of great events to board games that integrated VHS tapes. The videos repackaged otherwise dormant content from ABC's archives while stressing the network's role in documenting the important moments they displayed. Taking another stab at reviving *Monday Night*'s deteriorating halftime audience, in 1989 the network instituted a seventy-five-cent-per-call hotline where fans could vote among a selection of five plays of the week. *Monday Night* announced the winner later in the program—another effort to dissuade viewers from changing channels. Gifford voiced the call and ended each dispatch with an offer to buy a *Monday Night* videotape. Like the two-announcer format, the ploy lasted just one season. ABC stretched these efforts even further by creating a *Wide World of Sports* clothing line and convincing 650 JC Penny stores to install televisions featuring a loop of ABC Sports footage in their sportswear departments.[72]

As ABC scrambled to slow its dwindling sports ratings, the network's affiliates expressed heightened animosity toward ESPN. ABC received angry letters from a group of station owners after Koppel recommended that viewers watch ESPN's live coverage of the 1987 America's Cup on *Nightline* and Jennings did the same on *World News Tonight*. As Stanley S. Hubbard, owner of ABC's Minneapolis–St. Paul affiliate, wrote to Tom Murphy, "When ABC became involved with ESPN, we were assured by Leonard Goldenson and Fred Pierce that there would never be an occasion where ABC would use our facilities to promote ESPN—and especially in a manner that would be hurtful to affiliates."[73] Goldenson and Pierce, of course, were no longer running the network.

Cap Cities steadily gave ESPN greater attention and increasingly heeded Ohlmeyer and Martin's recommendation that the cable outfit could compose a less expensive alternative to the network's sports programming. By 1987, ESPN was more profitable than ABC and projected continued growth. ESPN used this rising credibility and budget to persuade the NFL to sign its first cable deal for a series of Sunday evening games titled *Sunday Night Football*. Evoking and cross-promoting ABC's prime-time franchise, *Sunday Night Football* attracted the highest ratings in the channel's history. Recognizing the NFL games' popularity, Cap Cities let select affiliates preempt their regular Sunday evening programming for ESPN's broadcasts—a substitution that satisfied viewers but cut into those affiliates' revenues. *Sunday Night Football*, as ESPN president William Grimes put it, made "ESPN legitimate in the eyes of the sports establishment" and led to a contract with Major League Baseball in 1989.[74] By the end of the 1980s, ESPN was carrying all the big-ticket sports that previously distinguished network TV.

Commenting on Capital Cities' incessant budget cuts in 1989, ABC sportscaster Jim Lampley prophesied "a day when ABC Sports is made up of three or four executives, one lawyer, two researchers and one or two announcers. Everyone else would be freelance." In 1991, *Monday Night* began using a crew made entirely of less costly part-time freelancers.[75] ABC Sports was inching ever closer to the streamlined and nonunion future ESPN portended with minimal regard for the aesthetic compromises that would inevitably accompany it.

ARLEDGE'S QUIET EXIT

By 1988, ABC Sports was mostly over the growing pains that came along with its new organizational reality. But the division was left with what the

Washington Post described as "its weakest lineup in history"—a menu head-lined by 97.5 hours of coverage from the Calgary Olympics.[76] Because of Calgary's $309 million price tag, which included an additional $100 million in production costs, ABC had to devote an even greater percentage of its coverage to commercials than in Los Angeles. It aired so many ads that it missed several goals during its live hockey coverage. Swanson lamented the overkill but argued that ABC had no choice given the event's expense. Despite the commercials, Arledge's swan song gathered rave reviews. It also lost $65 million. "I just don't think it's [the Olympics] a very good business for American networks to be involved in now," Swanson said after Calgary. Arledge saw the losses differently. "If you lose money," he said, "what better way to lose money than on something that captivates a global audience."[77] The Olympics, Arledge suggested, delivered ABC goodwill and prestige that were worth even major financial losses.

Arledge, of course, could afford to be idealistic on his way out. ABC Sports capped his final job with its presentation of Calgary's closing credits—a tradition the division began in 1976 that recognizes the hundreds who work on its Olympics coverage. McKay read many of the names as they scrolled atop footage of ABC's staff performing duties that otherwise receive no pub-lic notice. Beyond acknowledging ABC's crew, the credit roll—which typi-cally took more than ten minutes to complete—demonstrated the effort required to pull off a production of the Olympics' extraordinary scope. The credits always began with Arledge and spanned all the way to those who worked in wardrobe and food services. The credit roll from Los Angeles con-cluded with a logo for the Calgary Games and a cheerful reminder that the "Olympic tradition" would continue on ABC four years later. But Calgary's closing credits, set to an instrumental rendition of "Memory" from the popu-lar musical *Cats*, struck a somber tone. When Arledge appeared on-screen, McKay introduced him and wistfully remarked, "Some doubted that we'd do it together again. We did. Next time? Who knows?" The credits indicated that ABC's vaunted Olympic tradition had likely ended.

ABC withdrew early from the bidding for the 1992 Summer and Winter Olympics. CBS purchased the rights to the Winter Games in Albertville, France, for $243 million. NBC acquired the Barcelona Summer Games for $401 million and has carried every Summer Olympics since (and every Winter Olympics as of 2002) through a multibillion-dollar deal that emboldened it to brand itself "America's Olympics Network." Swanson maintained that the Olympics had become a financially untenable gambit. "I don't think we're out of the major sports business," he said after the 1992 rights were sold. "It's just that other people were willing to pay more—and at numbers we cared not to be associated with."[78] ABC was no longer the Network of the Olympics.

"The golden age of network sports has come to a close," wrote *Sports Illustrated*'s William Taaffe shortly before Calgary.[79] This golden age rose and fell with Arledge's reign at ABC Sports. Arledge's reflections on ABC Sports after his final assignment tended more toward reminiscing about the good old days than critiquing what the industry he revolutionized had become. But he did register some candid impressions shortly after Calgary. He shared them, oddly enough, on Cosell's short-lived syndicated TV talk show *Speaking of Everything*—an Ohlmeyer Communications Company effort that survived only three months. "I think that the networks didn't get to be networks just by being good bottom-line investments," Arledge told his former employee and antagonist. "They didn't get to be the institutions that they are in the country just by cost-cutting." While Arledge recognized the financial practicalities that drove profit-seeking entities like Cap Cities, he suggested these priorities hastily abandon the creativity that makes sports TV worth producing and consuming in the first place.

But even without the Capital Cities acquisition, ABC Sports was bound to change dramatically through the 1980s along with mounting rights fees, deregulation, the rise of cable and home video, and the introduction of Fox in 1986, a well-resourced fourth major network with a strong interest in sports. If nothing else, Capital Cities provides an identifiable dramatic foil that explains the amalgam of forces that drove ABC's transformation out of its golden age—a tidy and dramatic narrative not dissimilar from those Arledge made a career of concocting.

Conclusion

FROM *WIDE WORLD OF SPORTS* TO THE WORLDWIDE LEADER IN SPORTS

> I can see the day when there are only two networks in the sports business: CBS and NBC. ESPN will be the sports arm of Cap Cities.
>
> SETH ABRAHAM, HBO Sports president[1]

> The tail took over the dog. The tail outgrew the dog. The world has changed.
>
> FRANK GIFFORD[2]

BY 1992, SWANSON HAD REDUCED ABC SPORTS' losses by 85 percent through austerity measures that included budget cuts, layoffs, and buyouts.[3] While ABC Sports continued to gather critical acclaim, viewers—particularly the younger set—were steadily abandoning previously reliable programs like *Wide World*, *Pro Bowlers Tour*, and *Monday Night*. ABC Sports tried to curb these losses by hiring former America's Junior Miss champion Julie Moran to serve as *Wide World*'s first female studio host in 1994. "It's a new era," Moran said after accepting the position. "A new generation of kids doesn't know *Wide World*." The same year, ABC Sports teamed with *Sports Illustrated*—another legacy outlet that was losing customers at a similarly troubling clip—to produce segments that complemented the magazine's weekly features. Neither effort made much difference. *Sports Illustrated* editor Mark Mulvoy despondently called the coproduced *Wide World* segments "seven minutes that nobody watches out of ninety minutes that nobody sees."[4]

The growing Fox Network posed as much of a threat to ABC as cable. During its first years, the upstart unsuccessfully courted Arledge to run its news division and made a bid for *Monday Night*. Fox finally established viability by mimicking the youthful focus ABC adopted during the 1950s and had maintained to varying degrees ever since. It fastened its identity to trendy programs like *The Simpsons*, *In Living Color*, and *Beverly Hills 90210*. The junior network's appeals to young viewers came at the primary expense of ABC, which lost $50 million in projected revenues to Fox in 1993 alone.[5] Fox rode its mounting popularity to strike a four-year and $1.58 billion agreement to televise the NFL's National Football Conference (NFC) games— a contract CBS had held since 1955. It then invested in the production company New World Communications, which owned affiliates in several cities with NFC teams. On the promise of the NFL deal, New World switched twelve of its stations' affiliations to Fox. ABC lost three affiliates in the football-driven realignment. Fox's dual reliance on youth-oriented programming and sports transformed it into a legitimate fourth network—a strategy that borrowed from ABC and disproportionately impacted its market share.

DISNEY AND THE "CROWN JEWEL"

ABC's struggles did not deter the Walt Disney Company—which had transformed into one of the world's largest media conglomerates since the days when ABC aired *Disneyland*—from buying Capital Cities in 1996. The $19 billion stock and trade purchase was the second-largest corporate acquisition ever after Kohlberg Kravis Roberts & Co.'s $25 billion procurement of RJR Nabisco in 1988. While Capital Cities included a diverse portfolio, Disney was primarily interested in ABC's and ESPN's complementary strengths. "ABC has never had our resources, and we haven't had ESPN," Disney CEO Michael Eisner said after the purchase. "Put the two together and who knows what we get." Tellingly, Eisner praised ESPN—not ABC—as the "crown jewel" of the acquisition.[6]

Swanson retired as ABC Sports president shortly after the purchase, a move Disney unofficially encouraged. Disney replaced him with ESPN president Steve Bornstein, who would oversee both ABC and ESPN and tend to the still separate companies' previously underutilized potential for synergy. "We have long felt that the two divisions need to have a closer relationship to better coordinate their goals and activities," ABC CEO Bob Iger remarked after Bornstein's promotion. As Bornstein added, "The new structure will benefit the two programmers working together closer, promoting each other better and having a more dynamic combination." ABC and ESPN's first full-fledged coproduction came with the 1998 World Cup in France. "Everybody was on the same page," Geoff Mason recalls of the World Cup collaboration, "and once we put that under our belt, it was only a question of time before we got closer and closer."[7] But rather than blending the two entities, ESPN steadily began to drive the productions and receive top billing.

Disney gradually shed ABC Sports relics that did not complement the ESPN-driven image it was building for its sports programming. It canceled *Pro Bowlers Tour* in 1997 and pulled the plug on *Wide World* the following year. Though it abruptly shuttered *Wide World* after thirty-seven seasons, Disney remade it as a banner under which it presented all ABC Sports programming aside from college football and *Monday Night*. "Our focus groups suggest most people think all our sports programming is *Wide World* anyway," remarked an ABC spokesperson.[8] Disney scrapped the antiquated program but salvaged its still valuable title. It integrated *Wide World* markings, for instance, into its coverage of the 1999 Women's World Cup final—a match that instantly joined Battle of the Sexes in the pantheon of US women's sport history. Though not a *Wide World of Sports* episode, the final aired live in *Wide World*'s traditional Saturday afternoon time slot.

ABC Sports and ESPN renewed their respective contracts for the NFL's Monday and Sunday evening games shortly before *Wide World*'s cancellation. Disney leveraged ABC and ESPN's ramped-up synergies to convince the NFL to make ESPN its first exclusive cable carrier, a deal Bornstein called a "milestone for ESPN."[9] ESPN provided increased promotion for *Monday Night*, and the ABC telecasts began flaunting ESPN logos.

Disney's favoritism toward ESPN incited renewed antipathy toward the hotshot cable outlet within ABC Sports. When Bornstein was promoted to ABC-TV president in 1999, Disney returned to having separate executives run ABC and ESPN. It hired Howard Katz to helm ABC Sports and placed Bornstein underling George Bodenheimer in charge of ESPN. Katz, who began his career at the network under Arledge, was recruited in part to boost morale among ABC Sports' dissatisfied ranks. He immediately reassured employees and viewers that although ESPN's development was "an important corporate priority," it "shouldn't be at the expense of ABC Sports." He promised to restore the division's stature. "There was a time when ESPN felt totally inferior to ABC," Katz said. "Now, it's flipped. It's important for ABC to re-establish its leadership position."[10] He set about this task by turning his attention to ABC Sports' biggest remaining property.

Katz coaxed Ohlmeyer out of a cushy Southern California retirement to try to bring back the viewers *Monday Night* had lost. Ohlmeyer insisted he would not have returned to ABC if not for his relationship with Katz, a trusted confidant who worked at Ohlmeyer Communications from 1983 to 1993. The Arledge protégé aimed to reintroduce the "sense of danger" and "unpredictability" that made *Monday Night* special during the 1970s.[11] He most noticeably enlivened the program by hiring comedian Dennis Miller—famous for his acerbic rants and work on *Saturday Night Live*—to join the *Monday Night* booth. Miller, who had no previous sportscasting experience, generated the buzz Ohlmeyer sought—from amusement to indignation. Both *TV Guide* and *Sports Illustrated*, which had all but ignored *Monday Night* in recent years, featured cover stories on the experiment leading into *Monday Night*'s 2000 season. ABC emphasized Miller's vitalizing impact by opening his first *Monday Night* broadcast with a vignette featuring an elderly man lying in a hospital bed. The man's heart monitor begins to flatline, and a nurse bursts into the room to save him. Instead of performing CPR, the nurse places headphones on the man that are blaring the *Monday Night* theme. His pulse returns as the vivifying production commences. Miller did generate a brief spike in *Monday Night*'s viewing—particularly among the young consumers Ohlmeyer was seeking. But the novelty quickly wore off and the ratings leveled. Tired of the incessant traveling *Monday Night* required and out of ideas for how he might save it, Ohlmeyer returned to retirement after one season. ABC relieved Miller of his duties after two unremarkable years.

Alongside Katz and Ohlmeyer's fruitless attempts to reboot *Monday Night*, the US Postal Service issued a stamp to commemorate the program as part of its 1999 "Celebrate the Century" series, which honored fifteen important developments and events from each of the twentieth century's decades (figure 11). The *Monday Night* stamp was part of the 1970s—a decade that included stamps of the United States' bicentennial celebration, Earth Day, and Watergate. The stamp institutionalized *Monday Night* as a significant part of America's cultural past as its importance to the present declined.

Like its programs, ABC Sports' main figures faded as the century ended. Cosell retired from radio in 1992 and died in April 1995 of a heart embolism brought on by lung cancer. Most of ABC Sports' remaining old guard had passed away, left the company, or retired. McKay trimmed his duties to infrequent golf tournaments and horse races. NBC Sports boss Dick Ebersol, who began his career as McKay's researcher, negotiated with ABC to borrow the legendary sportscaster for NBC's 2002 and 2004 Olympics broadcasts.

FIGURE 11. The US Postal Service issued a *Monday Night Football*–themed stamp as part of its 1999 "Celebrate the Century" series.

McKay served as an essayist who lyrically commented on the Olympics' meanings and heritage. He lent the broadcasts a stately aura of nostalgia for viewers who grew up watching him work the Games. But like the *Monday Night* stamps, McKay's NBC guest spots tied his importance to a bygone era.

Arledge stepped down as ABC News president in 1997 and became its chairperson—a largely ceremonial post. He retired the following year and receded from public life after a prostate cancer diagnosis. As Arledge's health deteriorated, the National Academy of Television Arts and Sciences honored him with its first ever Lifetime Achievement Award in September 2002. It was his thirty-seventh and final Emmy. The congratulatory notes that cascaded into Arledge's mailbox doubled as sorrowful farewells. "Get well and strong and know that all of your many friends are pulling for you," Ted Koppel wrote to the executive who gave him his big break. Among the most moving letters came from Dennis Swanson, who gave up his "retirement" shortly after exiting

ABC to run the New York City NBC affiliate for which Arledge once produced puppet shows. "I am so sorry that you have had to suffer in this fashion," Swanson wrote. "I just hope that modern medicine can improve your circumstances."[12] Swanson's missive arrived on NBC letterhead that prominently featured the Olympic rings beneath the network's logo. Penned by the man who signaled the end of ABC Sports' Arledge era and advertising the Olympics' new TV home, the letter poignantly illustrated the changed sports television landscape that succeeded Arledge's career in sports. Underlying Swanson's affectionate dispatch was the unique bond he and Arledge shared. Both were once praised for their leadership and vision only to be recast as obsolete and replaced by a new parent organization's shifting priorities.

Arledge passed away on December 5, 2002. Ed Scherick—who had grown bitter toward Roone and publicly accused him of taking credit for ABC Sports' development—died of leukemia on December 3. The men who were perhaps the two most important people in modern sports television's birth passed away within forty-two hours of each other.[13]

ESPN SOUTH

In 1998, ESPN changed its motto to "The Worldwide Leader in Sports." It accompanied this makeover with a global and multiplatform effort that included an expanding menu of channels, licensed merchandise, and ventures into radio, print, and the web. Reflecting broader shifts in the TV industry, ESPN morphed into a media company rather than a cable outlet that used its increasingly robust web presence to market, augment, and build synergies among its other tentacles. ABC Sports only minimally participated in this digitally driven diversification. It published brief online articles that contextualized the college football games it was broadcasting, for example, and had a website commemorating the division's rich history. But all of ABC Sports' online activities were housed on ESPN.com, which was doing little to drive traffic to the network division's web pages. ABC steadily became a stagnant and old-fashioned alcove in ESPN's broadening empire. Disney returned to having a single executive oversee all sports content—not simply sports programming—by replacing Katz with Bodenheimer in 2003. As Bornstein fostered synergies between ABC Sports and ESPN, Bodenheimer initiated the divisions' consolidation. By 2005, ABC Sports and ESPN had fused all operations except production.

The following year, Disney eliminated the ABC Sports brand altogether and repackaged sports that appeared on ABC as "ESPN on ABC"—a title it unveiled with its college football coverage. "Our research revealed that with all things being equal (the event, the on-air talent, and so on), sports fans believed that *branding* a game as ESPN was a significant improvement in quality," Bodenheimer wrote. Alex Wallau, who had worked his way up to ABC-TV president since proving his mettle during the US Boxing Championships, claimed the transformation was long overdue given ESPN's status as "the biggest brand in sports television." Wallau also pointed out that "a generational transition had taken place" that eased the shift.[14] Beyond ESPN's brand equity, the company's multiplatform infrastructure built a "stickier" variety of sports media consumption that fed into, extended, and stretched beyond traditional TV viewing.

That same year, ESPN took over *Monday Night*, which had continued plummeting on ABC to the tune of nearly $200 million in annual losses. As *Monday Night* wilted, ABC enjoyed newfound success in prime time with the female-oriented melodramas *Desperate Housewives* and *Grey's Anatomy* that made it more willing to give up the program despite its thirty-five-year run. Bodenheimer explained that ABC "is focused on enter-tainment now" and added that "renewing *Monday Night Football* did not make smart financial sense for ABC." ESPN's *Monday Night* contract called for $1.1 billion annually—nearly double what ABC had been paying. The cable outlet absorbed these costs by raising subscriber fees. Moreover, ESPN made *Monday Night* the centerpiece of its weekly lineup and trans-formed it into "a full day experience" by pairing the broadcast with hours of related material across platforms. "It's a huge day for ESPN," Bodenheimer beamed. "Who would have thought 25 years ago that we'd have *Monday Night Football*, an American institution, on ESPN?"[15] *Monday Night*'s first season on ESPN attracted the highest ratings of any series in cable TV history.

But the ESPN-driven changes miffed purists. Barry Frank called the alterations a "further regression of ABC Sports from what was once the clear leader in sports, to ESPN South." Ebersol lamented the apparent loss of Arledge's legacy, which Keith Jackson claimed ESPN had "callously tossed aside." Besides concerns about ABC Sports' heritage, the *New York Times'* Richard Sandomir argued that the "ESPN on ABC" broadcasts failed to meet the division's formal standards.[16] Sports programming still aired on ABC, but it was no longer ABC Sports.

But the division did not completely disappear as Disney phased it out. ABC Sports trademarks, personalities, and footage continue to circulate intermittently through a stream of films depicting events it helped to make iconic. In 2001 and 2002, Jon Voight (*Ali,* 2001), John Turturro (*Monday Night Mayhem,* 2002), and Fred Willard (*When Billie Met Bobby,* 2001) played Cosell in films that portrayed Muhammad Ali, *Monday Night Football,* and Battle of the Sexes. Voight received an Academy Award nomination for his performance, which reproduced several quips Cosell uttered during his televised conversations with Ali. Other productions, such as Steven Spielberg's *Munich* (2005), licensed ABC Sports footage to lend their depictions authenticity. Spielberg's film, which focuses on Israel's covert efforts to avenge the Black September killings, sets the scene at Munich with footage of McKay commenting on Olympic events and includes sequences in which the terrorists watch ABC's coverage before German police terminate the domestic feed.

ABC Sports footage most frequently shows up in documentaries that use it in an archival capacity to build their historical narratives. Like *Munich,* the documentaries demonstrate the centrality of ABC Sports to the events and figures they represent while reinforcing the division's credibility and importance. HBO Sports' *Do You Believe in Miracles? The Story of the 1980 US Hockey Team* (2001) both employs ABC Sports footage to explain the United States' surprising victory over Russia at Lake Placid and uses Al Michaels's famous call—"Do you believe in miracles? Yes!"—during the game's final seconds as its title. In doing so, it conflates the event's history with ABC's rendition of it—a decidedly haphazard historiographical practice, but one that surely benefits ABC Sports.

Disney, of course, owns and controls ABC Sports' colossal archive. But this material seldom surfaces apart from infrequent specials on ESPN Classic, a channel devoted to sport's past that is unavailable with most basic cable packages, and scattered documentaries that use it to reflect on sport history. For instance, the short-lived ESPN Classic program *Classic Wide World of Sports* (1999–2000) celebrated *Wide World*'s legacy by repackaging old episodes for contemporary audiences. More prominently, ESPN's Academy Award–winning documentary *O.J.: Made in America* (2016) relied heavily on ABC Sports footage to explain O.J. Simpson's career—including his work at ABC Sports. The productions reinforce ABC Sports' position as the standard-bearer for network era sports TV while designating ESPN as the official keeper of the history it documented—a status that fortifies the media outlet's broader campaign to assert its "Worldwide Leader" status.[17]

While ESPN rarely uses archived ABC footage, it also ensures that no other entity may employ this content without paying a steep per-second licensing fee (content featuring Cosell requires additional clearance from his estate). Footage is not publicly available for researchers beyond scattered clips that have found their way into archives like the Paley Center for Media and Vanderbilt Television News Archive; out-of-print VHS tapes that ABC Video once produced; and material that has been digitized and uploaded onto the web by altruistic collectors, historians, and fans. The vast majority ABC Sports' material is sequestered within the vaults of a company that insists upon its historical importance while demonstrating little use for this footage, and even less interest in sharing it.

. . .

ESPN's extravagant *Monday Night* contract precipitated a boom in cable sports television. "Sports leagues increasingly decided to forgo broadcast's bigger audiences," *SportsBusiness Journal* reported, "for more money from cable networks that could write bigger checks, thanks to their dual revenue streams."[18] By this time, major sports organizations were beginning to establish their own cable networks, which gave them greater control over event broadcasts and ensured coverage would represent their parent organizations favorably. The United States' major networks also launched sports-themed cable channels—a group that includes CBS Sports Network (2011), NBC Sports Network (2012), and Fox Sports 1 (2013)—to compete with ESPN.

This swell in cable was primarily driven by live sports television's exceptional position as a scarce commodity in an abundant digital media ecosystem. "Sports absolutely overpowers film and everything else in the entertainment genre," media tycoon Rupert Murdoch asserted.[19] Event broadcasts are sold on an exclusive basis, yield predictable ratings, and maintain status as appointment viewing. They are one of the few types of content consumers still expect to view in real time—an exceptional "DVR-proof" status in an industry that increasingly caters to on-demand viewing. In short, traditional television's survival hinges in large part on sports programming.

Recognizing sports TV's unique value and scrambling to maintain its market share amid the surge in competition, ESPN began spending wildly to secure long-term contracts with prominent partners. Between 2011 and 2012, it pledged $15 billion to the NFL, $12.6 billion to the National Basketball Association, $5.6 billion to Major League Baseball, $5.6 billion to the NCAA for its College Football Playoffs, $1.5 billion to the NCAA's PAC-12 Conference, and $480 million to the Wimbledon tennis tournament. The spending sprees resembled the days when Arledge inflated contracts with his willingness to invest seemingly whatever it took to secure premium content. But while ABC passed the gargantuan costs Arledge incurred along to advertisers or absorbed them as promotionally rich loss leaders, ESPN continued to increase subscriber fees, which climbed to $7.21 per subscriber by 2017. Cable's next most costly channel at the time, TNT, gathered $1.76. The precipitous rise in rights costs and subscriber rates prompted *SportsBusiness Journal* to mull whether a volatile bubble in the cable sports TV market was forming.[20]

The bubble did not burst, but consumers began opting out of progressively pricier cable packages, "cutting the cord" for more affordable digital streaming services and smaller "over-the-top" (OTT) cable bundles that bypassed traditional distribution models and omitted ESPN. These consumers were understandably dissatisfied with cable packages that forced them to spend disproportionately for ESPN regardless of whether or how much they watched the channel. The streaming services and OTT packages provided previously unavailable alternatives. ESPN lost 13 percent of its subscribers between 2011 and 2017—a dip that outpaced overall declines in cable TV. A January 2016 poll revealed that 56 percent of cable subscribers would rather eliminate ESPN from their cable packages than pay the exorbitant monthly fees it demands. The results indicated that ESPN's traditional business model is obsolete and that its commanding status as an anchor driving cable subscriptions is wilting. The obstacles ESPN faces—sparked mostly by the internet, social media, and mobile devices—reflect the hindrances ABC Sports confronted as cable emerged during the 1980s. ESPN has responded to the challenges digital culture poses in much the same way: investing in the new media that are threatening it, cutting money-losing properties, implementing massive layoffs, and adjusting its aesthetics and branding to chase a younger set that increasingly gets its sports news and coverage through means other than cable TV.[21]

But as cable sports slips, network TV has experienced slight growth—though its overall viewership is nowhere near what it enjoyed during the late 1970s. Live network sports broadcasts—particularly mega events like the Super Bowl, Olympics, and World Cup—continue to draw record numbers through traditional distribution and streaming platforms. Better than any other genre, sports television has weathered the digital and postnetwork storm. As a result, sports leagues are turning back to networks that can, if nothing else, deliver consistently large audiences during a moment when they are harder to come by.[22]

As some of the only events that still draw truly mass audiences, network sports broadcasts have tremendous power to shape the world they depict and the industry they represent. This influence is still largely wielded through a language ABC Sports codified. But like all languages, sports television has transformed over time. The convergent and multiplatform coverage that took ABC Sports' place includes faster-paced editing, more graphic accoutrements to augment telecasts and discourage channel surfing, and efforts to sync viewers' TV consumption with their other and simultaneous media use. Given these shifts, most references to ABC Sports since the division's extinction depict it as a quaint emblem of a simpler media culture before sports programming could be consumed anytime and anywhere. It is emblematic of a time when kayaking not only could occupy space on a major network's Saturday afternoon schedule but could lead the ratings during its time slot; when athletes candidly spoke their minds rather than only divulging those platitudes their PR teams have deemed acceptably benign; when broadcasters who sought to provoke as well as explain were, in fact, provocative; when outfitting talent in garish yellow blazers seemed like a good way to establish their professional authority.

But beyond the nostalgia, ABC Sports' history usefully demonstrates what sports television can do and how those cultural and economic functions have shifted. There is now more sports television programming available than ever before. Nearly every prominent event—from college basketball games to horse races—is broadcast in some form and can be accessed if one has the resources and technological savvy. But as the sports media market crowds, the most prominent and best-resourced outlets tend to focus greater proportions of their overall energies on major sports that guarantee a predictable viewership. While coverage of bobsled races and volleyball can still be found, this type of material has never regained the visibility and accessibility ABC Sports occasionally offered it. Along these lines, a decades-long sociological study found that the percentage of TV coverage devoted to women's sports has actually decreased between 1989 and 2009—the same interval when ABC Sports faded from view.[23] Ironically, ABC Sports curated a more diverse picture of sports culture than the massive and convergent industry that succeeded it.

This is not to say, of course, that ABC Sports was driven by an altruistic effort to broaden sports fans' cultural horizons and increase diversity in sport (though Arledge did often proffer that virtuous perspective and gladly accepted the praise it yielded). Arledge would have traded *Wide World*'s demolition derbies for Major League Baseball games without hesitation, and most of the women athletes he put on the air did not look too different from the model he once hired to parade around the set of *For Men Only* in a bathing suit. But regardless of its motives, ABC Sports' intersecting cultural import and commercial success functioned through putting events into dialogue with their surroundings and showing that sports always somehow tap into bigger issues that help to explain the world in which they take place and the people they involve. This is particularly important given sports media's traditional tendency to avoid criticizing sport or acknowledging its political contours—a tradition that has only intensified as the crowding market makes outlets increasingly wary of upsetting partners that supply them with content. ABC's coverage of Ali and Mexico City, for instance, offers a frame of reference for more recent controversies surrounding African American athletes protesting during the pregame national anthem. The Battle of the Sexes still provides valuable perspective for debates about gender equity in contemporary sports. Cosell's self-aggrandizing candor simultaneously serves as the template for crusading sports television journalists and professional gasbags paid to spew semiscripted "hot takes" that prize incitement over intelligence and responsibility.

Network sports television is not dead; but ABC Sports is. Disney officially and unceremoniously put it to rest in 2006. Though ABC Sports is gone, the formal practices and industrial protocols it developed continue to animate contemporary sports television, which drives the symbiotic sports and TV industries, which illumine and shape culture. Few entities—within or outside sport and media—have had greater impact on US popular culture than ABC Sports. This is precisely why it is crucial to contextualize and critique this landmark organization, the forces that guided it, and its legacy.

Wide World of Sports *Inaugural Season Schedule, 1961*

April 29	University of Pennsylvania Relays, Philadelphia, PA
	Drake University Relays, Des Moines, IA
May 6	Syracuse University Old Timers Football Game, Syracuse, NY
	University of Oklahoma Old Timers Football Game, Norman, OK
May 13	Professional Bowlers Association World Championship, Paramus, NJ
May 20	FA Cup Soccer Championship, London, England
May 27	Indianapolis 500 Time Trials, Indianapolis, IN
June 3	World Championship professional tennis, Mexico City, Mexico
June 10	Canada Cup Golf Championship, Dorado Beach, Puerto Rico
June 17	Le Mans Grand Prix, Le Mans, France
June 24	National AAU Track Meet, New York, NY
July 1	Men's Softball All-Star Game, Clearwater, FL
	National AAU Track Meet, New York, NY
July 8	Masters Water Skiing Tournament, Pine Mountain, GA
	Daytona "Firecracker 250" stock car race, Daytona Beach, FL
July 15	National Gymnastics Championships, Dallas, TX
July 22	US-USSR track and field meet, Moscow, USSR
July 29	Japanese All-Star baseball game, Nagoya, Japan
August 5	Cheyenne "Frontier Days" Rodeo, Cheyenne, WY
August 12	World Hydroplane Championships, Seattle, WA
	National AAU Women's Swimming and Diving Championships, Philadelphia, PA
August 19	Arnold Palmer vs. Gary Player golf match, St. Andrews, Scotland
August 26	National AAU Men's Swimming and Diving Championships, Los Angeles, CA
September 2	World Water Ski Championships, Long Beach, CA
September 9	Inside Pro Football—AFL Game, San Diego, CA

ABC's Wide World of Sports
Athlete of the Year

1962:   Jim Beatty, track and field
1963:   Valery Brumel, track and field
1964:   Don Schollander, swimming
1965:   Jim Clark, auto racing
1966:   Jim Ryun, track and field
1967:   Peggy Fleming, figure skating
1968:   Bill Toomey, track and field
1969:   Mario Andretti, auto racing
1970:   Willis Reed, basketball
1971:   Lee Trevino, golf
1972:   Olga Korbut, gymnastics
1973:   O. J. Simpson, football, and Jackie Stewart, auto racing
1974:   Muhammad Ali, boxing
1975:   Jack Nicklaus, golf
1976:   Nadia Comaneci, gymnastics
1977:   Steve Cauthen, horse racing
1978:   Ron Guidry, baseball
1979:   Willie Stargell, baseball
1980:   US Olympic Hockey Team, hockey
1981:   Sugar Ray Leonard, boxing
1982:   Wayne Gretzky, hockey
1983:   Australia II, sailing
1984:   Edwin Moses, track and field
1985:   Pete Rose, baseball
1986:   Debi Thomas, figure skating
1987:   Dennis Conner, sailing
1988:   Greg Louganis, diving
1989:   Greg LeMond, cycling
1990:   Greg LeMond, cycling
1991:   Carl Lewis, track and field, and Kim Zmeskal, gymnastics

1992:   Bonnie Blair, speed skating
1993:   Evander Holyfield, boxing
1994:   Al Unser Jr., auto racing
1995:   Miguel Indurain, cycling
1996:   Michael Johnson, track and field
1997:   Tiger Woods, golf
1998:   Mark McGwire, baseball
1999:   Lance Armstrong, cycling
2000:   Tiger Woods, golf

Top Fifteen Television Audiences of All Time as of Roots' Premiere

1. *Roots*, part VIII	ABC	January 30, 1977
2. *Gone with the Wind*, part 1	NBC	November 7, 1976
3. *Gone with the Wind*, part 2	NBC	November 8, 1976
4. *Roots*, part VI	ABC	January 28, 1977
5. *Roots,* part V	ABC	January 27, 1977
6. *Roots*, part III	ABC	January 25, 1977
7. Super Bowl XI	NBC	January 9, 1977
8. *Roots*, part II	ABC	January 24, 1977
9. *Roots*, part IV	ABC	January 26, 1977
10. *Roots*, part VII	ABC	January 29, 1977
11. Super Bowl X	CBS	January 18, 1976
12. Super Bowl IX	NBC	January 12, 1975
13. *Roots*, part I	ABC	January 23, 1977
14. *Airport*	ABC	November 11, 1973
15. Super Bowl VII	NBC	January 14, 1973

Top Ten Most-Watched Wide World of Sports *Episodes*

Date	Event	Share	% of Audience
1. 10/25/1975	Evel Knievel motorcycle jump	22.3	52
2. 1/11/1976	Ali vs. Joe Frazier	21.0	43
3. 2/17/1974	Knievel jump/Cheyenne Rodeo	20.6	49
4. 1/14/1979	Harlem Globetrotters	20.3	40
5. 2/17/1980	Gymnastics/Frisbee Championship	20.2	42
6. 11/25/1972	Ali vs. Bob Foster/Olga Korbut	19.6	41
7. 9/14/1974	Knievel jump at Snake River Canyon	19.4	49
tie. 3/31/1973	Ali vs. Ken Norton	19.4	46
8. 1/27/1973	George Foreman vs. Joe Frazier	19.3	39
9. 1/13/1973	Globetrotters	19.1	41
10. 1/8/1978	Globetrotters/weightlifting	18.6	41

ABBREVIATIONS

FREQUENTLY USED PERIODICALS

AC   *Atlanta Constitution*

ADW   *Atlanta Daily World*

BG   *Boston Globe*

CD   *Chicago Defender*

CT   *Chicago Tribune*

LAT   *Los Angeles Times*

NYT   *New York Times*

SI   *Sports Illustrated*

SN   *The Sporting News*

WP   *Washington Post*

WSJ   *Wall Street Journal*

ARCHIVES

ABC   Avery Brundage Collection, University of Illinois, Urbana, IL

AMP   Agnes Moorehead Papers, Wisconsin State Historical Society, Madison, WI

HHC   Hal Humphrey Collection, University of Southern California, Los Angeles, CA

LA84   LA84 Foundation Archive, Los Angeles, CA

LGC   Leonard Goldenson Collection, University of Southern California, Los Angeles, CA

LNP	LeRoy Neiman Papers, Archives of American Art, Washington, DC
MMP	Mark H. McCormack Papers, University of Massachusetts, Amherst, MA
NYUA	New York University Archives, New York, NY
RAP	Roone Arledge Papers, Columbia University, New York, NY
VUTNA	Vanderbilt University Television News Archive, Vanderbilt University, Nashville, TN

NOTES

INTRODUCTION

1. Harry Wismer, "Greatest Contribution to Television Supplied So Far through Sports," *Variety*, January 8, 1947, 119.

2. National Opinion Research Center, "The Effects of Television on College Football Attendance," 1952, 4, HHC, Box 15, Folder "Sports"; Sports Committee of the Radio-Television Manufacturers Association, "Just What Has Television Done to Recreation—Communications?," 17, HHC, Box 15, Folder "Sports."

3. William O. Johnson, *The Super Spectator and the Electric Lilliputians* (New York: Little, Brown, 1971), 99; A. J. Liebling, *The Sweet Science* (New York: North Point Press, 2004), 5.

4. Liebling, *Sweet Science*, 21.

5. Roone Arledge, *Roone: A Memoir* (New York: HarperCollins, 2003), 30–31.

6. Herman Gray, *Watching Race: Television and the Struggle for Blackness* (Minneapolis: University of Minnesota Press, 1995), 9.

7. Michele Hilmes, "The Bad Object: Television in the American Academy," *Cinema Journal* 45, no. 1 (2005): 111–16. Some television scholars have treated sports television with the degree of seriousness it merits, such as Victoria E. Johnson and Markus Stauff.

8. James Michener, *Sports in America* (New York: Random House, 1976), 323.

CHAPTER ONE

1. Bert Sugar, *The Thrill of Victory: The Inside Story of ABC Sports* (New York: Hawthorn, 1978), 34.

2. William Boddy, *Fifties Television: The Industry and Its Critics* (Urbana: University of Illinois Press, 1992), 1.

3. "ABC-TV's Doing the Sportin' Thing—436 Hours of It," *Variety*, June 8, 1960, 23.

4. "The abc of ABC," *Forbes*, June 15, 1959, 15.

5. Leonard H. Goldenson and Marvin J. Wolf, *Beating the Odds* (New York: Charles Scribner's Sons, 1991), 140.

6. *United States v. Paramount Pictures, Inc. et al.* 334 U.S. 150, 167 (1948); Douglas Gomery, "Failed Opportunities: The Integration of the U.S. Motion Picture and Television Industries," *Quarterly Review of Film Studies*, Summer 1984, 219–28, 226.

7. Stewart Lewis Long, "The Development of the Television Network Oligopoly" (PhD diss., University of Illinois, 1974), 101.

8. Sterling Quinlan, *Inside ABC: American Broadcasting Company's Rise to Power* (New York: Hastings House, 1979), 27; "Twenty-Five Years Wiser about Show Business, Goldenson Finds TV the Brightest Star," *Broadcasting*, July 14, 1958, 84.

9. Jeff Kisseloff, *The Box: An Oral History of Television, 1929–1961* (New York: Viking, 1995), 538.

10. Goldenson and Wolf, *Beating the Odds*, 100; Gary Newton Hess, "An Historical Study of the DuMont Television Network" (PhD diss., Northwestern University, 1960), 104; US House 85th Cong., 2nd Sess., Network Broadcasting; "AB-PT's 'Full Speed Ahead Sets in Motion $30,000,000 Agenda," *Variety*, February 11, 1953, 1.

11. Long, "Development of the Television Network Oligopoly," 101; Timothy R. White, "Hollywood on (Re)Trial: The American Broadcasting–United Paramount Merger," *Cinema Journal* 31, no. 3 (1992): 19–36; Hess, "Historical Study of the DuMont Television Network," 140; Philip J. Auter and Douglas A. Boyd, "DuMont: The Original Fourth Television Network," *Journal of Popular Culture* 29, no. 3 (1995): 63–83. Paramount Pictures was one of DuMont's key shareholders, and there was some discussion of an ABC and DuMont merger, which DuMont's board of directors turned down. See "DuMont Network May Quit If Deal with ABC-TV Jells," *Broadcasting*, November 8, 1954, 27; "DuMont Live TV Headed for Pasture," *Broadcasting*, May 16, 1955, 127.

12. Martin Mayer, "Portrait of ABC," *Show*, October 1961, 59–63, 60; Ronald A. Smith, *Play-by-Play: Radio, Television, and Big Time College Sport* (Baltimore: Johns Hopkins University Press, 2001), 105.

13. Ron Powers, *Supertube: The Rise of Television Sports* (New York: Coward-McCann, 1984), 80.

14. "ABC-TV Settles for Big Games, Small Markets," *Variety*, May 27, 1953, 24; "Falstaff Reprises Network Ballcasts," *Variety*, March 3, 1954, 31; "ABC-TV's 'Game of the Week' Hits Snag," *Broadcasting*, March 22, 1954, 88.

15. Powers, *Supertube*, 81.

16. "ABC-TV Gets NCAA Grid Schedule," *Broadcasting*, April 26, 1965, 7; "ABC in Drive for Major TV Sports Shows," *Billboard*, May 1, 1954, 2; "ABC's NCAA Coup Points Up Web's Competitive Status," *Variety*, April 28, 1954, 23.

17. James L. Baughman, *Same Time, Same Station: Creating American Television 1948–1961* (Baltimore: Johns Hopkins University Press, 2007), 269; "Football TV Costs ABC $1,800,000," *LAT*, November 4, 1954, C1; "ABC-TV Set to Lose $1.8 Million on NCAA," *Broadcasting*, November 8, 1954, 84; "ABC-TV Drops 26 College Events," *Variety*, November 24, 1954, 24.

18. Oliver Treyz, "Television's Dangerous Drift: Programming in Kind," Address to Cincinnati Advertising Club, April 12, 1961, LGC, Box 57, Folder 10; Herman Land, "ABC: An Evaluation," *Television*, December 1957, 94.

19. Goldenson and Wolf, *Beating the Odds*, 149.

20. "The abc of ABC," 17.

21. US Federal Communication Commission, Office of Network Study, *Second Interim Report: Television Program Procurement*, pt. 2 (Washington, DC: Government Printing Office, 1965), 179.

22. "The abc of ABC," 15; "25 Years Wiser about Show Business, Goldenson Finds TV the Biggest Star," *Broadcasting*, July 14, 1958, 82–86, 84.

23. "ABC Rights to Disney Films Limited to TV," *Sponsor*, April 12, 1954, 33; "Disney's 7-Year ABC-TV Deal," *Variety*, March 31, 1954, 41; Fred Silverman, "An Analysis of ABC Television" (master's thesis, Ohio State University, 1959), 104. Disney purchased back its shares from ABC after their deal expired for a reported $17 million.

24. *Fortune*, April 1957, 248; "Corporate Health, Gains in Radio-TV Theme of AB-PT Stockholders Meeting," *Broadcasting*, May 21, 1956, 64. *Disneyland* left ABC for NBC, which offered to broadcast the program in color, after its ABC deal expired.

25. William Boddy, "The Studios Move into Prime Time: Hollywood and the Television Industry in the 1950s," *Cinema Journal* 24, no. 4 (1985): 23–37; Robert Canuff, "Selznick Talks about Television," *Television*, February 1955, 32, 67; Frank Orme, "Disney: 'How Old Is a Child?,'" *Television*, December 1954, 37; "The Critics' Verdict," *Television*, November 1955, 64; Bob Chandler, "Disney's Reaffirmation of TV," *Variety*, December 1, 1954, 1; "TV's Most Important Show," *Television*, June 1955, 85.

26. "ABC's Unique 'Big 3' Status as 'Propertyless' Network," *Variety*, July 27, 1955, 20; Boddy, *Fifties Television*, 145.

27. "Should Hollywood Get It for Free?," *Sponsor*, August 8, 1955, 32; "The Fan Who Runs a Network," *Sponsor*, June 15, 1957, 45; "The abc of ABC," 15.

28. Tom Moore, interview with Archive of American Television, Academy of Television Arts & Sciences Foundation, January 3 and 31, 2003.

29. "ABC-TV to Open Busy Sports Year," *NYT*, September 10, 1960, 43.

30. "Scherick Leaves CBS-TV to Head New Sports Firm," *Broadcasting*, September 24, 1956, 9.

31. Sugar, *The Thrill of Victory*, 38.

32. Chet Simmons, interview with Archive of American Television, Academy of Television Arts & Sciences Foundation, December 16, 2008.

33. Jim Spence, *Up Close and Personal: The Inside Story of Network Television Sports* (New York: Atheneum, 1988), 55.

34. "ABC-TV's Doing the Sportin' Thing—436 Hours of It," *Variety*, June 8, 1960, 28.

35. Tom Moore, interview with Archive of American Television.

36. "NBC's Gillette-Sponsored Friday Night Fights May Move to ABC," *WSJ*, March 16, 1960, 3.

37. Edgar J. Scherick, interview with Archive of American Television, Academy of Television Arts & Sciences Foundation, July 28, 2000.

38. Powers, *Supertube*, 113.

39. Goldenson and Wolf, *Beating the Odds*, 183.

40. Powers, *Supertube*, 113.

41. Roone Arledge, *Roone: A Memoir* (New York: HarperCollins, 2003), 21.

42. Benjamin G. Rader, *In Its Own Image: How Television Has Transformed Sports* (New York: Free Press, 1984), 103; Sugar, *The Thrill of Victory*, 49; "ABC Purchases NCAA Television," *AC*, March 16, 1960, 33.

43. "ABC Buys NCAA TV Grid Rights," *CD*, March 26, 1960, 18; "ABC-TV Grabs Off NCAA Grid," *Variety*, March 16, 1960, 25; Don Page, "NBC Peacock Sheds Its Prize Feathers," *LAT*, March 19, 1960, B5.

44. Powers, *Supertube*, 119.

45. "A Candid Conversation with Roone Arledge," *Playboy*, October 1976, 63–86.

46. Leonard Shecter, "Why It's Better to Watch the Game on TV," *NYT*, March 3, 1968, SM32.

47. Roone Arledge, Resume, RAP, Box 16, Folder 4, Series II.2.

48. Ibid.

49. Roone Arledge, Letter to James Caddigan, January 14, 1954, RAP, Box 16, Folder 4, Series II.2.

50. Roone Arledge, Letter to Orrin E. Dunlap, February 8, 1955, RAP, Box 16, Folder 4, Series II.2.

51. Arledge, *Roone*, 14.

52. Roone Arledge, TV Credits, RAP, Box 7, Folder 6, Series I.

53. Roone Arledge, Resume, RAP, Box 16, Folder 4, Series II.2.

54. Marc Gunther, *The House That Roone Built: The Inside Story of ABC News* (New York: Little Brown, 1994), 15.

55. Powers, *Supertube*, 144; Sugar, *The Thrill of Victory*, 60.

56. Roone Arledge, Letter to Hooper White, May 10, 1960, RAP, Box 16, Folder 4, Series II.2; Roone Arledge, Letter to Al "Jazzbo" Collins, May 23, 1960, RAP, Box 16, Folder 4, Series II.2; Powers, *Supertube*, 135.

57. Roone Arledge, and Gilbert Rogin, "It's Sport . . . It's Money . . . It's TV," *SI*, April 25, 1966, 92–106, 97.

58. "What Is a Roone Arledge?," *TV Guide*, February 29, 1964, 8–10.

59. Edgar J. Scherick, interview with Archive of American Television.

60. Arledge, *Roone*, 30–33.

61. Shecter, "Why It's Better to Watch the Game on TV," SM32.

62. *Wide World of Sports, 1965* (New York: American Broadcasting Company, 1966), 9.

63. Bruce Berman, "TV Sports Auteurs," *Film Comment*, March–April 1976, 34–36; Ralph Wiley, "Arledge's World Flowed with Ideas," ESPN.com, December 9, 2002, accessed February 9, 2014, http://espn.go.com/page2/s/wiley/021209.html.

64. Graham McNamee and Robert Gordon Anderson, *You're on the Air* (New York: Harper, 1926), 52.

65. Andy Sidaris, Letter to Ed Scherick and Roone Arledge, July 18, 1960, RAP, Box 5, Folder 1, Series I.

66. Randy Roberts and James Olson, *Winning Is the Only Thing: Sports in America since 1945* (Baltimore: Johns Hopkins University Press, 1989), 116; Shecter, "Why It's Better to Watch the Game on TV," SM32.

67. Roger Goodman, interview with author, December 19, 2015.

68. Richard Levine, "Wide World of News," *New Times*, January 23, 1978, 18.

69. "A Candid Conversation with Roone Arledge," 64.

70. Powers, *Supertube*, 149; Arledge, *Roone*, 35.

71. "NCAA Wants to Know What Gives with TV Grid Ratings and Com'ls," *Variety*, January 18, 1961, 27.

72. Shecter, "Why It's Better to Watch the Game on TV," SM32.

73. Dennis Lewin, interview with author, December 14, 2015.

74. "UCLA Band Salutes ABC and Football Sponsors," *Broadcasting*, December 19, 1960, 94.

75. William O. Johnson, *The Super Spectator and the Electric Lilliputians* (New York: Little, Brown, 1971), 130.

76. "$10,625,000 TV Deal for New Football League," *WP*, June 10, 1960, D8; David A. Klatell and Norman Marcus, *Sports for Sale: Television, Money, and the Fans* (Oxford: Oxford University Press, 1988), 137; Michael MacCambridge, *America's Game: The Epic Story of How Pro Football Captured a Nation* (New York: Random House, 2004), 133.

77. "ABC Bullish on AFL Gridcasts," *Variety*, July 25, 1962, 39; "The Upsurge in TV Sports: Football Helps ABC-TV to Catch Up," *Broadcasting*, October 10, 1960, 86.

78. Arledge, *Roone*, 64.

79. Spence, *Up Close and Personal*, 57.

80. "A Candid Conversation with Roone Arledge," 66.

81. "ABC-TV's Pro Grid (Untested League) Hits SRO Status," *Variety*, July 6, 1960, 28; Jeane Hoffman, "Richer TV Contract Will Keep Pro Grid Circuit Afloat," *LAT*, February 19, 1961, G3.

82. "Seating Capacity: 15,000,000," *Variety*, June 6, 1962, 20.

83. "The Upsurge in TV Sports," 86; "ABC's $15,000,000 Stake in Sports," *Variety*, May 4, 1960, 23; "ABC-TV to Open Busy Sports Year," *NYT*, September 10, 1960, 43; "How Many Firsts Make a Trend?," *Broadcasting*, October 16, 1960, 43.

84. Scherick became ABC's vice president in charge of sales and maintained his management of the sports broadcasts until leaving in 1963 to become ABC's head of programming, where he went on to develop shows like *Bewitched* (1964–72) and *Batman* (1966–68).

CHAPTER TWO

1. William Oscar Johnson, "Twenty Years and 199 Sports," *SI*, April 27, 1981.

2. Norman Chad, "Victory Not as Thrilling, Defeat Not as Agonizing, But 'Wide World of Sports' Still Spans the Globe," *WP*, August 28, 1987, C3.

3. Jim Spence, *Up Close and Personal: The Inside Story of Network Television Sports* (New York: Atheneum, 1988), 53.

4. Mark Mehler, "The Saturday Afternoon Revolution," *Variety*, April 22, 1991, 39, 48.

5. Ibid., 48.

6. Roone Arledge and Gilbert Rogin, "It's Sport . . . It's Money . . . It's TV," *SI*, April 25, 1966, 92–100, 97.

7. This iconic passage was not *Wide World*'s original introduction. The first episodes opened with McKay reciting, "The unending variety of sport unfolds on *ABC's Wide World of Sports*. Capturing the sights and the sounds; the beauty and record-breaking achievements wherever men gather to compete in this great wide world of athletics."

8. *ABC Wide World of Sports 1964* (New York: American Broadcasting Company, 1965), 16.

9. Ban Wang, "The Cold War, Imperial Aesthetics, and Area Studies," *Social Text* 24, no. 3 (2002): 45–65, 48.

10. Steve Rushin, "How We Got Here," *SI*, August 16, 1994, 35–66, 39.

11. Thomas Doherty, *Cold War, Cool Medium: Television, McCarthyism, and American Culture* (New York: Columbia University Press, 2005), 3.

12. Newton Minow, "Address to the 39th Annual Convention of the National Association of Broadcasters," in Newton Minow, *Equal Time: The Private Broadcaster and the Public Interest* (New York: Atheneum, 1964), 45–69, 52, 57.

13. Jack Gould, "Fabian, Julie Harris and WNTA-TV Sale," *NYT*, December 10, 1961, X21; Larry Wolters, "An 'Ugly' TV Show Sinks to a New Low," *CT*, December 4, 1961, C9; Cecil Smith, "Sordid Mishmash 'Wastes' Fabian," *LAT*, December 6, 1961, A16.

14. Gould, "Fabian, Julie Harris and WNTA-TV Sale," X21.

15. "ABC-TV Acted as Fagin of TV-Dodd," *Broadcasting*, May 21, 1964, 44.

16. Mary Ann Watson, *The Expanding Vista: American Television in the Kennedy Years* (Oxford: Oxford University Press, 1990), 134.

17. Jay Lewis, "Minow and the ABC Murder-Mayhem Rap," *Variety*, February 7, 1962, 30.

18. Michael Curtin, *Redeeming the Wasteland: Television Documentary and Cold War Politics* (New Brunswick, NJ: Rutgers University Press, 1995), 3.

19. Ibid., 8.

20. Leonard H. Goldenson and Marvin J. Wolf, *Beating the Odds* (New York: Charles Scribner's Sons, 1991), 194.

21. Lee Winfrey, "Meet the Man Who Put ABC on the Sports Map," *Philadelphia Inquirer*, January 15, 1976, B1.

22. Spence, *Up Close and Personal*, 53.

23. "A Sports Anthology That's a Best Seller," *Broadcasting*, July 11, 1966, 60–61.

24. H. L. Mencken, "October 30, 1947," in *The Diary of H. L. Mencken*, ed. Charles A. Fecher (New York: Knopf, 1989), 440–41.

25. *Variety*, August 30, 1950, 27.

26. Edgar J. Scherick, interview with the Archive of American Television, Academy of Television Arts & Sciences Foundation, July 28, 2000; William Taaffe, "You Can't Keep Him Down on the Farm," *SI*, July 18, 1984, 293.

27. Jim McKay, *The Real McKay: My Wide World of Sports* (New York: Dutton, 1998), 73–74.

28. Sean McManus, interview with author, January 6, 2016.

29. Roone Arledge, SportsCentury interview, January 25, 1999, RAP, Box 4, Folder 4, Series I.

30. Jim McKay, interview with the Archive of American Television, Academy of Television Arts & Sciences Foundation, October 28, 1998.

31. Ron Powers, *Supertube: The Rise of Television Sports* (New York: Coward-McCann, 1984), 165.

32. Sean McManus, interview with author, January 6, 2016.

33. Taaffe, "You Can't Keep Him Down on the Farm," 289; "Wide World of Sports' 4th Year," *LAT*, April 25, 1965, M8.

34. Jim McKay, interview with the Archive of American Television, Academy of Television Arts & Sciences Foundation, October 28, 1998.

35. *ABC Wide World of Sports 1964*, 8.

36. "A Cameraman's Fishy-Eyed View," *TV Guide*, August 4, 1962, 10–11.

37. The *Wide World* segment garnered a positive review from Red Smith—a boon for the fledgling program—who called it "remarkable." See Red Smith, "The Magic Carpet," *New York Herald Tribune*, September 12, 1961, 22.

38. Melvin Durslag, "Everything But the Pro-Am Clam-Digging Championship," *TV Guide*, April 1966, 24–25.

39. Jim McKay, *My Wide World* (New York: Macmillan, 1973), 261; *ABC's Wide World of Sports 1964*, 9.

40. "We Cover a Wide Range of Sports," *Variety*, November 7, 1962, 26–27.

41. Irving A Leitner, *ABC's Wide World of Sports: A Panorama of Championship Sport* (Racine, WI: Golden Press, 1975).

42. Roone Arledge, *Roone: A Memoir* (New York: HarperCollins, 2003), 43.

43. See Yale Richmond, *Cultural Exchange and the Cold War: Raising the Iron Curtain* (University Park: Pennsylvania State University Press, 2003).

44. Joseph M. Turrini, "'It Was Communism versus the Free World': The USA-USSR Dual Track Meet Series and the Development of Track and Field in the United States, 1958–1985," *Journal of Sport History* 28, no. 3 (Fall 2001): 427–71, 428.

45. Ibid., 430.

46. David Maraniss, *Rome 1960: The Olympics That Changed the World* (New York: Simon and Schuster, 2008), 9; see also Mary L. Dudziak, *Cold War Civil Rights: Race and the Image of American Democracy* (Princeton, NJ: Princeton University Press, 2000).

47. Art Woodstone, "U.S. Video's Sphere of Influence Abroad," *Variety*, July 15, 1959, 56.

48. Turrini, "'It Was Communism versus the Free World,'" 430–31.

49. Deane McGowen, "Sports All Over," *NYT*, February 11, 1962, 125.

50. McKay, *My Wide World*, 252 53.

51. McKay, *The Real McKay*, 254.

52. Ibid., 256.

53. "Russia & U.S.," *NYT*, July 22, 1961, 45.

54. Don Page, "U.S.-Russian Track Films on TV Today," *LAT*, July 22, 1961, B5; "Who Won Meet? Russians Hedge," *NYT*, July 16, 1961, 15; Shirley Povich, "This Morning," *WP*, July 16, 1961, A15; "Russians, U.S. Agree on Track Scoring," *AC*, July 12, 1961, 36.

55. Arledge, *Roone*, 56.

56. Ibid., 55.

57. McKay, *My Wide World*, 173.

58. Arledge, *Roone*, 55.

59. McKay, *The Real McKay*, 256.

60. Arledge, *Roone*, 53; McKay, *My Wide World*, 259.

61. *ABC Wide World of Sports: The First 25 Years* (New York: NYLAC Network, 1987), 194; Martie Zad, "Jim McKay: Little Agony, No Defeats," *WP*, April 20, 1986, TW9.

62. "ABC-TV's SRO on Five Sports Series," *Variety*, December 12, 1962, 24.

63. Deane McGowan, "Sports All Over," *NYT*, February 11, 1962, 125.

64. The following decade, ABC made Eleanor Riger the first woman to hold a full producership and executive position in networks sports. It did not place strictures on which types of sports Riger, who was married to Robert Riger, could cover. See "Eleanor Riger to Fill ABC Sports Executive Post," *LAT*, March 6, 1973, F14.

65. "Covering America's Cup Land-Sea-Air Operation," *Broadcasting*, September 24, 1962, 58.

66. McKay, *My Wide World*, 175.

67. Melvyn P. Leffler, *For the Soul of Mankind: The United States, the Soviet Union, and the Cold War* (New York: Hill and Wang, 2007), 187; Glenn T. Seaborg, *Kennedy, Khrushchev, and the Test Ban* (Berkeley: University of California Press, 1981), 160; Paul Mandel, "How Harriman 'Earned a Dinner' from Khrushchev," *Life*, August 9, 1963, 28–30.

68. "A Candid Conversation with Roone Arledge," *Playboy*, October 1976, 86.

69. Arledge, *Roone*, 61. See also "On the Scene," *Playboy*, August 1968, 131.

70. Leffler, *For the Soul of Mankind*, 187; Seaborg, *Kennedy, Khrushchev, and the Test Ban*, 245.

71. Leffler, *For the Soul of Mankind*, 187.

72. In November 1963, ABC produced "The International Language of Sports," a special dedicated to the memory of John F. Kennedy that celebrated sport and television's diplomatic potential by serving as the first telecast to link three continents—Asia, Europe, and North America. ABC broadcast the special as part of *Wide World*'s November 30, 1963, episode. See "International Language of Sports" [Internal ABC Memo], November 29, 1963, LGC, Box 57, Folder 10.

73. Arledge, *Roone*, 105.

74. "A Sports Anthology That's a Best Seller," 60–61.

75. *Broadcasting*, June 28, 1965, 44–45.

76. *ABCs Wide World of Sports 1965* (New York: American Broadcasting Company, 1966), 105.

77. Ibid., 106; See also "Early Bird Satellite to Bring U.S.-Russia Track Meet Live to ABC Viewers July 31 and Aug. 1. [Press Release]," July 22, 1965, HHC, Box 15, Folder "Sports."

78. Arledge, *Roone*, 105.

79. *ABC Wide World of Sports 1965*, 8.

80. Ibid., 106.

81. Ibid.

82. "ABC Sports' Hot Sales Pacing," *Variety*, April 15, 1964, 28; "Tele Follow-Up Comment," *Variety*, March 24, 1965, 51.

83. Richard Hoffer, "Spanning the Globe for 30 Years," *SI*, May 27, 1991, 88–93, 88; Don Page, "Enough to Make 'Em Forget Roller Derby," *LAT*, June 18, 1964, B3.

84. Hal Humphrey, "Athletes Clear Cold War Hurdle," *LAT*, April 27, 1965, C12.

85. "What Is a Roone Arledge?," *TV Guide*, February 29, 1964, 8–10.

86. "Action on the *Wide World of Sports*," *LAT*, May 26, 1993, D4.

87. Turrini, "'It Was Communism versus the Free World,'" 439.

88. The US-USSR track meets resumed through 1985 with cancellations in 1972, 1979, 1980, 1983, and 1984.

89. "He Keeps Widening the World of Sports," *Broadcasting*, January 1, 1968, 73.

90. Derek Gregory, "Imaginative Geographies," *Progress in Human Geography* 19, no. 4 (1995): 447–85.

91. Chet Simmons, interview with the Archive of American Television, Academy of Television Arts & Sciences Foundation, December 16, 2008.

92. Neil Amdur, "Bowling's Appeal Continues to Grow," *NYT*, January 11, 1983, C18.

93. Larry Stewart, "Even a Basketball Junkie Can't Watch All the Games," *LAT*, February 24, 1984, D3.

94. *ABC Wide World of Sports 1964*, 43.

95. *ABC's Wide World of Sports Quiz Book* (New York: American Broadcasting Companies, 1974), 4.

96. "ABC Sports Take Up Twentyfold since Arledge Went into QB Slot," *Variety*, April 26, 1967, 169.

97. *ABC Wide World of Sports 1965*, 9; "A Sports Anthology That's a Best Seller," 60–61.

98. Buck Biggers and Chet Stover, "ABC Comes in a Winner with Wide World of Sports," *AC*, June 26, 1973, 2C; Charles Maher, "College Football Loses, College Basketball Wins," *LAT*, July 15, 1975, D1.

99. Rich Setlowe, "Laughtrack on the Sports Grab," *Variety*, January 17, 1968, 28.

100. Durslag, "Everything but the Pro-Am Clam-Digging Championship," 24–25.

CHAPTER THREE

1. Dennis Lewin, interview with author, December 14, 2015.

2. William O. Johnson, *All That Glitters Is Not Gold: The Olympic Game* (New York: Putnam, 1972), 32–33.

3. ABC briefly considered pooling the rights to televise Squaw Valley with CBS and NBC to offset production costs. Leonard Goldenson, Letter to Louis Cowan, February 17, 1959, LGC, Box 57, Folder 10. See also "NBC & CBS Frozen Out of Winter Olympics? ABC-TV's Firm Offer; What about That 3-Way Pool?," *Variety*, May 20, 1959, 21.

4. Oliver Treyz, Letter to Prentis Hale and Robert King, June 10, 1959, LGC, Box 57, Folder 10; Oliver Treyz, Letter to Prentis Hale, June 12, 1959, LGC, Box 57, Folder 10; Prentis Hale, Letter to Oliver Treyz, June 11, 1959, LGC, Box 57, Folder 10.

5. "Squaw Valley's Squawck Forcing Olympic Airing," *Variety*, July 22, 1959, 21.

6. "CBS-TV Olympics: It's More Prestige Than Sponsorship," *Variety*, January 20, 1960, 33; Allen Guttmann, *The Olympics: A History of the Modern Games* (Urbana: University of Illinois Press, 2002), 218.

7. Roone Arledge, *Roone: A Memoir* (New York: HarperCollins, 2003), 67; Neil Amdur, "The Television Dollars Foster New Perceptions," *NYT*, October 30, 1982, 9; *ABC Wide World of Sports Year 1964* (New York: American Broadcasting Company, 1965), 8.

8. Arledge, *Roone*, 95, 66.

9. Geoff Mason, interview with author, November 30, 2015; Curt Gowdy, *Cowboy at the Mike* (New York: Doubleday, 1966), 191.

10. "Inside Sports on the New ABC," *Variety*, January 29, 1964, 40–41.

11. "Winter Olympics on Tube," *AC*, September 30, 1963, 17A; ABC Sports Press Release, "Olympic Preview Provided," January 2, 1964, HHC, Box 15, Folder "Sports."

12. Douglas L. Battema, "Going for the Gold: A History of the Olympic Games and U.S. Television, 1956–1988" (PhD diss., University of Wisconsin, 2002), 139, 74; "ABC Sports' Hot Sales Pacing," *Variety*, April 15, 1964, 28.

13. "Covering Olympics an Olympic Feat," *Variety*, January 22, 1964, 32.

14. *ABC Wide World of Sports 1964*, 42.

15. Jim Spence, interview with author, March 25, 2016; *ABC Wide World of Sports 1964*, 68.

16. "Olympics Fascinate Jim McKay," *Louisville Courier Journal*, February 1, 1976, 2.

17. Arledge, *Roone*, 68.

18. "ABC-TV Olympics Seen by 70% of US Homes," *Variety*, March 4, 1964, 31; Jack Gould, "ABC Does Fine Job at Olympics," *AC*, February 6, 1964, 41; "Here's Your Ticket to Winter Olympics," *AC*, January 29, 1964, 10.

19. "Sports Hottest Network Item," *Broadcasting*, September 30, 1963, 56, 58–59.

20. Jack Gallivan, interview with author, January 12, 2016.

21. Arledge, *Roone*, 72; Jim Spence, *Up Close and Personal: The Inside Story of Network Television Sports* (New York: Atheneum, 1988), 166.

22. "Voorlooper," *New Yorker*, June 11, 1955, 26–27.

23. Howard Cosell, *Cosell* (Chicago: Playboy Press, 1973), 128, 139. Young did not deny these charges, but he claimed he was not alone in yelling profanities while Cosell recorded. Dick Young, "Puff Piece on Howie a Study in Half-Truths," *New York Post*, August 25, 1983, 72.

24. Howard Cosell, "Letter to Bill Whitehouse and Oliver Treyz," September 13, 1958, LGC, Box 42, Folder 18.

25. Cosell, *Cosell*, 141.

26. Frank Deford, "I've Won. I Beat Them," *SI*, August 8, 1983, 67–82, 77; Ron Powers, *Supertube: The Rise of Television Sports* (New York: Coward-McCann, 1984), 199–200.

27. David Maraniss, *When Pride Still Mattered: A Life of Vince Lombardi* (New York: Touchstone, 1999), 359.

28. Powers, *Supertube*, 202; Arledge, *Roone*, 92.

29. Gary Deeb, "ABC Boss Pulls Out Stops to Back His 'Unique' Cosell," *CT*, January 18, 1980, E5; Powers, *Supertube*, 202; Arledge, *Roone*, 93.

30. Myron Cope, "Would You Let This Man Interview You?," *SI*, March 13, 1967, 70–85, 71. "Tele Follow-Up Comment," *Variety*, August 9, 1967, 41.

31. Cosell, *Cosell*, 53; William O. Johnson, *The Super Spectator and the Electric Lilliputians* (New York: Little, Brown, 1971), 199; Tom Tolnay, "Cosell Backs FCC Check on R-TV Sports B'Casters," *Variety*, October 6, 1973, 4; William Barry Furlong, "Arledge: Olympics Will Go On," *Variety*, January 16, 1980, 56; Gary Deeb, "TV Sportscasters Sell Out Fans," *CT*, December 19, 1973, B16; Johnson, *Super Spectator*, 201.

32. Alex Haley, "Interview with Cassius Clay," *Playboy*, October 1964, 67–82, 190–92, 82. Ali initially, and very briefly, changed his name to Cassius X before settling on Muhammad Ali.

33. David Remnick, *King of the World: Muhammad Ali and the Rise of an American Hero* (New York: Vintage, 1999), 150; Cosell, *Cosell*, 182.

34. Cope, "Would You Let This Man Interview You?," 72; Tony Kornheiser, "He Told It Like It Was, Like Only He Could," *WP*, April 24, 1995, C1.

35. Floyd Patterson and Milton Gross, "I Want to Destroy Clay," *SI*, October 19, 1964, 42–61, 43.

36. Cosell, *Cosell*, 182; Roone Arledge, SportsCentury interview, January 25, 1999, RAP, Box 4, Folder 4, Series I.

37. "Tele-Follow Up." *Variety*, August 10, 1966, 42.

38. Michael Arkush, *The Fight of the Century: Ali vs. Frazier* (Hoboken, NJ: Wiley, 2008), 3; Randy Roberts, "The Wide World of Muhammad Ali: The Politics and Economics of Televised Boxing," in *Muhammad Ali: The People's Champ*, ed. Elliot J. Gorn (Urbana: University of Illinois Press, 1998), 24–53, 44; Red Smith, "Patrioteers," *New York Herald Tribune*, February 22, 1966, 28.

39. See Michael Ezra, "Main Bout Inc., Black Economic Power, and Professional Boxing: The Cancelled Muhammad Ali/Ernie Terrell Fight," *Journal of Sport History* 29, no. 2 (Fall 2002): 413–27, 414.

40. Gilbert Rogin, "A Battle of the Lionhearted," *SI*, April 11, 1966, 32–37, 37.

41. Dave Brady, "Home TV Carries Clay-Cooper Fight," *WP*, April 26, 1977, G3.

42. Cosell, *Cosell*, *189*.

43. "Terrell Has Song for Cassius Clay," *CD*, January 21, 1967, 15.

44. Tex Maule, "Cruel Ali with All the Skills," *SI*, February 13, 1967, 19–21, 19.

45. Don Page, "Sports Version of a Godzilla Movie," *LAT*, February 11, 1967, B2; Don Page, "Fight Sewage and the Clay Pipeline," *LAT*, September 10, 1966, B2.

46. Cosell, *Cosell*, 95; Lee D. Jenkins, "Ali (Clay) Real Champion, Cosell's Antics Fizzle," *Chicago Daily Defender*, February 13, 1967, 24.

47. Lawrence Laurent, "Cosell Starts a Second Season of Sharp, Acerbic Comments on Monday Football," *WP*, September 19, 1971, 9.

48. Jim Spence, interview with author, March 25, 2016.

49. Representative Fletcher Thompson Speaking on Muhammad Ali and Un-American Activities, 91st Cong., 1st Sess., *Congressional Record*, October 23, 1969, vol. 115, p. 31249.

50. Jack Pitman, "Sports Whirly as ABC's 'Fifth Arm,'" *Variety*, December 27, 1967, 25; Rick Setlowe, "Laughtrack on the Sports Grab," *Variety*, January 17, 1968, 28; Roone Arledge, SportsCentury interview, January 25, 1999, RAP, Box 4, Folder 4, Series I.

51. Dennis Lewin, interview with author, December 14, 2015.

52. "One Olympics Team Is Loaded with Professionals," *Variety*, February 7, 1968, 30.

53. Sugar, *The Thrill of Victory*, 216. See also "Detail 'Fronges' in ABC's Bid for Mex. City Olympics," *Variety*, May 4, 1966, 173.

54. "ABC Sports, Early Bird's Best TV Customer, Tunes Up for Olympics," *Variety*, July 20, 1966, 34; "ABC to Telesport 1968 Olympiada," *Backstage*, March 17, 1967, 3; Clay Gowran, "ABC Bets 5 Million on '68 Winter Olympics," *CT*, December 31, 1967, F12.

55. "ABC to Preview Winter Olympics," *LAT*, February 1, 1967, E14; "ABC Opens New Promo Avenue for Olympics," *Variety*, January 31, 1968, 38.

56. Clay Gowran, "ABC Strikes Gold with Daily Olympics Telecast," *CT*, February 16, 1968, B23.

57. *Winter Olympics '68* (New York: ABC Sports and Rutledge, 1967), 95. Beyond its own cameras, ABC had access to an additional eighty cameras used by other members of the broadcasting "pool." It hired thirty interpreters to ease communications among the diverse group of TV professionals on site—a group that included Mexico's Telesistema Mexicano, Japan's NHK, and Europe's EBU. Steve Cady, "Ole for the Olympics: TV Gets 'Em in Mexico," *AC*, October 5, 1968, 15A.

58. Clay Gowran, "ABC Offers Look at Olympic Athletes, Fears Trouble at Mexico City Games," *CT*, October 6, 1968, NWA1.

59. "Segment of Olympics Eyed by Bewitched," *Variety*, August 28, 1968, 33. The episode, originally titled "Samantha and Darrin Go to the Olympics," was intended to showcase the titular characters watching events while Darrin was on a business trip

in Mexico City. The script was originally drafted in 1968, but the episode was delayed until 1969. As a result, the program cut the parts relating to the Olympics and was retitled "Samantha and Darrin Go to Mexico City." AMP, Box 47, Folder 4.

60. Damion L. Thomas, *Globetrotting: African American Athletes and Cold War Politics* (Urbana: University of Illinois Press, 2012), 150.

61. Richard Hoffer, *Something in the Air: American Passion and Defiance in the 1968 Mexico City Olympics* (New York: Free Press, 2009), 52.

62. Harry Edwards, *The Revolt of the Black Athlete* (New York: Free Press, 1968), 65.

63. Milton Gross, "TV's Eye in the Storm Center," *New York Post*, February 16, 1968, 84; Amy Bass, *Not the Triumph but the Struggle: The 1968 Olympics and the Making of the Black Athlete* (Minneapolis: University of Minnesota Press, 2002), 147; "The Olympic Jolt: 'Hell No, Don't Go!,'" *Life*, March 15, 1968, 20–29.

64. Douglas Hartman, *Race, Culture, and the Revolt of the Black Olympic Athlete* (Chicago: University of Chicago Press, 2004), 128; Don Page, "ABC Eyes Olympic Action," *LAT*, October 15, 1968, F20; Don Page, "Olympics Fiesta with a Siesta," *LAT*, October 19, 1068, C2.

65. Kevin B. Witherspoon, *Before the Eyes of the World: Mexico and the 1968 Olympic Games* (Dekalb: Northern Illinois University Press, 2014), 105; Bass, *Not the Triumph but the Struggle*, 112–14.

66. Guttmann, *The Olympics*, 129–30; Brundage, "The Olympic Story," ABC, Box 355, Folder: "Book Notes and Sources: The Olympic Story, 1968 Olympics, Mexico City."

67. David A. Klatell and Norman Marcus, *Sports for Sale: Television, Money, and the Fans* (Oxford: Oxford University Press, 1988), 177; Clay Gowran, "ABC Offers Look at Olympic Athletes, Fears Trouble at Mexico City Games," *CT*, October 6, 1968, NWA1; Dennis Lewin, interview with author, December 14, 2015; Cosell, *Cosell*, 52–53.

68. Hoffer, *Something in the Air*, 177; Avery Brundage, *Olympic Dreams*, ABC, Box 196, Series 26-20-37; Brundage, "The Olympic Story," ABC, Box 355, Folder: "Book Notes and Sources: The Olympic Story, 1968 Olympics, Mexico City."

69. Arledge, *Roone*, 96–97.

70. Don Ohlmeyer, interview with author, January 27, 2016; Roone Arledge, SportsCentury interview, January 25, 1999, RAP, Box 4, Folder 4, Series I.

71. Edwards cited Cosell as one of the few members of the media establishment whom he trusted to treat African Americans fairly. See Edwards, *The Revolt of the Black Athlete*, 31.

72. Olympics/Black Power, ABC News Evening News, October 17, 1968, VUTNA, Record no. 129; Brent Musburger, "Bizarre Protest by Smith, Carlos Tarnishes Medals," *Chicago's American*, October 17, 1968, 43.

73. Olympics (Commentary), ABC Evening News, October 18, 1968, VUTNA, Record no. 147.

74. John Bloom, *There You Have It: The Life, Legacy, and Legend of Howard Cosell* (Amherst: University of Massachusetts Press, 2010), 85; Dave Kindred, *Sound*

and Fury: Two Powerful Lives, One Fateful Friendship (New York: Free Press, 2006), 64–65.

75. Hoffer, *Something in the Air*, 194.

76. Commentary (Black Equality), ABC Evening News, October 22, 1968, VUTNA, Record no. 207.

77. Thomas, *Globetrotting*, 161; Bill Greeley, "ABC Coverage of Mexico Games an Olympian TV Remote Achievement," *Variety*, October 23, 1968, 38; Cosell, *Cosell*, 71.

78. Commentary (Olympics), ABC Evening News, October 25, 1968, VUTNA, Record no. 262.

79. Cady, "Ole for the Olympics," 15A; Jack Gould, "Vietnam War Turned into Nightly Experience," *NYT*, February 5, 1968, 71; "Nixon a Sponsor of ABC Olympics," *Variety*, September 18, 1968, 35.

80. "ABC Playing Politics For & Aft Olympicasts," *Variety*, June 5, 1968, 25; Jerry Reigel, "ABC-TV Works Up Load of Logistics for $15-Mil Mex Olympic Coverage," *Variety*, June 12, 1968, 39.

81. Robert Gordon and Morgan Neville's documentary on Buckley and Vidal, *The Best of Enemies* (2015), uses a boxing ring bell sound effect to emphasize their on-air debates' similarity to an athletic duel.

82. Jack Gould, "The Coverage Set Records, Too," *NYT*, November 3, 1968, 141; Robert Lipsyte, "Mexico City and the Loss of Innocence," *NYT*, September 25, 1998, S16.

83. "Peace Buffaloed," *St. Petersburg Times*, October 30, 1970, 1C.

84. Gary Deeb, "ABC Cuts Away from Peace Theme at Halftime of College Grid in Buffalo," *Variety*, November 4, 1970, 29; "ABC-TV Censors Halftime Show," *WP*, October 30, 1970, A11.

85. "American Big Brother Censors," *Spectrum* (University of Buffalo), November 2, 1970; "Radicalism Comes to the Rotary," *Reporter* (University of Buffalo), November 5, 1970, 3.

86. "In re: Complaint of the Student Association of the State University of New York at Buffalo," Federal Communications Commission, Decision and Reports of the Federal Communications Commission of the United States, Second Series, 73-246, March 12, 1973, 510–21.

87. Lawrence Linderman, "A Candid Conversation with the Fustian Oracle of Sport," *Playboy*, May 1972, 75–94, 82; John Walker, "They Say I Never Played the Game," *CT*, September 18, 1971, B3.

88. Stephen R. Wenn, "Growing Pains: The Olympic Movement and Television," *Olympika: The International Journal of Olympic Studies* 4 (1995): 1–22, 15; Allen Guttmann, *The Games Must Go On: Avery Brundage and the Olympic Movement* (New York: Columbia University Press, 1983), 219.

89. Ernest Weatherall, "Austria's '76 Olympics, or, Howard on a Helicopter," *Variety*, March 6, 1974, 42.

90. Julian Rubinstein, "The Emperor of the Air," *NYT*, December 29, 2002, E36.

CHAPTER FOUR

1. Roone Arledge, *Roone: A Memoir* (New York: HarperCollins, 2003), 100.

2. *Monday Night Madness: The Very Best of* Monday Night Football (ABC Video, 1989).

3. Tim Brulia, "A Chronology of Pro Football on Television: Part 1," *The Coffin Corner* 26, no. 3 (2004): 20–24.

4. Tom Moore, interview with Archive of American Television, Academy of Television Arts & Sciences Foundation, January 3 and 31, 2003; Ronald A. Smith, *Play-by-Play: Radio, Television, and Big Time College Sport* (Baltimore: Johns Hopkins University Press, 2001), 97. See also Michael MacCambridge, *America's Game: The Epic Story of How Pro Football Captured a Nation* (New York: Random House, 2004), 276. When Congress approved the AFL-NFL merger in 1966, it wrote into the arrangement that the National Football League could not play games on Friday evenings during the high school season.

5. Jeff Davis, *Rozelle: Czar of the NFL* (New York: McGraw-Hill, 2008), 357.

6. "Monday Morning Quarterbacking by Affils. on ABC," *Variety*, May 28, 1969, 43.

7. Bruce Berman, "TV Sports Auteurs," *Film Comment*, March–April 1976, 34–36.

8. Victoria E. Johnson, *"Monday Night Football*: Brand Identity," in *How to Watch Television*, ed. Ethan Thompson and Jason Mittell (New York: New York University Press, 2013), 262–70, 262.

9. Christine Acham, *Revolution Televised: Prime Time and the Struggle for Black Power* (Minneapolis: University of Minnesota Press, 2005); Donald Bogle, *Prime Time Blues: African Americans on Network Television* (New York: Farrar, Straus and Giroux, 2001); Herman Gray, *Watching Race: Television and the Struggle for Blackness* (Minneapolis: University of Minnesota Press, 1995).

10. Don Ohlmeyer, interview with author, January 27, 2016.

11. William O. Johnson, *The Super Spectator and the Electric Lilliputians* (New York: Little, Brown, 1971), 140; Wesley Hyatt, *Kicking Off the Week: A History of Monday Night Television on ABC Television, 1970–2005* (Jefferson, NC: MacFarland, 2007), 32.

12. Charles Maher, "The Next Problem," *LAT*, March 28, 1969, G2.

13. Richard Levine, "Wide World of News," *New Times*, January 23, 1978, 18; Val Adams, "Carson Refuses to Tape a Show," *NYT*, September 7, 1968, 59.

14. Maher, "The Next Problem," G2.

15. Davis, *Rozelle*, 360.

16. Hughes, in fact, attempted to purchase a controlling interested in ABC shortly before purchasing Hughes Sports Network. Industry commentators suspected the billionaire eventually aborted his pursuit because the acquisition would require the infamous recluse to appear before Congress.

17. Dave Brady, "Hughes Mines Pay-TV Gold," *WP*, March 23, 1969, 38; Dave Brady, "Hughes Plunges into TV, to Woo Major Sports," *BG*, March 24, 1969, 1.

18. Johnson, *Super Spectator*, 114; Arledge, *Roone*, 102.

19. "Sports Ready to Collect on Pay TV," *WP*, June 13, 1969, D1.

20. Roone Arledge, Letter to Pete Rozelle, RAP, Box 34, Folder 12.

21. "ABC-TV to Televise Regular Monday Night Football Games of the National Football League" (Press Release), May 27, 1969, RAP, Box 34, Folder 12; "Monday Night at the Stadium," *Broadcasting*, June 2, 1969, 66; Paul Jones, "Movies Made Just for TV Planned on ABC This Fall," *AC*, September 4, 1969, 12B.

22. Smith, *Play-by-Play*, 97, 101, 109; Arledge, Letter to Walter Byers, November 24, 1968, Walter Byers Papers, Vol. 47, Folder "TV: General 9/68–12/68," NCAA Headquarters, Indianapolis, IN.

23. Don Ohlmeyer, interview with author, January 27, 2016.

24. "With Apologies to the American Housewife, ABC Presents *Monday Night Football*," *Variety*, March 18, 1970, 40–41.

25. William N. Wallace, "It's a Seller's Market in Football TV," *NYT*, May 28, 1969, 50; Jerry Shnay, "Football Fans Get a Bonus from ABC," *CT*, June 9, 1969, A9.

26. Marc Gunther and Bill Carter, *Monday Night Mayhem: The Inside Story of ABC's* Monday Night Football (New York: Beech Tree Books, 1988), 35; Edwin Shrake, "What Are They Doing with the Sacred Game of Pro Football?," *SI*, October 25, 1971, 96–106.

27. Gary Deeb, "On the Defensive," *CT*, January 18, 1980, E5.

28. Howard Cosell, *Cosell* (Chicago: Playboy Press, 1973), 299.

29. Davis, *Rozelle*, 367.

30. "ABC Giving Deluxe Coverage to Primetime Grid with 9-Camera Setup," *Variety*, August 19, 1970, 32.

31. Robert Lipsyte, "One of a Kind in a Booth of His Own," *NYT*, April 24, 1995, C1.

32. Arledge, Letter to Joe Namath, September 22, 1970, RAP, Box 34, Folder 12.

33. Dan Jenkins, Letter to Roone Arledge, August 29, 1970, RAP, Box 34, Folder 12; Roone Arledge, Letter to Dan Jenkins," September 9, 1970, RAP, Box 34, Folder 12; Jim Murray, "An Insult to the Game," *LAT*, October 9, 1970, D1; Leonard H. Goldenson and Marvin J. Wolf, *Beating the Odds* (New York: Charles Scribner's Sons, 1991), 210.

34. Richard Sandomir, "25 Years Later, Monday Night Is a Fall Classic," *NYT*, September 4, 1994, S13; Arledge, *Roone*, 115.

35. Donald Freeman, "Monday Night Football Proved to Be a Big Hit," *San Diego Union*, December 16, 1970, A18.

36. Shrake, "What Are They Doing with the Sacred Game of Pro Football?," D1.

37. Don Ohlmeyer, interview with author, January 27, 2016.

38. Jack Craig, "SporTView," *SN*, December 29, 1973, 15.

39. Don Ohlmeyer, interview with author, January 27, 2016.

40. Leonard Shapiro, "Halftime Highlights Got You Down? Don't Blame Howard," *WP*, November 29, 1981, TV5; Travis Vogan, *Keepers of the Flame: NFL Films and the Rise of Sports Media* (Urbana: University of Illinois Press, 2014), 147–49.

41. Dorrance Smith, interview with author, January 29, 2016.

42. Shrake, "What Are They Doing with the Sacred Game of Pro Football?," 98; Cosell, *Cosell*, 344; Charles Maher, "The TV Sports Game," *LAT*, February 19, 1973, E1.

43. Percy Shain, "CBS Sends Archie, Rhoda against Monday Night Football," *BG*, June 9, 1975, 38.

44. "1975 NCAA Television Schedule Features 2 Monday Night Games," *ADW*, July 20, 1975, 6.

45. See William O. Johnson, "The Monday Night Alternative," *SI*, December 11, 1978, 70.

46. Dave Kindred, *Sound and Fury: Two Powerful Lives, One Fateful Friendship* (New York: Free Press, 2006), 155.

47. Mark Ribowsky, *Howard Cosell: The Man, the Myth, and the Transformation of American Sports* (New York: Norton, 2011), 213.

48. Richard C. Crepeau, *NFL Football: A History of America's New Favorite Pastime* (Urbana: University of Illinois Press, 2014), 65; Michael Lomax, "The African American Experience in Professional Football," *Journal of Social History* 33, no. 1 (Autumn 1999): 166–70.

49. Howard Cosell with Peter Bonventre, *I Never Played the Game* (New York: William Morrow, 1985), 129–30.

50. Douglas Gomery, "*Brian's Song*: Television, Hollywood, and the Evolution of the Movie Made for TV," in *Why Docudrama? Fact-Fiction on Film and TV*, ed. Alan Rosenthal (Carbondale: Southern Illinois University Press, 1999), 78–100, 84.

51. William Blinn, *Brian's Song* (New York: Bantam, 1972), 1; Cecil Smith, "Jimmy Caan Right for *Brian's Song*," *LAT*, November 29, 1971, 25.

52. More explicitly than *Brian's Song*, ABC complemented *Monday Night* with biopics and documentaries that celebrated NFL stars. It aired the Vince Lombardi film *Legend in Granite: The Vince Lombardi Story*, which starred Ernest Borgnine as the legendary coach, in December 1973. The following fall, ABC aired the George Romero O. J. Simpson documentary, *Juice on the Loose*. Both productions premiered in prime time during the NFL season.

53. Gale Sayers and Al Silverman, *I Am Third* (New York: Viking, 1970), 68.

54. Ibid., 62.

55. John J. O'Connor, "TV: Love Was Link to Tuesday and Wednesday," *NYT*, December 3, 1971, 83; Phil Casey, "Poignancy in Football," *WP*, November 20, 1971, B5; Charles Champlin, "TV Movies vs. Movie Movies: There Is a Difference," *LAT*, November 30, 1980, R2.

56. Michael McKenna, *The ABC Movie of the Week: Big Movies for the Small Screen* (Lanham, MD: Scarecrow Press, 2013), 51; William Blinn, interview with Archive of American Television, Academy of Television Arts & Sciences Foundation, October 7, 2005.

57. Howell Raines, "Lady Sings the Blues for All, Says Billy Dee Williams," *AC*, October 28, 1972, 3T; Don Page, "Delicate Beauty in *Brian's Song*," *LAT*, November 30, 1971, E19; Jim Murray, "A Game of Life," *LAT*, November 30, 1971, D1.

58. A. S. "Doc" Young, "Good Morning Sports," *CD*, December 1, 1971, 28; Howie Evans, "TV Portrays Sayers and Piccolo Friendship," *New York Amsterdam News,* November 27, 1971, D7. See also Marion Jackson, "Sports of the World," *ADW*, November 14, 1971, 10; Bill Lane, "People, Places 'n' Situwayshuns," *Los Angeles Sentinel*, November 25, 1971, B2A.

59. "Brian's Song Scores," *Broadcasting*, December 20, 1971, 42; Gomery, *"Brian's Song,"* 79; "Made for TV Movies Find Big Ratings," *WP*, April 9, 1972, TC27.

60. *Congressional Record*, December 15, 1971, 47230; John J. O'Connor, "Brian's Song Is Proving to Be a Film Phenomenon," *NYT*, January 29, 1972, 91.

61. Gomery, *"Brian's Song,"* 79. See also Elayne Rapping, *The Movie of the Week: Private Stories, Public Events* (Minneapolis: University of Minnesota Press, 1992).

62. Gomery, *"Brian's Song,"* 79.

64. O'Connor, "Brian's Song Is Proving to Be Film Phenomenon," 92; John J. O'Connor, "The Eagle, the Flag, and the Football," *NYT*, December 12, 1971, D23.

65. "Billy Dee Williams Is Gale Sayers in ABC Weekend Movie *Brian's Song*," *CD*, November 13, 1971, 25.

66. "Dandy Don Jilts Howard for NBC," *BG*, March 7, 1974, 59; Gary Deeb, "NBC 'Blandies' Award Dandy Don," *CT*, July 18, 1974, B7; Dan Lewis, "Two Big Egos, One Small Booth," *TV Week* (*The Sunday Record*), July 28, 1974, 2. At NBC, Meredith appeared sporadically in the TV drama *Police Story* (1973–78) and had a starring role in the TV movie *Banjo Hackett: Roamin' Free* (1976).

67. "The Hammer," *Life*, January 13, 1967, 12; Charles Maher, "The Hammer," *LAT*, July 14, 1974, C1.

68. Maher, "The Hammer."

69. Dave Anderson, "Three the Hard Way for the Hammer," *NYT*, July 9, 1974, 45.

70. James P. Murray, "Sportscasters Finally Making Progress," *New York Amsterdam News*, July 13, 1974, D13.

71. "Fred Williamson Joins Monday Night Football," *ADW*, July 16, 1974, 2; Fred Williamson, interview with author, January 25, 2016.

72. Gunther and Carter, *Monday Night Mayhem*, 163; Maher, "The Hammer," C1.

73. Jack Hurst, "Billy Dee Williams: The Once and Future King," *CT*, March 6, 1977, H20.

74. Gunther and Carter, *Monday Night Mayhem*, 166; Jack Craig, "SporT View," *SN*, July 27, 1974, 65; Gary Deeb, "The Hammer Could Nail ABC," *CT*, July 10, 1974, A4.

75. Fred Williamson, interview with author, January 25, 2016.

76. When Meredith rejoined *Monday Night*, ABC gave him a contract that guaranteed the ability to do some acting.

77. ABC started using *Monday Night*'s time slot beyond the football season in 1972 with a short-lived Monday evening sports special that Cosell and McKay cohosted. "ABC Sports Specials," *Variety*, March 1, 1972, 34.

78. Gary Deeb, "Baseball Fans Left Up in Air by ABC," *CT*, October 6, 1978, E5; Spence, *Up Close and Personal*, 15; Frank Swertlow, "Kuhn-Cosell Feud Threatens ABC's Baseball Deal," *TV Guide*, December 11, 1976, A3.

79. Frank Beerman, "ABC Scoops Up Baseball: Monday Sports All Year," *Variety*, March 12, 1975, 44.

80. Helen Taylor, "'The Griot from Tennessee': The Saga of Alex Haley's *Roots*," *Critical Quarterly* 37, no. 2 (1995): 46–62, 48; "Roots Biggest Event in TV History," *Broadcasting*, January 31, 1977, 10.

81. Leslie Fishbein, "*Roots*: Docudrama and the Interpretation of History," in *Why Docudrama? Fact-Fiction on Film and TV*, ed. Alan Rosenthal (Carbondale: Southern Illinois University Press, 1999), 271–95, 272.

82. See Matthew F. Delmont, *Making Roots: A Nation Captivated* (Berkeley: University of California Press, 2016), 129; William Marmon, "Why Roots Hit Home," *Time*, February 14, 1977, 69–75.

83. Paul Jones, "Roots Helps Other ABC Shows," *AC*, February 4, 1977, 3C; Gary Deeb, "NBC Plugs for Night Super Bowl in Prime Time," *CT*, June 22, 1976, C1.

84. Cecil Smith, "Roots Reaps Vast Harvest," *LAT*, February 1, 1977, G1; Quinlan, *Inside ABC*, 228; Huntington Williams, *Beyond Control: ABC and the Fate of the Networks* (New York: Atheneum, 1989), 80.

85. Fishbein, "*Roots*: Docudrama and the Interpretation of History," 273; Timothy Havens, *Black Television Travels: African American Media around the Globe* (New York: New York University Press, 2013), 54; Gary Deeb, "Roots TV Version Falls Prey to Big Bucks, Super Hype, and Prime Time," *CT*, January 24, 1977, A13; Robert E. Stephens, "The Role of Educational Media in Minority-Related Education," *Negro Educational Review* 29 (1978): 36; Ruth A. Protinsky and Terry M. Wildman, "*Roots*: Reflections from the Classroom," *Journal of Negro Education* 48, no. 2 (1979): 171–81; Alison Landsberg, *Prosthetic Memory: The Transformation of American Remembrance in the Age of Mass Culture* (New York: Columbia University Press, 2004), 101–6.

86. Delmont, *Making Roots*, 120–24. In addition to Moses, the production hired Joseph Wilcots, an African American, as director of photography.

87. Chuck Stone, "Roots: An Electronic Orgy in White Guilt," *Black Scholar*, May 1977, 39–40, 39; Stanley O. Williford, "Hollywood Has Produced Pablum," *LAT*, January 31, 1977, C5; see David C. Berliner, "Silverman: High Gear at NBC," *WP*, February 1, 1977, B1; Richard Schickel, "Viewpoint: Middlebrow Mandingo," *Time*, January 24, 1977, 56.

88. Lauren R. Tucker and Hemant Shah, "Race and the Transformation of Culture: The Making of the Television Miniseries *Roots*," *Critical Studies in Mass Communication* 9 (December 1992): 325–36, 335; Stuart Byron, "Family Plot," *Film Comment* 13, no. 2 (March–April 1977): 31.

89. David L. Wolper and Quincy Troupe, *The Inside Story of TV's* Roots (New York: Warner Books, 1978), 148, 48.

CHAPTER FIVE

1. Leonard H. Goldenson and Marvin J. Wolf, *Beating the Odds* (New York: Charles Scribner's Sons, 1991), 399.

2. Huntington Williams, *Beyond Control: ABC and the Fate of the Networks* (New York: Atheneum, 1989), 150.

3. Gwilym S. Brown, "TV Talk," *SI*, January 24, 1972, 8.

4. William O. Johnson, *The Super Spectator and the Electric Lilliputians* (New York: Little, Brown, 1971), 165.

5. Stephen R. Wenn, "A History of the International Olympic Committee and Television, 1936–1980" (PhD diss., Penn State University, 1993), 176; "Television Contract OOC-ABC," April 7, 1971, ABC, Box 204, Series 26-20-37b.

6. Bert Sugar, *The Thrill of Victory: The Inside Story of ABC Sports* (New York: Hawthorn, 1978), 223; *The Olympics* (New York: ABC Sports and Rutledge Books, 1972), 92; "'Carrying the Torch'—ABC Style," *Television/Radio Age*, August 21, 1972, 35; Don Page, "ABC to Deliver Summer Olympic Games from Germany," *LAT*, August 20, 1972, U1.

7. Isabelle Hall, "Networks' Prime Time Programming Curbed," *AC*, May 8, 1970, 3C.

8. "Prime-Time Waivers Settled on by FCC," *Broadcasting*, October 11, 1971, 8; "FCC's Yeas & Nays on Access Rule Waiver Favors, Mostly over Sports," *Variety*, October 13, 1971, 28; "One Sure Loser in the Olympics," *Broadcasting*, June 5, 1972, 46; "ABC Thrown for Loss on Access Bid Re Olympics," *Variety*, June 14, 1972, 29; "FCC Nixes Primetime Waiver for Olympics," *Variety*, May 24, 1972, 35; Robert J. Samuelson, "Olympic TV Battle Rages," *WP*, June 7, 1972, D3.

9. Earl Calloway, "ABC-Television Provides $20-Million for Olympic Games Telecast," *CD*, June 24, 1972, 22; Les Brown, "FCC: Is It Rule or Ruin?," *Variety*, January 20, 1971, 1.

10. John Martin, interview with author, December 15, 2015.

11. Bill Roberts, "Artist LeRoy Neiman: From Poverty to Playboy," *Indianapolis News*, November 23, 1972. See also Travis Vogan, "LeRoy Neiman and the Art of Network Sports Television," *American Art* 30, no. 3 (Fall 2016): 54–75.

12. *ABC Sports Olympic Journal*, November 1983 1, LA84; *The Olympics*, 92.

13. Jim McKay, *My Wide World* (New York: Macmillan, 1973), 120–21; Don Ohlmeyer, interview with author, August 6, 2016; *ABC Sports Olympic Journal*, November 1983, 2; "Summer Olympics," *NYT*, August 27, 1972, S5.

14. Anticipating a lucrative and Cold War–laden championship game between the United States and the Soviet Union, ABC persuaded the organizing committee to schedule the men's basketball final to coincide with prime time on the East Coast. The game did not begin until midnight in Munich.

15. "Weekend Olympics Top Timeslots but Trail Pair of Specs," *Variety*, September 13, 1972, 40; John J. O'Connor, "Olympic Games Make a Spectacular Show—Coverage of Events Is Technically Flawless," *NYT*, 30 August 1972, 75; Bill Greeley,

"17 Nights of Olympics May Give ABC Running Start on New Season," *Variety*, May 17, 1972, 32.

16. Greeley, "17 Nights of Olympics May Give ABC Running Start on New Season," 32.

17. See David Clay Large, *Munich 1972: Tragedy, Terror and Triumph at the Olympic Games* (New York: Rowman and Littlefield, 2012), 3.

18. Allen Guttmann, *The Olympics: A History of the Modern Games* (Urbana: University of Illinois Press, 2002), 3.

19. Roone Arledge, *Roone: A Memoir* (New York: HarperCollins, 2003), 128; Marc Gunther, *The House That Roone Built: The Inside Story of ABC News* (New York: Little Brown, 1994), 10.

20. William Taaffe, "You Can't Keep Him Down on the Farm," *SI*, July 18, 1984, 286–98, 286.

21. Joe Garner, *Stay Tuned: Television's Unforgettable Moments* (Kansas City, MO: Andrews McMeel, 2002), 184.

22. Goldenson and Wolf, *Beating the Odds*, 200.

23. Howard Cosell, *Cosell* (Chicago: Playboy Press, 1973), 1; Arledge, *Roone*, 137; Large, *Munich 1972*, 230; Mark Ribowsky, *Howard Cosell: The Man, the Myth, and the Transformation of American Sports* (New York: Norton, 2011), 268.

24. "ABC's Grim TV 'First,'" *Newsweek*, September 18, 1972, 67–68; "CBS and ABC Clash on Pooling of Satellite at Olympic Village," *Variety*, September 6, 1972, 31; Arledge SportsCentury interview, January 25, 1999, RAP, Box 4, Folder 4, Series I.

25. "A Story ABC 'Owned,'" *Variety*, September 6, 1972, 31.

26. "From Triumph to Tragedy in TV Coverage of Munich Olympics," *Broadcasting*, September 11, 1972, 22–23.

27. Simon Reeve, *One Day in September: The Full Story of the 1972 Munich Olympics Massacre and the Israeli Revenge Operation "Wrath of God"* (New York: Arcade, 2000), 124.

28. Don Ohlmeyer, interview with author, January 27, 2016.

29. Ibid.

30. Jim McKay, interview with the Archive of American Television, Academy of Television Arts & Sciences Foundation, October 28, 1998.

31. Guttmann, *The Olympics*, 140; Jim Murray, "Blood on Olympus," *LAT*, September 7, 1972, E1; Red Smith, "Again the Sandbox," *NYT*, September 8, 1972, 21; Cosell, *Cosell*, 14.

32. Geoff Mason, interview with author, January 22, 2016.

33. Les Brown, "Olympics Boost Web's Stature," *Variety*, September 6, 1972, 31; Ted Stevens, *Congressional Record*, September 19, 1972, 31164–65.

34. "Brought to You By . . .," *Time*, July 19, 1976, 62.

35. Dave Brady, "McKay's Wide World Includes Double Emmy," *WP*, May 24, 1973, D10.

36. "A Story ABC 'Owned,'" *Variety*, September 6, 1972, 31; Marc Gunther and Bill Carter, *Monday Night Mayhem: The Inside Story of ABC's* Monday Night

Football (New York: Beech Tree Books, 1988), 108; Reeve, *One Day in September*, 260; Les Margulies, "ABC Bid Avenges Loss of '80 Games," *LAT*, September 27, 1979, 31.

37. Sally Bedell, *Up the Tube: Prime-Time TV and the Silverman Years* (New York: Viking Press, 1981), 123.

38. Tony Schwartz, "ABC Had Adviser Known as a 'Psychic,'" *NYT*, March 13, 1981, C32; Bedell, *Up the Tube*, 115.

39. Bedell, *Up the Tube*, xiv; "The Man with the Golden Gut: Programmer Fred Silverman Has Made ABC No. 1," *Time*, September 5, 1977, 46–52; "ABC's Stock Rise on Drafting Silverman," *Variety*, May 28, 1975, 1.

40. Elana Levine, *Wallowing in Sex: The New Sexual Culture of 1970s Television* (Durham, NC: Duke University Press, 2007), 32; "Redd Foxx Jumps Over to ABC as Silverman Grabs Star Power," *Variety*, April 14, 1976, 57.

41. Gunther, *The House That Roone Built*, 24; David Frost, "Q&A with Roone Arledge," *Panorama*, September 1980, 24–28, 25; John J. O'Connor, "TV: Olympics as Entertainment and Selling Game," *NYT*, February 12, 1976, 47.

42. Frost, "Q&A with Roone Arledge," 25.

43. "ABC Radio Webs' Olympic Features as Ad-Less Inserts," *Variety*, June 30, 1976, 50.

44. ABC further reflected on the 1972 massacre after its 1976 Olympics coverage ended with the made-for-TV movie *21 Hours in Munich*, which starred William Holden as Munich police chief Manfred Schreiber. The film was framed with narration by an uncredited Jim McKay. The following year, ABC aired the telefilm *Murder at the World Series*, which centers on a disgruntled former baseball player who vows to exact revenge on the team that cut him by taking as hostage and killing a woman he believes is the wife of the player who replaced him. Reflecting made-for-TV movies' tendency to engage current events, the film's use of a mega sporting event as the backdrop of a violent crisis exploits the new environment Munich ushered in.

45. Frank Deford, "High Wide and Handsome," *SI*, August 2, 1976, 14–17.

46. "ABC-TV Wins in Prime Time and in a Big Way," *Broadcasting*, April 25, 1977, 38–39.

47. Goldenson and Wolf, *Beating the Odds*, 366; "The Man with the Golden Gut," 46.

48. Silverman reportedly campaigned for the position Arledge received. He left ABC to become president and CEO of NBC in 1978. See Bedell, *Up the Tube*, 218; "Arledge Deal Prexy ABC News Sports," *Back Stage*, May 6, 1977, 1; Les Brown, "Arledge Will Head ABC News; Disclaims Theatrical Flourishes," *NYT*, May 3, 1977, 81.

49. Gunther, *The House That Roone Built*, 24–25; Kay Gardella, "Roone Arledge at Crossroads," *New York Daily News*, October 12, 1976, 68; Jane Hall, "The Arledge Solution," *LAT*, January 5, 1992, G9.

50. Dorrance Smith, interview with author, January 29, 2016; Goldenson and Wolf, *Beating the Odds*, 399; Desmond Smith, "The Wide World of Roone Arledge," *NYT*, February 24, 1980, SM10.

51. Goldenson and Wolf, *Beating the Odds*, 274.

52. Tom Rosenstiel, *Strange Bedfellows: How Television and the Presidential Candidates Changed American Politics* (New York: Hyperion, 1994), 25; Gunther, *The House That Roone Built*, 25; "ABC's Wider World of News," *Time*, May 16, 1977, 79.

53. Dennis Lewin, interview with author, December 14, 2015, and September 7, 2016.

54. John Martin, interview with author, December 15, 2015.

55. Gunther, *The House That Roone Built*, 28; Jane Hall, "The Arledge Solution," *LAT*, January 5, 1992, G9.

56. See Marvin Kitman, "Rooneing the News," *New Leader*, April 10, 1978, 25–26.

57. Jeff Greenfield, "The Showdown at ABC News," *NYT*, February 13, 1977, SM9; see Charles Ponce de Leon, *That's the Way It Is: A History of Television News in America* (Chicago: University of Chicago Press, 2015), 141.

58. Tony Schwartz, "Arledge Fights, Yet Revels in, His Outsider Status," *NYT*, December 12, 1981, 53; Les Brown, "At ABC, the Winds of Change Are Blowing," *NYT*, March 4, 1977, 7.

59. Barbara Matusow, *The Evening Stars: The Making of a Network News Anchor* (Boston: Houghton Mifflin, 1983), 227.

60. Ibid., 232; Ted Koppel and Kyle Gibson, *Nightline: History in the Making and the Making of Television* (New York: Times Books, 1996), 16.

61. Richard Levine, "Arledge on Arledge," Alicia Patterson Foundation, RAP, Box 1, Folder 1, Series I; Ponce de Leon, *That's the Way It Is*, 145; John Dempsey, "Arledge Era May Boost News Salaries," *Variety*, August 24, 1977, 37.

62. Judy Flander, "Barbara Walters: No Vapors, Frills or Hostility," *Washington Star*, May 15, 1977, 13G–14G; John J. O'Connor, "ABC Is the Most Active New Game in Town," *NYT*, April 9, 1979, 31–32; "ABC News Opens Door to Documentary Makers," *Broadcasting*, January 29, 1979, 59.

63. "Going In: A Sampler of Arledgisms on TV News," *Broadcasting*, May 9, 1977, 30; "Roone Arledge and the Sherpas of ABC News," *Broadcasting*, May 9, 1977, 23.

64. Roone Arledge, Memo to ABC Sports Staff, July 8, 1977, LNP, Box 15, Folder IIB. Cosell was reportedly bitter toward Arledge for never allowing him to try his hand at anchoring the evening news. "I'd won another black mark in his secret book of grievances," Arledge later wrote of Cosell's anger. Arledge, *Roone*, 189; "Roone at the Top," *Newsweek*, May 16, 1977, 103–4, 104.

65. Schwartz, "Arledge Fights, Yet Revels in, His Outsider Status," 53.

66. Richard Levine, "Arledge on Arledge," Alicia Patterson Foundation, RAP, Box 1, Folder 1, Series I.

67. Roger Goodman, interview with author, December 15, 2015.

68. Sterling Quinlan, *Inside ABC: American Broadcasting Company's Rise to Power* (New York: Hastings House, 1979), 250; Gunther, *The House That Roone Built*, 70; Ellen Graham, "Serious Competitor: ABC Improves but Ratings Still Lag under Arledge Regime," *WSJ*, April 26, 1978, 1.

69. Tom Buckley, "Wide World of News," *Horizon*, September 1978, 66–70; Tom Link, "Roone Arledge," Academy of Television Arts and Sciences, RAP, Box 2, Folder 13, Series I.

70. ABC News Press Release, April 19, 1978, RAP, Box 1, Folder 4, Series I.

71. Susan Paynter, "Arledge's Goal: Better Newscasts," *Seattle Post-Intelligencer*, January 17, 1978, A11.

72. Richard Levine, "Arledge on Arledge," Alicia Patterson Foundation, RAP, Box 1, Folder 1, Series I; Sally Bedell, "Can Roone Make the Double Play at ABC?," *TV Guide*, June 10, 1978, 7–10; "Roone at the Top," 103–4; "Going In," 30.

73. Tom Shales, "Follow the Bouncing News with ABC," *WP*, July 11, 1978, C1.

74. Garry Trudeau, *Doonesbury*, November 7, 1977. Trudeau published two other comic strips satirizing ABC News' frenetic style the same month.

75. Richard F. Shepard, "Howard K. Smith Resigns from ABC," *NYT*, April 20, 1979, C30; Sally Bedell, "Escalating the War on the News Front," *TV Guide*, June 17, 1978, 27–34, 32. Cronkite eventually became an indirect victim of ABC's practices after Arledge began to pursue CBS's Dan Rather. CBS gave Rather—Cronkite's heir apparent—a new contract and pressured Cronkite to speed up his retirement. See Ponce de Leon, *That's the Way It Is*, 147.

76. Bill Carter, "The Impresario," Publication Unknown, June 1980, 34–35, RAP, Box 1, Folder 7, Series I.

77. Rick Kaplan, interview with author, January 11, 2016.

78. Arledge, *Roone*, 20; Jeff Denberg, "The High Priest of Prime Time," *AC*, January 6, 1980, 1E.

79. Kaplan, interview with author, January 11, 2016.

80. Howard Rosenberg, "Frosty Pomp at Lake Placid," *LAT*, February 15, 1980, H19; "Olympics and Iran Cause an Overload for ABC Latenight," *Variety*, February 13, 1980, 190.

81. Harry F. Waters, Lucy Howard, and George Hackett, "The Unflappable Koppel," *Newsweek*, February 16, 1981, 75.

82. Roger Goodman, interview with author, December 19, 2015.

CHAPTER SIX

1. Joan Ryan, "Only an Attack by Alligators Could Make Superstars Sporting," *WP*, February 25, 1977, D1.

2. Leonard Shapiro, "Superstars & the Sunday TVTKO," *WP*, February 14, 1982, TV3.

3. "NBA Back on Network," *Broadcasting*, May 11, 1964, 68.

4. Roone Arledge, *Roone: A Memoir* (New York: HarperCollins, 2003), 141.

5. "A Candid Conversation with Roone Arledge," *Playboy*, October 1976, 80.

6. "CBS Gets Pro Basketball; ABC Cries Foul," *Variety*, March 14, 1973, 39; Charles Maher, "ABC Sues CBS over TV Rights," *LAT*, June 2, 1973, D1; "ABC

Loses Basketball Suit," *Broadcasting*, August 6, 1973, 23; David Halberstam, *The Breaks of the Game* (New York: Ballantine Books, 1981), 246.

7. Arledge, *Roone*, 141. ABC first aired *The Superstars* as a two-hour special in February 1973 that led in to the network's NBA coverage. It rebooted it as a weekly series to compete against CBS's NBA coverage the following winter. Former Olympic figure skater and ABC commentator Dick Button developed the idea for *Superstars* decades before ABC picked it up. "In 1949, I was given the Sullivan Award as the best amateur athlete in the country," he said. "And yet, when I was in high school, there were 12 boys in my school, and I'd say 10 of them were better athletes than I was. So the question always with me was, who really is America's best athlete?" See Shapiro, "Superstars & the Sunday TV TKO," TV3.

8. Jack Craig, "SporTView," *SN*, February 23, 1974, 22; Halberstam, *The Breaks of the Game*, 248; David A. Klatell and Norman Marcus, *Sports for Sale: Television, Money, and the Fans* (Oxford: Oxford University Press, 1988), 155.

9. *Sports Illustrated*'s William Leggett coined the term *TrashSports*. See "Trash-Sport Should Be Canned," *SI*, April 18, 1977, 45; Lee Winfrey, "Father of All Trashsports," *BG*, January 11, 1979, 35; Don Kowet, "The Great TV Sports Hype," *TV Guide*, October 22, 1977, 28–31. Florida governor Reubin Askew was so thrilled that the program chose to stage its initial competitions in the Gulf Coast town of Rotonda that he issued a special proclamation declaring a statewide "Superstar Week" surrounding the event. See Reubin Askew," Proclamation: State of Florida Executive Department," January 12, 1973, MMP.

10. Frank Jacobs, "When TV Makes Full Use of Howard Cosell," *Mad* 150 (April 1972): 25–28.

11. Howard Cosell, *Cosell* (Chicago: Playboy Press, 1963), 360.

12. Frank Beerman, "Only the Best for Ol' Blue Eyes: Good Sport Arledge to Produce," *Variety*, August 14, 1974, 31, 41.

13. Les Brown, "Cosell TV Show Starts Tonight," *NYT*, September 20, 1975, 58.

14. Marc Gunther and Bill Carter, *Monday Night Mayhem: The Inside Story of ABC's Monday Night Football* (New York: Beech Tree Books, 1988), 185; Brown, "Cosell TV Show Starts Tonight," 58.

15. "Cosell Variety Has New Format," *Cincinnati Inquirer*, June 28, 1975, 27.

16. Robert Lipsyte, *An Accidental Sportswriter: A Memoir* (New York: Harper-Collins, 2011), 87.

17. James Bawden, "Cosell Given Variety Show in Television," *Ottawa Citizen*, August 25, 1975, B2; Jack Anderson, "Humble Howard Outlines His Variety Show Format," *CT*, July 29, 1975, B10.

18. Sally Bedell, *Up the Tube: Prime-Time TV and the Silverman Years* (New York: Viking Press, 1981), 119; "A Candid Conversation with Roone Arledge," 74.

19. Robert Lipsyte, interview with author, January 30, 2016.

20. John J. O'Connor, "Cosell, the Unpredictable, Opens New Series," *NYT*, September 22, 1975, 67; Gunther and Carter, *Monday Night Mayhem*, 187, 189; Robert Lipsyte, interview with author, January 30, 2016.

21. Robert Lipsyte, interview with author, January 30, 2016.

22. "Wide World of Sport Hit Rating Peak in 70," *Variety*, January 20, 1971, 28.

23. "Mathis Threatens Suit," *CD*, December 11, 1971, 29

24. "Tennis," *SN*, March 17, 1973, 25; Benjamin G. Rader, *In Its Own Image: How Television Has Transformed Sports* (New York: Free Press, 1984), 183.

25. "Riggs-King $1-Mil Lob for Tandem; ABC's Fast Sale," *Variety*, August 8, 1973, 26.

26. Billie Jean King and Frank Deford, *Billie Jean* (New York: Viking Press, 1982), 7; Howard Cosell, *Like It Is* (Chicago: Playboy Press, 1974), 61.

27. "The Ultimate Hustle," *AC*, September 16, 1973, 20D.

28. Selena Roberts, *A Necessary Spectacle: Billie Jean King, Bobby Riggs, and the Tennis Match the Leveled the Game* (New York: Crown, 2005), 124. "The producers told me exactly what to say," Casals confessed years later. "I think I was a sideshow. They wanted me to play a certain role."

29. ABC continued to tap the success of Battle of the Sexes by giving Riggs and King cameos on an *Odd Couple* episode two months after it took place. The episode, titled "The Pig Who Came to Dinner," has Riggs hustling the gullible Oscar out of nearly all his possessions through a series of bets. It culminates with Riggs and King playing a table tennis match as a reprise of their famous encounter.

30. Percy Shain and Jack Craig, "'Sexes' Match Had TV Sets Humming," *BG*, September 22, 1973, 21.

31. Melvin Durslag, "Libber, Lobber and Clobber," *SN*, October 6, 1973, 44; Charles Maher, "Riggs Butchered by Ms. King as Promoters Score a Million," *LAT*, September 21, 1973, 1.

32. Jim Spence, *Up Close and Personal: The Inside Story of Network Television Sports* (New York: Atheneum, 1988), 96.

33. Jack Craig, "SporTView" *SN*, March 16, 1974, 28.

34. Leigh Montville, *Evel: The High-Flying Life of Evel Knievel: American Showman, Daredevil, and Legend* (New York: Doubleday, 2011), 22.

35. Ibid., 217; Dave Anderson, "Mirror, Mirror on the Wall, Who Is . . .?," *NYT*, September 10, 1974, 47.

36. Jon Nordheimer, "Knievel Leaves Idaho in a Controversy," *NYT*, September 10, 1974, 20.

37. "ABC's Wide World of Evel," *Variety*, September 11, 1974, 54.

38. Jack Craig, "SporTView," *SN*, November 15, 1975, 17; Jack Craig, "Afraid of Bad Ratings: ABC Lacks Stomach for a Fight," *SN*, May 29, 1976, 47.

39. Jack Anderson, "Evel Leads Kids to Tragedy," *AC*, October 20, 1974, 22A.

40. John H. Murphy, *Congressional Record*, September 19, 1975, 29584–86, 29584; "Objection," *Broadcasting*, November 8, 1976, 44.

41. "ABC's Wide World of Evel," *Variety*, September 11, 1974, 54.

42. William Leggett, "A Free Look at the Champ," *SI*, April 21, 1975, 68.

43. See "Jewison's New 'Rollerball' Introduced on ABC Sports," *BoxOffice*, March 24, 1975, 7.

44. Marilyn Beck, "Conrad's Real Black Sheep," *AC*, November 13, 1976, 50T; Doug Wilson, Letter to Roone Arledge, May 10, 1978, RAP, Box 34, Folder 3, Series IV.

45. Paul Jones, "Actors' Prowess Isn't Limited to TV," *AC*, March 21, 1977, 3B; Elana Levine, *Wallowing in Sex: The New Sexual Culture of 1970s Television* (Durham, NC: Duke University Press, 2007), 17–18.

46. Bedell, *Up the Tube*, 199; Jack Craig and Alan Richman, "Sports No Longer Treated Gently by Networks," *LAT*, December 10, 1977, E5. *Saturday Night Live* mocked *Battle* in 1978 with a promo for a show titled "Battle of the T's and A's." The spoof featured slow-motion shots zeroed in on bouncing breasts and butts while an off-camera announcer promises the program will offer "the biggest stars, with the biggest T's, and the nicest A's!" The parody suggested *Battle* functioned as no more than an excuse to display women's bodies.

47. Neil Amdur, "How TV Leans on Sports," *NYT*, February 13, 1978, C1.

48. Spence, *Up Close and Personal*, 232; Arledge, *Roone*, 170; Jack Newfield, *Only in America: The Life and Crimes of Don King* (New York: William Morrow, 1995), 107.

49. Newfield, *Only in America*, 108; Alex Wallau, interview with author, January 18, 2017.

50. Newfield, *Only in America*, 110, 123; Alex Wallau, interview with author, January 18, 2017.

51. Jim Spence, interview with author, October 10, 2016; Jack Craig, "ABC Boxing: A Victim of King, *Ring*," *BG*, April 24, 1974, 85.

52. Mark Kram, "Keeping the Fight Game Afloat," *SI*, January 3, 1977, 20–23, 21; Newfield, *Only in America*, 113. It was later discovered that Kram had received money from DKP that compromised his neutrality. *Sports Illustrated* eventually fired the writer for misconduct and admitted one of its staffers was on the take. Robert H. Boyle, "Some Very Wrong Numbers," *SI*, May 2, 1977, 23–27. Kram maintained that the money he took from King was for a development deal for two boxing films. See also Michael MacCambridge, *The Franchise: A History of Sports Illustrated Magazine* (New York: Hyperion, 1998), 211–13.

53. Alex Wallau, interview with author, January 18, 2017.

54. ABC transcribed the telecast's references to *Ring*'s ratings as well as the postfight interviews and filed this material with its legal department in the event that separate lawsuits emerged. Betsy Goff, Letter to Chuck Smiley, August 14, 1977, RAP, Box 37, Folder 3, Series IV.

55. Cooper Rollow, "Arledge: ABC's Fights Not Rigged," *CT*, March 10, 1977, C1.

56. Ed Stone and Gary Deeb, "Indictments Neat in Boxing Scandal," *CT*, April 24, 1977, B1; "ABC Pulls Plug on U.S. Boxing Championships," *LAT*, April 17, 1977, B1.

57. "ABC Pulls Plug on U.S. Boxing Championships," B1. Muhammad Ali and the African American press charged that the suspicion against King betrayed the mainstream sporting press's racial prejudice. The African American press issued a statement that claimed, "We as newspapermen who uphold the tradition of the free press and a responsible press have examined the evidence before us and are forced to conclude that King has not been given fair play in the white press." See "Black Press

Supports King," *NYT,* May 4, 1977, 94; "ABC Pulls Plug on Boxing Tourney," *CT,* April 17, 1977, B2.

58. Jack Craig, "SporTView: Boxing Scandal Like Watergate," *BG,* April 21, 1977, 35; Gary Deeb, "Roone Arledge to Take Charge of ABC News," *CT,* May 3, 1977, A12.

59. "Boxing Investigation Finds Only Some Unethical Behavior," *Variety,* September 7, 1977, 67, 87.

60. "ABC Sports Names Ring Inquiry Head," *NYT,* April 20, 1977, 44.

61. Don King, Letter to Roone Arledge, June 13, 1977, RAP, Box 34, Folder 3, Series IV; "ABC to Telecast Norton-Young Bout under King Aegis," *Broadcasting,* July 11, 1977, 28–29.

62. Armstrong Report, August 25, 1977, RAP, Box 35, Folder 1, Series IV; see also Cooper Rollow, "ABC Won't Throw In Boxing Towel," *CT,* September 11, 1977, B9; "Manipulators Outside ABC Cited in Report on Boxing," *Broadcasting,* September 12, 1977, 56. *Ring* editor Nat Loubet published an August 1977 explanation that blamed ABC. See Nat Loubet, "The United States Boxing Championships—The Real Story," *Ring,* August 1977, 6–8, 44.

63. Forlenza Report, November 1, 1977, RAP, Box 34, Folder 4, Series IV.

64. Hearings Before the Subcommittee on Communications of the Committee on Interstate and Foreign Commerce, House of Representatives, 59th Cong., 1st Sess., October 3, November 2, and November 8, 1977; "Washington Hearings to Scrutinize TV Networks' Influence on Sports," *NYT,* October 30, 1977, 186; Jack Craig, "SporTView," *SN,* November 19, 1977, 59.

65. Hearings Before the Subcommittee on Communications of the Committee on Interstate and Foreign Commerce, House of Representatives, 59th Cong., 1st Sess., November 2, 1977, 127.

66. Federal Communications Commission Reports, Letter of Admonition Re: CBS, Inc. Tennis Match, March 16, 1976, 67 FCC 2d 969–76; Federal Communications Commission Reports, Letter of Admonition Re: CBS, Inc., July 12, 1978, 69 FCC 2d, 1082–96; "In Wake of Winner Take All, the Buck Won't Stop So Easily," *Broadcasting,* July 24, 1978, 32–33.

67. Jack Craig, "CBS Winner-Take-All 'Confession' Airs Today," *BG,* April 9, 1978, 72.

68. Federal Communications Commission Reports, Letter of Admonition Re: American Broadcasting Company, April 25, 1978, 78 FCC 2d, 1433–40. See also Ernest Holsendolph, "FCC Is Critical of ABC over TV Boxing Tourney: 'Should Have Acted Sooner' Tougher Warning to CBS," *NYT,* April 26, 1978, B8.

69. Chuck Smiley, Memo, May 30, 1978, LNP, Box 15, IIB.

70. Charles Stafford, Letter to Ted Levy, January 10, 1984, RAP, Box 34, Folder 4, Series IV.

71. "A Female Cosell? Billie Jean Signs to Tell It for ABC," *AC,* December 19, 1974, 1E.

72. Howard Cosell, Big-Time Sports in Contemporary America, NYUA, Howard Cosell file. Cosell taught a similar course at New York University.

73. Hearings Before the Subcommittee on Communications of the Committee on Interstate and Foreign Commerce, House of Representatives, 59th Cong., 1st Sess., November 2, 1977, 161.

CHAPTER SEVEN

1. William Taaffe, "It's Bottom-Line Time," *SI*, October 12, 1987, 50–54, 73.

2. Steve Daley, "Grumbles Aside, 'Calgary' Proves a Hit for ABC," *CT*, February 23, 1988, C1.

3. "ABC's New Overseas Sports Arm Gets a Boost from World Series," *Variety*, October 19, 1977, 204.

4. "Bird Is in Hand for Pay Cable," *Broadcasting*, October 6, 1975, 26; "HBO Hosts Thrilla from Manila," *Backstage*, October 17, 1975, 6. See also Patrick Parsons, "The Evolution of the Cable-Satellite Distribution System," *Journal of Broadcasting and Electronic Media* 47, no. 1 (2003): 1–17.

5. *Home Box Office, Inc. v. Federal Communications Commission*, United States Court of Appeals for the District of Columbia, Circuit 567 F.2d 9 (1977).

6. Travis Vogan, *ESPN: The Making of a Sports Media Empire* (Urbana: University of Illinois Press, 2015), 11–26.

7. John Martin, interview with author, December 15, 2015.

8. Merrill Brown, "ABC's Wide World of Risks," *WP*, January 16, 1983, F1; "ABC Bowl Deal Set for ESPN," *Variety*, December 23, 1981, 41; Jack Craig, "ABC Set to Make Deal with ESPN," *BG*, September 24, 1981, 65; "ABC Launches Sports Cable with Getty Oil," *Back Stage*, September 25, 1981, 81; Ron Arlidge, "ABC Plans an All Night TV Service That Could Be Better Than Good News," *CT*, May 13, 1982, C20.

9. "ABC's ESPN Interest," *Broadcasting*, January 9, 1984, 10; Laura Landro, "ABC Plans to Acquire the Rest of ESPN from Texaco in $202 Million Accord," *WSJ*, May 1, 1984, 5.

10. Don Ohlmeyer, interview with author, January 27, 2016; Laura Landro, "ABC Plans to Acquire the Rest of ESPN from Texaco in $202 Million Accord," *WSJ*, May 1, 1984, 5.

11. *NCAA v. The Board of Regents of the University of Oklahoma*, 468 US 85 (1984).

12. Michael Oriard, *Bowled Over: Big-Time College Football from the Sixties to the BCS Era* (Chapel Hill: University of North Carolina Press, 2009), 158–59.

13. Jim Spence, interview with author, January 7, 2016.

14. See Wenmouth Williams Jr. and Kathleen Mahoney, "Perceived Impact of the Cable Policy Act of 1984," *Journal of Broadcasting and Electronic Media* 31, no. 2 (1987): 193–205.

15. John Martin, interview with author, December 15, 2015; Dennis Lewin, interview with author, December 15, 2015.

16. Don Ohlmeyer, interview with author, January 27, 2016.

17. *ABC Sports Official Viewer's Guide to the XIV Olympic Winter Games* (New York: Pocket Books, 1983), 45.

18. John Denver, Letter to Arledge, March 6, 1984, RAP, Box 34, Folder 3, Series IV; Tony Schwartz, "Expansion of CBS News Is Resisted," *NYT*, January 25, 1982, C28.

19. "ABC's Countdown for Los Angeles Games," *Broadcasting*, July 9, 1984, 38–42; Sally Bedell Smith, "ABC Bars NBC and Affiliates from Olympic Broadcasts," *NYT*, February 17, 1984, C32; John Carmody, "TV Column," *WP*, February 17, 1984, E12.

20. "Record 63½ Hours of TV Coverage," *NYT*, February 5, 1984, S3; Sally Bedell Smith, "ABC Ratings Lag as Olympic Coverage Begins," *NYT*, February 9, 1984, C30; William Taaffe, "ABC: Too Many Hours, Not Enough Moments," *SI*, February 27, 1984, 30–31, 31.

21. "The Age of Television," *ABC Sports Olympic Journal*, September 1983, 8–12, 10, LA84.

22. John F. Burns, "Moscow Will Keep Its Team from Los Angeles Olympics," *NYT*, May 9, 1984, A1; "ABC Insures '84 Olympics with $200 Million Policy," *WSJ*, December 30, 1982, 2.

23. Marc Gunther, *The House That Roone Built: The Inside Story of ABC News* (New York: Little Brown, 1994), 195.

24. David Bergmann, "Olympics Scorecard," *Variety*, August 22, 1984, 89; Julius Barnathan, Memo, August 13, 1984, RAP, Box 36, Folder 3, Series IV.

25. Frank Beermann, "Greenspan—Olympic Storyteller," *Variety*, August 8, 1984, 38, 56.

26. Patt Morrison and Kenneth Reich, "IOC President Protests Focus of ABC's Coverage," *LAT*, August 3, 1984, H1; Tom Shales, "The Games TV Played," *WP*, August 13, 1984, B1.

27. Roone Arledge, *Roone: A Memoir* (New York: HarperCollins, 2003), 315; Kenneth Reich, *Making It Happen: Peter Ueberroth and the 1984 Olympics* (Santa Barbara, CA: Capra Press, 1986), 124.

28. David Bergman, "Gold, Goodwill . . . and Money," *Variety*, August 22, 1984, 89; see Robert Lindsey, "Private Sponsoring of Games Appears to Be Successful," *NYT*, August 6, 1984, C11.

29. Marc Gunther and Bill Carter, *Monday Night Mayhem: The Inside Story of ABC's* Monday Night Football (New York: Beech Tree Books, 1988), 310.

30. "Bowl Will Be Bright for ABC," *Broadcasting*, January 14, 1985, 70; Memo from J. Larre Barrett to Roone Arledge, February 22, 1985, RAP, Box 15, Folder 5, Series II.2; Peter Alfano, "A League Wonders If It Is at Its Peak," *NYT*, January 17, 1984, A19; NFL Survey, 1985, RAP, Box 35, Folder 2, Series IV.

31. John Bloom, *There You Have It: The Life, Legacy, and Legend of Howard Cosell* (Amherst: University of Massachusetts Press, 2010), 153; Howard Cosell with Peter Bonventre, *I Never Played the Game* (New York: William Morrow, 1985), 321; Mark Ribowsky, *Howard Cosell: The Man, the Myth, and the Transformation of American Sports* (New York: Norton, 2011), 388; Arledge, *Roone*, 286.

32. Arledge, Letter to Fred Pierce, May 24, 1983, RAP, Box 15, Folder 5, Series II.2; Cosell, Letter to Fred Pierce, RAP, Box 8, Folder 7, Series II.1. In response to Cosell's letter, Spence requested the grandstanding sportscaster "involve only responsible ABC Sports management in ABC Sports business. To involve the top management of this company in matters of this kind," he added, "is unnecessary." Spence, Letter to Cosell, RAP, Box 8, Folder 7, Series II.1.

33. Dave Kindred, "Fighting Mad, Cosell Walks Away from Sport Turned Spectacle," *WP*, December 2, 1982, D1.

34. William Cotterell, "Howard Cosell Apologizes for Monkeying Around," *ADW*, September 13, 1983, 5.

35. "Lowery Hits Cosell," *ADW*, September 8, 1983, 1. Two months later, a coalition of minority groups threatened to organize protests at the Los Angeles Olympics if ABC did not hire more minorities and change how it represented minority groups on and beyond its sports programming. Tony Castro, "Minority Protests Threatened at Games," *Los Angeles Herald-Examiner*, November 22, 1983, A3.

36. Bloom, *There You Have It*, 169, 170.

37. "Cosell Leaves *Monday Night Football*," *WP*, August 22, 1984, D2; Larry Stewart, "The Decline and Fall of *Monday Night Football*," *LAT*, September 5, 1986, C10; Norman Chad, "*Monday Night Football* Tackles Its Popularity Decline," *WP*, October 8, 1985, D5.

38. Larry Stewart, "Cosell, Tired of Football, Wants to Quit," *LAT*, July 14, 1984, D3; Norman Chad, "Sports Waves," *WP*, July 7, 1985, D12.

39. Cosell with Bonventre, *I Never Played the Game*, 352.

40. Bob Apter, Letter to Arledge, April 4, 1985, RAP, Box 8, Folder 7, Series II.1; "Fading Figure," *Broadcasting*, November 11, 1985, 7.

41. Al Michaels, Letter to Arledge, November 4, 1985, RAP, Box 1, Folder 7, Series II.2.

42. Cosell with Bonventre, *I Never Played the Game*, 302.

43. 1986 ABC Sports, RAP, Box 1, Folder 7, Series II.2.

44. ABC nearly merged with International Telephone & Telegraph (ITT) in the middle 1960s. ABC and ITT proposed the merger in 1965, which the FCC approved. The Justice Department, however, appealed the merger request and delayed its progress. ITT wound up dropping out in 1968. ABC Memo, December 8, 1965, HHC, Box 5, Folder "ABC."

45. Huntington Williams, *Beyond Control: ABC and the Fate of the Networks* (New York: Atheneum, 1989), 217; Capital Cities Communications Annual Report, 1985, LGC, Box 72, Folder 22; Ken Auletta, *Three Blind Mice: How the TV Networks Lost Their Way* (New York: Vintage, 1992), 36.

46. Auletta, *Three Blind Mice*, 37.

47. N. R. Kleinfeld, "ABC Is Being Sold for 3.5 Billion," *NYT*, March 19, 1985, A1.

48. Auletta, *Three Blind Mice*, 36.

49. Leonard Goldenson and Fred Pierce, Letter to ABC Employees, March 18, 1985, LGC, Box 72, Folder 22.

50. Jay Sharbutt, "Chairman of ABC Calls It Quits," *NYT*, January 10, 1986, G1.

51. L.J. Davis, "Can This Marriage Work?," *Channels of Communication*, July/August 1986, 20–29, 20.

52. Auletta, *Three Blind Mice*, 117.

53. John Martin, interview with author, December 15, 2015.

54. Rick Kaplan, interview with author, January 11, 2016.

55. Peter J. Boyer, "Arledge Gives Up ABC Sports Post," *NYT*, January 28, 1986, C18; Kevin Goldman, "Swanson Ordered to Stem Red Ink," *Variety*, January 29, 1986, 51, 68; Peter J. Boyer, "The Spendthrift Turns Miser at ABC," *NYT*, April 2, 1986, C26.

56. Kevin Golman, "New ABC Roles for Arledge and Swanson," *Variety*, January 28, 1986, 2.

57. Gunther, *The House That Roone Built*, 329.

58. Letter from Dennis Swanson to Roone Arledge, October 10, 1978, RAP, Box 15, Folder 5, Series II.2.

59. Norman Chad, "ABC Sports' New Chief Moves In, Admits Dollar Will Be Real Dictator," *WP*, February 15, 1986, D2.

60. Davis, "Can This Marriage Work?," 28.

61. Gunther, *The House That Roone Built,* 324; Arledge, *Roone*, 319; Dennis Lewin, interview with author, December 15, 2015.

62. Michael Goodwin, "Swanson Is the Man in Motion at ABC," *NYT*, April 16, 1986, B14; Jim Spence, interview with author, January 7, 2016.

63. Dennis Lewin, interview with author, December 15, 2015; Doug Wilson, interview with author, June 10, 2015.

64. ABC Sports, Memo, 1986, RAP, Box 1, Folder 7, Series II.2; David A. Klatell and Norman Marcus, *Sports for Sale: Television, Money, and the Fans* (Oxford: Oxford University Press, 1988), 32.

65. William Taaffe, "TV to Sports: The Buck Stops Here," *SI*, February 24, 1986, 20–27, 22.

66. Arledge, *Roone*, 312.

67. Stewart, "The Decline and Fall of *Monday Night Football*," C10; Norman Chad, "ABC's Coolness to Monday NFL Opens Possibilities," *WP*, December 15, 1986, C8.

68. Kevin Goldman, "ABC-TV Floats Sports Comp–Sport Swap," *Variety*, May 28, 1986, 33; Norman Chad and Tony Reid, "With Its Era of Dominance Past, ABC Now Looks to Regroup," *WP*, March 7, 1989, E3.

69. Goodwin, "Swanson Is the Man in Motion at ABC," B14.

70. Norman Chad, "More Events Means Tougher Choices," *WP*, August 1, 1988, C3.

71. John Carmody, "The TV Column," *WP*, December 24, 1986, C6; Michael Goodwin, "A Winning Game Plan for Minor Sports," *NYT*, April 20, 1986, H27.

72. "ABC Tests 'Place-Based Media' with Sports Shows at J. C. Penney," *WSJ*, May 11, 1992, B6; "Socks for Jocks: ABC Is Licensing Sports Clothes Line," *Variety*, February 25, 1987, 471; Meg Cox, "Programmers Bet Viewers Want to Interact with TV," *WSJ*, October 18, 1989, B1.

73. Stanley S. Hubbard, Letter to Tom Murphy, January 23, 1987, RAP, Box 15, Folder 6, Series II.2.

74. Elizabeth Jensen, "ESPN Syndie NFL Rights Return to Bite Cap Cities," *Variety*, July 1, 1987, 113; Brian Hewitt, "Rise of ESPN Is Cultural Explosion in a Nutshell," *Chicago Sun-Times*, March 26, 1995, 21; Vogan, *ESPN*, 28–34.

75. Chad and Reid, "With Its Era of Dominance Past, ABC Now Looks to Regroup," E3; "Outside Players Join Network Sports Teams," *Broadcasting*, July 22, 1991, 28.

76. Norman Chad, "Networks Fork It Over, but Fade, While Cable's Picture Expands," *WP*, December 16, 1988, D4.

77. "Network's Sports President Says Olympics, Baseball No Good Business Choices for ABC," *Broadcasting*, January 23, 1989, 128; Steve Daley, "Grumbles Aside, 'Calgary' Proves a Hit for ABC," *CT*, February 23, 1988, C1.

78. See Chad and Reid, "With Its Era of Dominance Past, ABC Now Looks to Regroup," E3; "ABC Sports Prez: Rivals Paid Too Much for Olympics," *Variety*, January 25, 1989, 52.

79. Taaffe, "It's Bottom-Line Time," 50.

CONCLUSION

1. Larry Stewart, "Sports, TV & Money," *LAT*, June 25, 1989, K4.

2. Richard Sandomir, "ABC Sports Is Dead at 45," *NYT*, August 11, 2006, D2.

3. Geoffrey Foisie, "Capital Cities/ABC's Finances Spelled Out," *Broadcasting*, December 14, 1992, 66; Richard Sandomir, "Nothing Further on Review," *NYT*, March 20, 1992, B13; "ABC Workers Accept Buyout," *WSJ*, February 9, 1993, B8.

4. "Sports People," *NYT*, January 5, 1994, B12; Michael MacCambridge, *The Franchise: A History of Sports Illustrated Magazine* (New York: Hyperion, 1998), 342.

5. Geoffrey Foisie, "Fox Hounds ABC-TV," *Broadcasting and Cable*, June 14, 1993, 65.

6. Bill Carter and Richard Sandomir, "ESPN: The All-Sports Trophy in Mr. Eisner's Big Deal," *NYT*, August 6, 1995, F1.

7. "Swanson Out as Head of ABC Sports," *WP*, April 11, 1996, D2; Richard Sandomir, "Thursday in the Park with Mr. Holy Cow," *NYT*, April 12, 1996, 11; Geoff Mason, interview with author, January 22, 2016.

8. Michael Hiestand, "ABC Opens New 'Wide World of Sports' Umbrella," *USA Today*, September 11, 1997, C3.

9. Press Release, "ABC Sports Renews 'Monday Night Football,' ESPN Becomes Exclusive NFL Cable Carrier," January 3, 1998, LGC, Box 109, Folder 11.

10. "Disney Names Katz of ESPN as President at ABC Sports Unit," *WSJ*, March 26, 1999, B8; Richard Sandomir, "ABC Sports President Named," *NYT*, March 26, 1999, D7.

11. Leonard Shapiro, "Hoping for a Happening on Monday Night," *WP*, March 10, 2000, D2; Don Ohlmeyer, interview with author, April 6, 2017.

12. Ted Koppel, e-mail to Arledge, September 13, 2002, RAP, Box 2, Folder 6, Series I; Dennis Swanson, Letter to Arledge, undated, RAP, Box 20, Folder 5, Series II.2.

13. Richard Sandomir, "The Mystery behind 'Wide World' Is Solved," *NYT*, April 27, 2001, D8.

14. George Bodenheimer and Donald T. Phillips, *Every Town Is a Sports Town: Business Leadership at ESPN from the Mailroom to the Boardroom* (New York: Grand Central Publishing, 2015), 233; Alex Wallau, interview with author, April 6, 2017.

15. Joe Flint and Stefan Fatsis, "ESPN Snatches NFL on Monday," *WSJ*, April 19, 2005, B1; Judd Zulgad, "*Monday Night Football* Gets a New Home: ESPN Instead of ABC," *Minneapolis Star-Tribune*, April 19, 2005, 1C; Mike Hughes, "ESPN to Expand the 'Monday Night Football' Franchise," *Gannet News Services*, July 14, 2006, 1; Leonard Shapiro and Mark Maske, "Monday Night Football Changes Channel," *WP*, April 19, 2005, A1.

16. Richard Sandomir, "Monday Nights Are Changing," *NYT*, April 19, 2005, A1; Richard Sandomir, "2nd Rate Broadcast for the Third Jewel of the Triple Crown," *NYT*, June 13, 2006, D4; Sandomir, "ABC Sports Is Dead at 45," D2.

17. See Travis Vogan, *ESPN: The Making of a Sports Media Empire* (Urbana: University of Illinois Press, 2015), 62–65.

18. John Ourand, "The Eyes Have It," *SportsBusiness Journal*, January 11, 2016, 16.

19. Brett Hutchins and David Rowe, "From Broadcast Scarcity to Digital Plenti-tude: The Changing Dynamics of the Media Sport Content Economy," *Television and New Media* 10, no. 4 (2009): 354–70; Brett Hutchins and David Rowe, *Sport beyond Television: The Internet, Digital Media, and the Rise of Networked Media Sport* (London: Routledge, 2013); Robert Milliken, "Sport Is Murdoch's 'Battering Ram' for Pay TV," *Independent*, October 15, 2016, accessed July 8, 2017, www.independent .co.uk/sport/sport-is-murdochs-battering-ram-for-pay-tv-1358686.html.

20. John Ourand, "How High Can Rights Fees Go?," *SportsBusiness Journal*, June 6, 2011, 1.

21. James K. Wilcox, "Most Cable Subscribers Would Dump ESPN to Save $8 a Month," *Consumer Reports*, January 16, 2016, accessed July 8, 2017, www .consumerreports.org/streaming-media-players-services/most-cable-subscribers- would-dump-espn-to-save--8-a-month/; Cork Gaines and Mike Nudelman, "ESPN Has Lost Nearly 13 Million Subscribers in 6 Years," *Business Insider*, September 15, 2017, accessed December 6, 2017, www.businessinsider.com/espn-losing-subscribers-

not-ratings-viewers-2017-9; Joe Drape and Brooks Barnes, "ESPN Layoffs: The Struggling Industry Giant Sheds On-Air Talent," *NYT*, April 26, 2017, B8.

22. Ourand, "The Eyes Have It," 16.

23. Cheryl Cooky, Michael A. Messner, and Robin H. Hextrum, "Women Play Sport, but Not on TV: A Longitudinal Study of Televised News Media," *Communication and Sport* 1, no. 2 (2013): 203–30.

INDEX

Academy of Television Arts and Sciences, 93, 142

Adam's Rib (ABC sitcom), 173

advertising, 13, 14, 18, 31; *Monday Night Football* and, 98; pulled from controversial programming, 36; young audiences and, 15

AFL (American Football League), 30–32, 44, 100

Ali (film, 2001), 7, 226

Ali, Muhammad, 1, 4, 95, 113, 118, 180, 230; ABC Sports gimmicks and, 168–69; boxing career, 72–83; "Fight of the Century" with Frazier (1971), 170; Knievel as kindred spirit in ballyhoo, 175, 176; outspokenness of, 6; portrayed in films, 226; "Rumble in the Jungle" with Foreman (1974), 177; "Thrilla in Manila" with Frazier (1975), 194; turn to Islam, 73

Ali–Cosell team, 5, 64, 68, 170; Ali's military induction refusal and, 77–78, 82–83; beginnings of, 72–74; Cosell as "Ali's Boswell," 74; Cosell's interviews with Ali on *Wide World*, 72–80, 91; critics of, 72–73; hate mail directed to, 115; *Monday Night Football* and, 112; TrashSports and, 180

Allen, Woody, 163–64, 166

All in the Family (CBS sitcom), 111, 143, 166

All League Clubhouse, 69

Almost Anything Goes, 182

Altman, Robert, 35, 118

American Football Conference, 104

American Sportsman, 12, 60, 102, 123, 193, 213

America's Cup yacht race, 52, 216

Ampex videotape recorders, 46, 50, 58

Anka, Paul, 167

anti-Semitism, 38–39, 70

antitrust battles, 10, 97, 98

Arends, L. C., 116

Arledge, Joan, 23

Arledge, Roone, 4, 7, 8, 191, 193, 228; ABC merger with Cap Cities and, 209–12; ABC News transformed by, 146–57; aesthetic of, 6, 9; Ali–Cosell team and,

82, 83; cameo in *The Odd Couple*, 164; career before ABC, 22–25; in charge of ABC News, 6; on Cold War sport events, 47, 49, 51, 53, 58; on Cosell, 71, 261n64; Cosell's departure from *Monday Night* and, 207; Cosell's failed variety show and, 166, 167, 168; departure from ABC Sports, 194, 216–18; as the "D. W. Griffith of sports TV," 27; on emotional involvement of audience, 34; on ESPN as farm system, 197; Fox Network and, 219; health decline and death of, 223–24; hired by ABC, 21–27; on importance of *World Wide of Sports*, 61; innovations of, 26–27, 29; Innsbruck Olympics coverage and, 143–44; on live broadcast from Kiev, 54, 55–56; Los Angeles Olympics coverage and, 200, 201–2; media infrastructure built under, 1; Mexico City Olympics coverage and, 64, 68, 85, 87–88; *Monday Night Baseball* and, 121; *Monday Night Football* and, 100–104, 106, 109, 118, 119; Munich Olympics crisis and, 127, 131, 134, 136, 137, 139, 141; on the Olympics, 63; persona, 28; on prime-time television, 97; revenge on CBS for NBA contract, 160–61, 213; on sports as show business, 3; on *SportsBeat*, 204; on University of Buffalo halftime protest, 95; US Boxing Championships scandal and, 184, 185, 186–87, 188; *World Wide of Sports* and, 38–39, 42, 45

Armstrong, Michael, 186, 187, 188

Arnaud, Leo, 84

ARTS cable channel, 195

Arum, Bob, 78

Askew, Gov. Reubin, 263n9

athletes, African American, 5–6, 49, 205, 230; converts to Islam, 86; inequitable treatment by the NFL, 112–13; *Monday Night Football* as racially integrated program, 98–99; OPHR (Olympic Project for Human Rights) boycott and, 85; protest at Munich Olympics, 132; reaction to Mexico City Olympics protest, 89–90; as sports commentators, 118–21. *See also* Ali, Muhammad; race and racial politics; Smith–Carlos raised-fist protest

athletes, as sports commentators, 28, 29, 51, 118–21

athletes, female, 4, 49, 51. *See also* "Battle of the Sexes" tennis match; women's sports

Athletic Revolution, The (Scott), 191

Atkinson, Al, 105

Aubrey, James T., 37

audiences, 3, 11, 32, 161; ABC Sports' wide appeal to, 72, 98; athlete announcers/commentators and, 13; cable television and, 194; Cold War sports events and, 46, 48; crossover, 175; emotional involvement of, 34; growth of ABC and, 17; national, 25; numbers viewing ABC, 4; regional, 30; for *Roots*, 123, 124; women, 6, 191; young, 14–15, 35, 219, 220

Auerbach, Red, 160

auto races, 44, 51

Axelrod, David, 166

Axthelm, Pete, 139

Baa Baa Black Sheep (NBC), 180

Babe Ruth: A Look Behind the Legend (documentary, 1963), 71

Bader, Marvin, 134, 136, 139

Bailey, Dick, 19, 100

Baltimore Colts, 25, 161

Bananas (film, dir. Allen, 1971), 163

Bannister, Roger, 40–41

Barnathan, Julius "Julie," 28, 200–201

Barringer, Dale, 44

baseball, 18, 33, 192; All Star Game, 121; minor-league, 2; National League Championship (1978), 211; World Series, 110–11, 121, 206. *See also* MLB, *specific teams and players*

Basilio, Carmen, 24

basketball, 18, 132, 213, 229. *See also* NBA; *specific teams and players*

Battle of the Sexes (film, 2017), 7

Battle of the Network Stars, 180–82, 191, 206, 213, 265n46

"Battle of the Sexes" tennis match (1973), 1, 6, 169–75, 264n29; debates on gender equity in sports and, 230; Knievel stunts as follow-up to, 176; in pantheon of US

women's sport history, 221; as subject of films, 226. *See also* King, Billie Jean; Riggs, Bobby

Bay City Rollers (rock band), 167

Bay of Pigs invasion, 34, 58

Bedell, Sally, 167

Beermann, Frank, 201

Bell & Howell Close Up! (documentary series, 1960–63), 37

Berger, David, 139

Bergman, Theodore, 12

Berlin Wall, 34, 57

Berman, Bruce, 26

Bewitched (1964–72), 85, 243n84, 250–51n59

Beyond Control: ABC and the Fate of the Networks (Williams), 126

Bionic Woman, The (1976–78), 143

Bird, Larry, 161

"Black Athlete—A Shameful Story, The" (Olsen), 112–13

Black Caesar (film, 1973), 119

Black September terrorist group, 6, 126, 134, 136, 140, 226; German police and, 137–38, 226; identified by Peter Jennings, 135; on sport as religion of the western world, 134

blaxploitation films, 117, 118–19

Blazing Saddles (film, dir. Brooks, 1974), 120, 159

Blinn, William, 114, 115, 124, 125

Blue Network, 10

Bodenheimer, George, 221, 224, 225

Bolotnikov, Pyotr, 55

Bonanza (NBC, 1959–73), 17

Bonnie and Clyde (film, dir. Penn, 1967), 173

Bonventre, Peter, 206

Borgnine, Ernest, 255n52

Bornstein, Steve, 220–21

Boudreaux, Johnny, 186

bowling, 21, 60

boxing, 2, 13, 19, 21, 80, 204–5; ABC Radio coverage of, 71; Ali's career in, 72–83; Budweiser Boxing Series, 213; cable television and, 195; Cold War and, 82; "Fight of the Century" (Ali–Frazier, 1971), 170; "Rumble in the Jungle" (Ali–Foreman, 1974), 177; "Thrilla in

boxing *(continued)*
  Manila" (Ali–Frazier, 1975), 194; US
  Boxing Championships scandal (1977),
  7, 182–90, 225, 265n57
Branker, Don, 177
Braverman, Al, 183, 184
Brian's Song (made-for-TV movie, dir.
  Kulik, 1971), 6, 99, 113–17, 120, 124, 180,
  255n52
Brinkley, David, 142
Broadcasting (trade journal), 30, 31, 32
Brooklyn Dodgers, 13, 69
Brooks, Joe, 60
Brooks, Mel, 120, 159
Brown, Bruce, 61–62
Brown, Drew Bundini, 74
Brown, H. Rap, 82
Brown, Jim, 112, 118, 120
Brown & Williamson, 39
Brumel, Valery, 49–50, 53–54
Brundage, Avery, 86, 87, 90, 91–92, 140
Bryant, Paul "Bear," 29
Buck, Jack, 31, 112
Buckley, William F., Jr., 92, 252n81
Buffalo Bills, 44, 118
Buffett, Warren, 208
"Bugler's Dream" (Arnaud, Olympic theme
  song), 84
Burke, Dan, 208, 209, 211
Burke, David, 149
Burke, Lynn, 51
Burton, LeVar, 122, 123
Bushnell, Asa, 20–21
Bus Stop (1961–62), 35–37, 56
Butkus, Dick, 117
Button, Dick, 23, 51, 159, 161, 263n7
Byers, Walter, 97, 102

Caan, James, 113, 180
Cable Communications Policy Act (1984),
  197, 198
cable television, 7, 156, 193–94, 219; "over-
  the-top" (OTT) cable bundles, 228;
  sports channels on, 194–98
Caddigan, James, 22
California Jam concert (1974), 177
cameras, handheld ("creepy peepy"), 26, 27,
  37, 48

Canadian Football League, 118
Candid Productions, 161
Cannes Television News Festival (France), 57
Cannon, Jimmy, 74
Capital Cities Communications, 7, 194,
  207–13, 220
capitalism, 56, 58, 202
Captain and Tenielle, The (1976–77), 145
Carlos, John, 90, 91, 95, 117. *See also* Smith–
  Carlos raised-fist protest
Caroline, J. C., 114
Carson, Johnny, 100, 111, 126, 166
Carter, Lynda, 181
Casablanca (film, 1942), 17
Casals, Rosie, 173, 175, 264n28
Casey, Bernie, 114
Castro, Fidel, 58
Cavett, Dick, 165
CBS (Columbia Broadcasting System), 10,
  11, 14, 92, 128, 166; commitment to pro
  football, 20; counterprogramming
  against "Battle of the Sexes" tennis
  match, 173; daredevil sports and, 179;
  Heavyweight Championship of Tennis
  scandal, 187–88, 189–90; Hollywood
  partnerships, 17; market dominance
  gained in "freeze" years, 12; McKay at,
  40–42; Munich Olympics hostage crisis
  and, 134, 137; NBA and, 160–61, 263n7;
  news department, 146, 147, 149, 150,
  153–54, 262n75; NFL and, 99, 101, 220;
  Olympic Games coverage of, 63, 64;
  response to *Monday Night Football*,
  111–12; Senate subcommittee investigation of violent media and, 36–37; stations and affiliates of, 12; as the "Tiffany
  Network," 17, 18; TrashSports and, 181,
  182; US–Soviet track meet rights purchased by, 57
CBS Sports Network, 227
CBS Sports Spectacular, 38, 193
Celebrity Challenge of the Sexes (CBS), 182,
  190
censorship, 26, 95
chain broadcasting, 9–10
Challenger space shuttle explosion (1986),
  142
Chamberlain, Wilt, 81

spectacle, 1. *See also* AFL; NFL; *specific teams and players*

Ford, Henry, II, 106, 107

Ford Motor Company, 97

Foreman, George, 177, 180, 188

Forlenza, Phillip, 186, 187, 188

For Men Only (variety program), 24, 25, 27, 230

Forte, Chet, 28, 104, 105, 157, 165, 214; "Battle of the Sexes" tennis match and, 171; resignation from ABC Sports, 212

Fox Network, 218, 219–20

Frank, Barry, 161, 189, 225

Frankle, Stanton, 20–21

Frazier, Joe, 161, 170, 194

Freedman, Mike, 48

Freeman, Ronald, 91

Friday Night Fights, 19

Friendly, Fred, 147

Frost, David, 143, 165, 178

Gagarin, Yuri, 50

Gallery, Tom, 20, 21

Gallivan, Jack, 68

Game of the Week, 13, 15

Garrett. Alvin, 205

Gator Bowl, 19

gender, 43, 132; *Brian's Song* and, 115; Cold War sports events and, 46, 48–49; "honey shot," 28; *Monday Night Football* and, 99–100, 102–3, 107. *See also* "Battle of the Sexes" tennis match

General Motors, 14

Gerlach, Joe, 179

Getty Oil, 194, 195–96

Gibson, Charles, 148

Gifford, Frank, 28, 70, 103, 107–8, 121, 214, 219; ABC News and, 148; "Battle of the Sexes" tennis match and, 171, 173; "Faultless Frank" nickname, 107; on Knievel, 177; on *Monday Night Football* as game within event, 97; outside commercial work of, 162; on status of the Super Bowl, 202

Gillette Cavalcade of Sports, 19

Gillette company, 19, 21, 25, 29, 39

Girl in Every Port, A (film, dir. Hawks, 1928), 114

Glickman, Marty, 24

Godfather, The (film, dir. Coppola, 1972), 111

Goldenson, Leonard H., 11, 12, 17, 18, 143, 204, 216; ABC's moves toward merger and, 207, 208; on condition of ABC News, 147; on creating new audiences for ABC, 14–15; on *Disneyland* success, 16; *Monday Night Football* and, 106–7; on *World Wide of Sports*, 38

golf, 42, 56, 182

Gomery, Brian, 116, 117

Gone with the Wind (film, dir. Fleming, 1939), 111, 123

Goodman, Roger, 28, 151–52, 157

Good Times (CBS sitcom), 180

Gordon, Malcolm "Flash," 183

Gowdy, Curt, 29, 42, 60, 103

Granath, Herb, 195

Grand Prix road race, Le Mans, 44

Great Depression, 9

Great Ecstasy of the Woodcarver Steiner, The (film, dir. Herzog, 1974), 62

Green Bay Packers, 71

Gregory, Derek, 59

Gregory, Dick, 85

Grier, Rosie, 174

Griffin, Merv, 165

Grimes, William, 216

Grossman, Larry, 23

Guest, Christopher, 166, 168

gymnastics, 43

Halas, George, 113, 114

Hale, Prentis, 63

Haley, Alex, 73, 122, 124

halftime events, 27, 29

Hamill, Dorothy, 145

Hamilton, George, 176, 177

Hammer, The (film, 1972), 119

Happy Days (ABC sitcom, 1974–84), 122, 142, 143, 179, 180, 181

Harlem Globetrotters, 191

Harriman, W. Averell, 52–53, 55, 200

Hawks, Howard, 114

HBO (Home Box Office) cable channel, 116, 194, 219, 226

Heavyweight Championship of Tennis scandal, 189–90

Notre Dame, 25, 31
NYAC (New York Athletic Club), 86, 87

Oakland Raiders, 204
Odd Couple, The (sitcom, 1970–75), 164, 264n29
"Ode to a Nightingale" (Keats, 1819), 158
Off My Chest (Brown, 1964), 112
Ohlmeyer, Don, 28, 88, 99, 104; on Battle of the Network Stars, 181; on ESPN, 216; on Monday Night Football "classic" lineup, 107–8; on the Munich Olympics hostage crisis, 139; on the NABA, 197; return to ABC, 221; on Up Close and Personal vignettes, 131
Ohlmeyer Communications Company, 195, 196, 218, 222
O.J.: Made in America (ESPN documentary, 2016), 226
Oliver, Chip, 112
Olympic Games, 1, 46, 100, 123, 142, 228; 1956 Summer (Melbourne), 40–41; 1960 Summer (Rome), 41–42, 49, 63; 1960 Winter (Squaw Valley, California), 19, 41, 63–64, 248n3; 1964 Summer (Tokyo), 67, 127; 1964 Winter (Innsbruck, Austria), 64, 65–68, 199; 1968 Winter (Grenoble, France), 68, 83, 84–85, 92, 129, 250n57; 1972 Winter (Sapporo, Japan), 126, 127; 1976 Summer (Montreal), 144–45, 182; 1976 Winter (Innsbruck, Austria), 143–44; 1980 Summer (Moscow), 193; 1980 Winter (Lake Placid, N.Y.), 155–56, 195, 198; 1984 Summer (Los Angeles), 4, 193, 198, 199–203, 211, 269n35; 1984 Winter (Sarajevo), 198, 199; 1988 Winter (Calgary), 198, 210, 217, 218; 1992 Summer (Barcelona), 217; 1992 Winter (Albertville, France), 217; "Bugler's Dream" (Arnaud) as theme song of, 84, 145; as global festival, 8; in Nazi Germany (1936), 86, 133; OOC (Olympic Organizing Committee), 63, 65, 84, 127, 133, 201; prerecorded coverage, 41, 199. See also IOC (International Olympic Committee)

Olympic Games, 1968 Summer (Mexico City), 5, 64, 68, 96, 125; cost for ABC rights to, 83, 127; Mexico's place in developed world and, 133; OPHR (Olympic Project for Human Rights) boycott, 85–89, 91; Tlatelolco Massacre and, 87. See also Smith–Carlos raised-fist protest
Olympic Games, 1972 Summer (Munich), 1, 159–60; ABC acquisition of contract for, 127–29; botched police ambush at end of crisis, 138–39; branded as the "Serene Games," 133, 135; continuation of games after hostage crisis, 140–41; live reportage of hostage crisis, 134–42; memorial service for slain athletes, 139–40; overshadowed by hostage taking, 6, 126–27; 21 Hours in Munich (made-for-TV movie, 1976), 260n44. See also Black September terrorist group; Israeli Olympic athletes (Munich, 1972)
on-demand content, 8
One Hour in Wonderland (1950), 15
One Man, One Canyon (documentary), 177
Opportunity Knocks (quiz show), 23
Orange Bowl, 128
Ort, John, 183, 188
Oswald, Lee Harvey, 134
Our Durable Diplomats (documentary, 1961), 37
Out of Their League (Meggyesy, 1970), 112, 115, 191

Paley, William S., 11
Paley Center for Media, 227
Paramount Pictures, Inc., 10, 240n11, 22
Parrish, Bernie, 112
Partridge Family, The (1970–74), 164
Patterson, Floyd, 74–75, 79, 80
PBS (Public Broadcasting Service), 23, 150
Peabody Award, 57, 116, 124
Penn, Arthur, 173
Perenchio, Jerry, 169, 170
Petit, Philippe, 179
Philadelphia Phillies, 13, 211
Phyllis (CBS sitcom), 111
Piccolo, Brian, 113, 114, 115, 116